conceived and skilfully executed detective story. It takes the author from dusty files in English garden sheds, through hair-raising taxi rides at night across the frontier into Ukraine, and over the Atlantic to a lakeside house in Quebec. Vera, who died in 2000, had tried hard to cover her tracks. But Helm, a dogged journalist by profession, has proven too good for her . . . A riveting story that is both serious and moving. If there's one big book you decide to read this summer, let this be it'
Scottish Herald

'Impressive and obsessive . . . a bizarrely fascinating – as well as a chillingly horrific – story. Helm gets as close to this secretive and cold woman as we are likely to get. Along the way, she sheds a harsh and revealing light on the still murky untold story of Britain's secret war'
Literary Review

'If you read just one biography this year then let it be this one. Sarah Helm, a former investigative reporter with the *Sunday Times*, has come up with a fine account of Britain's last and possibly greatest spymaster from the Second World War . . . impeccable work'
Metro (London)

'[A] fascinating account of the life of Vera Atkins'
Sunday Express Pick of the Week

A LIFE IN SECRETS

The Story of Vera Atkins and
the Lost Agents of SOE

SARAH HELM

To my parents

ABACUS

First published in Great Britain in May 2005 by Little, Brown
This paperback edition published in June 2006 by Abacus
Reprinted 2006, 2007

Map by John Gilkes

Papers used by Abacus are natural, recyclable products made from
wood grown in sustainable forests and certified in accordance with
the rules of the Forest Stewardship Council.

Typeset in Caslon by M Rules
Printed and bound in Great Britain by
Clays Ltd, St Ives plc
Paper supplied by Hellefoss AS, Norway

Abacus
An imprint of
Little, Brown Book Group
Brettenham House
Lancaster Place
London WC2E 7EN

A Member of the Hachette Livre Group of Companies

www.littlebrown.co.uk

CONTENTS

PART IV: ENGLAND

ACKNOWLEDGEMENTS

My meeting with Vera Atkins at Winchelsea in 1998 was the inspiration for this book. The power of her personality, impressed upon me on that occasion, remained with me throughout my research and writing.

Vera, however, would not have allowed her life-story to be written while she was alive. My greatest debt of gratitude therefore is to Phoebe Atkins, Vera's sister-in-law, and also to Zenna Atkins, Vera's niece, who in 2001 authorised me to write her biography. Phoebe and Zenna opened Vera's archive, encouraged others to assist me and offered constant advice and encouragement. I must also thank Phoebe and Zenna for their trust. They believed that Vera's life was a story that should be told, but they didn't know which way my research would lead.

Other members of the Atkins and Rosenberg families have generously given their time, hospitality and assistance. Ronald Atkins talked engagingly about his aunt and his father, Ralph Atkins. Without Karina and Peter Rosenberg, Hillel Avidan and Iris Hilke much of Vera's wider family history would have remained hidden.

The first idea for a book was taken up by my agent Natasha Fairweather, whose support, advice and patient encouragement saw the project to fruition.

I drew regularly on the advice of experts. Foremost among them were Duncan Stuart, the SOE adviser; Michael Foot, the official historian of SOE in France; Mark Seaman, at that time historian at the Imperial War Museum; and Dennis Deletant, professor of Romanian Studies at UCL. Jean Overton Fuller generously spared the time to talk about her ground-breaking investigations into SOE in the 1950s and her many encounters with Vera.

There were certain individuals from different sections of her life whom I returned to again and again for guidance about her character and motivation: among them were Annie Samuelli, Barbara 'Dicker' Worcester, Nancy Roberts, George Millar, John da Cunha and Sacha Smith.

At Little, Brown, I was indebted to Alan Samson, who first backed the project, to Ursula Mackenzie, who took it up with enthusiasm and gave greatly valued advice, and to Stephen Guise for his astute editorial suggestions.

For his support and guidance I am deeply grateful to my partner, Jonathan Powell, who read drafts and often cared for our daughters, Jessica and Rosamund, while I worked. I am also indebted to Katrina Barnicoat, Richard Tomlinson, Teresa Poole and Tony Rennell, who all read the first completed manuscript.

I am grateful for the assistance of researchers, archivists and librarians in several countries, particularly in London at the National Archives, the Imperial War Museum and the London Library. I am indebted to David List, specialist researcher at the National Archives, who followed leads through countless SOE and war crimes files; to Mihai Alin Pavel, who guided me through equally labyrinthine Romanian family trees, and to Dr Helmut Koch of the Stadtarchiv in Karlsruhe.

Countless people – too numerous to mention by name – who knew Vera or knew her world have willingly given time to talk to me, or offer practical help, in places as far apart as Galatz and Karlsruhe to the Special Forces Club and Winchelsea.

The family of Hans Kieffer, near Stuttgart, considered carefully whether to talk to me about their father, and their decision to do so was greatly appreciated. Dr Michael Stolle of Karlsruhe University gave invaluable advice on the Gestapo and on war crimes.

I wish to thank most profoundly each one of Vera's SOE colleagues, and their families, as well as those who worked with her on war crimes investigation. Tim Buckmaster readily advised on his father's work and friendship with Vera. Judith Hiller made invaluable contributions. I have been acutely conscious throughout my research that many of my inquiries led to the re-examination of the most personal and painful events. Yvonne Baseden, Robert Sheppard and Jean-Bernard Badaire survived the concentration camps and I am deeply grateful to them for sharing memories. Lisa Graf's vivid recollection of her imprisonment in Karlsruhe, and of the agents there, was an inspiration.

I should like to thank Vilayat Inayat Khan for his readiness, despite failing health, to talk so movingly about Noor and about the search for her, and I am also grateful to Claire and Hidayat Inayat Khan for their help. Anthony and Francis Suttill talked about their father and generously shared information on numerous occasions. Diana Farmiloe and Helen Oliver, whose sisters, Yolande Beekman and Lilian Rolfe, died in concentration camps, kindly recollected events and passed on papers and photographs. Without the help of these survivors and relatives I could not have begun to understand the suffering and the courage of the dead, whose memory I have sought to preserve. Without the help of all these people I could not have followed Vera's trail.

LIST OF CHARACTERS

SOE London
Colin Gubbins (M, later executive director of SOE (CD))
Maurice Buckmaster (F, head of the French Section (F Section))
Leslie Humphreys (first head of F Section)
Vera Atkins (FV, later F Int, later F)
Gerry Morel (F Ops, Operations Officer)
Major R.A. Bourne-Paterson (F Plans, Planning Officer)
Nicholas Bodington (FN, senior staff officer)
Penelope Torr (F Recs, Records Officer)
Nancy Fraser-Campbell (later Roberts) (secretary, later staff captain)
John Senter (head of SOE security section)

SOE Agents (Women)
Yvonne Rudellat (alias Jacqueline Gauthier, courier, Prosper sub-circuit)
Odette Sansom (later Churchill, later Hallowes, courier, SOE circuit)
Andrée Borrel (alias Denise, courier for Prosper)
Vera Leigh (alias Simone, courier Prosper sub-circuit)
Nora Inayat Khan (alias Madeleine, call-sign Nurse, W/T operator for Prosper sub-circuit)
Diana Rowden (courier, SOE circuit)
Cicely Lefort (courier, SOE circuit)
Pearl Witherington (alias Pauline, courier, Wrestler circuit, later organiser)
Eliane Plewman (courier, SOE circuit)
Yolande Beekman (alias Yvonne, W/T operator, SOE circuit)
Madeleine Damerment (alias Martine Dussautoy, courier to France Antelme, Prosper sub-circuit)

Lilian Rolfe (W/T operator, SOE circuit)
Denise Bloch (W/T operator, SOE circuit)
Violette Szabo (courier, SOE circuit)
Yvonne Baseden (W/T operator, SOE circuit)
Sonia Olschanesky (courier, Prosper sub-circuit)

SOE Agents (Men)

Francis Suttill (alias Prosper, organiser Physician circuit, known as
    Prosper circuit)
Marcel Garry (alias Cinema, alias Phono, organiser Prosper sub-circuit)
Gilbert Norman (alias Archambaud, call-sign Butcher, W/T operator,
    Prosper sub-circuit)
France Antelme (alias Antoine, Prosper sub-circuit)
Henri Déricourt (alias Claude, alias Gilbert, air movements officer)
Frank Pickersgill (alias Bertrand, organiser Archdeacon circuit)
John Macalister (alias Valentin, W/T operator, Archdeacon circuit)
Jack Agazarian (W/T operator, Prosper sub-circuit)
Henri Frager (alias Paul, alias Louba, organiser SOE circuit)
Marcel Rousset (alias Leopold, W/T operator, SOE circuit)
Francis Cammaerts (organiser Jockey circuit)
Maurice Southgate (alias Hector, organiser Wrestler circuit)
John Starr (alias Bob (and known as Bob Starr), organiser SOE circuit)

German Personnel

Hans Kieffer (counter-intelligence chief, Avenue Foch)
Josef Goetz (radio expert, Avenue Foch)
Hugo Bleicher (Abwehr intelligence officer)
Horst Kopkov (senior counter-intelligence officer, Berlin)
Theresia Becker (chief wardress, Karlsruhe prison)
Franz Berg (crematorium stoker, Natzweiler concentration camp)
Peter Straub (executioner, Natzweiler concentration camp)
Fritz Suren (Kommandant, Ravensbrück concentration camp)
Johann Schwarzhuber (camp overseer, Ravenbsrück concentration
    camp)
Christian Ott (Karlsruhe Gestapo officer)
Max Wassmer (Karlsruhe Gestapo officer)

Selected Family Members

Max Rosenberg, father

Hilda Rosenberg (later Atkins), mother
Ralph Rosenberg (later Atkins), brother
Ronald Atkins (son of Ralph and Hedwig), nephew
Wilfred Rosenberg (later Guy Atkins), brother
Phoebe Atkins (wife of Guy), sister-in-law
Zenna Atkins (daughter of Guy and Phoebe), niece
Siegfried Rosenberg, uncle
Arthur Rosenberg, uncle
Nina Rosenberg (née Mendl), wife of Arthur
Fritz Rosenberg (son of Arthur and Nina), cousin
Karen Rosenberg (née Gehlsen), wife of Fritz
Hans Rosenberg (son of Arthur and Nina, twin of George), cousin
George Rosenberg (son of Arthur and Nina, twin of Hans), cousin

PROLOGUE

I met Vera Atkins just once.

In May 1998, a few weeks before her ninetieth birthday, I visited her at her home in Winchelsea, on the East Sussex coast. A collection of immaculate white-boarded houses on top of a hill, Winchelsea has a post office, a shop, a pub and a tearoom, all set around a large church and a green. At the bottom of the hill is Winchelsea railway station and a collection of more modest houses. Vera lived at the top of the hill in a house called Chapel Platt.

I pressed a buzzer on what looked like a sophisticated intercom and found myself staring at a little smiley face on a sticker. GIVE ME TIME TO LOOK AT YOU it read. A few moments later a woman appeared at the door. She looked at me carefully. Perhaps I was not quite what the video intercom had led her to expect. Now ushering me inside, she stooped somewhat and leant heavily on a stick. As she turned to lead the way I found myself staring at a perfect roll of white-grey hair, tucked under at the nape of her long neck.

Vera Atkins was a woman who had preserved her good looks remarkably well, and at nearly ninety she was still almost pretty. Tall despite the stoop and poised despite the wobble, she led the way into the large entrance hall, where a portrait of her hung on the wall. It showed Vera in old age, with the fingers of both hands brought together under her chin, to produce a thoughtful pose. 'Brian Stonehouse painted that one,' she said. 'He was one of our agents. He survived four concentration camps.'

She told me to go on up to the living room on the first floor, as she would come up in 'the contraption'. I saw that she was referring to a disabled lift which seemed to have been installed in an old dumb-waiter shaft. Vera sat in it, and it was like a box with its top sliced off so that when I turned at the half-landing I saw her disembodied head emerging through the floor just above me.

It was such a distracting sight that I failed to notice the sea, which was visible from the window on the landing. At night, Vera told me, she could see the glow of the Dungeness Lighthouse as it flicked around. As we sat, I noticed that her face was brushed with powder, her lips touched with colour and a floral scarf was folded on her shoulders. Vera Atkins was an immaculate composition, disturbed only by clusters of very large diamonds on three rings which flashed each time she plucked a cigarette from a silver cigarette box – which was often.

I have never seen anybody smoke quite like Vera. Her selection of a cigarette was very slow and very deliberate; the neck of the cigarette was handled for quite a few moments then placed deep in the V of first and second fingers, before it was carefully inserted in the lips, which seemed to descend to take it in. The smoke was never inhaled, but taken into the mouth and then immediately exhaled so that she seemed to be permanently in a cloud of smoke. After a while – when she had made her judgement of me – she ceased to look at me at all and gazed straight in front, or over my head, through the window behind me and over the rooftops of Winchelsea.

I hadn't come to interview Vera about her own life, but found myself doing so from the beginning. She didn't tell me much. She never told anybody much. She said before the war she had been living with her mother in Chelsea, when, in February 1941, an 'anodyne little letter' had arrived out of the blue asking her for an interview at the War Office. This was how she came to join the London staff of Britain's newest secret service: the Special Operations Executive, or SOE.

SOE was created amid the panic of July 1940, when Hitler's advance through Europe seemed unstoppable. In April the Germans had launched assaults on Denmark and Norway and by May had surged through the Low Countries and penetrated France, forcing British and Belgian forces to retreat at Dunkirk. It was impossible to say how much time it would now take before Britain and its allies could amass a force with the strength to retake Europe. In the meantime, SOE was created to start an immediate fight-back. SOE was to organise a secret war: building up, organising and arming a resistance army from the peoples of the Nazi-occupied countries.

Inspired by Churchill's own enthusiasm for guerrilla warfare, SOE was opposed from the outset by many in government, who doubted that guerrilla tactics could achieve much against the mighty Nazi machine. Among rival intelligence services, particularly MI6, the Secret Intelligence Service, there was rancour and jealousy about the creation of a new secret body, to be staffed by amateurs, over which they, the established professionals, would have no control.

With little support, no time and only a handful of experienced staff, SOE set about recruiting, looking to the City and international business for its headquarters staff, who then organised SOE into country sections, covering Europe, the Middle East, the Balkans and Yugoslavia. In turn the headquarters staff looked for agents – anyone who was, first, able to speak the language of the country where they would operate and, second, brave enough to follow Churchill's famous edict to 'set Europe ablaze'.

When Vera was called for her interview in February 1941, SOE was still struggling to get properly started. It was nearly a year since the fall of France and nine months since SOE had been set up, yet its attempts to launch a secret war on French soil seemed to have stalled. Not a single British agent had yet been successfully infiltrated into France, from which Britain still seemed entirely cut off. There was not even any reliable information about the size or strength of any indigenous French resistance. General de Gaulle had set up his government-in-exile in London and his Free French were now also largely isolated from their homeland.

So, in the spring of 1941, the overwhelming priority for SOE was still to get British agents on the ground. Only with trained men in place could the potential of a civilian insurgency be assessed, and only once those agents had begun to form workable guerrilla cells could arms and supplies be dropped to the French resistance fighters. Vera would, by the end of the war, be playing a vital role in getting those agents behind the lines, but when she first joined, in April of that year, neither she nor most of her colleagues had much idea of what their role would be or how exactly this secret war was to begin.

When I probed Vera further about why she thought she had been chosen for this clandestine work she simply said: 'One didn't know.' Then she was silent for a minute. Realising I was waiting for more, she added: 'Let's leave it at that.'

I tried asking Vera about her family background as I had heard she was of Romanian origin. 'This is of no interest,' she replied. 'It is something on which I have closed the book. I have closed the book on many things in life.' Then she got up and offered me a drink.

But Vera had 'closed the book' on her past with such finality that it only made me more intrigued. The details of her life that were on the record at that time were these: Vera Atkins was born on 15 June 1908, somewhere in Romania. She came to live in England some time in the 1930s. In April 1941 she joined SOE and was soon appointed intelligence officer for F Section. By the end of the war she had become, in the words of a senior colleague, 'really the most powerful personality in SOE'.

Vera never worked in the field, but coordinated the preparation of more than four hundred secret agents who were to be dropped into France. She had knowledge of every secret mission, shared in the handling of each agent in the field and had sole responsibility for the personal affairs of every one of her 'friends', as she called the agents. The majority of these she saw off personally on their missions. She was most intimately associated with the women agents, her 'girls'.

When, after the war, more than a hundred of those agents had not returned, Vera launched and carried out almost single-handedly a search to establish what had become of them. On the first missing lists were sixteen women.

Across the chaos of bombed-out Germany she followed the agents' trails to the concentration camps and helped track down many of the Germans who had captured and killed them. She gave evidence at Nazi war crimes trials, was awarded by the French the Croix de Guerre in 1948 and the Légion d'Honneur in 1995. The British, by contrast, waited until 1997 to honour Vera Atkins, finally bestowing a CBE on her.

As I listened to her, however, I realised just how sparse the known facts about Vera Atkins were. Who was this woman? How could it be that she had reached the age of ninety without anyone knowing more than this about her? I looked around but the room contained no clues. It seemed unremarkable, quite comfortable but colour-less, with a pale-green carpet. At a glance I saw a few recent family photographs and lots of flowers – some in formal vases, some in little pots. The *Daily Telegraph*, open at the stocks and shares page, lay on a table in front of a very long sofa in faded pink. On the small table by Vera's chair were a magnifying glass, an open letter, a coaster and an ashtray. But there was not a book to be seen and only a few bland landscapes on the wall.

Vera returned with drinks and I tried once more to probe her. She was extremely well spoken; she articulated her sentences so carefully and her accent was so precisely English that it had, paradoxically, a foreign ring. But, for all its clarity, her voice was very hard to hear, because she spoke softly and in such deep tones.

I raised the question of SOE's most famous disaster, the collapse of the Prosper circuit, and we discussed the women agents. 'What did they have in common?' I asked. She considered, and I wondered which of the women were coming to her mind.

'Bravery. Bravery was what they had in common,' she said. 'You might find it in anyone. You just don't know where to look. Their motivations were all different. Many women made good couriers or had worked in coding and had fingers like pianists – they made good radio operators. They might be artists or fashion designers. Why not? They had to be self-reliant, of course. Physical appearance was important. They were all attractive women. It gave them self-confidence.'

'What about Madeleine?' I asked, mentioning the woman wireless operator whose story I had always found most compelling. Noor Inayat Khan, alias Madeleine, had worked with Prosper, the biggest F Section circuit. Noor, who took the English name Nora when she joined SOE, was the secret agent who played the harp and 'could not lie'. 'Do you believe today that it was right to have sent her?' I asked.

Vera thought for a moment. 'There were questions about Nora, about her suitability. But she wanted very much to go.'

She was now twisting a matchbox round and round in her hands and I strained to catch the words. 'I drove with her down to the aerodrome. It was a perfect June day . . . the smell of the dog roses. Taking the agents to the aerodromes . . . was very tiring.'

I asked when she had realised that some of the agents were not coming back. Her thoughts seemed to be moving on, but she was hesitant about whether to give voice to them. She turned and looked me straight in the face. Her expression was now quite blank, almost cold. I was quite sure she wanted me to leave. 'I'm really very tired, you know.'

After a few moments during which I fully expected her to rise and usher me out of the room, Vera suddenly turned and looked at me again. 'I went to find them as a private enterprise. I wanted to know. I always thought "missing presumed dead" to be such a terrible verdict.' Time suddenly telescoped to nothing, her voice was raised at least an octave and it was as if she was no longer peering into her past but setting off for Germany after the end of the war to follow the trail of her agents.

'I remember it was a bitterly cold day when I was collected by Staff Sergeant Fyffe, who drove from Berlin, through the Russian zone, to Bad Oeynhausen in the British zone. When we got there I said: "Who is in charge here?" I asked if he would have time to see Squadron Officer Atkins.

'Somerhough was his name. He had the quickest brain I have ever known. I just blew in that afternoon and told him I had arrived from Berlin by car. He received me and I explained in a few sentences what I wanted to do. I said: "I believe you have the camp Kommandants of Sachsenhausen and Ravensbrück in your custody. I would like to see them."

'He said: "They are tough nuts. One has escaped twice and the other has not yet been interrogated."

'I said: "I want to see them anyway." Next I had to persuade him to let me work from his HQ. He said there was no room for another officer – especially a woman officer. But I persuaded him. I stayed there until I had traced every agent we had lost.'

With these words Vera finished as suddenly as she had begun, and turned to indicate that now I really must leave. It was as if she had been waiting to see my interest awakened before calling a halt to our meeting.

It wasn't until after Vera Atkins's death on 24 June 2000 that I was able to start trying to find out more about her and her 'private enterprise'. I began my search in a garden shed in Zennor, Cornwall, that belonged to Phoebe Atkins, her sister-in-law. The shed contained Vera's personal papers.

It must be said that this was a very classy kind of shed. Vera would have approved of it as a home for her papers. It had a heater, a kettle and a sofa bed, and I was not really alone there as I could see the back of Phoebe's cropped white hair across the lawn as she read at her conservatory table. It was nice to know Vera was with us too. For she hadn't quite gone to her grave: her ashes were sitting on the shelf in Phoebe's conservatory next to a potted plant and a pile of Cornish liberal party leaflets.

It was at Phoebe's invitation that I had gone down to Zennor. She was the widow of the younger of Vera's two brothers, Guy, who died in 1988. Phoebe and Vera were always close and after Vera died Phoebe took charge of Vera's papers and had them carefully indexed. She wanted somebody to 'do Vera's life', as she put it, but she was unsure who the author should be. She had been advised by experts on SOE to select an established historian, somebody with 'gravitas'. But Phoebe, aged sixty-nine, who had trained at Camberwell College of Arts before moving to Cornwall to work as a farm labourer, said she was not interested in 'gravitas'. She wanted somebody who would write about 'Vera – Vera the woman'.

I began to trawl through the shed. There were a number of tempting boxes with neat labels such as 'Personal correspondence', 'SOE', 'Female agents A–Z', 'Male agents A–Z', 'War crimes'. Yet, as I started to pull out the papers, I was disappointed. Many files were just a collection of newspaper articles. 'War crimes' seemed to be about the erection of memorials. Most of the photographs just showed Vera as an upper-crust Englishwoman, often presiding at dinners, or being chummy with the Queen Mother. There was only one that interested me. This showed Vera as a very young woman, tall and handsome, almost beautiful, standing with another young woman by a newly planted sapling, but where it had been taken the picture did not say.

I started looking around for other files, which perhaps had not been indexed and which, I liked to think, might be called 'Romania', 'Childhood', 'Family', 'Education' or even 'Diaries'. They did not exist.

Instead there was a vast amount of material on the various media projects in which Vera had been involved over the years, including a large file called 'Controversial Books' which contained letters to and from authors about how they had got the SOE story wrong.

I came across a promising folder labelled 'Vera's letters'. These were in fact mainly postcards, most of them sent to her mother, so there was no room for Vera to say much, and they were in illegible, tiny, spiky handwriting. Here was one from Munich in February 1946, when, I knew, she had just arrived in the ruins of Allied-occupied Germany to start interrogating war criminals. But when I had patiently deciphered every word, I found the card filled with a bland list of places and no information at all: 'Dearest Ma, I've been on the move since last Sat: Frankfurt, Wiesbaden, Baden Baden (via Heidelberg) then on to Munich. Off to Nuremberg tomorrow. Fondest Love. V.'

When Vera did write at any length, the result was almost more frustrating than when she kept it short. Her longer pieces of prose – such as a synopsis I found for an autobiography – were so polished, so full of clichés, that I began to suspect that Vera herself would not have been the best person to tell her own story.

In another bulging box I found nothing but a pile of videos showing Vera's appearances in TV documentaries and alongside were film scripts for various movies that she had advised on. Here was the entire screenplay for *Carve Her Name with Pride*, the 1958 film about Violette Szabo, perhaps the most famous of the agents Vera had sent to France. Flicking through the script, I looked for Vera's lines.

'Violette carrying Tania in her arms hurries to open the door in the hall of Burnley Road to Vera Atkins; Vera tickles little Tania's cheek. "Pretty little thing, isn't she? Is she your sister, Violette?"

'"Well, no."

'"She's not yours, is she? You didn't say you had a baby, did you?"'

And in the next scene, watching Violette training, Vera says: 'It takes time to turn a pretty girl into a killer.'

But I didn't want to read others' scripts. By now Vera's personality was fading in front of my eyes, amid a pile of synopses and countless posed photographs. I was beginning to wonder if her life was really of any interest. Worse, I was beginning to wonder how much I liked her.

Phoebe's little dog, Zilla, was barking at the door to come in. It was raining. I shuffled around a little and looked through some drawers, which I had not yet inspected. Here was a whole row of as yet unopened files with titles such as 'Paris Files', 'Correspondence on Tracing', 'Buchenwald', 'Orders and Permits', 'Avenue Foch', 'Ravensbrück', 'Ravitsch case', 'Flossenburg', 'Mauthausen', 'Natzweiler', 'Karlsruhe Prison', 'Karlsruhe Gestapo' and many more. The files contained the original documents relating to Vera's investigation into the disappeared agents.

I pulled out a flimsy piece of brown paper. It was a statement made by a man named Franz Berg, who witnessed the killing of

women agents in Natzweiler concentration camp. I knelt on the
floor to read.

> I Franz Berg . . . make oath and say as follows: I am a waiter
> by trade, living in Mannheim. During my life I have
> received so far as I can remember twenty-two sentences of
> imprisonment. I cannot remember what they were all for but
> I can recall two cases of theft, several of obstructing the
> police and of causing bodily injury, and the last sentence of
> two years which I received for procuration.

Berg described how he started working in the crematorium at
Natzweiler in 1943 and had an assistant named Georg Fuhrmann,
who contracted an infection of the arm from one of the bodies that
was being cut up in the mortuary. He said the first crematorium outside the camp used to work on Wednesdays and Saturdays, but when
the new crematorium was built they used to burn bodies about three
times a week.

I got up from the floor and sat on the sofa bed. Berg said that two
English and two French women were brought to the cells in the crematorium building one afternoon in July 1944 around 3.30 and he
remembered in some detail what they were carrying. They had suitcases and coats over their arms and, he thought, one had a travelling rug.

> I was told on the evening of the day on which these women
> arrived to have the crematorium oven heated to its maximum
> by 9.30 and then to disappear. I went to the room in which I
> slept, in which were sleeping Georg Fuhrmann and Alex, a
> Russian from Leningrad.

A few minutes later the Kommandant of the camp and his men
came to make sure that Berg and his cellmates were asleep. Berg
pretended to be asleep.

> There was a fanlight over the door from which it was possible
> to see the corridor outside. Fuhrmann, who occupied the
> highest bunk, was able to look through this without standing
> up. He whispered to me that 'they are bringing a woman
> along the corridor outside'.

We heard low voices in the next room and then the noise of a body being dragged along the floor and Fuhrmann whispered to me that he could see people dragging something on the floor, which was below his angle of vision, through the fanlight.

I read on to the end of the statement, and saw that Berg had been interrogated by Squadron Officer Vera Atkins in April 1946. There was a tapping on the door. Phoebe was standing there, pointing at her watch. 'We're off to the Tinners for lunch,' she said. Her daughter Zenna had just arrived for a visit.

I hoped that in the pub Phoebe and Zenna would be able to tell me more about Vera's past than I had so far learned in the shed, but they said they didn't know much at all. 'We never talked about the past. With Vera one just didn't,' said Phoebe.

Zenna said she knew only 'the answers to the questions a child might ask' because she had talked to her Aunt Vera most when she was growing up. 'And Dad was paranoid – he didn't want anyone to know about his past.' As if to illustrate the point, Zenna put a packet of her father's papers on the table. He had written an instruction to Zenna on the envelope: 'Deposit these documents in your bank with instructions to be destroyed unopened on your death.'

What Phoebe and Zenna were able to tell me was this. Vera had two brothers, Guy and Ralph. Guy, the younger, who married Phoebe in 1964, was educated at Oxford and then took an MA at Prague in 1937. After the war Guy taught African languages at the School of Oriental and African Studies in London. He had a genius for languages. Ralph, Vera's elder brother, who died in 1964, was manager of an oil company in Istanbul before the war. Later he dabbled in business. Ralph had one son, Ronald, a journalist living in Lewes.

The mother of Ralph, Vera and Guy was Hilda Atkins, whose family came from South Africa, though of her precise origins they had no idea. Their father, Hilda's husband, was Max Rosenberg, who was originally German, they thought. He trained as an architect. Phoebe had earlier pulled a fork from her kitchen drawer, engraved with a large 'R', to show me all that remained of a set of family silver designed by Max. 'All the family possessions were stored on the docks and lost in the first bomb of the Blitz,' she explained.

Zenna and Phoebe passed on whatever stories they had over-

heard. Guy and Vera sometimes reminisced about an idyllic childhood in a large house somewhere in Romania. The children had a
pony and trap and a sleigh in winter 'with those curly bits on'. Vera
had a boat named after her on an ornamental lake.

Max Rosenberg was Jewish – of that they were sure – but they were
unsure about whether Hilda had Jewish origins. Max died sometime
before the war and the rest of the family took their mother's name.
'Guy changed his name before any of them,' said Zenna, who had also
changed hers. Her father, born Wilfred, took the name Guy as a young
man. 'Dad saw the dangers before any of them. After the war he still
believed it could all happen again, so he wanted me to have a nice
English name. He called me Lucy – but I didn't feel like a Lucy. One
day when I was in Bali I had a kind of nervous breakdown. I was about
sixteen. I just went off on my own for a long time and wandered round.
When I came back everyone was sitting there worried as hell and said:
"Lucy, where have you been?" They said I looked a little crazed. I said:
"I'm not Lucy. I'm Zenna." Tall and striking, with electric-red hair, just
dyed, Zenna indeed did not look like a Lucy. In fact in profile she had
the handsome allure of her Aunt Vera in her youth. 'An award-winning
social entrepreneur,' was how Zenna Atkins's website, detailing her
work with the socially excluded and the homeless, described her.

Although Phoebe and Zenna couldn't tell me much, they suggested
who might be able to, and gave me Vera's address book. They also gave
me advice: I should not expect to find information, as such, in the
shed. Vera stored most of the information she valued in her head, and
even this information she regularly erased. 'She could close things
down because she had a mental filing system,' said Zenna. 'I am the
same. Once I have dealt with a problem I erase it from my mind, then
I can't open it up again unless somebody hits the right trigger.'

But the two of them said I would find clues. For example, Zenna
had discovered photographs hidden behind other photographs in
Vera's frames. I should watch for 'little habits like that'. And she said
that although she had few facts to give me, she had heard a mass of
stories from Vera as a child. If I ever had a question about Vera, she
might be able to help as long as I 'pressed the right trigger'. It would
be a matter of luck.

Back in the shed that afternoon I stopped looking for answers and
found that this most secretive of women had indeed left clues of a

sort. I found love letters. They were more like snippets of love letters; snippets of great happiness. Here was a champagne bottle label in an envelope with a letter, in blue ink on blue notepaper, that said: 'My Sweet, My Lovely, My Darling – cross out the possessives if you like, but you are – My Darling, My Sweet.' The top of the notepaper had been carefully cut off. There was no signature at the bottom, except for what looked like a dollar sign.

Even those things that had been so disappointing that morning were now not so. Vera's postcards and letters to her mother seemed more interesting, precisely because they said so very little. And the posed pictures of Vera were more interesting now, when I put them together with other Veras I had begun to find. If I put the picture of her with permed hair, twin set and pearls next to the one of her in Paris – stylish suit, nipped in at the waist – she was simply not the same woman. And, tucked at random in a long, brown envelope, I found Vera on a mountain pony with a line of others on ponies, on the edge of a forest. A distinguished-looking man was having difficulty controlling his horse, and close to him was Vera, with bobbed hair and riding jacket, clearly in control of her mount. I turned the picture to find a date, 1932, and a list of names, including: 'Count Friedrich Werner von der Schulenburg. German Ambassador to Bucharest and negotiator of Molotov–Ribbentrop pact. Executed in the anti-Hitler plot 1944.'

The more I pulled out files and envelopes the more snipped letters or parts of papers or unidentified photographs would fall out. Books had notes or cuttings tucked in them. It began to feel as if Vera had left a deliberate paper trail for me to find. Rather than write anything down, she preferred what the SOE training schools called the 'flotsam' method of information dissemination. The flotsam looked like nothing on first examination but in fact had been deliberately placed to lead the interested party down a particular route – in this case, the biographer. For Vera must have known somebody would be 'doing her life'.

So the torn letters, the single page of a diary of her hunt for the missing, the carefully laid photographs which tumbled out before me were not the casual remnants of a life left behind, but a series of carefully considered signposts.

Then, as I packed things away, I noticed a card that had fallen to the ground. It had a photograph on the front, of a young woman whom I recognised as Nora Inayat Khan. This was a particularly beautiful picture of Nora. Faded and brown round the edges, it captured her unusual aura of gentleness and strength. It was all in her large, dark eyes.

Opening up the card, I saw there was writing inside: 'To Vera Atkins. With gratitude – a feeling I know Nora would have shared for your enterprise in following in her tracks in the German wilderness of the aftermath.'

The note was signed by Nora's eldest brother, Vilayat Inayat Khan, and dated 1948. I stared at the picture for some moments. Just lying there as it was on the floor, I could so easily have missed it.

PART I
ENGLAND

1

NORA

Vera Atkins did not, as a rule, take too much notice of the opinions of others. When it was a question of judging the character of a particular agent, especially a woman agent, she liked to make up her own mind in her own time – which was usually within a few moments of their entering the room where she first met them, at Orchard Court.

The flat in Orchard Court, just off Baker Street in London's West End, was a base used by SOE's French Section, or F Section, where headquarters staff could meet new recruits and also brief those departing on missions. Agents were never allowed into SOE's HQ in Baker Street in case they heard or saw something they did not need to know.

By the spring of 1943, when recruitment to F Section was fast picking up, a steady stream of young men and women would arrive at Orchard Court. The drill for new arrivals was by now well established. First, Park the doorman, in dark suit and tie, would lead the way (never asking names but always knowing exactly who a new arrival was) through the gilded gates of the lift and on up to the second floor. In perfect English or French, whichever they preferred, Park would then usher them into the flat and straight into a bathroom, because there was no space for a waiting room. 'Back in the bathroom, please, sir [or madam],' he would say if they wandered out, and here the agents sat on the side of a deep, jet-black bath, or on the onyx bidet, surrounded by black and white tiles, while they waited to see what would happen next.

Park would then lead the agent to meet Maurice Buckmaster, the head of F Section. A tall, slender, athletic figure (he once captained Eton at soccer) with angular facial features and fair, thinning hair, Buckmaster would shake the agent's hand vigorously, then, perching momentarily on his desk, legs swinging, make a few warm welcoming remarks. To any recruit who seemed inquisitive he would say, 'We don't ask questions,' firmly stressing the need for secrecy at all times. He would then stride off with the recruit down the hallway and, opening another door, say, 'And this is Miss Atkins.'

Nodding towards Vera, Buckmaster would then explain, 'Miss Atkins will be looking after you from now on,' and as the door closed the new arrival's eyes would fall on a woman seated at a table, who produced a smile – remote but welcoming. Vera then rose, tall and trim, in twin set or tweed suit, her fair hair rolled up at the nape of her neck. This mature woman in her mid-thirties, most recruits assumed, must be a woman of senior rank, though exactly what rank was not at all clear as there was no uniform and she was only ever called 'Madam' or 'Miss Atkins'.

After proffering a hand, Vera settled herself again behind a small table, showing off nicely turned ankles and smart court shoes that looked expensive but probably were not. She then slowly lit a cigarette and her blue-grey eyes fixed upon the new recruit.

Vera appeared to know everything about the new arrival, and without referring to any piece of paper she could talk to them about their country of origin, about their family and about their special knowledge in any field – for example, she knew if they could fire a gun, fly an aeroplane, read a map or ski.

And Vera knew exactly where the new recruit was living, and if they needed accommodation she would offer to arrange it. She knew of their financial circumstances as well and could offer cash advances on request up to a limited amount each month. All this was very reassuring, because until they met Miss Atkins many of these men and women had felt somewhat disorientated by the experience of 'special employment', as their new work was called.

Some of the women had, just days earlier, been mopping floors at RAF stations. Many recruits were civilians, spotted by SOE scouts, while some had just escaped across the Channel from France and had never been to England before. Few knew exactly why they had been picked out for this secret work, though it was almost certainly for little other reason than that they spoke native, or near native, French. Some were French, many had at least one French parent and most had a cosmopolitan background.

They had been invited first for a selection interview, perhaps with a Mr Potter, in a small, bare room numbered 055a, in the basement of the War Office. But Mr Potter would have said little about what exactly they would be doing. Once the MI5 search into their background had safely come back indicating 'no trace', they had been whisked off to sign the Official Secrets Act. But still they had no idea what it was they would be keeping secret.

Then the women went to Lilywhites to be measured for stiff new khaki serge uniforms, and found themselves transformed into members of the First Aid Nursing Yeomanry. The FANY, as this was known, was an organisation of ladies of a certain social standing (and in many cases with fathers or husbands in the officer corps) who volunteered for military work, driving perhaps or packing parachutes. All women agents joining SOE were obliged to join the FANY to give them 'cover' while in secret training, but none yet knew anything of what that training would be.

So, when the door had closed behind them and they were alone, and when Miss Atkins began to talk a little about why they had been chosen from so many others for this special work, things started to make more sense. Those recruits who had clandestine experience, such as working on resistance escape lines in France, felt that Vera had some direct knowledge of what they had been through. The less experienced felt flattered that somebody as impressive and courteous as Miss Atkins was now taking time with them. It helped, for example, to be told exactly how they should explain their new position to friends and family.

A young woman recruit named Nora Inayat Khan, seconded to SOE from the Women's Auxiliary Air Force, or WAAF, had expressed particular anxiety from the start about what to tell her mother about her new secret work. Miss Atkins suggested phrases Nora might begin to use – vague hints about going away – so that her mother, to whom she was evidently close, would get used to the ties between them loosening.

And as Vera went on to explain the set-up in some detail, saying how their care and training would be arranged, and how she would be following their progress day by day, the agents' confidence grew.

If before the meeting closed Miss Atkins should suggest a change in their address, their appearance or perhaps their name, naturally they did not demur. Nora Inayat Khan took the name of Nora Baker to disguise her Indian origins. Above all else, the new recruits left Vera's office with an impression that Miss Atkins was in control. Some now were even excited and eager to begin. They probably felt they had learned far more about their new work than in fact they later found they had. They had certainly learned nothing about Miss Atkins. All they knew was that she would be looking after them from now on.

————

More than fifty years later I discovered that those young men and women interviewed at Orchard Court still knew nothing about 'Miss Atkins'.

'My deaa booay,' said the former French agent Bob Maloubier, mimicking Vera's accent. 'For me everything about her was English.' 'Benenden and Kensington,' said another, asked to guess her background. 'I knew Atkins wasn't her real name,' said a third. How? 'I once saw something on her file.'

One former staff officer, though, had caught a unique glimpse of Vera in her very earliest days. He had met her at a bridge party at exactly the time she joined SOE. 'Now let's see,' said Peter Lee, reading through his diary for 1941. 'When was it exactly? The tenth of March. Ha! "Played bridge – Blitz – Boodles hit – windows out of Brooks – shaking like a jelly." I think it was round about then. It was at Elizabeth Norman's house in Thurloe Square.' Elizabeth, he explained, was the SOE secretary assigned to Room 055a, where SOE candidates were first interviewed. 'The room had two tables, two chairs and a skylight.'

Peter explained that he had befriended Elizabeth because he wanted a job with SOE. 'I had heard that her people were into cloak-and-dagger stuff and had the prettiest secretaries.' Elizabeth often held bridge parties at her home and on one occasion a mutual friend brought Vera along to make up a four. 'None of us knew who she was. But I remember she played a very good hand at bridge, probably because she carried everything in her head.'

Elizabeth Norman (now FitzGerald) recalled Vera at the bridge party as 'mysterious in some way'. She added: 'Or rather she covered herself in mystery. And she was gracious – rather too gracious in a way that none of us really were. I think a friend of mine had met her on an ARP [Air Raid Precautions] patrol and just brought her along when we were short of a fourth person. She seemed to have come from nowhere. You see, she was so much older than us other girls. She had no context at all that I discovered. And we didn't ask – one didn't then. We had a sort of code, you know.'

Elizabeth herself had started as a 'snagger', a filing clerk, in MI5, which was the Eton or Roedean of Whitehall. She then moved to SOE, and recalled that F Section was considered 'not quite top-notch', 'a mixed bunch, mostly City', whereas the Balkan Section had the really 'smart', wealthy types, brought in from Hambros or Courtaulds.

One of Elizabeth's jobs was to tick off recruits as they arrived for interview in 055a – 'they were all told it was life and death but it didn't seem to bother them.' Often she was called over to Orchard Court to help out, usually by chatting to agents, and drinking cocoa with them to set them at ease before their departure. In the early days some agents were landed in France by boat, but later most were dropped by parachute or landed in small planes. The infiltrations were always done at night during the full moon. 'I remember feeding éclairs to Odette as we waited for the moon to come up in the right place,' said Elizabeth, referring to the agent Odette Sansom, who in October 1942 was whisked from Orchard Court to the French Riviera and landed by felucca, a small sailing boat. 'And they also got their cyanide pills then.'

The atmosphere in Orchard Court was deliberately informal, with women smoking and handsome men always passing through and breaking into French, and nobody ever knew who anyone was as they all had aliases. Elizabeth herself had three aliases when she worked in the interview room. 'They would ring up and say, "You have an interview with so and so," and I would have to know the alias and whether that was an alias for somebody else. Then we picked up the green phone and said, "Shall we scramble?"' At this she started to laugh.

If there was an opportunity, Elizabeth and friends would nip down to the bar on the corner to relax, 'but if any non-SOE people came in we all had to shut up like clams'. There were a lot of 'bedtime stories', she said, 'and Gubbins was a lech', she added, referring to Colin Gubbins, who became Executive Director of SOE in September 1943.

I said I could not imagine how Vera could have fitted into the world Elizabeth described. 'In many ways she didn't,' she answered, looking up as if she was trying to picture Vera in her mind's eye. 'I often thought she seemed quite lonely.'

At weekends Elizabeth frequently used to go to Lady Townsend's tea parties at the Grosvenor House Hotel in Park Lane. 'It was all done so the men in town could meet a pretty girl.' The girls all had to be introduced by another girl.

'Would you have taken Vera?'

'Oh, no, she was much too old. Most of her age group were at that time off in the country looking after their children.'

Later Elizabeth moved to other work in the Cabinet Office, but she observed from afar as Vera 'reinvented herself' as she progressed through SOE and seemed, by the end of the war, to have virtually taken over F Section.

———

After meeting Vera and other F Section officers at Orchard Court, recruits left for an initial three weeks of assessment and training at Wanborough Manor, near Guildford, and then on to intensive para-military work – explosives, stalking and silent killing – for up to five weeks in the Western Highlands of Scotland. It was here that demolition training was also done and where agents – or so they claimed – became as familiar with plastic explosives as they were with butter. Then came parachute training at Ringway airfield, near Manchester.

Throughout their early instruction the agents were told they were undergoing straightforward commando training, and many still had little concept of what lay ahead. Then at Beaulieu, in the New Forest, where the agents at last began to learn the craft of clandestinity – using cut-outs (innocent intermediaries), *boîtes-aux-lettres* ('letterboxes', places where messages could safely be left) and basic Morse code – the reality of their likely missions became clearer.

Though she rarely visited the training schools, Vera received reg-ular reports from instructors as the agents progressed and she became quite used to sceptical, if not downright damning, comments that came back to her about the women she was responsible for. The male staff at the schools appeared awe-struck by the 'feminine' qualities of the women, who were 'painstaking', 'lacking in guile' and 'innocent'. What these young male officers really meant, in Vera's opinion, was that women should not be serving behind the lines at all.

It was in early 1942 that Colin Gubbins had first secured authority, albeit unofficially, to send women behind the lines. Colonel Colin McVean Gubbins, a wiry Scots Highlander, at the time was 'M', or head of military operations in SOE, and as such was eager to draw in the best recruits. A brilliant and high-spirited professional soldier, who won an MC in the First World War, Gubbins was known by colleagues as 'a whole hogger' and he saw no reason why women could not do the job of secret agent as well as many of the men.

An influential band of lawyers seconded to SOE (mostly in a batch from the City firm of Slaughter and May) were utterly opposed, as were officials at the highest levels of Whitehall. Although SOE already employed scores of women – mostly as typists, drivers and clerks – women in the Army, Navy and Royal Air Force were barred from any armed combat. The statutes of the three services simply did not envisage women bearing arms and therefore there was no legal authority for servicewomen to carry out the kind of guerrilla work SOE had in mind. Furthermore, protested the lawyers, though all SOE's agents would be without uniforms and therefore liable to be shot as spies, women agents would have even less legal protection in the field than men. The 1929 Geneva Convention and the 1907 Hague Convention on Land Warfare, the main legal instruments offering protection to prisoners of war, made no provision at all for protecting women, as women were not envisaged as combatants.

SOE operations in the field were organised around a system of circuits, or networks, each covering a specific sector of France. Circuits were structured around three key figures – an organiser, a courier and a wireless operator, or signaller – all normally recruited and trained in Britain.

At the head of the circuit was the organiser, whose job was to recruit local French men and women in his area, who were either already working with another resistance group or willing to start. The circuit organiser was also responsible for arming and supplying these local resisters, arranging with London, through encoded messages sent by his wireless operator, for aircraft or ships to deliver weapons. The organiser would then identify sabotage targets in his territory – railway lines, power stations, factories and dams – which were to be destroyed when the signal from London came.

Within the SOE circuit, argued Gubbins, it was the job of courier that could best be carried out by women. With no other secure means of communication on the ground, couriers carried messages between circuits and sub-circuits, travelling long distances, often by bicycle or train, memorising their messages or writing them on silk paper or rice paper, which could easily be hidden or destroyed. Because they were constantly on the move, couriers ran the highest risk of being stopped and arrested. For male couriers that risk became greater with every day the war went on. From early 1942 all young men in France were liable to be picked off the street and, unless they were classified as essential workers, were sent to Germany as forced labourers. Women, however, could invent a hundred cover stories as they moved around, and aroused little suspicion. It was also considered that because women were less likely to be bodily searched, their messages could be niftily tucked in hems of skirts or, better still, in underwear.

In April 1942 Gubbins's case for sending women was secretly nodded through by Churchill and his War Cabinet, but the decision was never to be avowed, and it was left to Gubbins to find a ruse both to get around the law and overcome opposition in the military. It so happened that his family and a senior FANY officer owned neighbouring estates in Scotland and, thanks to their informal talks, a solution was worked out. As a civilian organisation, the FANY was not subject to the rules governing the services, so deploying FANYs as armed agents could not be deemed to be breaching any statute. SOE's women recruits – even those few who would be drawn from the ranks of the WAAF – would therefore be commissioned as members of the civilian FANY corps for as long as they served behind the lines.

Although women were also recruited for other SOE country sections (and for MI6), the majority were hired for F Section, and Maurice Buckmaster, who fully supported the use of women, now had the 'knotty problem', as Vera once put it, of how to handle their affairs. If the use of women as guerrillas leaked out, the policy would have to be denied. Therefore neither the War Office nor any other government department could take official responsibility for the women and even the FANY, though offering 'cover', only saw its SOE members as 'cap-badge FANYs' and certainly took no responsibility for them in respect of, for example, pensions, training or welfare.

When in early 1942 Vera suggested to Buckmaster that, in addition to her other roles, she should take responsibility for the women, he therefore readily agreed. Miss Atkins, whom Buckmaster had promoted from secretary to junior staff officer, had already proved herself to be utterly loyal, tactful and discreet. She was obviously the right person for the job.

One year later F Section had already deployed eleven women behind the lines, most of whom were seen off by Vera, and each, in her view, had more than justified the decision to send them.

Yvonne Rudellat, born in France, was first spotted in the London hotel where she worked as a receptionist. A mature woman of forty-five, separated from her husband, Yvonne was nevertheless considered 'unworldly' by her instructors, although these same instructors also noted that this very quality would help her go unnoticed: 'Her air of innocence and anxiety to please should prove a most valuable cover asset.' By March 1943 Yvonne had not only bicycled hundreds of miles across the Loire region, delivering vital messages, but had also taken part in the blowing up of 300,000-volt electricity cables south of Orléans, winning the praise of her organiser, who said that she was 'an extremely valuable colleague' and was 'fast becoming a demolition expert'.

Rudellat was one of several women working with SOE's largest resistance group in France, led by a charismatic SOE agent named Francis Suttill, whose alias was 'Prosper'. Another of Vera's women, Andrée Borrel, was Suttill's personal courier, and had been praised by Suttill himself as 'really in every way the best of all of us'. Before escaping to England in 1942, Andrée had already worked with the resistance, smuggling shot-down Allied airmen out of France. So poor was Suttill's French accent that it was doubtful he could have got his organisation up and running without the savvy Andrée to act as his negotiator. The couple had travelled the length and breadth of central France posing as an agricultural salesman and his assistant but in reality recruiting followers, sabotaging railway lines and receiving arms drops. Over the first five months of 1943, 240 containers of arms and explosives had been dropped to Prosper's cells by aircraft flying from England.

By late May 1943 Vera was preparing two further women to join sub-circuits of the Prosper network. One, a Frenchwoman named Vera Leigh, who before the war worked in an haute couture hat shop in Paris, had proved an excellent trainee. 'Dead keen' and 'the best shot in the group', said her instructors. However, the second woman due to join Suttill was causing Vera some anxiety; this was the young WAAF officer Nora Inayat Khan.

So large was Suttill's network by now that he had urgently requested a further wireless operator (he already had two) to work with a sub-organiser and to act as back-up to his own wireless man. An acute shortage of qualified wireless operators meant that F Section had to pick out a new trainee, and the only one who was even near ready to go was Nora.

Twenty-nine-year-old Nora had a most unusual background. Her father, Hasra Inayat Khan, was descended from the 'Tiger of Mysore', the last Mogul Emperor of southern India, which meant Nora was by lineage a princess. Her father had also been a mystic teacher and philosopher who travelled the world spreading the word of Sufism, often taking his family with him. Nora was born in the Kremlin in 1914 as her father happened to be teaching at the Conservatoire in Moscow at the time. Nora's mother, Ora Ray Baker, was a relative of Mrs Mary Baker Eddy, founder of the Christian Science Church, and had been born in America of British stock.

Nora's origins, however, were not the concern; SOE agents often had unconventional backgrounds. What mattered to Vera was that Nora could pass herself off as French. This she most certainly could, for her main home as a child had been Paris, where she was educated, studying child psychology at the Sorbonne. After university she became a noted author of children's stories, adapting legends and folklore for children and working on children's programmes for Radio Paris.

However, Nora's 'childlike' qualities, particularly her gentle manner and 'lack of ruse', had greatly worried her instructors at SOE's training schools. One instructor wrote that 'she confesses that she would not like to have to do anything "two faced"'. Another said Nora was 'very feminine in character, very eager to please, very ready to adapt herself to the mood of the company, the tone of the conversation, capable of strong attachments, kind hearted, emotional, imaginative'. A further observer said: 'Tends to give far too much information. Came here without the foggiest idea what she was being trained for.'

Later, others commented that Nora was also physically unsuited, claiming she was so striking, with her Eastern, doll-like looks, that she would not easily disappear into a crowd. Physically tiny, Nora also received poor athletics reports from her instructors: 'Can run very well but otherwise clumsy. Unsuitable for jumping.' 'Pretty scared of weapons but tries hard to get over it.'

But, as Vera pointed out at the time, Nora was training as a wireless operator and in that field she was getting quite adequate reports. Her 'fist', or style of tapping the keys, was somewhat heavy, apparently owing to her fingers being swollen by chilblains, but her speed was improving every day. Like many talented musicians – she played the harp – Nora was a natural signaller. Furthermore, insisted Vera, her commitment was unquestioned, as another training report had readily confirmed: 'She felt she had come to a dead end as a WAAF, and was longing to do something more active in the prosecution of the war, something which would demand more sacrifice.'

So, when Suttill's request first came, Vera saw Nora as a natural choice, and although her final training in field security and encoding had to be cut short, she judged her ready to go.

Nora's new identity, or 'cover story', in France would simply have to be made to match her outwardly gentle character, said Vera. And by the time Nora came back to Orchard Court for her final briefings in May 1943, Vera had devised a cover story for Nora as Jeanne-Marie Renier, whose profession would be that of children's nurse.

Buckmaster wholeheartedly agreed with Vera that Nora should go to France and was furious when the commander of B Group Special Training Schools said in his final report on Nora: 'Not over-burdened with brains' and 'it is very doubtful whether she is really suited to the work in the field'.

'We don't want them over burdened with brains,' wrote Buckmaster on the report; 'nonsense . . . makes me cross'.

And yet, in Vera's view, Nora had always been something of a special case. Her mission would be a particularly dangerous one, precisely because she was not going as a courier but as a wireless operator. Nora was in fact the first woman wireless operator to be sent by SOE to France. So successful had the women couriers been that a decision was taken in early 1943 to use women also as wireless operators, which was even more dangerous work, probably the most dangerous work of all.

The job of a wireless, or W/T (wireless telegraphy), operator was to maintain a link between the circuit in the field and London, sending and receiving messages about planned sabotage operations or about where arms were needed for resistance fighters. Without such communication it was almost impossible for any resistance strategy to be coordinated, but the operators were highly vulnerable to detection. Hiding themselves as best they could, with aerials strung up in attics or disguised as washing lines, they tapped out Morse on the keys of transmitters, often for hours and usually alone, as they waited for a signal in reply saying the messages were received. If they stayed on the air for more than twenty minutes, their signals were likely to be picked up by the enemy and detection vans then traced the source of these suspect signals.

When the signaller moved location the bulky transmitter had to be carried, sometimes hidden in a suitcase or in a bundle of firewood. If stopped and searched, the operator would have no cover story to explain the transmitter. In 1943 an operator's life expectancy was six weeks.

But it was not only the special danger of Nora's mission that had caused Vera extra anxiety in this agent's case. Nora had also been harder to get to know than any of the other women; she had been harder to fathom. This unusually self-contained young woman had been brought up in an intensely spiritual way. There was something, as Vera saw it, 'otherworldly' about her. This impression was conveyed not only by her looks and manner, but also by her thin, quavering, pipe-like voice. And, as Vera had noticed during their first meetings, Nora's powerful bonds with her family were particularly hard to break. Nora's mother was a widow by the time the war started and was highly dependent on her, the eldest of four children. Furthermore, Nora had a special bond with her elder brother, Vilayat. By early May, when the decision was taken to send Nora to France, Vera's concerns had been allayed, but just as final preparations for the agent's departure were beginning, her anxieties were once again aroused.

In mid-month Nora parted from her family in London for the last time. She had been staying at a country house in Buckinghamshire, a place where agents had a final chance to adjust to their new identities and consider their missions before departure. Vera was in touch with the agents at this time through their conducting officer, a companion – female in the case of women – who watched over them in training, reporting on their progress to Vera in London.

Nora's conducting officer had told Vera that she had descended into a gloom and was clearly troubled by the thought of what she was about to undertake. Then two fellow agents staying with Nora at the country house had written directly to Vera to say they felt she should not go. Such an intervention at this late stage was most unusual. Vera decided to call Nora back to London, to meet and talk. They arranged to meet for lunch at Manetta's, a restaurant in Clarges Street, Mayfair. Manetta's was the kind of place Vera liked to meet: it was lively but had secluded corners.

———

Vilayat Inayat Khan remembered trying to stop his sister going on her mission at exactly the time of the meeting at Manetta's. I spoke to him at the family home in Suresnes, near Paris. Nora's harp sat in a corner.

'You see, Nora and I had been brought up with the policy of Gandhi's non-violence and at the outbreak of war we discussed what we would do,' said Vilayat, who had followed his father and become a mystic. 'She said, "Well, I must do something but I don't want to kill anyone." So I said, "Well, if we are going to join the war we have to involve ourselves in the most dangerous positions, which would mean no killing."

'Then, when we eventually got to England, I volunteered for mine-sweeping and she volunteered for SOE, and so I have always had a feeling of guilt because of what I said that day.'

'Might you have been able to stop her?' I asked.

He said no, though in May 1943, when he was on leave, she came suddenly to him and showed him a pill that, if she was captured, she should take to commit suicide, and 'I was shattered, shattered. I knew what it meant. I said, "No, no this is going too far. Let's go and say you are not going to do it any more." She said, "I can't do that," but I think she was very disturbed.'

I asked Vilayat if Nora ever talked about the people she was working with or the job she was going to do. 'No, because it would have broken her code, but somehow it all came through to me to some extent. I knew she was landing in France and I was scared stiff. And I was aware of new people in her life, somehow controlling her. I was aware of their presence. And I learned later, of course, that she had been given this code by Vera Atkins and the others to withdraw and say nothing and so on. But it was so difficult for her to be secretive with me. I could read right through her. I would not say that she betrayed her code, but I could read through what she was saying. That was her whole teaching.

'Have you read her stories: *Jakarta Tales*?' he asked, referring to one of the books Nora wrote for children. 'It is all about a man who cannot lie.'

Did he remember Vera Atkins?

Yes, of course, he said, he had met her when the war was over. 'I would have said she had short hair maybe, or it was pinned up. Was it? And I remember her as elegant. Not pretty, but she looked distinguished. She was not charming but rather remarkable in her way.'

———

When Vera arrived at Manetta's, Nora was already there waiting. Vera ushered her downstairs, where red-leather seats lined the wall. She did not wish to unsettle Nora in any way or give the impression that she or Buckmaster had any doubts about her. But she did wish to talk about the worries she had heard.

Above all else she wished to confirm that Nora believed in her own ability to succeed. Confidence was the most important thing for any agent. However poor Nora's jumping or even her encoding, Vera knew that those agents who did well were those who knew before they set off that they could do the job. Her intention was to let Nora feel that she had an opportunity to back out gracefully should she so wish. Vera began by asking if she was happy in what she was doing. Nora looked startled and said: 'Yes, of course.'

Vera then told her of the letter she had received and what was said in it. Nora was upset that anyone should think she was not fit for the job. 'You know that if you have any doubts it is not too late to turn back,' Vera said. 'If you don't feel you're the type – if for any reason whatever you don't want to go – you only have to tell me now. I'll arrange everything so that you have no embarrassment. You will be transferred to another branch of the service with no adverse mark on your file. We have every respect for the man or woman who admits frankly to not feeling up to it.' She ended by adding: 'For us there is only one crime: to go out there and let your comrades down.'

Nora insisted adamantly that she wanted to go and was competent for the work. Her only concern, she said, was her family, and Vera sensed immediately that this was, as she had suspected, where the problem lay. Nora had found saying goodbye to her mother the most painful thing she had ever had to do, she said. As Vera had advised her, she had told her mother only half the truth: she had said she was going abroad, but to Africa, and she had found maintaining this deliberate deception cruel.

Vera asked if there was anything she could do to help with family matters. Nora said that, should she go missing, she would like Vera to avoid worrying her mother as far as possible. The normal procedure, as Nora knew, was that when an agent went to the field, Vera would send out periodic 'good news' letters to the family, letting them know that the person concerned was well. If the agent went missing the family would be told so. What Nora was suggesting was that bad news should only be broken to her mother if it was beyond any doubt that she was dead. Vera said she would agree to this arrangement if it was what Nora really wanted. With these assurances Nora seemed content and confident once more. And doubts in Vera's mind were also now settled.

Vera always accompanied the women agents to the departure airfields, if she possibly could. Those who were not dropped into France by parachute were flown there in Lysanders, which were short-winged monoplanes and light enough to land on very small fields. The planes were met by a 'reception committee' made up of SOE agents on the ground and local French helpers. The reception committees were alerted to the imminent arrival of the plane by a BBC action message inserted as a *message personnel*; these were broadcast across France every evening, mostly for ordinary listeners wishing to contact friends or family separated by war. The messages broadcast for SOE, agreed in advance between HQ and the circuit organiser, usually by wireless signal, sounded like odd greetings or sometimes aphorisms – '*Le hibou n'est pas un éléphant*' ('The owl is not an elephant') – but the reception committee on the ground would know that the message meant a particular operation would now take place. '*Roméo embrasse Juliette*', for example, might mean a Lysander flight was coming in that night.

Nora was to fly by Lysander with the June moon to a field near Angers, from where she would make her way to Paris to link up with the leader of a Prosper sub-circuit named Emile Garry, or Cinema, an alias chosen because of his uncanny resemblance to the film star Gary Cooper.

Once on the ground, Nora would also make contact with the Prosper organiser, Francis Suttill, and take on her new persona as the children's nurse Jeanne-Marie Renier, using fake papers in that name. To her SOE colleagues, however, she would be known simply by her alias, which was to be Madeleine.

There were two Lysanders leaving that June night in 1943. Also departing would be two other women: Diana Rowden, who was going out as a courier to the Jura area in the east of France, and Cicely Lefort, who would be doing the same for the Jockey circuit in the south-east, as well as an agent named Charles Skepper, who was going to Marseille.

Two open-topped cabriolets took the group to the airfield at Tangmere, near the Sussex coast east of Chichester. It was a gorgeous afternoon and the hedgerows were smothered in dog roses. Nora hardly talked on the journey and to Vera she appeared serene.

By the time they reached the cottage at Tangmere that was used as a base for the pilots – members of the so-called 'Moon Squadron' – night had fallen and inside the cottage supper was being prepared. Places were laid along two trestle tables in front of bare, whitewashed stone walls. Part of the cottage had once been a chapel and random numbers around the walls were thought to have denoted the Stations of the Cross.

After the meal, Squadron Leader Hugh Verity, the genial head of Lysander operations, led the group into another small living room, which had been converted into an operations room. On a table were a black telephone and a green scrambler, and on one wall was a large map of France bearing red marks, mostly over the coast, which Verity explained were high-risk areas for flak.

Vera and the three agents pulled up chairs as Verity started his briefing. The weather forecast, just telephoned in from the Met Office, was fair, with a slight risk of mist at ground level. Verity indicated the flight path on the map and showed the agents a photograph of the landing field, 3 kilometres north-north-west of Angers, which had been taken by an RAF Photo Reconnaissance Unit. It showed a tiny open space surrounded by woods and a river looping towards the southern end. Verity explained that, from their seats under the glass hood of the plane, they would be able to follow the loops of the Loire, which on a clear night like this would be lit up by the moon. They would be surprised how quickly they got used to the moonlight, he said, and it was quite adequate for reading a map – or even for finding the hip flask of whisky stowed in front of their seat. Verity always tried to relax the 'Joes', as the SOE passengers were called. Nobody was allowed to know their names. And as he talked, Vera constantly watched for signs of nerves in her agents, observing just the occasional shaking cigarette.

After the briefing Vera said a few words. Air Ops in London had called to say that the BBC message announcing their arrival had already gone out, which meant the reception committee would be in place. She then took each agent to one side, to go over cover stories one last time and to carry out her final checks of their clothes and equipment.

It was Vera's job to look meticulously through pockets, checking labels, laundry tags, examining every article of equipment and clothing for any telltale signs that these people had come from England. Then she completed their disguises with a packet of French cigarettes, a recent French newspaper or perhaps photographs of a 'relative' to go in a pocket or a bag. If any last-minute adjustment to clothing was needed, Vera could deftly stitch on a French manufacturer's label or a French-style button. As she knew, the tiniest tricks could sometimes perfect a disguise.

Instructors had warned that Nora was so distinctive she could never be camouflaged, but on this operation Vera felt just as worried about Cicely Lefort's poor French accent and Diana Rowden's English looks. Born in England of Irish descent, forty-three-year-old

Cicely had married a French doctor and lived for a number of years in France yet had never lost her English intonation. Diana was thoroughly bilingual, having grown up in the South of France, where her family had a villa and a yacht. But she was English and educated at an English girls' private school, and this showed – even down to the bow in her fair wavy hair.

The checks complete, Vera gave each agent a chance to see her alone, should they wish. She took Nora up to the bathroom, and as they spoke for a moment on the landing Vera was relieved to find that she seemed quite relaxed, almost elated. She even commented on a silver bird pinned to Vera's lapel. 'You are so clever, Miss Atkins. You always make sure you wear something pretty.' Vera responded by unpinning the brooch and pressing it into Nora's hands.

Just before 10pm a large army Ford station wagon arrived at the cottage. The group were then driven out to the tarmac, where the moonlight was now bright enough to light up the Lysanders. The group got out and stood huddled together as Verity briefly explained take-off procedures, describing how luggage was stowed under the wooden hinged seat.

Then Verity nodded to Vera, who moved forward, embracing Nora, Diana and Cicely and shaking Skepper's hand, before taking several paces back.

The pilots signalled their passengers to step up to the ladder and climb into the plane. Nora, heaving both her ordinary suitcase and a much heavier one containing her wireless, was the last to board. She was so slight she could hardly get a foot on the ladder and an airman moved forward to give her a leg up.

Within moments the engines had started and were left ticking over for several minutes as the pilots carried out their checks. The engines briefly opened up to full throttle and then returned to fine pitch. As the first 'Lizzy' turned its nose towards the runway, Vera looked up towards the silhouetted heads in the passenger seats and waved goodbye.

Back at the cottage, Vera paused only to collect up the few oddments left behind by her agents – a novel, a coat and a small vanity case – and then asked her driver to take her back to London. The moon was now high in the sky. June had been an excellent month for the Lysanders.

2

DISASTER

Just as Vera's colleagues knew nothing of her background, so nobody I spoke to in my researches knew what her real role was within SOE. Penelope Torr, F Section's records officer, said she was 'nothing special – the same as me'. But Pearl Witherington, perhaps SOE's most outstanding surviving woman agent, said: 'For me Vera Atkins was SOE. She still is.'

Details of Vera's service would be in her personal file, I was told. SOE personal files were still secret. I would have to see the 'SOE adviser', who turned out to be an amiable man in a dark suit who wore a French beret out of doors. His secretary, Valerie, led me down a deserted corridor in the bowels of the Old Admiralty Building to find him. It got darker and there was quite a chill. She pointed to where Ian Fleming's office once was and we talked about the suggestion that Vera was Miss Moneypenny, M's alluring secretary in the James Bond books, as mooted in an obituary. Valerie thought this most unlikely as Fleming worked in naval intelligence, although he might have caught a glimpse of Vera when she came to Room 055a, which was also down here somewhere, along a corridor that connected to the old War Office.

Up stone steps, Valerie stopped outside a door bearing a picture of Maurice Buckmaster in late middle age, looking kindly, almost ecclesiastical, and smoking a pipe. The door swung open on to a tiny room and amid a pile of files – stamped 'Secret' or 'Most Secret' – sat the SOE adviser. 'Closed until 2020,' it said on one file identified by a yellow sticker as 'pending release'.

The intention after the war was that all these files would remain secret indefinitely. SOE was closed down in January 1946, its staff sworn to secrecy and its papers locked away. But versions of the SOE story emerged anyway; in particular about the many agents who lost their lives. Sinister conspiracy theories were elaborated about SOE's true wartime role and debate began about whether the organisation had served any useful purpose at all. So persistent were the questions that an official with experience in secrets was appointed to 'advise' the general public by reference to these files. But the questions kept on coming. So now, explained the SOE adviser, the files were finally being opened up and people could read what happened for themselves.

However, he added, I would have to wait at least a year or two to see the files, as before their release they were being declassified. This meant that all sensitive material was being weeded out for ever. Sensitive material meant anything the people 'upstairs' – the MI6 'weeders' – felt should not be seen. I asked if Vera Atkins's file had already gone upstairs and Valerie went to see.

In any event, the adviser told me, personal files often had nothing much between the parachute training and the casualty report. 'Look at this,' he said, picking up a file on one of the agents, Vera Leigh, which held two or three scraps of paper. 'Born, Leeds. Abandoned by mother,' said a note. She had once been put up for a George Cross but this was not pursued, and there was no explanation why.

'The fact is that in those days if people died they scrubbed their files because they were of no further interest. You see, effectively whole periods of history were just junked. Only 13 per cent of the files remain.'

'Why 13 per cent?'

'I don't honestly know. It was a figure handed to me by my predecessor.'

Immediately after the war many files were supposed to have been lost in a fire, but of course, said the adviser, 'those conspiracy theorists' did not believe in the fire. They thought the files had been deliberately destroyed as a cover-up.

Valerie then brought in a thick brown folder; Vera Atkins had not yet gone upstairs.

The adviser opened it and started to read very fast: '"Rosenberg, alias Atkins. Vera May. ARC number: 334 Bow Street Magistrates 1937. Identity papers: expired Romanian passport."'

He paused. 'That's interesting,' he said.

I asked what an ARC was.

'Aliens Registration Certificate,' he replied. 'Now, let's see – "Languages spoken: French, German, English. Status: Single. Political views: None. Private means: Yes. 'Do you ride, swim, ski, shoot?' Answer: 'Yes.' 'Do you drive a car, a motor cycle or a lorry, do you sail a boat, mountaineer, run, bicycle, fly an aeroplane, box, sketch or transmit Morse?' Answer: 'No.'"'

'She says she is fluent in German and French with some knowledge of Romanian. "Countries visited prior to 1939: Romania, France, Turkey, Greece, Austria, Germany, Italy, Switzerland, Egypt, Syria, Palestine, Hungary – etc. 'What districts are you most familiar with?' 'Sussex.'"'

'She was put through the cards and there was "no trace". Everyone was "put through the cards" – which meant checked for anything suspect in their background. If they found "no trace", there was "nothing recorded against".'

Vera's personal file contained a jumble of information but among it all was the hitherto hidden fact that she was still of Romanian nationality, and so an 'enemy alien', when she worked for SOE. 'She must have had important backers,' said the SOE adviser, who advised me to find her naturalisation papers 'if they haven't been destroyed'.

———

Vera always arrived at work by the same black cab. She had an arrangement with a driver, a Mr Lane, who collected her from her flat, where she lived with her mother, at Nell Gwynne House, Sloane Avenue, every morning and dropped her outside an office block in Baker Street. Through lack of space in Whitehall, Baker Street had become the address for SOE and several buildings here had acquired discreet plaques saying 'Inter Services Research Bureau'. Staff called it 'the firm', 'the org' or 'the racket'. Vera told acquaintances she had 'a boring little job in Baker Street'.

The headquarters of SOE was at 64 Baker Street, where the executive director, known as CD, had his office, with most country sections located over the road at Norgeby House. On arrival Vera took the lift up to the second floor and walked down the corridor of F Section to reach her office at the end, overlooking Baker Street, just before the door marked 'F'.

The symbols for country section desk officers indicated their country and sometimes, though not always, their role. Maurice Buckmaster, as head of F Section, was simply 'F'; the operations officer, Gerry Morel, was 'F Ops'; the head of planning, Bourne-Paterson (nobody knew his first name), was 'F Plans'; Nicholas Bodington, Buckmaster's deputy (until he was removed for other duties), was 'FN'; and Vera, in June 1943, was 'FV'.

Buckmaster, who caught the bus to work, would usually be in before his staff arrived, and was always in before Vera, who was last of all to arrive. Once he tried to get every staff officer to sign in every morning, which Vera adamantly refused to do. Mornings, she told people, 'are not my time of day'. But she was always in the office in time for Buckmaster's morning meeting, held promptly at ten.

Forty-one-year-old Buckmaster had not been an obvious choice for a top job in SOE. Although he had served in the British Army's Intelligence Corps at the outbreak of war, and was evacuated from Dunkirk, he had no knowledge or training in guerrilla warfare. The son of a Midlands entrepreneur, Buckmaster had shown an academic bent at Eton and gained an exhibition to study Classics at Oxford, which he then could not take up as his father had just gone bankrupt.

Instead he went on a cycling tour of France and stayed there, taking several jobs but showing a particular flair for public relations. Eventually he secured a responsible post as a manager with the Ford Motor Company in France, and it was his knowledge of French industry, gained with Ford, which caught the attention of SOE. But Buckmaster's superiors had also been impressed by his 'tireless zeal'.

Decision-making in SOE was rarely carried out by discussion. If a view was needed from a colleague a note was dictated, tucked into a brown envelope, picked up by a passing trolley and delivered. It would then come back marked 'approved', 'I agree' or sometimes 'rubbish' and also marked 'F' or 'F Plans', or perhaps 'FV'. Anything important was copied to whoever needed to know. SOE had scores of messengers running around and a large typing pool, and every staff officer had a secretary or even two. Vera, by the end of the war, had three. And although the European country sections were largely in one building – Belgium, Holland and Poland were just above France – there was little contact between sections for fear of leaks.

The 'Ops' (Operations) room was on the first floor of Norgeby House and was shared, but each country section had its own separate board with hooks on it. On this a duty officer would hang up notices detailing each section's separate operations for the day – usually flights dropping weapons or agents – on their board, and then draw a curtain across it.

Even communication with the high command across the road was mostly carried out on paper. Neither CD nor his senior officers ever felt the need to cross to Norgeby House. Country section heads ran operations without day-to-day direction from above. Periodic council meetings were held to discuss policy, but in general the SOE hierarchy was built on trust and it went without saying that everyone was working to the same end.

If, therefore, 'F' needed a view from the top he could simply mark up a note for CD, AD/E (Assistant Director/Europe) or perhaps 'C', head of MI6, the Secret Intelligence Service, though relations between these two covert agencies were not good. MI6, protective of its territory, feared that SOE's sabotage operations would endanger the quiet gathering of secret intelligence, which was its domain.

Also constantly at loggerheads with SOE was Bomber Command, which thought acts of sabotage on the ground less efficient than bombing from the air.

Country sections had little useful contact with MI5, the Security Service, either, though MI5 was constantly trying to exert oversight over SOE, which it knew (from bitter experience) was wide open to enemy infiltration.

Buckmaster's section had not only to defend itself against rivals in Whitehall, however, but was also constantly wary of the Free French. General Charles de Gaulle, having set up his government-in-exile in London in June 1940, had established his own secret service department in a house in Duke Street, which ran entirely separate guerrilla operations into France and gathered its own intelligence on the resistance. The fact that the British were setting up their resistance circuits 'infringed the sovereignty of France', according to de Gaulle, so that relations between SOE and the Free French were little short of poisonous. A special section of SOE, known as

RF Section, was established purely to coordinate operations with the Free French.

F Section staff therefore welcomed their morning meeting in Buckmaster's office as an important opportunity to talk in confidence to trusted colleagues. Only the inner circle attended the meeting: Major Morel, Major Bourne-Paterson, Major Bodington – if he was in the office – and one or two other senior staff. Buckmaster, whose rank was Lieutenant Colonel in June 1943, also liked Miss Atkins to be present, because, although she was of junior status, her views, when offered, were invariably pertinent. As he had recently noted on Vera's personal file, she had 'a fantastically good memory and quick grasp', whereas he had a tendency to get 'enmeshed in detail' and 'lacked fixity of purpose', as his superiors had, in turn, observed about him.

By June 1943 Vera had informally been assigned not only responsibility for overseeing the women recruits but also the task of intelligence officer, which largely meant sifting all intelligence about life on the ground in France. In her encyclopedic brain Vera stored away the latest information on what papers an agent would need to move about; on whether ration cards were issued monthly or weekly; on the hours of curfew; or on the latest trend in hats in rue Royale. Gleaning the facts from magazines, intelligence sources or returning agents, she circulated highlights in little leaflets for the staff called 'Titbits' or 'Comic Cuts' after popular magazines.

Absorbing such information demanded considerable mental acumen, though as a mere GSO III – a General Staff Officer, grade III, the equivalent of an army staff captain – Vera did not enjoy a grade, salary or symbol that reflected her responsibilities. And she was not the only woman at the morning meeting. Penelope Torr, who dealt with records, had the symbol 'F Recs' and also carried the three nominal 'pips' of a staff captain, was present too.

The mood at F's morning meetings in mid-June 1943 was generally positive. There had been setbacks in the spring – not least the capture of an organiser, Peter Churchill, and his courier, Odette Sansom – but a number of promising new agents had recently been sent out to the field. Vera reported, for example, on the successful departure of several agents during that month's full moon. On the night of 15–16 June she saw off two bright young Canadians, Frank Pickersgill and John Macalister. Dropped by parachute to a reception committee organised by a Prosper sub-circuit, the Canadians' mission was to set up their own new circuit, Archdeacon, near the town of Sedan, in the Ardennes region of north-eastern France.

Vera also reported on the double Lysander flight of the following night, carrying Nora Inayat Khan and three others, who landed safely north of Angers. On the ground to meet them was Henri Déricourt, F Section's new air movements officer, who was Buckmaster's prize new recruit. A trick aviator who became a pilot with Air France, Déricourt had escaped to England in 1942 to look for work. Buckmaster, at that time in urgent need of an airman to organise his night landings and pick-up operations, had snapped him up and had him parachuted back into France with the alias Gilbert. As all at the morning meeting were agreed, air operations in and out of France were, thanks to Déricourt, running more smoothly now than ever before.

There was, nevertheless, anxiety in F Section in mid-June. This centred on Francis Suttill, alias Prosper. Educated at Stonyhurst College and a barrister by training, thirty-two-year-old Suttill had shown himself to SOE instructors to be highly resourceful and smarter than most. Although he caught polio as a teenager, leaving him with a slight limp, he had overcome the disability and had displayed a certain athleticism and daring in training, which Buckmaster had admired. With his obvious flair for leadership, Suttill soon became the natural choice for F Section's most challenging job: to establish a circuit based in Paris, covering a vast chunk of central France. Having supposedly chosen his own alias – Prosper was a fifth-century French theologian who preached predestination – he keenly took up his mission, which was to rebuild blown circuits and then recruit afresh. His commitment to the task was beyond question. Raised in Lille by an English father who worked in the French wool industry and a French mother, Suttill had volunteered for the paratroops, saying: 'My one wish is to be used in France.'

Such had been Suttill's success in recruiting followers that by June 1943 his circuit, named Physician, was already poised to spearhead a general resistance uprising, planned to coincide with the Allied landings. Though the date of the landings was not yet known, the talk in French resistance circles was that it could happen as soon as autumn 1943. Suttill, always thinking ahead, had reported to

London in April that he was already planning for the landings by strategic placement of arms caches. He personally intended to 'follow the enemy' as they retreated.

Since then, however, Suttill's normal ebullience had evaporated. Returning to London for briefings in mid-May, he seemed jaded and voiced fears of penetration of the circuit. Two of his best local agents, sisters who provided a 'letterbox', had been captured in April and a somewhat desperate bid to negotiate with the Germans for their release in return for cash had backfired. Instead of the handover of the two sisters, two prostitutes were produced.

Suttill was parachuted back into France on 20 May, but his most recent report home suggested that his mood had not improved. He named a colleague who was not to be trusted, encoding the name for fear his report might be intercepted. Most notable was Suttill's intense antagonism towards desk officers back at HQ.

'Your conception of a letterbox', he had complained 'appears to be a place where an agent usually covered in mud, carrying an obvious suitcase, can turn up at an unreasonable hour to be lodged and fed and laundered for anything up to three weeks.' He even complained about Déricourt, alias Gilbert, the new air movements officer. 'There has been a good deal of confusion this month over the Lysander receptions owing to Gilbert's insufficient instructions. Henri, for instance, on arriving was given a bicycle and left to his own devices. As he cannot ride a bicycle he had to walk and came to me.'

The concern in Baker Street was that Suttill's network, made up of intellectuals, farmers, communists and aristocrats, was riddled with rivalry, which was spreading distrust. Perhaps the network was simply too big for one man to manage.

Reading between the lines, it sounded to headquarters staff as if morale in Suttill's own immediate team might be flagging too. He had asked HQ for 'a short personal letter' for his women couriers, Andrée Borrel and Yvonne Rudellat. Not that their morale needed 'bucking up', but they had been rather left out of it as far as personal messages were concerned, said Suttill.

On top of Suttill's 'show of nerves', as HQ saw it, another member of Prosper, a wireless operator named Jack Agazarian, had flown home on leave with the June moon, bringing news of further arrests in the group.

During periods of uncertainty like this it was Vera's practice to spend as much time as possible in Room 52, the SOE signals room. In late June she was waiting every evening for the first messages of the departed agents to come in, and was particularly anxious for a message from Nora.

It was, in fact, not necessary for Vera to be physically in the signals room. Until early 1943 all SOE signals had been handled by MI6, but, under a new, more secure system, messages for SOE were now received first by wireless telegraphy staff at an outstation known as Home Station, where they were decoded before being passed to Baker Street over a secure teleprinter link.

The country section would be alerted by Room 52 over the scrambler that a message had come through, and that message would then be passed to a superintendent to classify according to a classification board – 'Top Secret', 'Most Secret', 'Secret' and so on – before being marked in an 'in and out' register and sent out for distribution. The messages would then be colour-coded according to where they were going and from where they had come: white for outgoing traffic, green for live traffic and pink for service traffic.

And there were five duplicating machines, so once a message had arrived in Baker Street distribution clerks rolled off sufficient copies and messengers distributed the messages on a trolley every half-hour during the day and every two hours at night. Country sections saw only their own signals, but every message that came in went to Colin Gubbins, whose secretary would sort them by colour code and tie them all to treasury tags.

On receipt of a 'priority' message an operator at Home Station signalled the word 'flash' to London HQ, whereupon extra paper and carbon was inserted at the London end and the 'flash' copy was stripped off the teleprinter without correction. It was stamped 'subject to confirmation' and immediately passed to the dispatch clerk, who sent it off by special messenger.

Rather than wait for the messenger's trolley, however, Vera liked to be in the signals room in person. In her role as intelligence officer she insisted on seeing all telegrams in order to build up as accurate a picture as she could of all developments affecting every circuit in France. She knew nothing herself of signals operations and had never studied Morse code. But for staff officers in London, most of whom had never been in the field but at times felt that this was where they too should be, there was nothing to compare with the sound of the teleprinter's clacking. The messages created the illusion of instant communication with the agents, and with France, which by June 1943 had been entirely cut off from England for more than three years.

Immediately on entering the signals room, which was blacked out and was approached via a cordoned-off outer area, Vera could look up at a large blackboard high on the wall to see the call-signs of agents for whom a listening watch was being maintained.

In the middle of June, Vera was looking for the call-sign 'Nurse'. Each wireless operator had a call-sign, most often referring to an article of clothing but sometimes to an occupation, in addition to an alias and a street name, to go with a cover story. The call-sign was part of the operator's 'signal plan', which was designated as their particular set of frequencies, codes and transmission times. Nora Inayat Khan's alias was Madeleine but her call-sign was 'Nurse'.

Vera knew precisely what Nora's 'scheds', or transmission times, were: on Sunday she would come on from 9.05, on Wednesday from 14.10 and on Friday from 17.10. But as there was always a chance she would transmit much later than her designated time, Vera would often wait late into the evening, eating perhaps in the SOE canteen.

Four days after Nora's departure Vera was still watching for 'Nurse'. Nora should by now have made contact with her sub-circuit organiser, Emile Garry (Cinema), and should also have been in touch with Prosper's own people, based just outside Paris. The circuit's core group met at an agricultural research college, the Ecole Nationale d'Agriculture, at Grignon, near Versailles, and several of the college's staff worked for Prosper.

Nora might have tried and then failed to make her signal heard, but Vera had checked with Home Station over the two-way microphone and there had been nothing at all. She might have already been 'DF'd', or blocked by German direction-finders. (When the Germans isolated an enemy signal they first sent a beam out from a radio station and jammed the frequency, which for both the operator and receiver produced a high-pitched ringing noise.)

Then, on 20 June, instead of 'Nurse' the call-sign 'Butcher' came up on the blackboard. This was the call-sign of Gilbert Norman, alias Archambaud, who was Suttill's principal wireless operator and the person most likely to have news of Nora.

The message from Norman, transmitted fast and clear, said Nora had safely arrived. She had not transmitted because her wireless set was damaged on landing, and Norman requested a replacement radio for her 'soonest'. He said he was giving her instruction in W/T from his own set, out at Grignon. Norman's message was copied round F Section and set minds at rest. Two days later, on 22 June, 'Nurse' came up on the board, and, using Norman's set, Nora sent a hesitant first message confirming her arrival. She could have had no better instructor in the field than Norman, whose own wireless training reports had been among the best F Section had ever had. Vera knew that Nora was now in good hands.

But within a few days more worrying news had reached London, again from Francis Suttill.

Wireless messages, though the most immediate, were not the only means of contact between the field and HQ. Agents could also send back longer, more detailed reports in SOE mailbags. These reports were written '*en clair*' – that is, not encoded – though any ultra-sensitive details, such as names, places or signals details, were supposed to be encoded. As well as arranging the pick-up of agents on the landing fields, the air movements officer Henri Déricourt (Gilbert) was the 'postman' who collected agents' mail from 'letter-boxes' and put it on the Lysanders.

The report Suttill sent on the last flight of the June moon was his bleakest yet. Dated 19 June, it reached Baker Street five days later and said that Madeleine (Nora) had narrowly escaped arrest a few days previously. Suttill was blaming London for sending her to France with details of a 'blown letterbox'. The letterbox was unsafe because the person who provided it had been in touch with another F Section circuit, known to have already been infiltrated by the Gestapo, as Suttill himself had warned London four months previously. 'Had Madeleine gone there yesterday afternoon she would have coincided with one of the Gestapo's periodical visits to the flat!' he wrote. In a fury with whoever was responsible, he accused London of breaking a cardinal rule by allowing one circuit to be contaminated by contact with another. He then demanded that HQ take disciplinary action immediately against everyone involved.

In this case it at once becomes superabundantly clear that similar circumstances can arise at any time and that therefore the whole system of giving to any agent a letterbox of another circuit is an obvious invitation to disaster for that circuit.

I hope I have made myself clear. I state, in parenthesis,
that it is now 0100 hours 19 June and I have slept seven hours
since 0500 hours 15 June.

Suttill went on to warn London that all his letterboxes and pass-
words now in force would be cancelled from midday 19 June until he
received a message from London saying: 'The village postman has
recovered,' which would mean his rule was taken on board.

'If you are not prepared to accept my suggestion I will of, course,
on your instruction, immediately reinstate the letterboxes uncondi-
tionally. In such case please file this report carefully for production
on the inevitable eventual "post mortem" of the "feu" ['the late'
(i.e. dead)] Prosper organisation.'

With this report Suttill had also sent a letter for his wife, Margaret,
a GP near Plymouth, thanking London for allowing him to write
home. Personal mail carried by Lysander was a privilege not all
agents received. One of Vera's jobs was to pass on the mail, checking
first for security breaches. 'Dear Child,' was how Francis Suttill
always began letters to his wife. 'It is nice to have the boys with me,'
he wrote, referring to the fact that after his last home leave he had
brought a photograph of his two baby boys with him back to France,
which was against the rules.

HQ had no chance to take action on Suttill's threat. The following
day, 25 June, a 'flash' message came out of the teleprinter in the signals room. It was from an F Section local recruit in Paris. Extra
carbon paper was placed in the teleprinters by FANY clerks and the
dispatch riders were put on stand-by.

The message said that Suttill, along with his main radio man,
Gilbert Norman (Archambaud) and his courier, Andrée Borrel
(Denise), had 'disappeared, believed arrested'.

'To be confirmed' was stamped on the signal 'flimsy', which was
duplicated and transported around the building in Baker Street, with
copies going to F, F Ops, F Plans, F Recs, FV and FN, and over the
road to CD and his senior staff, who, already dealing with emergen-
cies in Yugoslavia and the Middle East, had little time to intervene
in F Section's crisis. An even greater catastrophe had hit the Free
French. Jean Moulin, the leader of the Gaullist resistance, had been
captured in France at almost exactly the same time.

*

Although Vera knew nothing of signals telegraphy, her presence in the signals room was never irksome to the signals staff. On the contrary, she was valued because she had a particular flair for reading mutilated messages: those that were hard to understand because letters were garbled or words were missing as a result of enemy jamming or poor transmission.

Each agent had a unique 'fist', rather like a fingerprint in Morse. Tapping on the key of their transmitter, some made a long 'dah' and some short; some used long breaks between words and some clipped their 'dits'.

Vera also knew the different 'signal plans': the coding system, transmission times and frequencies ascribed to each agent. For security, each agent was assigned their own exclusive frequencies – usually two – which could be located only by inserting a device called a 'crystal' into the wireless set. If the agents wanted to change frequencies, new crystals were sent out by London, deliveries of which Vera might often arrange.

Vera also made it her business to know an agent's coding system. Many agents encoded their messages using a favourite poem – typically one they learned at school or university – which they chose and memorised before leaving for the field. Others used a Playfair cipher, based on a square containing twenty-five letters and numbers. Nora had been given a simplified code as she had left in such a rush.

Because Vera knew the coding systems and poems, she was well equipped to unscramble an 'indecipherable'. This might occur simply because an agent had mistransposed a letter in their Playfair or misspelled a word in their poem, which Vera was often able to spot. Each agent had a characteristic set of mistakes. And although she was not qualified to identify the technical aspects of a 'fist', Vera certainly knew individuals' styles of communication as well as anyone. For example, some agents liked simply to sign off 'Goodbye', while others sent 'Lots of Love' and one of Nora's hallmarks was 'Tallyho'.

Buckmaster, like Vera, had never trained in clandestine communications of any sort. But he did have a talent for crosswords and even claimed he finished the *Times* crossword every day on the bus to work. Not surprisingly, he liked to try his hand at transposing garbled messages. It was quite a common sight to see Vera, often with Buckmaster, bent over a piece of paper, transposing letters or debating whether an agent might have transliterated in error, using perhaps 'mite' instead of 'might' or 'peace' instead of 'piece' to 'code up' a particular word. Both of them also enjoyed dreaming up BBC 'action' messages, which were used not only to alert agents on the ground to a landing operation, but to signal that a prearranged arms drop would now go ahead or an act of sabotage should now take place. One of Vera's tasks was to deliver BBC messages to Bush House, ready for broadcast.

For now, however, no messages of any sort could be sent to the Prosper network. All anybody could do was wait for more news. The silence – particularly from Gilbert Norman's radio – did not bode well. 'Butcher' was simply not coming up on the board.

If Suttill had been caught, his people all knew, he would try to hold out under torture for forty-eight hours without talking. In that time word would spread like lightning down the lines and Prosper's followers – several hundred of them, counting all his sub-circuits – would be running for cover, closing down letterboxes, abandoning safe houses, destroying messages and burning their papers and codes. More information was bound to reach London soon. But at the moment nobody at HQ could be sure what was happening in France, because no messages were coming in.

Then, on 7 July, the call-sign they had so much hoped would come back up was chalked on the board. 'Butcher' – Gilbert Norman – was trying to transmit. His message came through. Prosper 'captured', he confirmed.

Coming from Norman himself, the dismal news was hard to question. Yet the consolation was significant: Norman, since he was transmitting, was evidently free. To that extent at least, the disaster was limited. The vital wireless link to London was still in place.

And yet, as some in the signals room were swift to see, Norman's message was peculiar. It was mutilated, which might have been caused by atmospheric conditions, but his tapping was uncharacteristically clipped.

Most surprising was that Norman had forgotten to include the secret security check, carried by each agent, which gave London absolute confirmation that a wireless operator was transmitting freely. Each agent was given a bluff check and a true check, which they had to insert in a message. These took the form of spelling mistakes or secret signals, agreed with London, that were inserted in the text to show the sender had not been caught. A 'bluff' check was one that could, under torture, be yielded to the Germans. The one that mattered was the true check. If the true check was not present it meant the agent was captured.

A number of explanations were posited for the peculiar message. At first Vera considered that the message had perhaps been transmitted by Nora, who had been practising on Norman's set. Another suggestion was that Norman was on the run and operating in difficult circumstances. Few, though, were prepared to countenance the possibility that he might be operating under German control.

As F Section was aware, the Germans had sent messages back to London over the radios of captured operators before. As recently as April 1943 an F Section wireless operator named Marcus Bloom, alias Bishop, had been captured and peculiar messages had been sent over his radio, but this case was seen as a one-off.

For the Germans to be operating Norman's radio, however, Norman himself must have passed over his codes and crystals. 'He would rather have shot himself,' exclaimed Buckmaster when the possibility was proposed by Penelope Torr, the records officer.

Norman, an accountant by profession and an earnest young man, had passed every test in training with flying colours, and security in particular had become 'second nature', said his instructors, whose only criticism of him was that he tended 'to talk too much'.

Miss Torr pointed out, however, that Home Station had examined Norman's back traffic and found that he had sent 149 near-perfect messages since going to the field and had never forgotten his security check before. Buckmaster was unmoved. There was only one explanation for Norman's mistake and that was carelessness. 'You have forgotten your double security check,' he replied as soon as the operator's next sched came up. 'Be more careful next time.'

F's morning meetings were now dominated by Prosper as staff pored over the latest reports on who was captured and who was not. Among those reported safe was Nora, who was said to be lying low with France Antelme, another key Prosper man, who had escaped the round-up. But the clatter of messages now coming in was reporting mass arrests. The Gestapo were raiding all of Prosper's arms depots. Names of several traitors, among them key Prosper lieutenants, were already being mentioned in messages. Somebody was obviously talking. But none of the reports could be verified and the position still remained anything but clear.

There was even some uncertainty now about the fate of the two Canadians, Pickersgill and Macalister, who had not signalled to London since they arrived on 16 June.

Meanwhile Miss Torr had compiled another report for Buckmaster detailing the latest analysis of Norman's 'peculiar' message. The cryptanalysts were now insisting that the fist was 'very out of character' and 'unusually hesitant' and the message 'could quite easily be the work of a flustered man doing his first transmission under protest'.

Buckmaster, however, pointed out that all Norman's messages had been technically quite normal since he had been reminded about missing his 'true check'. He ordered staff to continue sending messages to Norman, particularly to ask him for news of Suttill. Where had he been taken? Was he injured? The replies never answered the questions.

For a better picture, F Section could only wait for the July moon, when France Antelme was due to fly back, bringing first-hand news.

———

'I did like tidy records and nobody had really bothered with records before,' Penelope Torr told me. She talked very fast and recalled being accused by her male superiors at SOE of being 'a talky bitch'.

'I had a new kind of flip-flop file: you pulled a card out and had different colours for each circuit so you could see exactly what had happened in that circuit. When the messages came in they brought them to me and I filed them and Buckmaster used to come and ask me to get them out so he could remind himself what they had said and what had happened, because he often didn't seem to know. He never wanted to believe anyone was captured. All his geese were swans.

'The horrifying thing was that when somebody had been captured you had to take a card out and put it in another file and then later I discovered the agents had been strung up on meat hooks.'

Did Vera ever come to see the records? I asked her.

'Oh, no. She would never speak to me. She wasn't interested in me. She was abrasive and tiresome. She was abrasive in a quiet way. She didn't say much. But she was sarcastic. "What are you doing here, you upstart" sort of tone. She always seemed to be very pleased with herself – she had an "I know best" attitude. I don't think she could stand the fact that there was another woman of equal rank who could attend the morning meetings.'

Sitting in her flat on the Banbury Road in Oxford, in a block of sheltered housing, Penelope Torr seemed suddenly haunted by the very thought of Vera. 'I found it disturbing when she came into a room for the morning meeting. I thought, now what, you know,' she said, and laughed nervously. 'I dislike what I remember of her.'

Then she paused a while and said: 'It sounds like a terrible thing to say but I have been waiting till Vera died before I ever said anything of this. I never wanted anything I said to get back to her. I was worried she would immediately call me up and start belittling me.'

———

A businessman before the war, France Antelme, a broad-shouldered, handsome British Mauritian in his mid-forties, had been sent to France by SOE, charged with arranging finance and supplies for Allied troops after the landings. Arriving back in London in mid-July, Antelme, normally resilient and proud, was a shaken man. Events were unfolding even as he had left the field, he said, and he himself had only missed being caught up in the disaster because he had left Paris for a rendezvous with a contact in Poitiers.

Antelme reported for sure that Suttill had been arrested in Paris on 24 June but he did not know how. He also revealed other arrests as yet unknown to London, including that of Yvonne Rudellat and her sub-circuit organiser. Scores of other local recruits had been rounded up in the days after Suttill was taken and either shot or put in prison at Fresnes, near Paris. The arrests seemed systematic and based on very accurate information.

Nora had survived the round-up, the Mauritian confirmed, but only just. On the day of Suttill's arrest she went to the agricultural college at Grignon, intending to meet up with Gilbert Norman and to practise transmitting, but Norman had not turned up. The area was swarming with Gestapo. Later the base was raided by the Germans. Serge Balachowsky, another Prosper man, a distinguished biologist, hid whatever equipment he could in the grounds of the college, including Nora's wireless transmitter, which he buried under lettuces. Balachowsky himself was then later arrested.

Antelme said he had done what he could to put Nora on her feet before leaving for England. He had spent the last two weeks with her in Paris, hiding out in a safe house. Before leaving he had placed her in contact with Henri Déricourt, who needed a W/T operator and would no doubt be able to guide her. Nevertheless, now he himself was safely back, Antelme was evidently concerned that he had left Nora in such danger.

Considered a shrewd judge of character, Antelme was then pressed for his view on what had become of Norman, but he could not say for sure if he had or hadn't been arrested. Antelme had been to Norman's flat since the disappearance and it appeared not to have been searched. Everything looked tidy and there were two bicycle clips lying next to Norman's bicycle, which was leaning against the wall.

If Norman was still free, Antelme thought it was surprising that he should have transmitted badly, as he always transmitted with extreme ease and often chatted away while he was tapping out messages. He remembered hearing Norman telling Nora to memorise her plans and codes and then burn them, which suggested he would have done the same himself. And if Norman were free, Antelme was puzzled as to why he was refusing to answer questions in his latest messages about Suttill's whereabouts.

Penelope Torr, who then examined Norman's recent traffic with Antelme, wrote Buckmaster another long note: 'The sequencing of the events described in his messages makes no sense,' she reported. 'The only explanation I can think of is that Archambaud may have coded up a number of his messages and left them somewhere for transmission in rotation. If they were then found by one of the traitors after his arrest they would naturally send them in rotation to maintain normality, not realising that part of the text was now hopelessly out of date. I hope somebody can find a more favourable explanation.'

Buckmaster still insisted that nobody could have imitated Archambaud, but Penelope Torr suggested exactly how it might have been done, adding: 'There is no reason to suppose that the Gestapo have not prepared for just such an eventuality by providing trained W/T operators of their own.'

She added that Antelme had now told her that Norman had 250 BBC messages in his wallet, which he took to the field last time, and he suggested they be cancelled.

On 19 July there was good news. The call-sign for John

Macalister, Frank Pickersgill's signaller, finally came up on the signals room board.

———

'Would Vera have ever challenged Buckmaster?' I asked another F Section staff member, Nancy Roberts. Nancy was closer to Vera than anyone in F Section. I had hunted for memos, notes or jottings from Vera at this time – any hint of what views she might have formed about suspect radio traffic. But, unlike Penelope Torr, Vera had committed nothing to paper, or if she had, it had not survived. Yet Vera was studying the messages as closely as anyone. She had Buckmaster's ear. What would she have said to him in the summer of 1943?

'Vera didn't think like a woman,' said Nancy. 'She didn't have irrelevant, womanish ideas like the rest of us.' We were talking in the drawing room of the Special Forces Club in Knightsbridge. 'She didn't waste time wondering what to do. And though the men around her hated to admit it, they knew she was always right.'

'So might she have told Buckmaster he was sometimes wrong?'

A portrait of Vera was gazing out over our heads, and I couldn't help wondering if she wasn't a little irritated still by the design of the upholstery. She resigned in a huff from the committee of the Special Forces Club in 1971 because she was right about the redecoration plans and the committee was wrong. 'She would not have told him he was wrong exactly,' said Nancy. 'She was always loyal to Buck. And I always had the impression she was in awe of Buck. He didn't have her dexterity of mind. But he was very much the officer class and she admired all that.'

We carried on up the stairs to the bar, passing all the famous faces: Suttill, Baseden, Szabo. And here were Buckmaster and Vera. She was in WAAF uniform. 'But Vera didn't get that uniform until very late in the war,' said Nancy. 'Buckmaster always wanted her to join the FANYs but she knew that was a Cinderella corps. She waited until she could be commissioned in the WAAF.'

Sinking into a chair under a picture of the Queen Mother, Nancy explained: 'You see, Vera was very ambitious. It was she who recruited me for F Section very early on, before Buck was even head.' People were perching on green leather stools while a barman squirted spirits from upturned bottles.

'How did she recruit you?' I asked.

'In the Ladies' in Norgeby House.'

'To do what?'

'To take over her job as secretary to BP.'

'Why?'

'So she could move on, I suppose.' Vera had never let anyone know that she had started out at F Section as secretary to 'BP' (Major R.A. Bourne-Patterson).

Before joining F Section, Nancy was with the Air Liaison, or AL, section on the first floor. 'There was no mixing between sections,' said Nancy, 'but of course we powdered noses together in the Ladies' and picked up the gossip.' The women's cloakroom was on the half-landing and it was here that Vera came to take an interest in Nancy. Even at this time Nancy was aware of Vera's reputation and was flattered that she should pay attention to her, although Nancy too had a reputation – as an auburn beauty with a mind of her own. In those days, as Nancy Fraser-Campbell, she also had an impeccable upper-crust name and a Scottish pedigree to match.

Nancy didn't like working for BP. A City accountant before the war, he was 'a snide man', said Nancy, laughing as she described how he used to swing back on his War Office wooden chair while dictating. 'One day he lost his balance, fell in a heap to the floor, rolled under his desk, climbed back on to his chair, and never for a moment stopped talking.'

At the time that Vera was trying to secure Nancy a job as BP's new secretary, F Section was deeply divided over who should be its new head, after a recruit from Courtaulds was sacked for getting nothing done. Buckmaster was eager for the job and Vera backed him early on. It was when Buckmaster took over as F, towards the end of 1941, that Nancy took Vera's job and Vera was given officer status by Buckmaster, no doubt partly as a reward for her loyalty.

Nancy and Vera always remained close friends. 'I know she admired me and it touched me a great deal. I was quite useful to her, I know that. And she used to imitate me. She used to try to dress like me. I was even invited to meet her mother and to have dinner at their flat. It had a rather eastern European feel. It was dark, with rugs on the wall.'

Given that Vera was 'always right', what view did Nancy think she would have taken about the confused radio messages? I asked again.

Sometimes, she told me, she would see Vera enter 'Buck's' office and the door did not always fully close behind her. Through the crack she would hear them talking, in quite insistent, though never heated, terms.

Might she have told him she thought an agent had been captured?

'She would not have said anything as direct as that,' said Nancy. 'But she might have simply said something like, "Perhaps we should look again at a message," or "Perhaps we should reconsider," or something to that effect. She would have taken a much more practical view than Buck, who was somewhat up in the clouds.'

'And what would Buckmaster have done?'

'He would have shrugged, gone silent and turned to look out of the window.'

———

It was not until 7 August that Buckmaster finally accepted that Gilbert Norman was caught or, as he put it, 'Butcher is a gonner', but his decision did not come in time to save Jack Agazarian.

Amid the continuing confusion of mid-July 1943, Nicholas Bodington, then Buckmaster's deputy, was pressing to go out to Paris in person to investigate the collapse of Prosper. Sending such a senior London staff officer to the field was highly controversial; staff officers knew so much that it could be catastrophic if they were caught. But Bodington, a former Reuters man in Paris, had always been a law unto himself. At the outbreak of war he had applied for 'anti-fifth column work' with MI6 but was rejected as unsuitable and taken on by SOE instead. A loner, considered by colleagues to have a high opinion of himself, Bodington was unpopular with everyone except Buckmaster, who admired him as a hustler who could get things done.

So, with Buckmaster's authority, Bodington planned to fly to France, first contacting Norman by radio, asking for a rendezvous in Paris and giving the BBC message, which would be broadcast when he arrived: 'N'oubliez pas de renvoyer l'ascenseur' ('Don't forget to send the lift back'). Norman's message came back, giving an address for the meeting at rue de Rome.

Bodington then insisted on taking his own wireless man with him for the trip, and chose Jack Agazarian, even though Agazarian was just back from the field on leave.

On the night of 22 July, Bodington and Agazarian flew out and were received by Déricourt. A week later a message reached London that Agazarian was captured. Agazarian, not Bodington, had gone to the prearranged meeting with Norman and the Gestapo were waiting.

When he returned to London Bodington's report was anxiously awaited in Baker Street. 'The entire Prosper organisation is destroyed,' it said. 'No element of it should be touched.' Arms dumps had been seized and arrests were still ongoing. 'Prosper should be considered dead.' Referring to the new Archdeacon circuit, which was to have been set up by the Canadians Pickersgill and Macalister in the Ardennes, Bodington wrote: 'No one has the slightest knowledge of the Ardennes group, which must be considered lost.'

Bodington also told HQ on his return of other 'alarming' stories he had heard in Paris, passed on to him by one of F Section's most experienced agents, Henri Frager, who ran the important Donkeyman circuit in north-west France. Frager claimed to have been told that the Gestapo knew of Bodington's presence in Paris but had not arrested him because they wanted him to 'run for a while'. Frager's story was a strange and complicated one as it had come direct from a German who introduced himself to him only as Colonel Heinrich. Frager claimed to have met the German by chance at the Monte Carlo café in Paris. Heinrich worked for the Abwehr, the German armed forces intelligence, which loathed the Gestapo. For reasons of his own – possibly jealousy of his Gestapo rivals – he passed on to the British agent what he had heard about the Gestapo's 'nationwide drive'. He also warned Frager that 'l'homme qui fait le pick-up' – the head of the British Lysander operations, who was obviously Henri Déricourt – had been 'infiltrated'.

These allegations were 'obviously not true', commented Bodington, who then mentioned another claim Frager had made. Frager had also alleged that his reports back to London, sent in SOE mailbags, were being copied before they left France and given to the Gestapo. He appeared to have some evidence for this, and accused Déricourt of somehow passing the reports to the Germans. Nevertheless, Bodington concluded that these allegations also were 'obviously untrue'.

Bodington's report on the lost circuits evidently painted an unsettling picture for Baker Street, but Buckmaster saw no reason to take further action over the reports on Déricourt, which he dismissed.

One action Buckmaster had taken, however, even before he had read Bodington's report, was to recall several agents who might have been contaminated by the Prosper debacle. Some were told to return by the August moon and others to escape across the Pyrenees. But one agent who was not ordered back at this time of acute danger was Nora Inayat Khan. Probably the most contaminated agent of all, she was nevertheless now considered F Section's most important remaining radio link between Paris and London. Nora had become overnight one of Buckmaster's foremost agents in France.

Vera, watching in the signals room, could tell that Nora was now operating under the greatest stress. Her communication had become erratic and often did not occur at her regular sched time. She appeared to be constantly on the move and Home Station had been instructed to set up an emergency listening watch for her each day at 1500 hours.

Yet Buckmaster knew that if F Section was to have any chance of recovering from the disaster, Nora's continued presence in Paris was vital. And on 15 August, as other agents were heading back, Buckmaster instructed signals staff: 'If Nurse does not take the message no. 6 on her QRX [schedule] at 17.30 today will you please ensure that it is sent on the first possible occasion as it is extremely urgent. I particularly want to get it to her before 1500 hours tomorrow 16 August.'

Buckmaster's 'message no. 6' was an instruction to Nora to meet up with Frank Pickersgill and John Macalister, who were working to form the Archdeacon circuit in the Ardennes. Contrary to what Bodington concluded in his report, Buckmaster did not believe the Ardennes circuit was 'lost'. He saw the meeting between Nora and the two Canadians, which was to take place in Paris at the Café Colisée in the Champs-Elysées, as a first move to reconstitute the Prosper circuit. Reports later reached London that the meeting was successful. Nora passed on useful contacts to Pickersgill and Macalister, and further meetings were arranged.

When mail from Nora arrived with the August and September moons, Baker Street had cause to be cheered by her high morale – as well as unnerved by her glaring lack of security. In one long letter in her own girlish, looped writing, she requested a series of new scheds and crystals, setting out precisely what they were to be '*en clair*' and thereby breaking the security rule that required all sensitive information to be encoded. She wrote: 'From Madeleine – Ops – Please arrange everyday scheds also using 3407 – if sched is missed possible recontact at 1800 GMT same day – Please send another 3408 crystal.' The letter also asked: 'Someday, if possible please send white mac FANY style. Thanks a lot. It's grand working with you. The best moments I have had yet.'

Also with the mail came a letter from Nora to her mother and one to Vera:

> Dear Miss Atkins, (excuse pencil) your bird has brought me luck. I remember you so often. You cheered me up so sweetly before I left – lots of things have happened and I haven't been able to settle down properly. Still my contacts have started to be regular and I am awfully happy. The news is marvellous and I hope we shall soon be celebrating. In fact, I owe you a date. Lots of love, Yours Nora.

The 'marvellous' news was the Allied invasion of Sicily and the fall of Mussolini.

3

THANKS FROM THE GESTAPO

'There was a large empty hangar. The planes were out over on the tarmac. It was night, and we were lit up only by the moonlight.'

Yvonne Baseden was describing flying off to France from Tempsford airbase, near Cambridge, in March 1944. Just twenty-one, she was one of the youngest SOE women to be dropped by parachute. As we spoke in her flat in Putney, a purple balloon bobbing above her said, 'Happy Eightieth Birthday'. On the wall was a photograph of a female silhouette descending by parachute against a night sky.

'Who was in the hangar?' I asked Yvonne.

'When I think back I can see only the two of us: Vera and me. I can see Vera sitting at the desk and I was standing in front. I was in my jumping suit. I can just picture her in the gloom. I think she was smoking. Checking things off on the list. She wasn't saying anything exactly, but one was conscious that if there was anything one wanted to ask or say, she was there. I remember being told how much money to put in my jumping suit so I didn't have anything to carry in my hands – things like that. And I had a feeling that she was thinking; that she wanted to say something. It was as if she didn't want to miss a single thing. You felt she was involved.

'She was the link, you see. It was Vera we would turn to in those last few weeks. She was the last link, you might say. Because we had cut off from our own families – I mean, automatically, during our training, we had cut off from the outer world.

'And one was physically extremely fit and all one could think of was the mission. Because you had only just heard about your mission. In a sense, you see, your life had been taken apart and rebuilt.'

She paused. 'And Vera was in control of things. As a mother might be, I suppose. But I wouldn't have called her exactly motherly. She had a lot of responsibilities. And she was already in the picture as to who your mother was and who your father was. I knew she would remain in contact with my parents in a sort of distant way.'

'In the hangar, to what extent do you think Vera was feeling the stress?'

'I am sure she was, quite a lot. I think she was trying to put us at ease by looking herself at ease, as if it was something which a lot of people were doing and that it was nothing out of the ordinary. I think she was trying to shoulder the stress that everyone might be feeling. She knew that she had to keep everything moving along, under control. And for us, you see, she was the remaining link as we walked out too. And, well, for me as well, she was the first person I saw when I came back.'

Yvonne talked for some time longer, each word carefully chosen from memories which were deeply scarred. At the end her eyes welled up with tears.

———

By the autumn of 1943 Vera was spending more and more of her time at airfields, seeing agents off on missions to France, a number of them women. Since the Prosper disaster of the summer, she had grown in stature within F Section. Throughout the crisis Vera's support for Buckmaster had never wavered, and though she still held junior rank, he no longer addressed her as 'Miss Atkins' but always as 'Vera'. The two were nearly always together in the signals room or at Orchard Court; if not, they would be walking through the Ops room or sharing a late evening meal in the SOE canteen.

Relations between them were not always smooth. As Buckmaster noted on Vera's personal file, she was 'somewhat disinclined to accept instructions without argument. Requires handling'. For the most part, though – whether it was to compose an *aide-mémoire* or choose a sabotage target – Buckmaster found that Vera was now the most reliable person to consult. After the losses of the summer Bomber Command had threatened to withdraw flights from SOE, using the Prosper collapse as yet further proof that planes and pilots were being wasted making drops to an ineffective resistance. Colin Gubbins, however, had fought back, defending F Section and exhorting Buckmaster in the strongest terms to prove Bomber Command and other critics of SOE wrong.

Although the date of D-Day was still a closely guarded secret, all the signs at this time were that it would take place sometime in the first half of 1944. As the invasion plans gathered pace, Buckmaster was left in no doubt of the central role that Gubbins expected F Section to play. He was also left in no doubt that, in order to succeed in its D-Day role, the section must brace itself for the sacrifice of very high numbers of agents.

'Strategically France is by far the most important country in the Western Theatre of War,' declared Gubbins, and the morale of the resistance 'is a vital factor in our success'. He went on: 'I think therefore that SOE should regard this theatre as one in which the suffering of heavy casualties is inevitable. But will yield the highest possible dividend. I would therefore increase to the maximum possible peak SOE aid to the French field from now on and so maintain it until D-Day.' The instruction called for the hiring, training and dispatching of new agents to France as fast as possible, whatever the risks. As Buckmaster strove to achieve these aims, nobody gave him more support than Vera did.

The closing months of 1943, however, were not easy for F Section, and there were many new alarms. Several highly valued agents simply vanished, among them an expert in explosives who disappeared on his way to Pickersgill and Macalister's Archdeacon circuit in the Ardennes.

Wireless operators had also caused new fears. Extra security measures, agreed after the loss of Prosper, had brought in stricter rules on composing messages. For example, in addition to using his bluff check and true check, an operator named Marcel Rousset was instructed to sign off '*adiós*' or '*salut*' if all was well, and 'love and kisses' if he was caught. Over a nerve-racking weekend in Baker Street in September, Rousset sent a series of strange messages which suggested that he had forgotten his new rules. Buckmaster, without any senior staff to consult, anxiously showed the messages to the duty secretary, Nancy Fraser-Campbell, and asked for her advice, but the messages soon reverted to normal and fears were dispelled.

A technique called 'electronic fingerprinting', by which a wireless operator's 'fist' could be electronically recorded by a machine before departure, had also been introduced. This 'fingerprint' allowed

London to compare a message sent later from the field with the 'fingerprint' that the agent left behind. But often there was little time to make such checks, because of the volume of F Section activity in the field. Among operations carried out around this time was the bombing of the Michelin factory at Clermont-Ferrand, set up by one of Buckmaster's most trusted organisers, Maurice Southgate, alias Hector, with the assistance of his resourceful courier, Pearl Witherington. At the same time, another of F's best men, Francis Cammaerts, who had built up the highly successful Jockey network in the south-east, was blowing up railway locomotives about to be taken to Germany.

It was Nora Inayat Khan who caused the most regular alarms in Baker Street during the autumn of 1943. In early October a message had come in saying an informant, unknown in London, called Sonia had reported: 'Madeleine had an accident and in hospital', which clearly meant 'burned', or infiltrated, if not captured. Sonia's reliability was never confirmed and the anxiety sparked by her warning then passed, until, in November, somebody drew attention to a report from Paris that said that nobody in the field had set eyes on Nora for nearly two months. Buckmaster held his nerve, saying she must be sensibly lying low. The fact that no handwritten letters had come from Nora since September was, in Buckmaster's view, another sign of her new concern for security. Her latest request to London for a new letterbox had been properly encoded and sent by wireless message. The message detailing these changes had come in from Nurse at 14.15 GMT on 17 October:

'MY CACHETTE UNSAFE. NEW ADDRESS BELLIARD RPT BELLIARD 157 RUE VERCINGETORIX RPT VERCINGETORIX PARIS PASSWORD DE PART DE MONSIEUR DE RUAL RPT DE RUAL STOP. THIS PERFECTLY SAFE. TRUE CHECK PRESENT. BLUFF CHECK OMITTED GOODBYE.'

Anxieties about Nora were therefore once again dispelled until, at Christmas, she caused further jitters in F Section. This time the operations officer, Gerry Morel, was letting it be known that he was not happy about Nora's 'fist'. A respected figure, and one of the few Baker Street staff who had experience in the field, Morel was not a man to voice concerns lightly. Vera offered a solution: to send a test message for Nora containing questions of a personal nature that only she could answer. The message was designed to settle the doubts about Nora once and for all. If the questions were wrongly answered, it would have to be accepted that she was in German hands. Although slow in coming, the answers were in Vera's view quite satisfactory, and Buckmaster's confidence was immediately restored.

Cheering Christmas messages from other agents had also lifted his spirits, among them one from Frank Pickersgill. Buckmaster had been warned by Bodington back in August that Pickersgill's Archdeacon circuit 'must be considered lost', but he was now more convinced than ever that Bodington was wrong.

———

Kay Gimpel (née Moore), who worked for another branch of SOE, told me she saw in a flash that Pickersgill's Christmas message meant he was caught, but she never dreamed of telling Buckmaster. Like Pickersgill, Gimpel was a French Canadian and the two had long been friends. 'He was a brilliant, charming boy,' she said. 'Tall and gangly with a very sharp wit.' Before his mission Pickersgill and John Macalister, who was a Rhodes Scholar, used to spend time at Kay's house at 54a Walton Street. 'We all yacked a lot and Frank loved to go off and make lots of tea.'

Kay used to travel into work on the same bus as Buckmaster, who, one day in December 1943, sat down next to her and asked if she could think of a Christmas message for Frank. 'I said tell him the samovar is still bubbling at 54a.' The reply came back a few days later: 'Thank you for your message.'

'It was an awful moment,' said Kay. 'If he was all right I knew he would have said something personal and secret to our little group.'

Why had she not told Buckmaster of her fears?

'He would not have listened to somebody like me. I was junior in rank.'

———

In January 1944 there were new crises to face. One agent who had been held briefly by the Gestapo at their Paris headquarters in Avenue Foch claimed that Prosper was cooperating with a German named Boemelburg and with another named Kieffer. Prosper was said to have plotted a large map for the Gestapo showing F Section circuits. 'Total provocation. Obviously untrue,' noted Buckmaster.

Allegations of treachery against Henri Déricourt, first made the previous summer, had also spread. So persistent were the accusations against the air movements officer that in February 1944 Buckmaster was obliged by MI5 and SOE's own security directorate to recall him for investigation. Déricourt flew back to England on the night of 8–9 February, bringing with him his wife, Jeanne. He protested his innocence and was reassured by Buckmaster, who told him he had nothing to fear from the charges, and put him up in the Savoy.

Déricourt had won Buckmaster's trust from the moment they first met. The thirty-five-year-old from Château-Thierry, birthplace of La Fontaine (whose fables he loved to cite), had an easy manner, a quiet confidence and muscular physique, with fair hair curling into a quiff. His charms had impressed not only Buckmaster and most in F Section but also the pilots of 'Moon Squadron'. The self-educated son of a postman, he had been drawn to the thrill of flying from a young age, going on to organise aerial events before training as a commercial pilot. In 1942 Déricourt had been promised a job by British Overseas Airways, but when offered a role with SOE he had readily accepted this instead.

MI5, who checked the Frenchman's history, warned Buckmaster at the time that they were 'unable to guarantee his reliability'. The reason they gave was that, after he was first offered the job with British Overseas Airways, Déricourt had delayed coming to England, spending several more weeks in France. During this time, 'he would have been a likely subject for German attention', cautioned MI5, but Buckmaster saw nothing to fear.

As Déricourt's interrogation began in February 1944 Buckmaster conceded that, should the allegations against the air movements officer prove true, every agent landed in France by air over the previous ten months, and every agent brought back to England, would be contaminated. But Buckmaster refused to believe the allegations would ever be proven and declared it an 'SOE war objective' to clear Déricourt's name.

Throughout this time Vera had remained as loyal and diligent as ever and Buckmaster recorded in another effusive note: 'An extremely able, hard working, capable and loyal officer. Nothing is too much trouble for her.' While Buckmaster's dependency on Vera was by now quite evident, however, few could have been aware just how dependent she was on him, particularly at the turn of the year. In January and February 1944 small notices appeared in the personal columns of the *Kensington News* and *West London Times*, and Buckmaster was probably the only one of Vera's colleagues to be aware of them. 'Notice is Hereby GIVEN that Vera May Atkins (otherwise Rosenberg) of 725 Nell Gwynne House, Sloane Avenue, SW3 in the County of London, Spinster, is applying to the Home Secretary for Naturalisation,' read the announcement.

Vera's first application for naturalisation as a British citizen had been made in February 1942 and rejected. No reason was given, although, as Buckmaster was well aware, senior figures in SOE's security directorate were suspicious of her Romanian and Jewish origins. So, to ensure her application was not blocked again, Buckmaster himself was this time backing Vera's request for naturalisation.

———

A former SOE staff officer told me he recalled 'a stink' and 'a smell' in the office when Vera first joined SOE. The same person recalled a further 'stink' when Vera first applied for naturalisation in 1942. When I asked him the reason for the 'stink' the man said: 'Something in her background.' He then thought for a moment and added: 'I am not anti-Semitic but I am not very keen on Jews. They are always touching and pawing one, and the fleshy nose and all this flesh at the back of the neck,' and he then reached for the back of his neck.

Another officer, Anghais Fyffe, employed in SOE's security directorate, gave an even more graphic account of the prejudice Vera faced from anti-Semitic officers at the most senior levels of SOE. One day in December 1942 Major General John Lakin, then head of the security directorate, came to him and said: 'Morning, Fyffe.' Fyffe replied: 'Morning, sir.' Lakin then asked: 'Have you heard of a woman called Rosenberg?' and the conversation continued until he said: 'That damn fair-haired Romanian Jewess has applied to be naturalised. I've put a stop to it.'

———

In February 1944 Vera's renewed application for naturalisation came up for decision by the Home Office, and she hoped that a long letter from Maurice Buckmaster backing her claim would bring success this time. Buckmaster, whose second wife was part Jewish, did not tolerate anti-Semitism in his section and openly criticised anti-Jewish prejudice in other sections when he encountered it. Many of F Section's most motivated agents were themselves Jewish exiles.

Furthermore, Vera's lack of British nationality had been inconvenient to Buckmaster in the office, not least because her origins had to be kept strictly secret in case SOE's detractors got to hear. MI6, always ready to do SOE down, might well have made much of the fact that F Section's intelligence officer was an enemy alien, as might De Gaulle's fractious Free French. It was an SOE rule that, for reasons of security, only British subjects by birth should be employed in HQ.

By February 1944 Vera's nationality had become more than inconvenient: it was now standing in the way of Buckmaster's D-Day plans. As he told the Home Office in his letter supporting her application, Vera had been chosen to run a forward station in France to coordinate post-D-Day operations. 'If Miss Atkins goes overseas as a Roumanian subject we fear that she will be both obtrusive and much restricted in her movements.'

Buckmaster's letter explained: 'In as large a city as London we hope that the true nationality of Miss Atkins might not be known, but in any move overseas where papers will have to be shown such a fact could not be concealed. This consideration is one of great delicacy, but one of tremendous importance if enemy penetration is to be successfully resisted.'

On 25 February Vera was interviewed at the Home Office, where she said: 'It is essential that many of the people whom I meet should not know that I am a Roumanian.' The fact she was not British continued to be 'a great hindrance', she told her interviewer, and 'a point has now come in the work she is doing when it would present even greater difficulties'.

The officer wrote: 'Miss Atkins impressed me as being a woman of intelligence and discretion, well able to keep her own counsel' and finally added: 'Nothing detrimental recorded at New Scotland Yard.'

During the month of February SOE's air operations over France suddenly expanded at a rapid pace. Churchill himself had given orders that the arming of the resistance was now a priority and no longer could the RAF hold back the supply of planes for F Section drops. Among the F Section agents to be dropped by parachute in February was a team of three led by France Antelme, who had so luckily escaped the Prosper round-up. A man who, according to his instructors, had 'plenty of guts, stalks well and uses his head' was evidently wasted in Baker Street and Buckmaster wanted him back on the ground to fulfil his pivotal role of overseeing supply lines for the Allied forces after D-Day.

Antelme was given the finest courier Vera had in training, Madeleine Damerment, a remarkable young woman who had escaped from France after being involved in the highly dangerous work of rescuing Allied prisoners. A devout Catholic, she had made her home in England, at a French convent in Hitchin. 'She does not know how many prisoners she handled but said it was a considerable number,' said an official who interviewed Damerment on her arrival in England. 'She was modest and looked upon the whole matter as something very natural. She said many French women are willing to do this sort of work every day.'

Antelme's radio operator for the mission was an experienced man named Lionel Lee. As always, the agents were told before departure that their task was a risky one, but nobody told Damerment or Lee of the most immediate and potentially catastrophic risk they faced. They were to be dropped to a reception committee organised by Nora's circuit, now called Phono. Furthermore, the plans for the drop had been made over Nora's radio, despite yet further fears, now shared by several staff officers, including Gerry Morel and Penelope Torr, that she might be in German hands.

If Vera had her own renewed doubts about Nora, she made little obvious attempt to make them known. Buckmaster was in no mood to change his mind about the planned drop, and her personal relationship with him had never been more delicate. While Antelme, Damerment and Lee were waiting to fly out to France, her own naturalisation application was being decided and at no time since joining SOE had Vera been more determined to maintain Buckmaster's support.

Yet somebody did instruct Antelme, in a note on his mission statement, to 'cut completely with the Phono circuit on landing', which suggested an attempt by a hidden hand to warn him of possible penetration. And in the days before the drop Vera certainly invited Antelme himself to look at Nora's recent wireless messages and make up his own mind as to whether or not she was free. After all, Antelme knew Nora as well as anyone and was widely believed to have developed an intimate affection for her when they were thrown together, hiding out in Paris the previous July. Had Vera been entirely sure of Nora's 'fist' herself, no consultation with Antelme would have been necessary. In any event, Vera made it very clear to anyone who asked later that Antelme was reassured when he saw Nora's messages and it had been his own personal decision to go.

The flight was delayed for several days owing to bad weather, but on the evening of 29 February the skies suddenly cleared. The pre-arranged BBC message was broadcast to the reception committee, who then knew that they were to prepare to receive agents on a ground near Rambouillet. The flight was cleared to go and Vera was on the tarmac at Tempsford to see the agents off.

The Halifax, due to take off at 2100 hours, was even able to leave a little early. On his return the pilot reported that the lights from the reception committee on the ground had been particularly good.

—

Penelope Torr told me that Antelme was by no means reassured by reading Nora's messages. 'He knew he would not be coming back. You see, by this time we were engaged – well, anyway, he had been talking to me of things we might do after the war. He took me out to dinner on Valentine's Night, before he was due to go. That was when he told me he would not come back. He had a premonition.'

'Yet he still wanted to go?'

'I know,' she said. 'I can't explain it. There was a very unreal atmosphere in the office at that time.'

—

By early March nothing had been heard from Lionel Lee, Antelme's radio operator, but strange messages had come over from Nora's radio saying that, on landing, Antelme had fractured his skull. Subsequent messages gave bizarre medical reports on his worsening condition. London sent messages back giving Antelme's medical history for the French doctors and cheering him with the news that he had won an OBE. Antelme was 'very pleased and touched by the award', said one reply from the field. Then a week later he had 'deteriorated' and on 2 May it was announced that he 'died after an attack of meningitis'. He was 'buried by moonlight' and 'deepest sympathy' was sent to his family.

Penelope Torr produced an analysis of these messages and even sought the opinion of a doctor, who said the position of the head fracture as described in one message was 'very unusual for a landing accident'. Penelope's analysis, however, went unheeded and the next time she raised questions about messages from the field – by taking her concerns to an MP – she was removed from her job for 'letting sentiment override her duty'.

*

In April 1944 the date of the Allied landings was still not known, but SOE's role in the run-up to D-Day was now clear to every agent: all circuits were to organise the destruction of German lines of communication in order to prevent enemy troops reaching the landing beaches. D-Day action messages directing circuits to blow up railways, telephone lines, fuel depots and dams could now go out at any time.

The briefing of agents going out to the field at this moment demanded the utmost calm and so Vera's presence at Orchard Court was often required; she was now at the height of her powers. On 24 March she had been issued with her certificate of British naturalisation. Just two weeks later, on Buckmaster's recommendation, she secured a promotion and was at last officially designated F Section's intelligence officer, with the symbol 'F Int'.

Among the agents that Vera was now briefing for their first mission was a spirited, attractive young woman by the name of Violette Szabo. Born in Paris, Violette was the daughter of a British First World War veteran, Charles Bushell, who had met and married a Frenchwoman after serving in France. The Bushell family had returned to live in England and Violette had grown up in Brixton, south London, where as a teenager she worked at Woolworths and gained a reputation in shooting galleries as a talented shot. In 1939, soon after the outbreak of war, Violette married a French Foreign Legionnaire named Etienne Szabo, and by the time she walked into Vera's room at Orchard Court she was, at twenty-three, a war widow with a baby. Violette's instructors said she was 'mature' in certain ways 'but in others very childish'. Vera was impressed.

'You have probably not met this young woman who is a new and fairly promising trainee,' Vera wrote to the SOE finance department. 'Mrs Szabo has a one-year-old child and is very anxious to know, at once, what pension arrangements would be made for her in the event of her going to the field. Provision for her child is such a primary consideration to her that I am sure she feels unsettled about her training and future until this question has been dealt with . . . I wish we could give more precise assurance to our women agents with children.' A note on Violette's file from a FANY officer read: 'This girl has a young baby. I wonder if she fully realises what she is doing.'

Sorting out the affairs of women agents such as Violette was now taking up much of Vera's attention, but if she didn't do it, nobody else would. Suddenly there was so little time. In March alone six women were infiltrated into France to work for F Section circuits, the highest number in any month so far. Vera had guided each through training and preparation, and seen each of them depart. In April six more women were dropped or landed in France, including Violette, who landed by parachute with her organiser on 5 April, with the cover story that she was Corinne Reine Le Roy (taking her French mother's maiden name), a commercial secretary. Her mission was to find out if a suspect sub-circuit had indeed been penetrated. After ascertaining beyond doubt that it was blown, Violette flew back to England three weeks later.

As D-Day became imminent doubts arose again in the signals room about certain F Section wireless operators and by the end of April senior staff officers felt such concerns could no longer be ignored. Gerry Morel and Major Bourne-Paterson had analysed back traffic and together they told Buckmaster precisely how far they thought the penetration had spread. Nora was captured – of that Morel was now certain. Anyone who flew to her circuit must have landed directly in German hands. Many other connecting circuits must have been contaminated and Marcel Rousset was one of several further wireless operators who had clearly been in enemy hands for some time. Also now suspect, said Morel, was the Archdeacon circuit set up by Pickersgill and Macalister.

The implications for Buckmaster were unthinkable. Just as he was about to realise Colonel Gubbins's command by getting a maximum number of agents into the field ahead of D-Day, he was being told by his two most senior lieutenants that several of his most valued circuits had been penetrated.

It was not until the following month that Buckmaster finally accepted some of the evidence of penetration. Even then, in a memorandum on the matter to his superior officer, he pleaded that since the collapse of Prosper 'there had been no reason to believe that Nurse was captured'. He failed to mention the many earlier warnings. And against the typed letters of her call-sign Nurse, Buckmaster wrote carefully, in his own handwriting, Nora's official name, 'Princess Inayat Khan'.

Buckmaster still rejected Morel's conclusion that Archdeacon was also blown. Morel, fearing that Pickersgill and Macalister's sub-circuits had contact with other groups dangerously close to areas where the landings might take place, was determined to convince Buckmaster before it was too late. The fear was that Germans, posing as SOE agents and fully armed by SOE, might now be taking up positions near the landing beaches in the guise of French resistance fighters. By now senior figures in MI5 knew of these dangers and were urgently voicing precisely these concerns.

Morel's recourse was to test Archdeacon's integrity conclusively by speaking with Pickersgill in person by means of an 'S phone', a directional microwave transceiver which allowed air-to-ground communication. On 8 May the contact was arranged and, flying overhead at an agreed location, he began to ask Pickersgill questions. The person on the ground spoke English with a heavy guttural accent, Morel reported. It was not Pickersgill. Buckmaster, however, was still not convinced, maintaining that the voice must have been distorted by 'atmospheric conditions', and he ordered that drops to Pickersgill and Macalister should continue even now.

On the evening of 5 June 1944, as the first vessels of the D-Day invasion fleet were almost in sight of the French shore, hundreds of SOE action messages were broadcast to circuits and within hours messages came back to the signals room in Baker Street from wireless operators reporting that sabotage operations had begun. Overnight Tony Brooks, organiser of the Pimento circuit, had seen to it that all railway lines between Toulouse and Montauban in the south-west were cut. Francis Cammaerts of the Jockey circuit had been equally efficient in the Marseilles area. Pearl Witherington, who had taken over from her organiser, Maurice Southgate (Hector), after his capture by the Gestapo, had taken charge of a thousand resistance fighters who were cutting railway lines throughout the Indre region in western central France.

On 6 June, amid the chaotic surge of messages about resistance activity now pouring in from the field, came a stream of peculiar messages from the agents identified by Gerry Morel as definitely captured. On that day Marcel Rousset's call-sign came up on the board. The message tapped off by the teleprinter was soon in the hands of Buckmaster and Vera. 'Many thanks large deliveries arms and ammunition have greatly appreciated good tips concerning intentions and plans.' The sender signed off 'Geheime Staatspolizei' – the Gestapo.

Soon afterwards the call-sign for Pickersgill's radio operator, Macalister, came up. This message thanked London for the stores which had recently been delivered, stating that unfortunately 'certain of the agents had had to be shot' but that others had proved more willing to do what the Germans asked them to do. Again the signature was that of the Gestapo.

Buckmaster, apparently disorientated by the Gestapo's macabre little game, spent some time composing jovial responses, such as: 'Sorry to see your patience is exhausted and your nerves not so good as ours.'

Vera, however, was impatient to be at the airfields where the next dispatch of SOE agents was about to begin, along with a wave of SAS men now being parachuted behind the lines as the invasion got under way. On 7 June she said goodbye to Violette Szabo, who was being parachuted into France for a second time to play her part in keeping advancing German Panzer divisions from reaching the Normandy beaches.

—

'Did Vera ever question whether it was right to send out Violette – a woman with a baby?' I asked Nancy Roberts when I met her again.

'I think Vera admired strong women,' she said. 'She was not a feminist in the modern way but she always stood up for women and believed in their abilities. I saw her take the younger girls into her office and sit down with them as they wrote letters to their parents, which she would post for them when they had gone. I think it made it easier for some to leave, knowing that their families would get their very own handwritten letters.'

'What would they write?'

'Oh, just something vague and general: "All is well. Keeping busy." Vera was good at thinking of things like that.'

'Which of the agents was she closest to?'

'She certainly admired Nora tremendously. Everyone loved Nora. And there was no doubt that Violette held a fascination for Vera. All of them did, you know. They were intriguing. I thought so too. We all did.'

What did she mean by intriguing?

'Just that they were fascinating creatures. To be prepared to do what it was they went to do.'

Nancy considered a moment and then revealed: 'I have never said this before, but I think that Vera was sometimes jealous of me. I think she was jealous of me over Violette. Vera guarded the women agents very closely. And she was jealous that it was me who took Violette to the field and not her. Vera was only able to come down later to take over, after the flight had been delayed.'

How had it come about that Vera didn't go with Violette at first? I asked.

'It was very close to D-Day and Vera had many responsibilities. I think she just was elsewhere. So I was asked to drive up to Tempsford with Violette.' Nancy described how they arrived at Hasell's Hall, the country house where the departing agents were attended to by FANY women. Violette had to wait for three days as the first two attempts to fly her out were aborted because of poor weather, but she remained calm throughout. 'The first two attempts I had to take her out and get her ready in the hangar and make sure she had everything and say goodbye, and then it didn't happen. And then we just had to wait. I will never forget it. Ever. Where we were, it was beautifully sunny and there was Violette sitting on the lawn with this young Polish man who was going too. They were laughing and chatting and Violette was playing a gramophone record over and over and over again. I can still hear it: "I want to buy a paper doll I can call my own."

'I can see her now. She was wearing a pretty summery dress with blue and white flowers and shoes she said she had bought in Paris, and she had a rose in her hair. I can still hear that damn song going round and round in my head.'

'Did she talk about what she was going to do?'

'No, not at all. She just chatted to that Polish boy about film stars. I was overawed by it more than anything. I was so young and here was this other young woman and a mother going to do this. Why was this young woman who was so attractive going to do this? She had so many advantages. I was intrigued by what made them brave enough to do it, when I knew I never could.

'And she slept at night like a baby,' said Nancy, who explained that escorting officers even shared a room with departing agents, should they suddenly need support or help of any sort during their last night. I slept in the bed next to her. But she never wanted anything. She slept through the night without stirring.'

On the third day Vera appeared to take over, said Nancy, and so it was Vera who spent the last night and day with Violette, while Nancy was sent back to London. 'Vera always wanted to do it all

herself. I knew that. To be there when they left was the most exhil-
arating thing. This was what we were all there for after all – to send
these brave people off – particularly with a girl like Violette.'

'Why?'

'Well, she was really very pretty. She was an entrancing creature,
to men and women alike. Everyone had wanted to see Violette off;
she had bewitched the whole of Baker Street.'

'Why do you say that Vera was jealous of you over this?'

'I just know she was. Because of the way she never spoke about it.
Because of the way she behaved. She never mentioned that anyone
had been with Violette during those last days except her.'

Nancy appeared uncomfortable.

'And because Violette was very attractive,' she added.

'Are you saying that Vera was attracted to Violette?'

Nancy considered.

'Was Vera attracted to you, Nancy?'

It was evidently a question she had considered before.

'I never felt that Vera was attracted to me in that way. She never
made a pass at me in that way, but in those days nobody would. But
I do know that she admired me greatly. She had a very manly brain.
I don't know if that made her in any way bisexual. I think, like me,
she was just intrigued by these young women. She was always very
protective of them. You see, she didn't want anyone else to know
about the agents. She saw the care of them as her personal role. And
that was why she saw it as her personal role to go and look for them
later. And then they tried to stop her.'

'Who tried to stop her? Was it Buckmaster?'

'No, it was higher up they tried to stop her.'

'Why?'

'Because she was a woman.'

'You mean, because they thought she wasn't capable as a woman?'

'Because they didn't think she had the authority to do such a
thing. And because she was doing these things they knew they
ought to be doing but had not thought of doing themselves. They
just thought if they waited the agents would all turn up.'

When I asked if Buckmaster would have gone to trace the missing, Nancy said he did not have the strength, and she paused again,
thinking back. 'I was in the office when the news of Oradour-sur-
Glane came in,' she said. On 10 June 1944, just after D-Day, in the

tiny French village of Oradour-sur-Glane, SS troops murdered 642 people, including 190 schoolchildren. The attack was in reprisal for resistance attacks on German troops moving towards the Normandy beachhead.

'Maurice read the telegram and he just couldn't believe it. I remember he was very shocked. It was a Sunday morning and only he and I were in the office. He was wandering around, very angry. He was a very emotional person, in a way that Vera was not. He could not believe the Germans would do anything so awful as that.'

4

TRACES

In mid-September 1944 Vera was at her desk in Baker Street scrutinising documents, underlining a word from time to time with a black fountain pen or correcting a spelling. The building was almost deserted. The Ops room was still and only the occasional clatter of a teleprinter could be heard in the signals room. At her side Vera had a row of flip-flop card indexes, an inventory of names, addresses and aliases of every F Section agent, each with a small photograph attached. Almost all the information here was already in her head, but even so she liked to keep the cards close to her. If she wanted to confirm a detail of an agent, she could run a fingernail along the top and a mass of little faces would appear, flipping over on the roller.

Vera was scanning the documents for names of missing agents. And if she made a note on a card it meant she had found another 'trace'. Occasionally a messenger would appear and pass to Vera another file from a trolley. Nobody else from F Section was here. Buckmaster was in France starting his victory tour of F Section circuits, code-named the Judex Mission, and with him was Bourne-Paterson. In early 1944 Bodington had been dispatched to lecture Allied forces on conditions in France and had not been seen since. Gerry Morel had been recruited to work with a new intelligence body that was planning for the liberation of Germany.

Vera, however, had chosen – or rather, she had insisted most forcefully – to stay on in Baker Street. To move office or accept a different assignment would be to desert the men and woman pictured on these cards. It was three months since the Normandy landings, yet of the four hundred F Section agents sent to the field more than a hundred were still missing, sixteen of them women. Her responsibility, as she saw it, was to remain in place until every one of them was accounted for.

In the turmoil after D-Day there had been little time to consider where everybody was, who was captured and who was not. Gradually snippets of news began to come through, perhaps from those who had escaped or from Allied troops, who were by then pushing through the areas where SOE's circuits were active.

In mid-June Violette Szabo – alias Corinne Le Roy, Seamstress or Vicky Tailor – was reported to have been arrested on 9, 10 or 11 June and taken to the German part of Limoges. What had happened to Violette next, nobody knew; she had been moved to a 'destination unknown'. Buckmaster wrote on her casualty report that she had fought off elements of an SS Panzer Division using a Sten gun before collapsing exhausted. A report had also arrived soon after D-Day giving news of Yvonne Baseden, stating that she was captured and last seen in prison in Dijon. She and her organiser had been cornered in a barn stacked high with cheeses. Yvonne's organiser had taken his suicide pill and others had been arrested. The source of the news was a member of her circuit who had been able to avoid detection and escape to Switzerland. Another woman agent, Muriel Byck, died of meningitis after just six weeks fearless work in the field.

Many agents were known to have been captured well before the Allied invasion. Odette Sansom, one of the first women couriers to go into France, arrested in April 1943 in St Jorioz, near Annecy, was reportedly then imprisoned at Fresnes, along with several others. At first it was thought possible that Allied prisoners held in these French jails might have been left behind when the Germans retreated. But, as France was liberated, not a single prisoner was found. There were reports that Berlin had given orders for all Allied prisoners to be killed before the retreat. Others said that this was nonsense and that the Germans wanted all British agents alive because they might be useful as hostages.

Vera herself had spent a short time in Paris immediately after the city was liberated in late August 1944. She, along with Buckmaster, had crossed the Channel by navy gunboat to assess priorities now that the war in France was nearly over. The initial task had been to set up a base where agents could make contact when they began to come in from the field. The Hôtel Cecil, in rue St Didier, was hardly the 'forward station' on the grand scale Buckmaster had envisaged for SOE back in February. De Gaulle himself had blocked all plans for SOE to have any more significant presence. So determined was the victorious de Gaulle to implant in the minds of his people that it was they alone who had liberated France, that immediately after D-Day he had set about scotching any traces of SOE's contribution.

Nevertheless, the two bedrooms requisitioned by SOE served a purpose and many familiar faces pushed through the hotel's revolving doors, to find Vera, or later Nancy Fraser-Campbell, upstairs ready to greet them. Pearl Witherington arrived to be showered with accolades after her magnificent command of a group of *maquisards*, and Francis Cammaerts, the former teacher from Beckenham and Penge County School, who had won a reputation as '*un des grands*' of the SOE circuits, also reported to the Cecil. The dashing George Millar, who set up the successful Chancellor circuit just before D-Day, had no sooner arrived at the hotel than he had whisked Nancy on a bicycle up to the bars of the Champs-Elysées.

Some agents at first believed captured now returned safe, while others were scooped up by Vera in person. Lise de Baissac, working under cover as a poor widow in a Normandy village, had followed orders to stay put after the Allied landings and await instructions. In early September a black car turned into the village and out stepped Vera, who handed Lise a brand-new FANY uniform and told her to put it on as she was taking her home.

Soon, however, there was little more Vera could do in France. The revolving doors of the Cecil stopped turning and the euphoria of the first homecomings passed. Paris was now awash with accusations of collaboration and treachery, and hard information about what had happened to individuals or how SOE's circuits had collapsed was difficult to come by. The French security police had taken control of the few German records which had been salvaged and were limiting any British access to French collaborators. Vera returned home; but her search for missing agents had only just begun.

In September news of the missing might reach Baker Street from any quarter and Vera was starting to file casualty reports. These carried the headings: 'nature of casualty', 'when and where agent was last known to be free', 'source of report', 'estimated degree of accuracy', 'date and place of burial' and 'remarks'.

Information on the courier Cicely Lefort, sent to Cammaerts's Jockey circuit, was unusually detailed. A French source had made contact saying they now had an address for her in Germany: 'Kunz Lager, Ravensbrück, Fürstenberg, Mecklenburg'. This was the first Vera had heard of Ravensbrück, though she knew Mecklenburg was a vast area, studded with lakes, north of Berlin.

Vera was now building up as much intelligence as she could on camps where Germans might be holding prisoners, but she could never learn enough. The Red Cross provided details on the network of more than two hundred PoW camps, spread right across Germany, but Vera considered it more likely that agents would have been taken to civilian internment camps, or possibly even concentration camps. Colleagues in SOE's Polish Section had access to the most up-to-date information on concentration camps, but Vera was now urgently seeking reliable data on the precise number of these camps and on the categories of prisoners held there. Weekly intelligence reports provided by SHAEF (Supreme Headquarters Allied Expeditionary Force) listed names of known concentration camps and gave a broad analysis of their organisation and function, but SHAEF admitted that its information was often 'hearsay'. For good anecdotal evidence about the nature of these camps Vera monitored the press, spoke to exile groups and sifted data from the British General Post Office's Postal Censorship department. Mail reaching, in particular, the Jewish Agency had consistently told a story of concerted horrific atrocity. But nowhere had Vera seen mention of a camp named Ravensbrück.

Information on most agents was not only limited but also usually very old; even so, it was all noted down. News of the arrest of Yolande Beekman of the Musician circuit, which had happened six months previously, had reached Vera in September by pure chance. A woman who worked in a pharmacy in St Quentin (near Amiens), where Yolande had been based, had travelled to the British embassy in Paris to report that Yolande was arrested in the town on 13 January 1944. 'She was brought back four days after her first arrest to the pharmacy. Her face was very swollen and she had obviously been badly treated. She was then taken away again to the local prison,' reported the woman, who added that she had tried to get food to Yolande but she was being held in solitary confinement. The woman also heard that at the end of February Yolande had been taken to Paris by two members of the Gestapo.

In rare cases, captured German agents had provided information. MI6 had passed to Vera a report from one captive who had talked of 'three men and one woman dropped together with a supply of arms near Rambouillet'. One of the men was described as 'a tall English captain (a very tall muscular type)'. The Germans had been waiting for the plane and knew the precise time it was due to land. The parachutists were rounded up by the Gestapo and taken direct to Gestapo HQ in Avenue Foch.

This information clearly referred to France Antelme, Madeleine Damerment and Lionel Lee. Mention of a fourth man appeared to be an error. Vera noted on the forms of the three agents 'believed captured' in February 1944. The fact that they were dropped direct to waiting German hands had been clear to her for many weeks. She saw no reason, however, to note this extra detail on the files.

Other reports were so vague that it was hardly worth filling out a casualty form. The form might just state: 'Missing believed captured' or often 'Source unreliable'. Of Francis Suttill, for example, all that could be said was that he was 'believed captured June 24th 1943 and last seen in Avenue Foch'.

Of Gilbert Norman there was no confirmation of the date of capture even now, and the report simply said: 'Presumed arrested'. Under 'When and where last known to be free' was written: 'Middle of July 1943 Paris'.

And of Nora Inayat Khan there had as yet been no trace, not even a hint about when or where she had been captured, or where she might have been taken. Nobody seemed to have seen her at all. Of all the captured agents, Nora had most completely disappeared.

Vera had requested colleagues in every service, including the Red Cross, to pass all possible traces of missing agents directly to her. Sometimes only the tiniest of clues about a missing agent, or their circuit, would appear in a report or an interrogation and only Vera knew every alias, every cover story and every detail of the agent's secret life well enough to pick out these clues. She feared, however, that others – particularly her own colleagues in SOE's security directorate – were deliberately keeping back information. John Senter, head of the security directorate, had requested all F Section's files be sent to his Bayswater headquarters, but Vera was resisting. Senter had also dispatched his own officers to Paris to carry out investigations, quite separate from Vera's, into what had happened to SOE circuits.

By mid-September one important report, which Vera had urgently requested from Senter's men in Paris, had at last arrived and it was occupying all her attention. It was an interrogation of an F Section wireless operator named Marcel Rousset, alias Leopold. Rousset, one of F Section's Mauritian agents, was another unexpected figure to have walked into the Hôtel Cecil. He was 'reported captured' many weeks earlier when his call-sign had come up in the signals room on D-Day with a 'thank you' message from the Gestapo.

Vera had heard about Rousset's arrival at the hotel from Nancy Fraser-Campbell. A small man with red hair and moustache, he had walked up to Nancy and said: 'You are coming with me right away. I am going to show you the blood on the walls.' He had then led Nancy to 3a Place des Etats Unis, a building which, until a few weeks earlier, had been used as a Gestapo prison. He showed Nancy into the torture room and forced her to look at the blood of SOE agents now dried brown on the walls. Rousset was a very bitter and angry man. He told Nancy how stupid everyone at HQ had been; how they had risked agents' lives. He said he had done everything to warn London that he was captured, but nobody had noticed. According to Nancy, he was damning about Buckmaster, Bourne-Paterson, Vera – everyone involved.

Turning to the first page of Rousset's report, Vera read swiftly over the early headings: 'Arrival in France and mission', 'Landing and subsequent events' and 'Organisation of circuit'. She noted that he had been in touch with Gilbert Norman and Francis Suttill soon after his arrival in France in March 1943. He was arrested on 7 September 1943, when twelve Gestapo men walked into the house in Paris where he was having lunch.

Under 'Interrogation of Source at Avenue Foch', Rousset told his interrogator that as soon as he arrived at the Gestapo headquarters at Avenue Foch he was informed that they knew his alias was Leopold, which he denied.

He was then taken to a room on the third floor and confronted with some of his messages which had been decoded. In spite of this incriminating evidence he continued to deny he was Leopold. Next Rousset was confronted inside Avenue Foch with Gilbert Norman who told the Germans that Rousset was, indeed, Leopold. Norman told Rousset that the Gestapo had full information about SOE and that 'in view of this knowledge he and Prosper had decided to admit everything, in order to save their lives'. Archambaud advised Rousset to do likewise.

Vera underlined this paragraph. It was the first credible reference to Francis Suttill since his arrest in June 1943. It appeared to support gossip, which Vera had heard from French sources in Paris, that Suttill and Norman had together decided to make a pact with the Germans 'to save lives'. 'Archambaud then went on to say that they had been betrayed by somebody in London and named as the traitor Gilbert (Henri Déricourt).'

The interrogator noted that 'Rousset's personal opinion was that Gilbert was not a traitor. He had had contacts with Gilbert and if Gilbert had wanted to have them arrested before he could have done so.'

As Vera knew, MI5's investigations into Henri Déricourt's case had only just been wound up and at the beginning of September 1944 he had been told he was free to go.

Rousset then told his interrogator how he was taken to another room on the third floor of Avenue Foch, where there was a large map of France. 'On this plan was marked the organisation of the French Section with Colonel Buckmaster's name at the top and all the circuits underneath with names of organisers and radio operators.'

Vera read on:

Next source was shown his W/T set. This is divided into compartments and on one side of the lids source had put his extra 'scheds', his frequencies and his 'Playfair' code, but not his poem. It is possible that the Gestapo discovered the poem messages under the carpet and were thus able to decode source's messages.

When the Gestapo was sure of Rousset's identity they asked him to work for them, but he refused. They asked him about the speed of his transmissions and he replied that sometimes he transmitted at high speed and sometimes more slowly.

The Germans then asked him to check messages sent by his organiser, Max, to see if they were in Max's style 'saying they knew all about the organisation and were going to have some "sport" with HQ'.

[. . .] Rousset agreed to do this, but states that he did everything possible to mislead the Germans, giving them a method of stating coordinates for a ground which he had been absolutely forbidden to use, saying that he put his security checks (which they must have found) after the date, when in fact he put them at the end of his message; [and] that he signed his messages with the words 'Love and kisses' whereas he used '*adiós*' or '*salut*'. This went on for five or six days.

As Vera knew, London had received a series of confusing messages from Rousset at about this time.

She now read down a list of all other F Section agents Rousset had seen at Avenue Foch as well as at the prison in Fresnes and the Gestapo prison in Place des Etats Unis. Underlining names as she read, she also updated several cards on her card index. On his first stay at Avenue Foch, Rousset had seen the agent John Starr, alias Bob. Vera's casualty report for Starr stated: 'reported arrested in June [1943]', and she now updated it to: 'seen in Avenue Foch. October 1943. Source reliable.' Rousset had told his interrogators that Starr 'seemed to be on good terms with the Gestapo and working for them'.

In the prison at Fresnes, where he was taken next, Rousset saw Jack Agazarian. Vera had heard nothing of Agazarian since Bodington had returned from Paris in the summer of 1943 after the disastrous trip to investigate the collapse of Prosper. It was on that trip that Agazarian had walked into a Gestapo trap. Bodington had said, on returning home, that he and Agazarian had tossed a coin to decide who should go to the rendezvous and Agazarian had lost. 'Agazarian told Rousset that he had been arrested in the month of August 1943 after his arrival in France with Major Bodington. He was arrested when going to a meeting with Archambaud, but Archambaud had been arrested before this time, and a *souricière* [trap] had been placed. Agazarian told Rousset that Archambaud was double-crossing the Germans in order to save the lives of all the agents under arrest.'

Rousset told his interrogator that on 27 October 1943 he was taken back to Avenue Foch and then to the Gestapo prison in Place des Etats Unis. 'There were sixteen prisoners in this prison,' he told his interrogator. 'Source was in solitary confinement in a cell which had a view on to the staircase and through a hole in the wall he was able to see various prisoners coming and going.' Rousset also 'spoke' to prisoners in adjoining cells, tapping Morse code. Vera now underlined more names, correcting occasional spellings, as they were mentioned one by one. All were F Section agents, all were on her list of the missing and all were glimpsed at the Gestapo prison by Rousset through the hole in the wall of his cell.

The first of the sixteen to be mentioned was a man named Jacques Michel, an explosives expert who Vera knew had been sent out to work with Pickersgill and Macalister's Archdeacon circuit in September 1943 and had vanished. Rousset saw Michel in the Gestapo prison the following month. 'He told Rousset he had been tortured and that he had done everything possible to avoid giving information to the Germans and had finally tried to hang himself.'

When Michel was taken away 'to an unknown destination', Vera read, he was replaced in the cell by Pickersgill himself. 'Pickersgill told Rousset he had been dropped in France in June 1943 and both he and John Macalister were arrested three days after their arrival, in a village which was surrounded by SS troops. Pickersgill had tried to escape from a cell by jumping from a second-floor window but fell and broke his elbow and received two bullet wounds. He was recaptured and taken to hospital. Here he was operated on and during his operation he was given an injection and has no recollection of what he may have said after that.' Vera's casualty reports for Pickersgill and Macalister simply said: 'believed arrested', but gave no date or place. Nobody had imagined the two Canadians had been arrested as early as June 1943. This meant Germans had been operating the Archdeacon circuit in the Ardennes for precisely one year.

She read on: 'Rousset was told by Pickersgill (who was in the cell next to him) that in the cell on his other side was an agent called Cinema.' Cinema was the first alias for Emile Garry before it was changed to Phono. He was Nora's organiser. Pickersgill described Cinema as 'very dark; aged 30–35 and wore spectacles'.

And then Rousset told his interrogator: 'Cinema's Wireless Operator was called Madeleine, who, Pickersgill supposed, was at Avenue Foch. The Germans were using her wireless set.'

Vera had read only halfway through the report, yet already it had produced the most devastating news. Now at the bottom of page six, just tucked away in the middle of another long list of missing agents seen or heard by Rousset, was the name Madeleine.

Rousset clearly didn't know who Madeleine was, but he had been told by Pickersgill that she was Cinema's W/T op, which was enough to make Vera quite sure that this was Nora Inayat Khan. Cinema was the name of the sub-circuit leader Nora was first sent out to work with in Paris. It was the first trace Vera had found of Nora. And yet it was hardly even a trace. It was really just a rumour, a tapping on stone from one agent to another through a cell wall. Pickersgill 'supposed' Madeleine was at Avenue Foch.

And here now was France Antelme, arrested on landing at Rambouillet, coming into Avenue Foch. 'Through a hole in the wall of his cell Rousset saw the arrival of Antelme, alias Antoine.' Rousset saw nothing more of Antelme, who was not mentioned again.

But an agent named Guy Schellens, alias Goat, was reported on at length by Rousset. Schellens was with the Belgian Section, not the French Section, but Rousset had known him at an SOE training school. Around the end of November or beginning of December 1943, Schellens attempted to escape, by attacking a guard. The guard (an SS man) shouted and three other SS guards arrived on the scene. Schellens received a bullet and died a minute later. Thereupon all the prisoners were driven out of their cells with blows and shown Schellens's body. They were told that this was the fate they could expect if they tried to escape. After this the treatment received by the prisoners was much more strict and severe.

On the following pages Rousset's graphic reporting took Vera further and further inside the Gestapo's cells, revealing more and more traces of other F Section agents: each new sighting, each new confirmation of capture, produced another scribble on another card or a note on a casualty report.

After the death of Schellens two new agents were put into Rousset's cell and Vera was able to fill in more details on their cards.

Then suddenly, as Vera reached the final pages, the agents Rousset had seen or spoken to started to leave for 'unknown destinations'. Under 'Transfer to Germany' she read: 'Rousset remained at the prison in Place des Etats Unis until 18 April 1944. On that day he and several other agents were summoned for transfer to Germany.' Among the agents listed in the group were Frank

Pickersgill (Bertrand), John Macalister (Valentine) and Gilbert Norman (Archambaud)

'Archambaud', Rousset told his interrogator, 'had arrived at Place des Etats Unis the previous evening in a lamentable condition. He was limping terribly and he later said that he had tried to escape and then had been wounded by three bullets from a "mitraillette" [submachine gun]. The agents were taken to a bus in which there were other agents which they recognised.' There were nineteen altogether, reported Rousset. The group were driven to the outer suburbs of Paris. Here the bus stopped and still more agents joined it. The bus started up again and they arrived at the railway station at Vaire-sur-Marne 'in company with a group of women from Fresnes'. Vera underlined this reference and read on. 'They travelled for four days to Germany via Maastricht, Düsseldorf, Leipzig and Dresden to Breslau. Before arriving at Breslau the women left the train.'

Vera knew something of Breslau, if only as the name of a station. It was somewhere on the River Oder in Western Silesia. Suddenly the group Rousset had been imprisoned with had been taken many hundreds of miles across Europe. 'From Breslau,' said Rousset, 'the men travelled on to the penitentiary at Ravitsch.' Vera had never heard of Ravitsch. It made little sense that prisoners should have been transferred so far to the east. In the spring of 1944 the Red Army was already crossing the Carpathian Mountains, advancing westwards.

And what had become of the women who 'left the train at Breslau'?

As the interrogation drew to a close, Rousset described his escape. He had been imprisoned at Ravitsch, in Silesia, with the others until 19 May 1944 and then, for reasons he was not told about, was awakened at 1am that day. 'He immediately thought he was going to be shot.' Instead he was put in a car with four others, among them Pickersgill and Macalister, and driven to Berlin. From there they were all flown back to Paris for reinterrogation, though they did not know why. They were placed again in the prison at Place des Etats Unis. 'Pickersgill later informed Rousset that he and Macalister had been reinterrogated and during that interrogation had been rendered drunk.' Rousset was given a cell that looked out on to the garden at the back, facing a convent. 'He had a job now sweeping the stairs and corridors. He befriended two of the guards who were

Georgians. One day he noticed that there was a door leading out into the back garden and on the morning of 8 June 1944 he perceived that this gate was not locked. He immediately knocked out the SS guard, escaped through the garden, jumped over the side wall (which was supposed to be electrified) and reached the street through the adjoining house.'

Rousset went into hiding in Paris. He tried to arrange the escape of the others, still imprisoned in Place des Etats Unis, and made contact again with the Georgian guards, but it was too late. 'He was informed that all the agents had been removed from the prison.' Rousset remained in hiding until the arrival of the Allies in Paris, when he was able to give this report – the most dramatic evidence so far that prisoners had been systematically transferred to Germany.

Vera now asked the Foreign Office and War Office for information on PoW camps at Ravitsch and Breslau. She then sent out instructions for a series of new 'good news' letters to be sent to families of the missing. Although in many cases the news was very bad, reports were still contradictory and, in Vera's view, too vague to be passed on to relatives. In any case the continuing need for secrecy about SOE operations meant that even the families of those known for sure to have been captured were not to be told the truth.

'Dear Mrs Baker Inayat,' wrote a junior official to Nora's mother on 29 September 1944, 'I am glad to be able to tell you that we have good news of your daughter.'

Christian Rowden, the mother of Diana Rowden, received an identical letter. 'Dear Mrs Rowden,' wrote the same official on the same day, 'I am glad to be able to tell you that we have again had good news of your daughter Miss D. Rowden.' Diana's mother always replied straight away to letters about her daughter. Writing from her flat in Cornwall Mews West, Kensington, on 3 October, she said: 'Thank you for your letter of 29 September which I was so glad to receive yesterday. It always seems such a long time between letters and when they are a week or two late it seems like a lifetime. Actually it is 16 months only since I saw my daughter and it seems much longer owing to being unable to send letters to and from her.'

A month later the news was even worse. No more agents had come forward in Paris. There had been several more disturbing confirmations that the agents were captured, including another report from the Gestapo headquarters at Avenue Foch.

In October British officials were finally given access to Avenue Foch. Dated 9 October, a report of what was found reached Vera's desk soon afterwards. 'I visited the torture chamber at Avenue Foch where inter alia Kieffer had an office,' reported an intelligence officer, referring to Hans Josef Kieffer, the senior German counter-intelligence officer in Paris. 'I found a moving inscription from men and women who knew they had lost everything, except their honour. Names underneath are those present in the cells. Their ultimate fate is unknown to me but I was informed during the last few days before the departure of the Germans that several people had been taken downstairs into the courtyard, placed against the wall and shot.'

The officer then gave a list of names he had found, which included: 'S/O D.H. Rowden. 4193 WAAF OFF. 22.11.43. 5.12.43' and 'A/S/O Nora Baker'. He added: 'The dates are, I understand, those of the arrival and departure of the various people at Avenue Foch.'

Vera was quick to identify her two women agents. S/O D.H. Rowden was obviously Section Officer Diana Hope Rowden, and the dates given against her name were, as Vera could see, consistent with the date when she was believed arrested. Although there were no dates against her name, there was little doubt that A/S/O Nora Baker was Assistant Section Officer Nora Inayat Khan. Nora Baker was her main alias. While the report provided corroboration that Nora – and now Diana too – had been held at Avenue Foch, Vera did not accept the rumour that they may have been shot. These were not the first reports that agents had been shot before the German retreat, but Vera took the view that the shootings probably did not involve her people. From French sources she had now heard that all the captured British agents were taken to Germany, where they could be used as hostages or in prisoner exchanges.

Nevertheless, it was now time to change the tone of the family letters from 'good news' to bad. On 15 October a letter went to Nora's mother at the family's home in Taviton Street, Bloomsbury.

Dear Mrs Baker Inayat, I am extremely sorry to have to inform you that we have recently been out of touch with your daughter. Due to the confused state of affairs in France we were not unduly worried, but I am afraid now your daughter must be considered as missing although there is every reason to believe that she will eventually be notified as a prisoner of war . . . I would impress upon you in the interests of your daughter's safety that you make no enquiries with regard to her except through me.

On the same date a letter went to Mrs Rowden, in almost exactly the same terms, stating similarly that there was 'every reason to believe' that Diana would be notified as a prisoner of war. Mrs Rowden was not so sure. 'Thank you for your letter of 15 October with its very bad news. It certainly is, as Diana would have put it, a very bad show. I do hope she may have gone into hiding and will turn up again soon. In fact I have been expecting her home daily lately. However, you believe she is a prisoner of war and will eventually be all right. I hope this will prove so.'

5

'NEED TO KNOW'

In the early months of 1945 Vera was often to be found lunching at the Causerie in Claridge's, or maybe at Fortnum's. Her guests – perhaps a young airman, a personal assistant to an air vice marshal, or else an influential secretary with channels to the Air Ministry – were flattered to be invited out in such generous style. And by the time the meal was over the guest would also have been impressed by Vera's argument that she must immediately have a commission, preferably as a squadron officer in the WAAF.

As Allied forces closed in on Germany, Vera's mission to follow the trails of her agents was fixed so firmly in her mind that anyone who encountered her at this time saw she could not possibly be deterred. There was, as she pointed out, nobody else to do the job.

Nevertheless, it was unclear exactly how, as a lone woman with no military status and as yet no passport, Vera was to proceed. By January 1945 her personal position had once again become precarious. Her naturalisation had come through a year ago, but she still had no passport, owing to a regulation time delay. Within SOE her status was unquestioned, but F Section was now reduced to a rump, and there was already talk of closing SOE down at the end of the war, so she could soon be out of a job. Official indifference about SOE was such that nobody would be kept on to care for the affairs of the missing agents, whose files would simply be stamped 'missing presumed dead' and closed.

Vera was therefore pulling every string she could to secure a commission, in order to bolster her authority to continue her search. As she also pointed out to those she lobbied, her lack of status was already badly hampering her ability to operate. Early in January she had been on an abortive trip to France. On the invitation of the French Sécurité Militaire, which was investigating treachery against members of the resistance, she travelled with another SOE officer to discuss French investigations into penetration of SOE circuits. It was a gruelling trip which involved taking another gunboat – this time across a rough winter sea – followed by several hours in the back of an army lorry to reach Paris. Vera had hoped to hear what the French were finding out, particularly about the Prosper case and about Henri Déricourt. She was disappointed. No sooner had she and her colleague arrived than the French police made it clear that they had nothing to say to the British after all. General de Gaulle himself had apparently got to hear of their arrival and declared the SOE personnel 'persona non grata in France'. Vera returned home angered by the snub, but determined that next time she went to Paris she would go with more authority.

Her main frustrations, though, were much closer to home. Even as the first PoW and concentration camps were being liberated in the east by Russian forces, one of Vera's own SOE colleagues was trying to put a stop to her search. In a lengthy memorandum Vera had argued that, given the speed of the Allied advance, it was now essential that the names of missing agents be distributed widely. She suggested that the names be supplied to other branches of the military, to the International Committee of the Red Cross, to the Russians and other Allies, and to any forces or bodies likely to be crossing German frontiers or contacting prisoners held in camps. On sight of Vera's memo, John Senter, head of SOE's security directorate, commissioned as a Commander in the Royal Navy Volunteer Reserve, immediately pulled rank, saying her search should, in effect, be stopped.

'Top Secret and Confidential. Strictly Addressee only,' wrote Senter in a memorandum on Vera's proposals. 'I think the set-up suggested in Vera Atkins's note, and the annotations, is frankly unworkable,' he stated, adding that she should confine herself to 'welfare work'.

A barrister, noted for his gleaming white hair, Senter had begun his working life as legal adviser to the Scottish Boot and Shoe Company and was a stickler for the rules. He had always disliked Vera – or 'Rosenberg', as he called her – precisely because she broke his rules.

Senter wanted total control of investigations into missing SOE agents. As security director his interest in their personal fate was slight: rather he wanted to know who had survived in order to be first to interrogate them and to find out how the Germans had penetrated so many circuits. Given the sensitivity of the investigation, in which both MI6 and signals intelligence would take an interest, only personnel with the highest security clearance could be involved. Vera had no such special clearance and no need to know.

Not only was Senter angered by Vera's attempt to take over his interrogations; he was also opposed on principle to her methods of tracing the missing. To circulate names of agents, he argued, broke all the rules of a secret service by alerting others – possibly the enemy – to the fact that secret missions had taken place. Vera, however, argued that rules had been broken to get agents out there, particularly in the case of the women. Now rules needed to be broken to get them back.

The anomalous status of the female secret agents was becoming Vera's prime concern. It was not clear, for example, which department of government would maintain contact with them or their dependants after the war, or who would 'carry' them if disability benefit were ever necessary or in the case of future welfare payments. Now Vera was also having to grapple with how the women's limbo status could affect their very chances of survival.

Male agents either carried commissions or honorary commissions in the regular services, so they could correctly tell their captors they were officers, albeit not in uniform. This gave them at least a slim chance of claiming prisoner-of-war status, which was automatically denied to civilians or irregular combatants.

But even this feeble hope of decent treatment did not apply to the women who were commissioned in the voluntary FANY corps, a civilian organisation. Those women who had been in the WAAF before joining SOE, or who, more recently, had been accepted as honorary WAAFs, carried some possible claim to treatment as PoWs, but those who were mere 'cap badge' FANYs were the most vulnerable secret agents of all.

Vera's anxiety, however, also had a more immediate cause. The reality was, whatever Mrs Rowden and other next of kin had been told, that SOE agents were, by any legal definition, spies. Once identified as such they were liable to be shot rather than treated as PoWs.

The only way agents were likely to survive German captivity would be by disguising their true role in some way, perhaps by claiming to be ordinary French resistance members, or by escaping, or by sheer luck. The question was: how could those agents who survived be identified in the chaotic aftermath? By early 1945 no name – neither male nor female – of any missing SOE agent had been passed to a single organisation outside Baker Street. No SOE name, real or alias, had been placed on any military casualty list or any missing lists designated 'secret' or otherwise. The idea, in particular, that women's names should be circulated was anathema to the authorities as this would be to admit that women had been deployed. SOE names had certainly not been passed to the International Committee of the Red Cross, the British Red Cross or SHAEF (Supreme Headquarters Allied Expeditionary Force). No organisation which might be responsible for looking for the missing, whether it was liberating camps or repatriating prisoners, had a single SOE name on its lists.

Under international law the Germans had a duty to notify the Red Cross if any names on its missing lists were found in their hands – dead or alive. But as no SOE name had been posted, none would be notified, even if they had managed to get into a PoW camp.

If, after liberation, Allied forces found British agents alive among the mass of displaced people who would by then be flooding across Europe, they would have every reason not to believe their stories, as they would not be on their lists. And the agents would not be entitled to repatriation or welfare of any kind. Once again the FANYs would have the greatest difficulty of all in convincing British or Allied military of their bona fides. Despite this, Senter was still refusing publication of their names because 'security' might be jeopardised.

By early February 1945 Vera's case for publishing names became daily more urgent. Russian forces were advancing fast and vast numbers of prisoners who had been held in eastern camps were being marched west by the Germans before the Russians' arrival. Meanwhile Allied prisoners in camps liberated by the Russians, fearful of heading west into German lines, were reportedly making their way east and turning up in places such as Lublin in liberated Poland and Odessa on the Black Sea. Vera hoped her people might be among them. The fortress of Ravitsch, near Breslau, was liberated by the Russians in mid-January. Vera knew that several SOE agents were prisoners there, among them France Antelme and Gilbert Norman.

The Ravitsch prisoners might even now be making their way home. 'Given the Russian advance . . . special attention should be given to the problem of ensuring that our prisoners shall be identified and released as quickly as possible following the liberation of their area,' she wrote, requesting that the British embassy in Moscow and British diplomats in Lublin and at a military mission in Odessa be given the agents' names.

In February the entire government bureaucracy seemed paralysed by the enormity of the PoW catastrophe now unfolding in mainland Europe. Perhaps as many as two hundred thousand British and Commonwealth prisoners were among more than two million Allied nationals (including Russians) now believed to be held in more than two hundred German PoW camps, and rumours were rife that all might perish on Hitler's orders.

In these circumstances nobody had time to pay attention to the fate of a few missing secret agents. But Vera was asserting, more forcefully than ever, that they should be given special attention. The Red Cross was pushing hard for access to concentration camps and trying to negotiate prisoner exchanges. Vera argued that it should keep 'a special look out' for SOE prisoners and should give them priority on release and repatriation, but it must be given lists of names. 'This is not an unreasonable request given the special hardships they have undergone and the special risks they have taken in preparing for an Allied landing,' she wrote.

Then, just as agreement neared on publishing names, the bureaucrats started quibbling over what to call them. 'Which of the secret agents' many names – real and false – should be published?' asked one. Buckmaster, at last back from his celebratory tour of France, opined at length on how to classify an F Section casualty, only to conclude that in any event 'we have every reason to believe that they will be recovered at the cessation of hostilities'.

By early March, Vera had new cause to worry that her men and women might never be recovered. The French had found an inscription on prison charts kept by the Germans at Fresnes, and it was passed to her. The inscription referred to a man named John Hopper, who had been captured as a spy and imprisoned in Fresnes before being transferred to Germany. 'Hopper. John. Cell No. 288,' it said, and in a remarks column were the notes '*N+N*' and '*Ständig gefesselt*' ('permanently chained'). Hopper, it seemed, had been singled out for special treatment. He had been chained, and when Vera asked her sources about the meaning of '*N+N*' she discovered that it referred to a category of prisoner to be dealt with under the *Nacht und Nebel* order. Issued by the Reich towards the end of 1942, this ruled that resisters and spies should be categorised '*N+N*'. Nobody – family, fellow resisters or anybody else – should ever know what became of them. It would be as if they had disappeared in the 'night and fog'.

Another inscription had also been found in Fresnes prison: 'Frank Pickersgill, Canadian Army Officer 26.6.43.' Pickersgill's little scratches confirmed that he was taken there soon after his arrest. But what Vera so desperately needed was a clue as to where he was now. She knew Pickersgill had once been in Ravitsch. Perhaps he was marching east.

Even more tantalising were letters from her agent Ange Defendini. The letters had been written by the Corsican while he too was held at Fresnes and were apparently smuggled out to a friend, who had passed them to the French police, but the French could make neither head nor tail of them.

Written in a complex code based on a film of the novel *Le Fantôme de l'Opéra*, the letters had flummoxed everyone except Vera, who succeeded in deciphering them and found they contained a daring plan for escape: 'Get for me two small revolvers with ammunition, some cyanide or mercury poison and four small metal saws.' But the letters contained no clues about where Defendini was eventually taken. The only clue they did contain was a warning about Déricourt. 'I have confirmation here from my mistress that Gilbert is a swine.' The word 'mistress' was code for Defendini's Gestapo captors.

By March families of the missing were clamouring for news. The destruction of Dresden by Allied bombers had exacerbated fears that Hitler would take revenge at the eleventh hour by slaughtering all prisoners held in the camps.

Vera invited those relatives who requested meetings to see her in a hotel just off Trafalgar Square. The Victoria Hotel, in Northumberland Avenue, had been requisitioned by the War Office at the outbreak of war. SOE candidates were sometimes interviewed in Room 238, and it was here that Vera now met their next of kin. Sitting at a small wooden table in what was once a single bedroom, she tried to assure the relatives, as she had in letters, that when hostilities were over there was every reason to hope the missing would be found. But few who came here believed the reassurances of the elegant officer in her brand-new powder-blue uniform. Vera had at last secured her commission. She was now a flight officer in the WAAF; the higher rank of squadron officer had been refused.

———

'There may have been a basin in the room. I think there was a gas fire. It was a horrible little room,' said Helen Oliver, sister of Lilian Rolfe. Lilian had been landed by Lysander near Bléré in May 1944 and her family had heard almost nothing from the War Office since.

'What did Vera say?' I asked Helen.

'I can't remember. I think she may have told me about how Lilian had been captured – how brave she had been. She could tell me nothing about what had happened to Lilian – that's all I remember. But I already knew Lilian was dead.'

'How?'

'I had had a dream about her,' said Helen, who explained that she and Lilian were mirror twins and often had premonitions about each other. 'My crown went one way and Lilian's the other. She played the piano beautifully and I played the violin. We were very similar. But Lilian was not as strong as me. She nearly died of rheumatic fever before the war. Our mother nursed her back to health.'

I asked what happened in the dream.

'I saw Lilian. She came to me. She was crying. She was dressed in brown. She was in terrible distress. Just crying. I knew something awful had happened to her.'

'When was the dream?'

'It was on 11 February 1945 – not long before I saw Vera Atkins. I now know that was the night she died, although Vera Atkins gave a different date later, but I know she was wrong.'

Was there anything else that Helen could recall about Vera at the meeting in the Victoria Hotel?

She thought about this. 'I remember I disliked her. She smelled.'

———

After every meeting with the families Vera took the chance to update the next-of-kin register, annotating her personal copy with details so it read like a personal inventory of the F Section family. Here were brothers, sisters, husbands – estranged or otherwise – stepfathers, daughters, illegitimate children, lovers. Vera had learned of all of them, and recorded them here for future reference. Yvonne Rudellat, she had noted, was estranged from her husband and first contact should be with her twenty-two-year-old daughter. Violette Szabo 'leaves a small girl in the care of a guardian whose name I do not know. She also has a father who is a very bad type and she wishes at all costs to prevent that any money of hers should fall into his hands or that he should have any say in the guardianship of her daughter.'

Madeleine Damerment's next of kin was listed simply as: 'Mother Superior, St Mary's Convent, Hitchin'. In another case a stepbrother had been in touch 'but is not known to our friend'.

In a cupboard in Room 238 Vera was also guarding the scaffolding of the agents' lives: in boxes were rental agreements for temporary housing, bank details, copies of wills, club membership cards and odd photographs. There were little personal notes about what should be done if such and such should happen and whether a mother could be telephoned on her birthday or a suit collected from a tailor's. And Vera's job was to ensure that the pay of the missing, including allowances for dependants, was sent to bank accounts.

And then there were the physical remnants of the missing which had also been left under Vera's supervision: a vanity case, cravats, gramophone records – all these things were left behind in the rush as they departed. Violette Szabo left a camel-hair coat wrapped in a brown paper bag; Diana Rowden a diary, a map and a pair of plimsolls; Andrée Borrel a large blue suitcase containing another smaller brown suitcase. Vera knew exactly what was here and if the items were not noted, they were all filed in her head, along with the aliases and cover stories, the last-known colour of hair – all of which would enable her, and her alone, to trace her agents.

By early March 1945 the Allies had crossed the Rhine and the final collapse of Germany was expected at any time. Vera was scanning telegrams and telexes, monitoring the flow of paper from every possible source, so that no detail, however small, that might identify somebody could possibly slip by.

Papers were flying from Vera's office to Buckmaster, to Senter's men in Paris and to officials in the War Office, as everyone suddenly seemed acutely conscious of the need to get ready for the moment when liberation would happen – though nobody knew what to expect.

Lists and more lists of the missing, with aliases and details of next of kin, were passed around and checked and double-checked. Vera was arranging for enlargements of photographs of all the agents to be sent to Paris, where some of the first returnees were expected to arrive.

'Is the list of FANYs enclosed a complete one: Beekman, Bloch, Borrel, Damerment, Inayat Khan, Lefort, Leigh, Nearne, Sansom, Plewman, Rowden, Szabo, Baseden, Rolfe?' asked a note from FANY HQ on Vera's file.

Even before the Allies reached the first camps in Germany, prisoners had started to trickle back across frontiers. Some were escaping and others were at last being exchanged.

The first traces of F Section names came in, often picked up from interviews with early returnees and then passed on. Vera's advice was swiftly sought. 'Top Secret. Is Celestin Rept. Celestin. Brian Stonehouse?' said a signal from Paris, clearly referring to the agent Brian Stonehouse but saying nothing about where or how he was. Vera replied: 'Our operator Celestin is Brian Stonehouse arrested approx Oct 22. If any interesting information comes in I am sure you will let us have it.'

And another signal from Senter's men in Paris gave news of Yvonne Rudellat, but nothing definite. 'Top secret. Yvonne Rudellat. Only meagre particulars available . . . Now believed prisoner in Germany. She is down in the Kardex as a FANY and French by birth, which presumably means she is British by nationality. Is she also British by upbringing and education?' Again the question was referred to Vera, who alone could supply the answer.

Pouring over the wires and filling newspapers were ever more horrific stories of atrocity and horror, and in response politicians were suddenly preparing the ground for the possibility of war crimes trials. SOE received a memorandum from the newly formed War Crimes Commission saying that evidence of war crimes should be gathered wherever possible from any returning agent. A note from a senior

Foreign Office diplomat suggested that the fate of SOE agents had suddenly drawn attention: 'Anticipating that in the near future Allied armies will overrun some of the camps in which these officers are held it is now desired to institute some procedure whereby the welfare of the officers can be cared for.'

On 4 April Vera remarked that 'at last' the head of SOE's security directorate had sanctioned that short particulars of SOE agents should be published in the PoW casualty lists, 'to ensure that they get into the P/W stream'. Vera stressed: 'We are anxious to get on with the job as quickly as possible.' And also, at long last, somebody somewhere had decided she had been right after all and that it was now 'in the best interests of our officers if we supply to casualties branch a list of all who have been arrested or who are missing'. Vera sent a memo to a liaison officer in Whitehall: 'Herewith ten copies of our casualty lists which please forward MOST URGENTLY to the War Office Casualties Branch . . . I have heard that it is most important that we get this documentation out since those returning are most handicapped by not being identifiable.' Somebody in the SOE hierarchy was even now suggesting sending officers to Germany with advancing troops to look for missing SOE agents, but the plan was dismissed by others as 'impracticable' in view of the pace of the war. Vera now sent an internal minute arguing that lists of agents be provided to the displaced persons branch of the Allied Control Commission, which was preparing to take over the administration of Germany. Senter had objected.

By the first week of April a tidal wave of returnees from Nazi Germany was already swamping France and PoWs were reaching England by the thousand. Senter's men in Paris were overwhelmed trying to keep track of reports of missing agents and interrogating those with news. Asked by Senter to explain why his interrogations were taking so long to process, a Major Wells replied that a 'mountain' of paperwork had been produced by one interrogation. 'I cannot tell you the size of it in pages and words but it is written on very thin paper and I weighed the whole bundle on the kitchen scales it is just short of 4 kilos.'

Vera, meanwhile, kept only mental notes, so that when a colleague complained of a failure of communication with London another commented: 'The reason for the failure is that the information is in Miss Atkins's head and not elsewhere.' On another question of identity an official in Paris commented: 'Suggest you irritate F/O Atkins.'

Names of more and more concentration camps were now cropping up in Red Cross intelligence reports. On 8 April Vera finally had a reply to her request of weeks earlier for more information from the Foreign Office.

> With reference to your enquiry about the Ravensbrück and Buchenwald [concentration] camps we have just received the following information from the War Office on the subject:
>
>   'Ravensbrück camp as such is comparatively unknown to us, and we have no record of any British civilian internees being in Brandenburg now. Recently, however, our Embassy in Paris informed us that women returned from that internment camp said it had been transferred to Weimar, and we are making further enquiries.
>
>   'With regard to Buchenwald – no further information is forthcoming other than that given in March – i.e. that it is a concentration camp for German nationals, although a certain number of Poles and Czechs have been reported there. The War Office telegraphed Bern again on 6th of this month asking for a report on the present position.'

Then at precisely 11.55am on 13 April 1945, a teleprinter in a Bayswater office shook suddenly into life and started spilling out the truth about Weimar concentration camp, which, from that moment on, the world would know as Buchenwald:

> Most Immediate. Rpt Most Immediate. Top Secret. Rept
>   Top Secret.
> To Senter from Delaforce.
>   Have interrogated French Officer deported with number of our male agents to WEIMAR concentration camp.
>   On 11 September 1944: ALLARD BENOIST DEFENDILI [*sic*], DETAL HUBBLE? LECCIA MAYER MACALISTER PICKERSGILL RECHENNMANN SABOURIN STEELE: Executed by hanging.
>   On 5 October: FRAGER MULSANT WILKINSON: Executed by shooting.

On 21 October: YEO THOMAS: executed by shooting.
October (date uncertain)
BARRETT: Executed by shooting.
October (date uncertain)
4. SOUTHGATE: Possibly still Alive
5. Full report follows this afternoon. Contents this message NOT repeat NOT communicated to anyone except A.M. (above mentioned).

A man with white hair was standing by the teleprinter tearing off the piece of paper. He then called SOE's signals room to make sure the teleprint was marked secret and circulated to nobody else. He wrote: 'In particular it must not be seen by the country section'. John Senter meant that the information about the F Section dead at Buchenwald should not be seen by Vera Atkins.

6

'BUCHENWALD BOYS'

Vera read through the names of the dead listed in the report from Buchenwald and ticked off her 'boys'. The Free French agent Bernard Guillot had escaped from Buchenwald a few days before the liberation. When he arrived in Paris on 7 April 1945, Guillot reported to Senter's men revealing the names of all the British agents who died at the concentration camp. Guillot was one of the first to give eyewitness testimony of Buchenwald's horror.

Senter's men, however, did not at first believe what Guillot said. They were sceptical partly because they had never considered that Britons might be taken to a concentration camp. And, like most other British officials at their level, these officers considered that Nazi atrocity stories were largely propaganda. So Senter marked Guillot's report 'secret' while he checked its accuracy.

An inner circle of senior British officers and politicians had been keeping secret what they had known about the concentration camps and death camps since the start of the war. From as early as 1939, SS signals encoded by German Enigma machines had been intercepted and decoded by cryptanalysts at Bletchley Park in Buckinghamshire. The resulting decrypts, known as ULTRA, revealed early evidence of a Nazi extermination programme, but for security reasons nobody outside the inner circle – which included the Prime Minister – was allowed to know. The fear was, or so it was said later, that if information from ULTRA were to spread, the Germans would guess that the Enigma code had been broken and would change the codes.

Vera made an effort to inform herself about concentration camps from other sources, but most of her colleagues did not. A mere SOE staff officer had no access to ULTRA traffic. Those who briefed SOE agents made a point of setting out the risks they faced if captured, but concentration camps were never mentioned.

The 'secret' stamp on Guillot's report proved a futile gesture. A few days later, on 11 April 1945, the US Third Army, commanded by General George Patton, stumbled on Buchenwald, 8 miles north of Weimar. It was the first concentration camp liberated by Western troops. General Patton himself now decided that there should be no more secrets about concentration camps and called for photographers and reporters 'to get the horrid details'.

Vera read on, now making notes from Guillot's report. Here was Ange Defendini, the author of those desperate letters from prison to his 'mistress' – hanged at Buchenwald. Here too were Frank Pickersgill and John Macalister – also hanged. Also on the list was Henri Frager. Guillot passed on comments made by Frager as he went to his death. 'Louba [Frager] said that a double agent called Gilbert was responsible for his arrest.' Vera had dearly hoped to talk to Frager about Déricourt (Gilbert). There were many other F Section men here too: all correctly identified and all shot or hanged.

Guillot's story had begun with a description of a transport leaving Paris by train for Germany on 7 August 1944, four months later than the transport described by Marcel Rousset. And Guillot's transport had headed further south than Rousset's. 'The men were handcuffed two by two. In addition to the men, there was a party of twenty-five women who left at the same time.' Vera underlined this last sentence. Guillot continued:

As there had been a bombardment, the line was broken and the train stopped for a day then reversed. At a small station they were put into two requisitioned French lorries – one for the men and one for the women – and took the road to Châlons-sur-Marne. There they changed lorries and went on to Verdun, where they slept the night, leaving again the next morning for Metz. There they remained for four hours at the Gestapo HQ and here Guillot saw the women again. Out of the photographs shown him, he was only able to recognise Denise Bloch. He thought he recognised one other but said

he had spent so little time with the women he hardly
remembered them. After Metz they lost sight of the women.

Vera made a note on Denise Bloch's card. A Jewish Frenchwoman, Denise had been reported captured just before D-Day and
nothing had been heard of her since. If she was among this group of
prisoners, others captured at about the same time might have been
with her. On a piece of scrap paper Vera now jotted the names of
Violette Szabo, Eileen Nearne and Yvonne Baseden.

Leaving the women behind at Metz, Guillot's convoy of men
moved on. They were taken by lorry to Saarbrücken, where they
spent four days.

They were chained together in fives by their feet and were
made to run round and round in small circles so that
obviously they kept falling down. On the fourth day they
were put in a *voiture cellulaire* [secure carriage] at Saarbrücken
station, and taken by train to Weimar, passing through
Frankfurt and Kassel. They arrived at Buchenwald camp near
Weimar at midnight on 16/17 August 1944.

They were at first told they were to be put in a gas chamber
but this did not happen. Instead they were robbed of everything
they possessed, their hair was cut off and they were disinfected.
They were then taken to Block 17. At 1.30 on 9 September a list
was brought round from the SS Direction with about fourteen
names. These men were immediately taken to the prison in the
interior of the camp where they were shut in cells. During the
night of 11–12 September they were all hanged in the cellars of
the crematorium and burned immediately. On 5 October
another special bulletin was issued and the named men were
called to present themselves and were shot at 3 in the afternoon.
These men were shot two by two at two stakes and their bodies
burned immediately afterwards.

Vera now selected seventeen cards from her index and on each one
she noted: 'Believed executed at Buchenwald.' She also wrote a note
to Buckmaster saying that Guillot's report suggested the executions
were probably the result of a specific order from on high. Vera had by
now seen intelligence on Hitler's *Führerbefehl*, or Commando Order,

issued on 18 October 1942, which stated that 'all terrorist and sabotage troops of the British and their accomplices who do not act like soldiers but rather like bandits will be treated as such by the German troops and will be ruthlessly eliminated in battle wherever they appear'.

Those 'bandits' who were arrested by police were to be handed over to the SS for execution. The Buchenwald deaths suggested that SOE agents arrested in France fell into the second category of the Commando Order. They had been systematically executed.

Fast on Guillot's story came another report from Buchenwald by a man named Professor Serge Balachowsky, one of Prosper's people. Balachowsky, the biologist who had worked at the agricultural college at Grignon, corroborated Guillot's story and added new detail, picked up from prisoner-guards. The first group, he said, was hanged at 5.30 in the afternoon and were first beaten 'as was customary'. He added: 'They were simply hung by a rope on hooks a few metres from the ground so that they died of strangulation and not by breaking the spinal cord, thus taking 5–10 minutes to die. The bodies were burned but traces of blood were found on the floor.' Balachowsky said Hubble's notebook had been passed to him after it fell from the SOE man's body as he was hanged.

Now everyone expected the remainder of the group to be executed and Balachowsky, who had friends among them, devised an escape plan. He was working in the typhus laboratory, part of the medical experimentation block, and arranged for dead bodies of typhus victims to be exchanged for the condemned prisoners and then smuggled out. For help he first approached leaders of the camp's German communist clique, but they did not wish to save those who were not in their group. Then he approached the head of the typhus laboratory, an SS officer, 'who had shown a good deal of pessimism about Germany's fate in the war' and was persuaded to help if his own life was spared by the Allies.

The plan was for three men to be saved at first. The first two were already chosen, but there was debate about whether the third should be a Free French agent named Stéphane Hessel or the SOE agent Henri Frager; 'after hesitation' Hessel was chosen. As the escapes were being planned, quite suddenly another list of names was published and the men were ordered to be shaved. This was on 4 October and the following day, at 4pm, all, including Henri Frager, were executed. 'They were all supremely brave and nobody showed any weakness,' said Balachowsky. Frager had negotiated with the

Germans that this time the men be shot, not hanged.

Vera passed on what she was learning to colleagues who she felt might need to know. 'The attached document shows people it is intended to make disappear,' she wrote in a note referring to a paper brought back by 'one of the Buchenwald boys'. She stated: 'I believe the cross shows they are dead and those underlined that they are pending execution. I have spare copies should anyone require them.'

She had also started settling the affairs of the dead. Casualty reports were filled out. A uniform draft letter to the next of kin was composed with blanks for the appropriate names. The letter was then sent to a junior officer to sign. Personal effects were also now returned. 'Thank you for your note concerning Mrs Macalister. Her husband's kit is being dispatched today,' wrote Flight Officer Atkins. Hubble's notebook was sent to his family.

The bureaucrats who had argued earlier about how to classify the missing were now wrangling about how to classify the dead. The War Office insisted that SOE dead should be classified 'died as prisoners of war', but Vera was determined they should be 'killed in action'. She wrote: 'It was one of the peculiar risks of SOE work that being in civilian clothing they were liable to be executed by the enemy . . . their execution was caused directly by their work for us. It is felt strongly that next of kin of these officers should be treated quite as generously as had their husbands fallen in battle.'

Vera was also pushing finance officers regarding the status of FANY women and, in particular, who would pay for 'possible claims arising from disabilities as a direct result of their treatment in enemy camps'.

On 15 April 1945 British forces had reached the concentration camp at Belsen, north of Hanover, and soon hundreds of thousands of witnesses to atrocity were streaming over European borders. Senter's men in Paris were overwhelmed: 'Warden to Senter,' signalled one. 'Greatest possible confusion concerning repatriates from Germany. Stop. Some individuals interviewed by all and sundry including local press and others not seen at all and disappear into various parts of France, many in too sick condition for interviews. Stop. On constant lookout for people who may have news of our agents but no controlling body with whom we can work. Stop.'

'Victims stacked in heaps at Belsen,' headlines declared, but Vera had moved on to trace Belsen's living, and among the survivors was a

Polish woman who had known a British prisoner there called Jacqueline Gauthier. Vera knew Jacqueline Gauthier to be Yvonne Rudellat, one of the first SOE women sent to France, who worked with Prosper. The Polish woman said 'Jacqueline' had been marched to Belsen from Ravensbrück and when last seen was in an 'awful condition' and suffering loss of memory. 'She had arrived morally strong but became very ill and by 10 April she knew she was dying,' wrote the woman. 'I do hope she lived to know the camp was liberated so she rested quietly knowing her work had been of use and rewarded.' Vera urgently sought information on Rudellat from the Red Cross and from British forces now scouring the camp. Locating her was urgent, 'not least because she is an important witness to the Prosper collapse'.

For all the horror now emerging, Vera still clung on to hope wherever she could. There had already been miraculous escapes. 'Southgate, possibly alive,' Bernard Guillot had said and not long afterwards came news that Southgate had indeed walked alive from Buchenwald. Yeo-Thomas, first reported dead at Buchenwald, had escaped thanks to the Balachowsky plan, along with Harry Peulevé, one of F Section's best men. And then from Belsen Vera received copies of detailed camp records, including meticulously produced 'nominal rolls' of inmates. On one list she found the name Jacqueline Gauthier. The record said she was still at the camp four days after the liberation. Vera wrote: 'I cannot believe that anyone can die or disappear without trace after the liberation.'

A man believed to be the F Section agent Robert Sheppard was reported by a Frenchman early in April to have been seen at Dachau concentration camp. 'His morale was wonderful,' said the returning prisoner. And, when Dachau was liberated by the Americans on 29 April, amid the thousands of corpses of people who had died the previous week were thirty-three thousand survivors, including Sheppard and his friend Brian Stonehouse. A few days later the two men stepped on to the tarmac at RAF Lyneham in Wiltshire, wearing American boots with their trousers tucked into them and decked out in yards of blue silk dotted with white and wound around them as scarves. They had found the silk in the Industriehof, the workshop attached to the camp at Dachau. Vera was on the tarmac to meet them.

'Close-shaven heads, hollow cheeked, very bright eyed. Both of them tall, needless to say, slim, Brian very dark brown eyes, long sensitive face. Bob, fair, blue-eyed, round amused robust face. With these two no emotion other than joy,' was how Vera remembered their arrival fifty years later.

'Smart in her uniform. Standing by a car. I think Buck was there too. Vera – obviously pleased to see us. Welcome home, boys. No emotion,' was how Robert Sheppard remembered Vera.

'Did she ask you questions?' I asked him.

'Not as I remember, no. And we would not have been able to tell her much at that time,' he said. 'Suddenly we had come back to the normal world. The abnormal world was in the past – gone – and everything with it.'

'When did you leave the normal world?'

'We left the normal world in Paris. Even Paris with the Gestapo had been the normal world. Things happened there that were not nice. Often they were brutal. But, relatively speaking, they had been normal. Then, when the train went off to Germany, we had no idea what was going to happen. I had never heard of concentration camps. We travelled all night and next morning we stopped at Saarbrücken. And suddenly we entered Neuengamme. We realised at once we had left a normal world for another one where there were entirely different rules, a new mentality, another way of living – even between the prisoners; this was something new. The first morning they asked me to beat a prisoner in front of the others. He was a Russian. And I refused. And the SS officer, he took the stick and he went and he did it. And we had to adjust but many didn't. I saw people who died within three or four days because they stopped believing. People committed a kind of suicide because they could not believe this world.

'And then we went to Mauthausen and then to Natzweiler and Dachau and so many people died we took no notice. And in this abnormal world there was no human contact with the SS, you see. We had no idea what the SS guards' names were. And there were rules but there were no rules. Why were those others from SOE killed and why were Brian Stonehouse and I allowed to live? We don't know. There is no answer.

'Then, when we came back from the camps, we had to be careful what we said. We could see very quickly nobody wanted to know about the abnormal world. It was a strange feeling: we were not proud at all of what we had been through.'

'Did Vera understand?'

'I think that Vera had this reaction – she had an intelligence to understand without trying to know why. I expect that Vera, on her own, must have thought and analysed many things. But she had the intelligence never to ask a question which could have put us back in that situation. It is difficult to analyse, always, with Vera.'

'Why did she choose to go and find out about the "abnormal world"?'

'I am not sure she wanted to know too much about it. I think she went with a feeling of responsibility. She was reacting – she had a personal responsibility, having been what she was in SOE. You might ask why did she enter SOE, knowing what she was going to do and sending people she didn't know to their deaths.'

———

Of SOE agents not yet traced, the strongest hope lay with those in camps taken or about to be taken by the Russians in their continuing westward advance. It was now three months since the fortress prison of Ravitsch, on the German-Polish border, had been liberated and not a word had been heard of the twenty-five agents there. When the Russians took the camps there was no system for prisoner repatriation, and evidence now suggested that any prisoners found there were often left to make their way to freedom as best they could. Prisoners still appeared to be heading east towards Odessa, rather than west, where they feared they might run into German lines. By the end of April the British military mission in Odessa had reported many PoWs turning up. Remarkably, information had also somehow reached the offices of solicitors acting for an agent named John Hamilton, one of the SOE Ravitsch prisoners, saying he was safe in hospital in Odessa. Such news naturally inspired optimism in Baker Street. Vera was trying to check the report on Hamilton and wrote: 'I am hopeful that all those whom we believe to have been overrun by the Russians in January 1945 in the Fortress of Ravitsch may be somewhere in Russia.' Reports of the bravery of SOE agents as they went to their deaths were also giving cause for pride. One uncorroborated story alleged that the agent Guy Bieler had so impressed his captors at Flossenburg concentration camp that he received an SS guard of honour as he was marched to execution.

But nothing caused greater optimism than unexpected news of

Francis Suttill brought by a returnee from the camps called Wing Commander Harry Day. He was no ordinary returnee. 'Wings' Day was one of the masterminds of the great escape from Stalag Luft III in March 1944. On recapture he had been sent to Sachsenhausen concentration camp, from where he had also escaped in September 1944, only to be returned to Sachsenhausen's Zellenbau, or prison block. It was there, in late January or early February 1945, that he saw Suttill and another SOE man, a racing driver named Charles Grover-Williams. 'They were both well. They were in solitary confinement but able to communicate with others, as usual. They were receiving reasonable basic rations but not parcels.' Vera now immediately wrote to Margaret Suttill: 'I am pursuing this clue and will certainly keep you informed if it should give results. In any case it is good news that at that time he was well.'

If Suttill and Grover-Williams had survived until the liberation, they too might also be making their way towards Odessa. So encouraged was Buckmaster by this prospect that he offered to go to the Black Sea port at once himself to repatriate survivors. Showing a sudden active interest in the missing, he wrote that an SOE presence in Odessa was 'the only likely way of seeing our people again in the reasonably near future (if at all)'. Buckmaster, now backing Vera's demand, also insisted that names of the F Section missing – to date totalling 118 – should be circulated to every relevant authority in Russia.

There was still resistance to circulating names of women, because, said senior SOE staff: 'the including of such names would defeat the desire for normality for the rest of the list'.

Buckmaster, however, made sure that the names of the women were now included. He told officials he would rather rescue an agent 'even though that agent were blown to the Russians than to leave him to die or rot in a Russian prison'.

And Vera had another good reason for hope. By the end of April none of the missing women had been found in the western camps liberated by the Americans and British, apart from Yvonne Rudellat, last seen at Belsen. For Vera no news of the other women was good news. There was strong evidence that they too had also been taken east, probably to the concentration camp of Ravensbrück, which would be reached by the Russians any day. In the confusion that was bound to accompany the Russians' arrival these women might also start the tramp east. Or they might be released in the prisoner exchanges that were suddenly happening. Exchanges administered by the Red Cross were due to start at Ravensbrück in the last days of April, ahead of the Russian liberation.

Vera could not conceal her optimism from Mrs Rowden, writing on 1 May to Diana's mother: 'I am sorry that we are still without news of your daughter. I can tell you however quite definitely that she has not been in any of the camps so far overrun. We have reason to believe that she may be in a camp which is about to be overrun by the Russians and therefore we are hoping for news shortly.'

Vera very soon had cause to believe her optimism justified. On 3 May a telegram came in from the British mission at Malmö saying a young British woman had turned up with a Swedish Red Cross convoy bringing prisoners out of Ravensbrück. Vera recognised the description and plans were made to fly the woman to Scotland so that she could catch the overnight train to London. Vera arranged to meet her.

7

EUSTON STATION

Euston Station was almost deserted. The clock said eight and the night train from Glasgow was pulling in. Doors swung open and figures stepped down hauling baggage, then dispersed. A single female figure was left on the platform; she appeared to be waiting for somebody.

The woman was carrying just a brown paper bag. She wore a thick woollen coat that hung loosely from her shoulders and looked far too heavy for the time of year. She looked uncomfortable and nervous. Two weeks earlier Yvonne Baseden had been in Ravensbrück concentration camp.

Yvonne was one of about fifty women who were released to the Swedish Red Cross on the eve of the camp's liberation in April 1945. The women were driven in coaches across the ruins of Germany to the Danish border and then on to Sweden. On the docks at Malmö, the women, many fainting with weakness, were herded into steam-filled tents for cleaning and delousing. Then they were housed in hospitals or tents; Yvonne's first nights of freedom were spent on a mattress on the floor of Malmö's Museum of Prehistory, sleeping under the skeletons of dinosaurs. She was then flown to Scotland and put on the train to Euston. She had been told there would be somebody to meet her. But it was now 8.15am and nobody was here.

———

'I saw a telephone and I decided to call the Air Ministry,' Yvonne told me. 'I had a number on a piece of paper but it was Sunday morning and I wasn't expecting anyone to be there. And I didn't know what to say, you see, so I said: "I'm sorry, but I am a WAAF officer and I have just come from Germany and I am at Euston and I don't know what to do." A voice – I suppose it must have been a duty officer – said: "Don't move. Hold on a moment." Then a few moments later the voice said: "Miss Atkins is on her way."

'I waited on the platform and then after a while Vera suddenly appeared. I think she was wearing a suit and looked just the same. She probably signalled to me and I walked over to join her. I was quite weak. There was no emotion. I was quite confused, you see, and just pleased to see a face I knew.'

'What did she say?'

'Oh, very little at first. Just pleasantries. I think she may have asked about the journey and apologised for keeping me waiting. She was quite distant – cold almost, at first. Suspicious even. On reflection I realised what it was. You see, she had reason to be quite suspicious of me.'

'Why?'

'Well, I think she must have thought – you know – why had I been released? What had I done to be released and not the others? I think that must have been why she was a little wary of me.

'Then she took me to a waiting car. When I asked where we were going she said, "I am taking you home to your father." You see, my father lived quite close by, in Brockwell Park, and he had been told, of course, that I was coming back.

'Then, as soon as we were in the car, I remember the first thing she said to me was: "What do you know of any others?"'

'Who did she mean?'

'Well, I thought she must mean the others who were in Ravensbrück with me – Violette Szabo, Lilian Rolfe and Denise Bloch. So I told her the whole story: how I saw them first at Saarbrücken on the way to Germany. I was taken in a convoy from Dijon and we stopped first at Saarbrücken, which was like a big base – a kind of holding camp for all the prisoners going east, with lots of sheds. And I was taken into one of these sheds and there they were in this shed.'

'What was it like?'

'I am trying to visualise that hut, which was quite dark and full of women. Packed with beds. I looked round and began to see these faces that I knew and I thought, My God, the whole of Baker Street is here! I expected to see more.'

'How did they seem?'

'They were in quite a good state at that time – particularly Violette. They were sitting on beds. But there were a lot of people around and we could not speak easily. And they were very wary of me – suspicious really – because they would have thought, What is she doing here arriving on another convoy? And, you see, they would not have known the circumstances of my arrest, so they would have been wary of me. And I don't even know if we spoke English. I doubt it because I didn't want people to know I was English. You see, as far as the Germans knew, I was just a French woman with the resistance. That is how I survived. They never knew I was a British agent, but the other girls had been through some sort of process. They had already been put in a different category. They went on in a different transport to Ravensbrück from me. They left before I left and, thank goodness for me, I did not go with them.'

'What did you think was going to happen?'

'We had no idea. I had just come from the prison in Dijon in solitary confinement. The others had come from Paris. They seemed quite confident – particularly Violette. Lilian and Denise seemed more subdued, but I remember Violette was sitting quite casually and she had obviously made an effort to get whatever clothes she was wearing clean. She had taken her shirt off and had washed it. She had lost none of her vivacity – or else she had been in prison longer than the others and had got used to the atmosphere.

'But later it occurred to me they had been constrained in some way as a group and I have an idea they had chains on their feet. I sensed it afterwards.

'Then they all left for Ravensbrück and I went on there a few days later. But I didn't see them again, so I could not tell Vera much, except that I heard they had been sent out on a work commando to a factory. They were gone for many weeks. I told Vera that I had heard one day they been brought back from the factory to Ravensbrück. I didn't see them when they came back. All I had heard was that they had then been taken off again and we didn't see them any more. I heard that their clothes had been suddenly handed back to one of the block guards, but nobody knew for sure what had happened to them. I think Vera had hoped I would be able to tell her more.'

'Did Vera ask you about the camp, about what it was like?'

'Oh, no,' said Yvonne. 'We reached my father's house and then she left me.'

———

Nobody – not even Vera until recently – had suspected there was such a thing as a concentration camp for women. Despite the concerns that SOE women would not be covered by the rules of war, it had been tacitly understood that women prisoners – simply because they were women – would receive better treatment than men. Now Vera was learning fast about Himmler's purpose-built women's concentration camp. By the time Yvonne arrived back in Britain Vera had already studied the reports from Paris of scores of other women detainees at Ravensbrück, mostly French, who had been released to other Red Cross convoys.

Ravensbrück, she had learned from one French prisoner, was built on Himmler's own estate, near a large lake north of Berlin. The SS guards were housed in villas dotted around the woods. The camp was surrounded by walls and electrified fences and machine guns were trained on the prisoners from pillboxes. The camp was mined. One French returnee had described how commando parties (i.e. work parties) of women were marched to the lakeside to unload coal barges. Others were sent to factories. Another returnee described how pink cards were given to those women not fit for work. They were put in a sub-camp called the *Jugendlager*, once a youth camp but now a place where the sick and aged waited to be selected for death. Parties of women were taken from this sub-camp, placed on lorries in nothing but chemises and coats, and never seen again.

Picking over these reports, Vera hunted always for any sighting of her girls. In January 1945 three women parachutists were hanged at the camp. The reason given was 'false identity', but no names were known. There were French women survivors here who had evidently worked with Prosper. One woman reported that a fellow prisoner told her, before being sent to the gas chamber, that '*Gilbert nous a trahies*' ('Gilbert has betrayed us'), another reference, it seemed, to Henri Déricourt.

The women returnees had been shown photographs of all the missing SOE women. One thought she recognised a picture of Eileen Nearne. The person was an actress in private life and left on a commando party in summer 1944.

Several witnesses identified Cicely Lefort, the courier with the Jockey circuit, who had arrived at Ravensbrück as early as autumn

1943. She quickly became critically ill and was issued with a pink card. Witnesses said she had been gassed. There had been one possible sighting of Odette Sansom. Of all the others, though, there was no firm news. Nobody could tell Vera more about Violette, Lilian and Denise. And on her own missing list she wrote 'no trace' against the names of Andrée Borrel, Madeleine Damerment, Nora Inayat Khan, Diana Rowden, Eliane Plewman, Yolande Beekman and Vera Leigh.

But then, on 6 May, there was more good news, from the HQ of the United States First Army in Allied-occupied Germany:

Subject: Nearne, Eileen, alias Duterte, Jacqueline, alias Wood, Alice, alias ROSE.

Subject claims to work for an intelligence organisation run by a Colonel 'Max Baxter'. Subject stated she was flown to a field near ORLEANS. Subject encoded messages and signed them ROSE but claims she has forgotten her agent's number. In July 1944 Subject's transmitter was detected and Subject was arrested by the Gestapo. She claims that despite being tortured she did not reveal any information detrimental to the British intelligence service or its agents.

On 15 August Subject was sent to the extermination [*sic*] camp of Ravensbrück, where she stayed for two weeks, then to a camp near Leipzig. From that last camp, Subject claims, she managed to escape on 13 April 1945. Subject creates a very unbalanced impression. She often is unable to answer the simplest of questions, as though she were impersonating somebody else. Her account of what happened to her after her landing near ORLEANS is held to be invented. It is recommended that Subject be put at the disposal of the British Authorities for further investigation and disposition.

SECRET.

As Vera saw in a flash, nothing in Eileen Nearne's story was 'invented'. On her return home she made a statement for Vera describing how on arrival at Ravensbrück she had been sent on the same work commando as Violette, Denise and Lilian. They all worked in the fields for two months, near the town of Torgau, 120 miles south of Ravensbrück, before Eileen was moved to work in a munitions factory. At the factory she heard a rumour that two English girls had escaped from Torgau but she did not know if it was true. Eileen was then sent to work near Leipzig, labouring twelve hours a day on the roads.

One day in early April they told us we would be leaving this camp for a place 80 kilometres away. Two French girls and I decided to escape and while we were passing a forest I spotted a tree and hid there and then joined the French girls in the forest. We stayed in a bombed house for two nights and the next morning walked through Markkleeberg and slept in the woods. We were arrested by the SS, who asked us for papers. We told them a story and they let us go. We arrived at Leipzig and at a church a priest helped us and kept us there for three nights and the next morning we saw white flags and the first Americans arriving and when I said that I was English they put us in a camp.

Then another message came in from the US First Army HQ, dated 7 May: 'FLASH/PRIORITY EMERGENCY STOP ODETTE SANSON [*sic*] RPT SANSON F SEC AGENT AND WIFE OF PETER CHURCHILL RPT CHURCHILL NOW 20 KEFFERSTEIN STRASSE LUNEBERG STOP PLEASE ARRANGE COLLECT AND REPATRIATE UK SOONEST'.

Odette Sansom, also imprisoned in Ravensbrück, was the third of Vera's girls from the camp to be heading home. Her escape from Ravensbrück was no less extraordinary than Eileen Nearne's. Odette, aged thirty-two, born in Picardy and married to an Englishman, was marked out early in her SOE career as a 'shrewd cookie'. When captured with her organiser, Peter Churchill, in 1943, she was clever enough to call herself 'Mrs Churchill', believing that the name might help her.

At first Odette received no favours. She told Vera on arriving home how, in prison in Fresnes, her toenails were extracted and she was burned on the back by an iron bar but she gave nothing away.

She was sent in May 1944 on a transport with other SOE women to a civilian prison in Karlsruhe, where she stayed for at least two months. Odette was then separated from the other Karlsruhe prisoners and taken on her own to Ravensbrück. There, although she was kept in solitary confinement, she was favoured by the camp's Kommandant, Fritz Suhren, who kept her alive. When the Russians were about to seize the camp, Suhren packed a small bag, put it in a car and brought

Odette from her cell, telling her she was going to leave Ravensbrück with him. Together they drove towards the American lines, where Suhren hoped that Odette would attest to how well she had been treated, thereby sparing his life. Odette did nothing of the sort. Instead she told the Americans exactly who Suhren was and then asked to be taken home, taking with her the Kommandant's bag. When she met up with Vera, Odette was able to display the contents of the bag, including Suhren's personal pistol, a writing case and a pair of pyjamas.

Though intrigued by Odette's escape, Vera was far more interested in her journey to Karlsruhe and she particularly wanted to know the identities of those women who went with Odette. Karlsruhe, close to the French–German border, seemed an unlikely place for any prisoners to have been taken and Vera knew nothing until now of any transport of women there. Odette said she travelled to Karlsruhe with seven other SOE women. She didn't know the women, but after looking through photographs and jogging her memory for names, she confidently identified six of the seven. They were: Madeleine Damerment, Vera Leigh, Diana Rowden, Yolande Beekman, Andrée Borrel and Eliane Plewman. Where these women had been taken after leaving Karlsruhe, Odette had no idea, though she had heard reports that Andrée and two others may have been moved to Poland in mid-July.

Odette was sure the staff at the prison would know where the women went, and she gave Vera the name of a 'Fräulein Beger', the chief wardress, who was about sixty, 'a Quaker and very correct'.

With Odette's evidence Vera now had traces of almost all of the twelve missing women. Cicely Lefort was the only one of the group who Vera felt sure was dead, but in all the other cases she was still holding out hope. Violette Szabo, Lilian Rolfe and Denise Bloch were last seen at Ravensbrück, and Eileen Nearne, who had escaped, heard rumours that at least two of those three might also have escaped. Hope had not been abandoned for Yvonne Rudellat, last known to be at Belsen, and now Odette had named the other six untraced women, all last seen alive and well at a correctly run civilian prison in Karlsruhe.

There was one woman, though, of whom Vera still had found no trace at all in Germany. She had expected Odette to identify Nora as the seventh woman on the Karlsruhe transport. But as Vera noted at the time: 'There was also one other woman whom Mrs Sansom described as somewhat Jewish looking, small, slight. I have been unable to identify her. It is not Nora Inayat Khan.'

8

'GESTAPO BOYS'

The grandeur of Avenue Foch was favoured by Himmler's security chiefs for their Paris headquarters. The magnificent nineteenth-century villas, set back from the vast boulevard, offered seclusion, yet were only a short distance from the restaurants of L'Etoile and Place des Ternes. It was here that, in the last year of the occupation, the Nazi Party security service apparatus, the Sicherheitsdienst, or SD, had its headquarters for the whole of France. The SD was often seen as synonymous with the Gestapo, the secret state police. Indeed, Vera and SOE agents always referred to the Germans of Avenue Foch as 'Gestapo', when, in fact, the SD was a separate intelligence organisation. At 84 Avenue Foch Sturmbannführer Hans Josef Kieffer, of the Sicherheitsdienst, was in charge of hunting down spies, terrorists and commandos sent to France to aid the resistance.

A few months after the war Vera came to 84 Avenue Foch to look around, before the inscriptions on the walls of the cells were plastered over and any other traces of her people removed. She came also to learn more about Kieffer. She wanted to know how it was that he and his 'Gestapo boys', as one agent had described Kieffer's men, persuaded so many of her people that the game was up in the summer of 1943.

So much had Vera heard by now about Avenue Foch from return-ing agents that she almost knew her way around the building. She also already knew a lot about Kieffer. She had heard he was strongly built; he was once a gymnast; he had dark, curly hair; he sometimes wore glasses. She had heard all about the sweets and biscuits he distributed to prisoners on Sunday mornings, the Louis XV furniture in his fourth-floor office and his secretary, Katya, who was also said to be his mistress. Vera knew that Kieffer liked to bring his prize prisoners down to his rooms and chat about public schools and the English officer class. The SOE agent Brian Stonehouse was even asked on one occasion to explain who was the heir to the British throne. 'And what does the English officer class think of Churchill?' Kieffer asked him.

Kieffer kept his most valued F Section prisoners on the fifth floor, in twelve attic rooms directly above his office. At one end of the corridor on the fifth floor was a bathroom and at the other end was a guardroom with a small library of books. And Kieffer kept a large chart on a wall showing all the names of the SOE senior command and details of training schools, with Maurice Buckmaster's name at the top of an F Section family tree.

The evidence that Kieffer knew everything about F Section had come as something of a surprise in Baker Street. Section heads like Buckmaster had known in general terms about their German opposition; they knew that Amt (Department) IV of the Reich Security Head Office (Reichssicherheitshauptampt, or RSHA), directed by Himmler, was concerned with counter-intelligence operations against saboteurs and spies. This much information was given in lectures at the training schools.

But they devoted little time to understanding German counter-intelligence methods. A man at the Beaulieu SOE training school in Hampshire used to dress up as a Gestapo chief, wake trainees with a rifle butt at night and take them off for a mock interrogation. Nora Inayat Khan was terrified by the mock grilling but most agents told the officer to 'bugger off' and let them get back to sleep. For the most part, SOE agents adopted an attitude of contempt for their German enemy – and for the French police who collaborated with them – an attitude also displayed by SOE instructors who had rarely been in the field.

And there had been little attempt inside SOE to find out about the individual Germans they were up against. In F Section they had heard Kieffer's name by the spring of 1944 but they thought this might be an alias for Colonel Heinrich of the Abwehr, the armed forces intelligence, who had many aliases and was known by then to have caused F Section a great deal of trouble. But then it was decided that Heinrich and Kieffer could not be the same person because, according to one reliable report, 'Kieffer bullies and shouts' while

Heinrich had a reputation for being 'extremely nice and polite'.

Then, in June 1945, a month after the end of the war, the confusion between the two men was finally cleared up. Colonel Heinrich was arrested in Amsterdam and turned out to be the Abwehr's wily spy-catcher Hugo Bleicher, who impressed his MI5 interrogators with his professionalism. For his part, Bleicher was impressed by 'a very pretty young woman officer' who also interrogated him. 'She turned out to have more aplomb than all the other officers put together,' he wrote of Vera, in his memoirs. 'She boxed me in with astonishing ease and con-summate tactics. Luckily my memory is good or she might well have put me in an awkward position. She seemed also quite tireless in her questioning and if the conducting officer had not felt hungry at lunchtime and urged her to break off the interrogation, she would have kept me on tenterhooks for a good deal longer.' Bleicher, however, had few of the answers to Vera's most urgent questions. By the time of the Prosper collapse, in the summer of 1943, the Abwehr, along with Bleicher, was largely a spent force. By then the Sicherheitsdienst ran counter-intelligence in France, and the man who launched the real war against F Section was Kieffer. It was he who had rounded up Prosper and many of Vera's other men and women. And for some time Kieffer had kept them here – in a certain style – at Avenue Foch.

The first people to describe the inner workings of Avenue Foch for the British were the French collaborators who were arrested after the end of the occupation. After long negotiation the French had finally allowed British investigators to interrogate these prisoners before they were executed. Vera had read every word they said, scan-ning the reports for any clue about agents held here – when they left or where they went. These collaborators included the notorious Bony–Lafont gang, whom Kieffer used as his bully-boys. There were also drivers, cleaners, bodyguards, interpreters, and all talked about their Nazi employers, among them 'the Colonel'. Some talked of a 'Dr Goetz' and of 'Ernest', who looked like a boxer and had an American accent. There was a man named Placke who had the appearance of a 'Boer'. The French collaborators talked of British agents arriving at landing fields, sometimes drunk, speaking such bad French that they could have been picked up just by opening their mouths. The British used cafés openly as letterboxes and meet-ing places, not thinking that they would be watched, but Kieffer had made sure he had a man in every bar in Paris. Agents could be spotted wearing brogue shoes of a style rarely seen in France or carrying obviously fake ration cards. And the British agents used wads of brand-new large-denomination notes to pay small bills, immediately drawing attention. Buckmaster, after reading some of these stories, wrote sarcastically on one report: 'very interesting!'

Rose Cordonnier, who cleaned the fifth floor of 84 Avenue Foch, where the prisoners were held, and was the mistress of one of Kieffer's aides, had been interrogated for hours in the hope that she would identify who had been held there and when. In the end she had produced a confused jumble of names and aliases, but tangled in her memory was a clear recollection of a British agent named John Starr, whose alias, she said, was 'Bob'. Bob, she claimed, had a German mistress inside the building and worked on the third floor sending wireless messages on sets captured from British operators. Rose Cordonnier also referred to 'a dark English girl named Madeleine who gave nothing away under torture, except that she was working for her country'.

When Vera entered Kieffer's office on the fourth floor she observed the chandeliers and the views over grassy lawns where, one of the returnees said, a German officer arrived each day on horseback in full army riding gear. Kieffer, on the other hand, favoured informality around the building and always wore 'civvies'. Kieffer was not a remarkable figure; he did not impress his prisoners with any great sophistication or even with any particular love of Hitler. Rather he gave the impression of being a somewhat bluff professional policeman. He did not even speak good English or French and always used a translator. Yet he had certainly won the trust of many of his prisoners.

The testimony of the Avenue Foch survivors showed just how each of them had been lulled into a sense of security; encouraged to feel that they were privileged and sometimes even on equal terms with their captors. The prisoners ate the same food as Kieffer and his men. The agent Maurice Southgate (Hector) arrived at Avenue Foch 'to find myself taken to the guardroom on the fifth floor and fed with a large piece of *pain de fantaisie* in the morning, with butter and jam or cheese, hot black coffee, with two pieces of sugar. Lunch consisted of meat and two vegetables and dinner of soup, cold German sausage with bread and coffee.'

Southgate also recalled how, as he ate for the first time on the fifth floor, he heard, coming from a nearby cell, an English voice singing the words of 'It's a Long Way to Tipperary' to the tune of 'Rule Britannia'. He commented: 'I must say this cheered me up a lot.' According to Rose Cordonnier, Kieffer's secretary 'seemed to fall in love with Southgate'.

More than one of the returnees told their debriefers that they had been treated as gentlemen and one added that this was 'despite being without any of the normal attributes of [a gentleman] such as necktie, shave or a clean shirt'.

Southgate was invited one evening to join Kieffer and his men for dinner and when he refused they made promises to be 'honourable'. 'They said I would be treated as a prisoner of war and that I had no real reason for refusing food from other soldiers.' This time he recalled being fed with 'real chocolate, Spam and American K rations', adding, 'I must say that their ways were most polite and gentle, pumping me up with English cigarettes and English coffee. We were treated extraordinarily well.'

Interrogations in Avenue Foch were 'never about business', said Southgate, who was led to understand that the German officers were interested only in preventing arms and supplies getting into the hands of communist *maquisards* – or 'bandits', as they called them. The British officers and the German officers were really in the fight together, Kieffer had suggested, and had a common interest in stopping the communists.

Above all else, it was Kieffer's grasp of the workings of SOE that had so clearly stunned many agents and thus weakened their resolve. His knowledge went far beyond the details of F Section shown on the wall chart at Avenue Foch. Kieffer's man Ernest would greet new arrivals with a knowing smile. 'How about it, Mr Hector?' he cajoled Southgate, deliberately using his alias. And a little later: 'Well, Mr Southgate, the game is up.'

Southgate said he had been so staggered by the depth of Kieffer's knowledge that he had told him: 'You seem to know more than I do.' Kieffer did not understand Southgate's words immediately. But then, on hearing the translation, he jumped to his feet and laughed with great excitement, relishing the flattery. 'We know much more even than you think!' he exclaimed. 'The documents that were sent to your country were read by our people before they were read by yours.' Then he paused for a moment, perhaps realising that he was being somewhat indiscreet: 'Do you know Claude?' he asked.

Observing the surprise on Southgate's face, Kieffer continued: 'He is a very good man of ours. From him we get reports, documents and names of people.'

Claude, as Southgate well knew, was another alias, in addition to Gilbert, used by Henri Déricourt. Southgate told his British inter-rogators: 'Personally I can only state the fact that this German colonel told me himself that Claude was his agent.' And for good measure Southgate added that while he was in Buchenwald he had heard from another prisoner who experienced Avenue Foch a little later that Kieffer had 'gone raging mad' when he heard that Claude had been returned to England for investigation in January 1944.

Vera also had the impression that Kieffer went out of his way to be liked. He enjoyed contact with the agents, and once took Robert Sheppard, a fair-haired young man of twenty, for a stroll around the pond outside the 'house prison' in Place des Etats Unis. Kieffer showed Sheppard his shotgun and tried to shoot a pigeon. It became clear to Sheppard that Kieffer was showing off. He seemed to have taken a liking to him, and Sheppard was to recount many years later that he had feared momentarily that the German's interest in him was homosexual. Vera had also learned of a famous occasion when Kieffer went swimming in the same pond with Bob Starr.

Kieffer would sometimes even mention his children to his F Section prisoners. On one occasion he drove Sheppard in the back of his own car to the prison in Fresnes. On the way he turned round and offered him a sandwich, saying it was made by his daughter.

Harry Peulevé, an escapee from Buchenwald, was another SOE agent who had been bowled over by the extent of the Germans' knowledge. When he arrived at Avenue Foch and tried to deny his real identity he was told: 'It is useless denying this as of course you realise we have in Orchard Court an agent working for us, and we know the real identity of all your agents.'

Ernest, his interrogator, 'made a great show of producing a lot of photographs of agents who I recognised and asking me if I knew any of them. When I denied this, he smiled and said: "Well, we will see!" Afterwards he enquired as to the health of F Section officers.'

Peulevé was shown a photograph of Francis Suttill, and was told of a 'pact' Prosper had made with Kieffer in order save his people's lives.

Of all the questions Vera wanted answered, the mystery of Prosper's 'pact' with Kieffer was perhaps the most urgent of all. Much had been said about it by returnees, but nobody in London believed that Suttill could have done a deal with the Gestapo. It was a damaging story, nevertheless, and in the summer of 1945 was widely recounted by certain Frenchmen, who blamed the British for the massive loss of French lives, which they claimed was caused by the pact.

And the account of Peulevé and others about what might have happened to Suttill after capture certainly carried some conviction. The Germans told Peulevé that for a long time Suttill had been resolute under interrogation and had refused to give any information. It was only when he was shown a photostat copy of a report he had sent to London, giving all details of his circuit, that Suttill had finally broken down. Another agent said he was told that Suttill held out under torture but broke down when he was shown his last letter home to his wife, Margaret. In any event, the story went, Suttill became convinced that Kieffer knew all about SOE and said: 'Well, since you know everything I am prepared to answer any questions.'

According to Peulevé's account, the 'pact' involved an agreement to give Germans information about all the circuits' and sub-circuits' arms dumps. In return the Gestapo had then guaranteed the lives of everyone in the network. 'They told me that in many cases the presence of Prosper with them in visiting these arms dumps helped to convince the people that it was all over and that it would be better not to resist.' Peulevé had also been told that the 'pact' had been agreed to by the RSHA in Berlin, and that Prosper was by then already in a camp in Germany.

Such stories were at best second-hand. So swiftly had Suttill been taken to Germany that no F Section survivor had actually set eyes on him at Avenue Foch or heard a word about the 'pact' directly from Suttill himself. Yet what the stories suggested was that agents who were brought in later were one by one convinced, perhaps like Suttill before them, that Kieffer already had the full picture so they might as well cooperate and tell him what they knew. Several agents had told Vera that Gilbert Norman met them at Avenue Foch and said the Germans knew everything so there was no point in refusing them information. And a number of agents had said that most of what the Germans had discovered they had found out direct from London by working the wireless sets and then monitoring the BBC's *messages personnels* on the Avenue Foch radio.

Peulevé, whose SOE alias was Jean, described how a BBC message, sent apparently as a warning to others of his capture, was heard inside Avenue Foch, immediately alerting Kieffer's men to the identity of three of Jean's resistance helpers. 'During one interrogation – it was about ten o'clock at night – a German I had previously seen came rushing down to the office and asked me: "Who is Nestor?" I said I did not know. He then said: "That is very surprising, we have just heard a BBC message saying: 'Important message for Nestor – Jean very ill, Nestor go immediately to Maxime or Eustace and not to contact Jean.'" I said it was probably another Jean but of course the Gestapo fully realised this message applied to me. This put me in great difficulties as up to now they were unaware of the existence of Nestor, Maxime and Eustace.'

By now Vera had her own information showing how much the Germans learned through radio deception. Recently she had been asked to comment on German documents captured at Stuttgart which showed that the Germans knew about F Section's plans to increase sabotage against railways well before this had begun. In a memo she wrote: 'They appeared to know of the pact with the RAF who agreed to cease their attacks against French rail traffic if we could prove we were capable of taking on the job by sabotage. They ordered a strengthening of guards. I assume they obtained this advance information through the controlled W/T traffic they were running for the various Prosper circuits.'

Several of Vera's agents had now explained how the radio deception was done. An officer named Dr Goetz was the radio mastermind. His office was on the third floor at Avenue Foch. Southgate said the cracking of the codes began with Suttill's arrest. Many of the wireless operators' codes and crystals were captured in that round-up. 'But for a long time,' he said, 'the Germans did not realise that there were two checks on outgoing telegrams – one true check and one bluff check.' Therefore they sent out their telegrams with one check, which should have been clearly phoney to London. 'Time after time for different men, London sent back messages saying: "My dear fellow, you only left us a week ago. On your first message you go and forget to put your true check." You may now realise what happened to our agents who did not give the true check to the Germans, thus making them send out a message that was obviously phoney, and after being put through the worst degrees of torture, these Germans managed, sometimes a week later, to get hold of the true check, and then sent a further message to London with the proper check in the telegram and London saying: "Now you are a good boy, now you have remembered to give both of them."'

This had happened first to Archambaud, who had been totally demoralised by it. But Southgate said it had happened to several others. He considered that the officer responsible in London should have been court-martialled. 'He was responsible for the death and capture of many of our best agents, including Major Antelme for one, who was arrested the minute he put his foot on French soil.'

After reading Southgate's comments, Buckmaster wrote: 'this is the report of a very tired man.' Vera, however, wanted to learn more. In particular, she wanted to hear the evidence of Bob Starr, the agent who, according to Southgate's report, knew the most about the 'radio game' because he had 'cooperated' with Kieffer and thereby collected all the evidence of London's 'foolishness' for a long time.

Vera wanted to find out exactly what 'evidence' Starr had and what he might intend to do with it. For many weeks Starr had been on Vera's 'missing' list but he had suddenly turned up – one of the very few SOE survivors of Mauthausen concentration camp, from which he had cleverly escaped by slipping in among a group of French prisoners being taken out on a Red Cross convoy.

On arriving home Starr told Vera that his 'cooperation' with Kieffer began when he first arrived at Avenue Foch. Kieffer himself had immediately showed him a large drawing of all the F Section circuits. He then asked him to print the name of his own circuit in the space provided. Starr did so, and found he caused much excitement, not because he had given his circuit name – this was already well known to the Germans – but because of his artistry in printing the name.

A graphic artist by trade, Starr had taken some trouble with the lettering. As a result Kieffer asked him to draw the whole chart for him in similar fashion, and he readily agreed. So delighted was Kieffer with his graphics that he assigned more and more similar tasks to Starr, who became, in effect, Kieffer's artist in residence. He even painted portraits of the Avenue Foch Gestapo, including the Sturmbannführer himself.

The quite extraordinary sight of Starr at work painting charts of F Section circuits, joking and laughing with the Gestapo and singing 'Rule Britannia', was what first struck most new British arrivals when they were captured and brought to Avenue Foch. Starr was seen translating the BBC news for the German guards and correcting the spelling on the trick radio messages. 'Thumbs up for England,' he would boast to Kieffer, and on one occasion he played 'God Save Our Gracious King' on the accordion. Kieffer, Dr Goetz and Ernest all took it very well. 'The Gestapo boys are quite decent when you get to know them, you know,' he told Southgate. The two men, who both grew up in Paris, had been boyhood friends.

Southgate said he asked Starr one day why he was doing all this. 'If I don't do it somebody else will, and in doing it I am gathering very valuable information which may come in useful sometime,' Starr explained. 'At one time Starr told me that the materiel [arms and explosives] received by the Germans through the mistake of London not realising that if a man did not send out his true check there was some very good reason for it amounted to tons,' said Southgate. 'Most of these grounds were in Normandy where in the months of June several of our organisations were in German hands and had been receiving British materiel for months and months. I was amazed at HQ Gestapo to see the quantities of British food, guns, ammunition, explosives, that they had at their disposal.'

Southgate had said he did not think ill of Starr's 'cooperation' with the Germans because he told him he intended to make use of all the information he was gathering as soon as he got the chance. And Starr had twice tried to escape, the second time from Avenue Foch 'with a girl and a French officer'. Peulevé's impression was that Starr thought he was being cleverer than the Gestapo, and didn't give any secrets away. But, Peulevé added: 'His presence was unfortunate in that it may have been used to give confidence to newly arrested agents that they would be well treated, and in fact Starr was used by the Germans as a living example of the way in which they would keep their word.'

Many did appear to believe that Kieffer would keep his word. Kieffer had let it be known that he had secured the authority of Berlin that the F Section agents should not be killed. And even now those who had returned from the camps did not believe that he really expected or knew that they had been sent to concentration camps. But one person who had evidently never trusted Kieffer, and had scorned all German approaches to her from the start, was Nora Inayat Khan, as Vera had heard in detail from Starr.

Starr said Nora had arrived at Avenue Foch one day in early

October and had never shown any desire to engage in conversation with him up on the fifth floor and said nothing except: 'Goodnight. Good morning.' One day, Starr said, Nora had tried to get out on to the bathroom window sill. Ernest, as her interrogator, had had to coax her back in. Starr did not think this was an escape attempt but an attempt to commit suicide. There had been a lot of fuss at the time and Starr had taken pity on her and slipped a note into her cell, telling her not to worry and that if she wished to communicate with him she could do so by means of written messages placed in certain spots in the lavatory.

It was by this means that they had plotted their escape. Teaming up with a French prisoner, Léon Faye, the head of an important resistance network, they removed the bars from the windows of their cells, and by using face cream and face powder provided by Nora, who was allowed such things by Kieffer, they made plaster to hide the damage done to the walls. Starr got on to the roof with the Frenchman by trailing a blanket and using a cord, but unfortunately Nora could not remove her bars until two hours later. She eventually appeared on the roof and they started on their way down to the street, but suddenly there was an air-raid alert and all the cells were inspected. All three were caught by Kieffer's men and brought before him.

According to Starr's account, Kieffer was fuming with rage at the escape attempt. It was as if he had been badly let down by his prisoners. He told them he would shoot them on the spot, but then, after a short discussion with them, he relented. Instead he said that, if the three of them gave their 'word of honour' not to escape again, they would be spared and could return to their cells. Starr gave his word of honour and went back to his cell, but Nora refused to do so, as did Faye. Still in a fury, Kieffer ordered the two of them to be taken to prisons in Germany, Starr said.

Starr believed that Kieffer sent Nora to an ordinary German prison simply to stop her trying to escape again. He was sure Kieffer would not have sent her to a concentration camp.

When Vera had debriefed Starr for the last time, in the late summer of 1945, she remained extremely wary of him and both she and Buckmaster decided that they should keep their distance from him. Starr would be made to feel most forcefully that he had let his comrades down. However, Vera did give some credence to certain points that Starr had made. She was inclined to trust his view of Kieffer, believing that perhaps the German had intended that Nora should be fairly treated.

In a comment on her debriefing she wrote: 'Bob Starr said Madeleine had shown extreme bravery and great courage and was therefore respected by the Germans. He does not think that she was in any way ill-treated after her attempt to escape. But he does not know where she was moved.' She also stated: 'The time has not yet come to give up hope of those who have not yet returned.'

PART II
ROMANIA

9

CONFIDANTES

Vera told me she had closed the book on her Romanian past when I met her in Winchelsea, and, since her death, I had been unable to prise it open. Her papers gave few clues about her family's story before the war. Her colleagues knew nothing of her origins; nor did her own close family.

'Of course, Vera had the great art of selecting within the family people whom she found compatible and sticking to them, and not being sidetracked by people for whom she might feel sorry but actually had nothing in common with,' commented Janet Atkins, wife of one of Vera's cousins, writing to Phoebe Atkins just after Vera's death. 'I remember her once uttering that sentiment. I was always intrigued to know where her family came from in Romania and where they were educated but one never really liked to ask. And she did not volunteer any scenes from childhood. I would think a biographer might have quite a difficult time finding out about her youth.'

More distant relatives – particularly those who lived abroad – I hoped, might yet tell me more. A cousin in Canada possessed a Rosenberg family memoir, written by Vera's Uncle Siegfried, but the document was lying in a garden shed in Quebec, buried under several feet of snow. Waiting for the Canadian thaw, I could only seek out more clues, some of which had been squirrelled away by Vera herself, in the fading memories of her most trusted friends.

Though Vera never spoke of her past in the normal way, I found she had sometimes passed on confidences, usually very late at night, in almost inaudible tones, to listeners who remembered them as little more than tales.

Vera's favourite confidante in later years was probably Barbara Worcester. Vera often used to travel down to stay with her at her cottage in Martinstown, near Dorchester, taking the cross-country train known as the 'Little Sprinter'. Vera never learned to drive; she liked to be driven or to travel by train.

'You could tell Vera had grown up in the countryside as she loved wild flowers,' said Barbara, taking me up her narrow garden path so we could smell the scent of the Peloponnese. Vera and Barbara often used to wander up this path, admiring the plants. 'This is my Mediterranean bit,' she said, pointing to a bed of herbs and grasses. The daughter of an explorer, Barbara liked to travel and bring things back to preserve: a chipped tile of a bird; a ceramic bowl full of stones and shells 'with a dash of bleach in to keep them from going fuzzy'. Vera met Barbara through her ex-husband, David Worcester, who worked with Vera in Germany, investigating war crimes.

'She loved dogs and horses. But she particularly noticed flowers,' said Barbara, who liked to pamper Vera on her visits. 'I always used to take her breakfast in bed. She liked a glass of very cold water first "to get the system going". If I overdid the butter on her toast Vera would take her knife and scrape it off. She said: "You must always make an effort – you must never give up.' She wasn't beautiful but she was stylish. She had no bosom or waist – all of a piece really. And she was just as likely to turn up in a Crimplene dress she had found in Oxfam as anything expensive. She never wore trousers – ever.'

Barbara had heard people say that Vera was cold, but she had never found her so. 'I think she just kept it all inside her, in case she showed too much. She was always very controlled. You know, she had a rule – never to smoke or drink when she was on her own, otherwise she knew she would either die of lung cancer or become an alcoholic.'

On her visits Vera liked to mingle with the Dorset 'nobs'. 'We once bumped into the local hunt and I remember she was most impressed. She told me: "Now, Barbara, these are the kind of people you should know." She couldn't see what frauds they were. I think Vera wanted so much to be English but she always got her Englishness a little wrong. She was surprisingly naive in a certain way.'

Vera also mixed well with Barbara's real friends – writers, travellers, retired spies and even former F Section agents – all of whom gathered in Barbara's tiny sitting room, books packed under the very low beams.

But mostly, when Vera came to stay, Barbara preferred to be alone with her and listen. After dinner Vera would settle amid the scatter cushions by the log fire and talk for hours. 'After a while the voice was just a low rumble.' What sort of things had she heard? I asked. 'I got the impression there had been many men,' Barbara replied.

From others I had heard gossip about Vera's relationships. Some speculated that Maurice Buckmaster might have been a lover. He certainly had a love affair early in the war, but he divorced his first wife for Anna Melford Stevenson, the wife of a prominent lawyer, and not for Vera. Some I had spoken to wondered about Vera's sexuality, and one confidante heard her talk of a blissful summer in the company of another young woman.

But the lovers Barbara got to hear about were always men, and all of them from Vera's very distant past. Early in her life there had been a White Russian prince named Wittgenstein. 'She told me he gave her a complete set of diamonds and amethysts: earrings, a necklace and a tiara. But Vera refused to take them from him. She only kept the earrings.' I wondered if Barbara ever saw the earrings. 'No, never. Vera always wore clip-on, paste earrings. But she had wonderful rings. And she wore an amber necklace which came right down to her navel.

'And I often used to hear about the German ambassador who Vera knew in Bucharest, Von der Schulenburg. He was certainly an admirer and would drive Vera around in his car. She used to tell him she would not get in the car if the swastika was flying. So he would say: "For you, Vera, it will not be unfurled."'

A woman colleague from SOE days told me she always felt 'uncomfortable' with Vera but Barbara said: 'She never made me feel uncomfortable. She was certainly very protective towards me, particularly since David left me. And I suppose I felt sorry for her too. I felt sorry for her having sent those girls out there, and for her having to worry about whether it was right. It must have been terrible looking for them. I think it always haunted her. She told me once that one of the witnesses she went to look for, she found in a blood-stained apron in a butcher's shop.'

During several late-night conversations Barbara had heard pieces of one particular tale which, she felt sure, was an account of Vera's first true love. 'He was an English pilot. She met him on a marvellous journey which began with a trip to Alexandria. For her twenty-first birthday present Vera's father gave her a first-class ticket on a steamer to travel to Alexandria, as well as a red vanity case with a £20 note tied to the handle. I had the impression Vera was very close to her father.'

It was sometime on that trip or soon after it, said Barbara, that Vera had met the pilot.

'The ship was so smart it had crêpe de Chine sheets in pastel colours which were changed each night; Vera liked yellow the best.' She sailed back from Alexandria via Smyrna, where her brother, Ralph, was en poste as a manager with an oil company, said Barbara. 'I think it was there, or perhaps earlier on the trip, that she met this young pilot and they fell in love.' Vera told her friend that she and the pilot had arranged to meet again – in Budapest, Barbara thought, though it might have been somewhere else. 'In any case he was killed and they never met again.'

Vera had never given a name and Barbara had not asked. 'All I remember was that he was English and he was a pilot. I had the feeling that he was the most important. She often mentioned him.'

Alice Hyde, a neighbour of Vera's in Winchelsea, was another confidante who used to hear tales from Vera's distant past. 'Often if she was alone she would ask me over and we would get something out of the freezer and eat. Then we would sit and she would talk and talk for hours.

'She would talk sometimes of Romania and of her childhood, but it was always so hard to hear. As she talked her voice dropped several octaves. I remember one story which came up often. It seemed to go on and on for hours and involved a long and terrible journey which all ended in Canada. I think the story was about some great tragedy which Vera had been involved in and at the end the people in Canada said to Vera: "You must not worry. We will always remember you. You have been very brave. To us you will always be a heroine."'

Alice apologised for not remembering more. 'I think she only talked to me about it because she knew my hearing was poor and I was rather muddled. She knew her secrets were safe with me and that I would never be able to pass them on.'

Christine Franklin, who also lived in Winchelsea, had, like others, collected Vera's squirrelled-away secrets, but Christine's collection was of a different kind. For many years she had been Vera's cleaner, though from the very beginning she had evidently been far more than that. Sitting on her living-room floor, cross-legged in jeans and a T-shirt, and with long, blond hair and pink lipstick, she told me about her interview. 'Miss Atkins called me in first and I sat on the chair next to her and she lit up a cigarette and put it up in the air and looked at me. I said I had good references and she blew out the smoke and said: "I don't think I need other people's views. I am a good judge of character."' Christine laughed.

'And sometimes when I was talking she would hold her hand up for silence. I knew she meant nothing by it but some were put off by it. She was very particular in lots of ways. She could not abide toilet roll that divided at the perforated edges.' And then there were the flowers, said Christine. 'She wouldn't ever let me throw them out if there was a bit of life in them. "They are not dropping. They are not dropping," said Christine, imitating Vera. 'So I had to take them to the kitchen and snip them back.

'And she was a hardy type – she always slept with the window wide open in just a flimsy nightdress. She had lots of old nightdresses. "It was an extravagance of my youth," she said to me once. When there was a gentleman to stay she would ask me to put her best nightdress out. I think she thought to herself, They still find me attractive.'

In other ways, Christine observed, Vera was not particular at all. She was not tidy and would sit in her office surrounded by piles of papers. Her cupboards were full of hundreds of old shoes. 'And the kitchen was full of any old thing. Miss Atkins would leave the ratatouille in the fridge for days and then she'd eat it. She'd drink the vegetable water because it had vitamins in it.

'And she certainly didn't like to be wrong.' Christine laughed again. She was recalling numerous occasions when Vera insisted she had paid a bill, but the gas board, the electricity board or BUPA said she hadn't. 'She'd let them cut off the gas rather than admit she'd made a mistake.'

I had heard several people say how hard Vera found it to admit she was wrong. Joan Atkins, wife of another cousin, remarked one day when visiting Winchelsea that Vera was growing carrots in her garden. 'They are not carrots,' said Vera firmly. Joan said they certainly looked like carrots from the foliage. 'They are not carrots, dear,' said Vera adamantly. 'But those are carrot leaves,' persisted Joan. 'I don't grow carrots,' said Vera, at which point Joan tugged at the leaves and dangled a carrot in front of Vera's nose. Vera turned on her heel, still muttering that she didn't grow carrots.

'But she was very fair to me,' said Christine, to whom Vera once lent money to start up a business. 'And when I had a tragedy in my family which upset me very badly, Miss Atkins tried to help. She could see I was in a bad way and she asked if I wanted to talk about it. I told her what it was. She said: "Well, Christine, you have been badly hurt. But you must say to yourself that it is over now. It is finished and done with. I must forget it and move on."'

As the years passed Vera found that Christine had many uses and the two women became firm friends. 'What would I do without my wise owl,' Vera once wrote to her. And Vera had promised to leave Christine and her husband one or two small souvenirs, including a horseshoe she had found at Belsen. The daughter of a south London market trader, Christine loved to collect things. 'I found this in a bin bag after Miss Atkins died,' said Christine, producing a horseshoe out of a shoebox. It had a pink ribbon tied around it.

When, after Vera's death, her possessions and papers were packed up and taken off to Phoebe's shed in Cornwall, Christine had a poke through the rubbish left behind, where she told me she found the horseshoe and other oddments which she decided to salvage and take home. She showed them to me. One item was a book entitled *Felbrigg, The Story of a House*.

Christine said she had found some letters and photographs with the book. The pictures showed Vera with a young man; they were certainly taken before the war, as Vera looked to be in her twenties. Vera and the young man were in the mountains. He had fair, wavy hair, looked freckled and wore a tweed jacket. Vera had on heavy leather ski boots and wooden skis were leant up against a little hut. She was smiling in a way I had not seen in any other photograph: she looked radiant.

Then Christine showed me the letters she had found with the book and the photos. The first letter was typed. The sender's address was Headquarters, Royal Air Force, Middle East, and the date was 8 November 1941:

Dear Miss Atkins, A Standing Committee of Adjustment has been set up at this Headquarters to deal with the effects in this country of all missing personnel amongst whom is R.T.W. Ketton-Cremer who was so reported on 31 May 1941. We join you in the hope that he is in fact safe and well. Among his correspondence, which has been forwarded to this Committee, is a letter from which we have taken your address. Further news, when it is received, will be sent to his next of kin. If you wish it to be sent to you also, or if there is anything else that we can do for you, we hope that you will let us know.

The next letter Christine produced was handwritten, bore the date 30 September 1941 and had been sent from Felbrigg Hall, Roughton, Norwich:

Dear Miss Atkins, Thank you for your letter which I ought to have answered sooner, I'm afraid. I think every possible enquiry about Dick is being made, from a variety of sources in addition to the Air Ministry: and I am afraid there are so few data which could help your brother in Istanbul. But if anything further comes through I will let you know, especially if it is of a nature which would give your brother something to look for. With my many thanks.
    Yours sincerely
       Wyndham Ketton-Cremer.

From the letter it appeared that Vera had written first to Wyndham Ketton-Cremer, who was the brother of Dick, the missing airman. Vera must have suggested that her brother, Ralph, then with an oil company in Istanbul, might be able to help in the search for Dick, but Wyndham Ketton-Cremer had not wished to take up the suggestion. He did not appear to know Vera and his letter to her seemed somewhat cold.

I flicked through the guide to Felbrigg Hall. It was written by Wyndham Ketton-Cremer, who in the last chapter spoke most movingly of the loss of his younger brother, Dick. Dick loved to fly and had his own plane. On the outbreak of war Dick had joined the RAF hoping to be a pilot but his poor eyesight prevented him from flying and instead he became an equipment officer with a bomber squadron and was posted to the Western Desert. 'He said goodbye to us in January, and to Jester his large horse, and Mimi his little cat, both of whom were to live with me for many years. We never saw him again,' wrote his brother. It seemed from the book that Dick's fate remained unclear until well after the end of the war.

Vera's friend Barbara Worcester had heard her story of a young English pilot whom she had met long ago in her days in Romania and who was killed. Perhaps the young pilot was Dick Ketton-Cremer, who went missing in action in 1941. Dick had travelled widely in the 1930s. His brother wrote in the book: 'He spent months – sometimes years – in travel. He went all over the world. A few photograph albums are all that remain of those gay and carefree years.' Or was this pilot, his picture salvaged from a bin, part of a different tale?

Though I had peered at her many times, I had not expected to find Annie Samuelli. I had peered at Annie in a photograph I had found tucked inside an envelope in Phoebe's shed. Brown with age, it showed a long line of people sitting on what appeared to be mountain ponies on a wooded hillside. On the back was written '1932' and a few names. I assumed it had been taken in Romania but I didn't know where. I could easily identify Vera, in the middle, wearing jodhpurs and boots with riding crop in hand. According to the list, the man second from Vera on the left was Friedrich Werner von der Schulenburg, the ambassador to Bucharest that Barbara had heard about. At the other end of the row was a girl with dark hair and the faintest of smiles. Now here she was. Annie Samuelli was the first person I had met who did not just have stories of Vera's distant past; she was part of it. Aged ninety-two, Annie was now nearly blind. Sitting in her Paris flat, she adjusted a lamp and also peered at the photograph, trying to think back. At first Annie told me her memory of the pre-war years was not good, but after several cups of her favourite Whittards tea she began to remember more and more.

Over many hours she recalled Vera at little girls' tea parties at the Bucharest country club and later, as a young woman, at debutante balls, often at the Athénée Palace, the smartest hotel in Bucharest. She remembered that as a young girl Vera was 'very calm, extremely reserved, highly intelligent and very good at everything she did, but Vera would never do things she wasn't good at'. And she was the sort of person people wanted to 'suck up to', said Annie. 'People would not want to be in her bad books.'

Studying the photograph again, Annie described in remarkable detail the mountain gathering. It was a Whitsun celebration at the mountain home of one of Vera's uncles, somewhere in the Carpathians towards the border with Transylvania. She then told me exactly who was in the photo, identifying the figures one by one. What she remembered most about the weekend was a ceremonial sacrifice of new-born lambs. She had never been able to forget the screaming of the lambs.

How could I find the place? She didn't know. That part of Romania had gone back to Hungary in the war, and the property would have been destroyed. Vera and her family all left Romania well before the war, but, Annie said, she had stayed on. In 1949, while working in the press office of the British legation, she was seized by the communists, who had by then taken over in Romania. On trumped-up charges, laid against all Romanian nationals working for the British legation, Annie and her sister, Nora, were imprisoned for twelve years.

'You might find Crasna, though,' said Annie suddenly, as if I would know the name. Crasna, she explained, was where Vera mostly lived. Her father had had a large estate there with thousands of acres of woods. Where was it? I asked, but Annie didn't know, except to say it was in the north, probably in the region of Bukovina.

Annie had given me the vital clue. With a name of a place, I could at last travel to Romania and begin to search there. Yet there were at least five Crasnas in Romania, I subsequently found, three of them in the area Annie had directed me to. As I was about to leave for Bucharest to try my luck with the various Crasnas, Annie rang, saying she had found out more. Her friend Prince Mihai Sturdza, a descendant of one of the most illustrious families in Romania, said that the place I was looking for was no longer called Crasna at all; and it wasn't even in Romania. I had to find a place called

Krasno'illshi, which was somewhere near the town of Czernovitz, across the border of northern Romania in Ukraine. There were bandits, and I would need a Ukrainian visa.

'Visas take three days to process,' said the woman at the Ukrainian consulate in Notting Hill. 'But I'm leaving in three days' time,' I told her.

'So you will have to apply today,' she said. 'We close in one hour.'

10

THE DANUBE DELTA

When I emerged from the Hotel Boulevard, on Bucharest's Calea Victoriei, Ion Rizescu, my driver, interpreter and guide, was bent under the bonnet of a battered yellow Mercedes. His torso eventually appeared and straightened. He was a tall, craggy man, dressed in a thick, black anorak. It was likely to be icy up there on the border, he said in slow, gravelly French.

We planned to leave by 8am in order to reach Galatz, on the Danube delta, and find Vera's birthplace before nightfall. From Galatz we were to head north to Ukraine in search of Crasna – or, as I now knew it to be called, Krasno'illshi – which had been Vera's main childhood home. Then we would turn back towards the south-west, cutting deep into the Carpathians, where we would try to find the spot where Vera, family and friends gathered for a Whitsun picnic in 1933.

I had everything which might help me find the places I was look-ing for: compass references, photographs, maps and, most important, I now also had Vera's Uncle Siegfried's memoir. When the snow had finally melted in Quebec, Vera's relatives in Canada had dug out this ninety-nine-page family history and put it in the post.

Steam spewing from the bonnet of the car, we left Bucharest and struck out across vast flats of brown, tilled soil running into a February sky.

With me I also had Vera's birth certificate. Nobody I had spoken to ever knew exactly where she had been born. Fortunately, before she died, a historian at the Imperial War Museum in London asked her to declare in an interview for the sound archives the actual city of her birth, to which she responded in her best drawl: 'I was born at Galatz on the Danube delta.'

The interviewer then dared to press her further: 'Why were you born in Galatz?'

Vera took a deep draw on her cigarette (on the tape I could hear the intake of breath) and after a long pause she quipped: 'Because my mother was there, I suppose.'

Once Galatz was pinpointed, it was not hard to get the facts of Vera's birth.

Her original birth certificate, found in the archives in Galatz, read as follows: '*Certificat de Nastere. Numele de familie: Rosenberg. Prenumele: Vera-May. Sexul: Femeiesc. Data nasterji, Anul 1908; Luna Junie, Ziua 2. Locul, Galati, 135 Domneasca str.*' In the Romanian calendar her time of birth was given as 2.30am on 2 June, which, in the Western calendar, was 15 June, and this was, of course, the date she always used.

The more complicated question of how Vera had come to be born in Galatz had been answered for me by Uncle Siegfried's family history, with help from a South African rabbi.

Vera's father, Maximilian Rosenberg, was born in Kassel, Germany, in 1874, the eldest of the five children of Simeon Rosenberg, a prosperous Jewish farmer and trader, and his wife Freda (née Hermann). The Rosenbergs had lived near Kassel for several generations.

Max had a sister, Bertha, whom Siegfried described as 'very intelligent and brave', and three brothers: Siegfried himself, Arthur and Paul. After an idyllic childhood – 'We had a nice pond with lizards . . . On Sundays we got the geese out of their cages and held a goose race' – the three brothers started work in their father's timber import–export business in Kassel. Max, however, changed direction and went to Hamburg to train and work as an architect. In 1892, when Hamburg was devastated by a cholera epidemic, he looked for a new beginning and, like many Jews of his generation, he made for Cape Town, where he was taken under the wing of a powerful businessman named Henry Atkins.

At this point Rabbi Hillel Avidan, one of Vera's South African cousins, took up the story for me, saying he was not surprised I had found Vera's history hard to fathom. The family liked to hide its Jewish roots.

Vera's maternal great-grandfather was born in 1766, in Gomel, Belorussia, and his name was Jehudah Etkins (or perhaps Etkin or Etkind). Jehudah's children, including Vera's grandfather, Henry (formerly Heinrich and before that Hirsch Zvi) Etkins, were also born in Gomel. This isolated town near Chernobyl, north of Kiev and south-east of Minsk, was, by the nineteenth century, in the heart of the Pale of Settlement, where the majority of Russia's Jews were forced to live by the tsars, trapped in towns and shtetls. As many as twenty thousand Jews lived in Gomel in the nineteenth century, which was half its total population, and when, in the late nineteenth century, pogroms became a common occurrence, the Etkins family began to flee. Henry left from Odessa in the late 1870s, just before a spate of anti-Jewish riots.

Travelling via London, he moved on to Cape Town, then to Kimberley, where he supplied pit props for diamond mines. Henry Etkins and his wife Katherine (née Foyen) then returned to London and in 1881 Zeffro Hilda was born in the sub-district of Saint Mary in the County of Middlesex, according to her birth certificate. The family's address was given on the certificate as 105 Christian Street, Brick Lane, London. Other Etkins brothers from Gomel were now settling in England and Rabbi Hillel Avidan's grandfather had bought two tobacconist's shops in Streatham High Road, south London.

Vera's grandfather, Henry, however, was soon back in Cape Town accumulating wealth. He became a friend of Cecil Rhodes and other pioneers of the diamond fields. By the turn of the century, as more and more eastern European Jews poured into South Africa, Henry Atkins had successfully erased his own Russian roots and was now passing himself off as a true Englishman, which enabled him to join Cape Town's prestigious Garden Synagogue. No eastern European Jew was allowed in this synagogue – only Jews of English or German origin.

Henry then started new businesses, including the export of ostrich feathers. During the Boer War he sold large quantities of Australian frozen canned meat, flour and oats to feed the British Army. He later purchased the Lace Diamond Mine and became one of the biggest property developers in Cape Town.

*

By the time Vera's father Max Rosenberg arrived in South Africa in the last decade of the nineteenth century, Henry Atkins was an influential patron. 'With the boom in building at that time my oldest brother became very rich,' wrote Siegfried Rosenberg. 'He built houses and raised mortgages wherever he could.' He also became engaged to Henry Atkins's eldest daughter, Zeffro Hilda, known as Hilda, and the couple travelled to England for their marriage, which took place at the Central London Synagogue on 12 November 1902. Hilda, already born in England, no doubt hoped to entrench her English roots by making sure her marriage vows were exchanged here too. Afterwards the couple returned to live in South Africa, where their first child, Ralph, was born in 1905.

By this time the Boer War had precipitated a reversal in Max's fortunes. As Siegfried recounted, prices fell and Max, unable to recoup his debts, left South Africa. 'When he wanted to sell the buildings he could hardly pay back the mortgages so he decided to sell all his houses and leave.'

While Max had been in Cape Town, two of his three brothers, Arthur and Siegfried, had set out from Kassel to exploit the timber of Bukovina – the name means 'beech forest' – which then lay on the eastern fringes of the Austro-Hungarian Empire. They then ventured further to exploit the forests of Romania. Exporting timber from the Danube ports through the Black Sea to Rotterdam, Arthur and Siegfried were, by 1908, making a name for themselves on the Danube delta, where they had founded a successful shipping agency.

Paul, the youngest of the four brothers, stayed in Kassel and handled the German end of the business, now called Gebrüder Rosenberg Handlung.

'We had a good business so we told our older brother who had lost everything in South Africa to come and join us,' wrote Siegfried. 'He came and took over the shipping agency at Galatz and at Constanza.' When Max arrived in Galatz, he brought with him his new young wife, Hilda, and their son, Ralph. So this was how Vera's mother happened to be in Galatz in 1908 at the time when Vera was born.

Vera always regretted her father's decision to move from South Africa to Romania. In a unique moment of self-revelation, she said so openly during an interview with a British Home Office official when she was seeking naturalisation.

'Miss Atkins told me', wrote the official, 'that her father was unfortunately persuaded to enter the family timber business in Romania and they all went there to live.' Had he stayed in Cape Town – even just for another three years – Vera would have been born in an English colony, with an automatic right to be English, which was what she wanted all her life. Instead, Vera was born in Romania. History would dictate that as a result she would have to fight to be recognised as English and would never really know – and nor would anybody else – quite who she was or where she belonged.

Our Mercedes approached the western side of Galatz, dominated by the towering graveyard of iron that was the Sidex steelworks, one of Ceauşescu's most monstrous bequests to his nation. The Danube, a mile wide at this point, stretched out ahead of us in a vast brown expanse, across which chugged a single dredger, attempting to remove decades of deposited mud and silt. When Max Rosenberg arrived here in the early twentieth century the delta was crammed with vessels lapping up every opportunity for profit offered by this huge transcontinental waterway.

At that time Galatz itself had a thriving economy, owing in large part to the prosperous local Jewish community. The city's Jewish population was nearly twenty thousand strong – mostly small traders but also a substantial number of rich bourgeois Jews who, unable by law to own land, put assets into business or banking.

The Jews of Galatz had come from all over Europe, but the majority had arrived in the nineteenth century after fleeing persecution in Russia and other parts of eastern Europe, particularly Poland. They had been allowed to install themselves in certain parts of the city. One of these was the area around the central market. And here was 135 Domneasca Street, the house where Vera was born. An elegant single-storey villa, shaded by linden trees, Vera's birthplace lay in the heart of the wealthiest Jewish quarter, now the poorest part of the city, abandoned in many places to beggars and gypsies.

At the time of Vera's birth Max Rosenberg was fast rebuilding the fortune he had lost in South Africa and soon he had started his own shipping agency, exporting the timber from his brothers' mills. He also began to borrow again, to build shipyards in Galatz and Constanza. By 1908, the year Vera was born, the family was able to adopt the luxurious colonial lifestyle which at that time prevailed among Romania's expatriate community. As nations vied for their slice of trade and political influence in the Balkans, diplomats and international businessmen poured into the ports of the Danube delta and Max's position as a powerful businessman gave him an automatic entrée to this set. Soon the family had moved to a larger house in Braila, another flourishing Danube port.

However, the atmosphere in the family home was not always happy, in large part because Hilda was homesick for South Africa, or, as Vera put it in her Home Office interview, 'my mother did not settle well' in Romania. Hilda nevertheless did her utmost to ensure all the 'Englishness' she had absorbed in colonial Cape Town and on her visits to London was maintained, and English was the first language the children learned. Indeed, though French culture dominated much of Romania, Englishness was the height of fashion in Romania before the First World War, especially after the arrival of the much-loved Queen Marie, granddaughter of Queen Victoria, who married King Ferdinand of Romania in 1893 and imposed her own very English style on the country's royal court.

The Rosenberg family's entrée into the highest echelons of Romanian society came about also through their close connections with the Mendl family, one of the most prominent Jewish families in Braila. The Mendls, originally from Trieste, also had strong ties with England.

Perhaps during a visit to see her sister in Galatz, May Atkins, Hilda's elegant younger sister, met Anthony Mendl, a wealthy businessman. Anthony and May were married in London, and soon afterwards Nina Mendl, a cousin of Anthony's, married Max's brother Arthur.

Teresina Mendl, another cousin of Anthony's, whom I met in Paris just a few days before her hundredth birthday, recalled with a smile 'la vie coloniale' which they all enjoyed in the Danube ports at this time. 'We all had big houses, we had servants.'

The rich, especially German-speaking Jews, looked to Vienna for culture and entertainment. 'In Vienna,' Teresina told me, 'they went shopping, consulted the renowned specialists, had check-ups and cures. They enjoyed Viennese operettas and great opera singers. From Vienna they ordered their furniture and brought the latest style in embroidered tablecloths and so on.'

In those days, Teresina said, the young men might be educated abroad – perhaps in England. Vera's elder brother Ralph was sent to an English prep school as soon as he was old enough. But the girls were educated at home and never went out unchaperoned. So Vera, by the age of six or seven, would have had a governess who accompanied her at all times.

Teresina then revealed that she remembered Vera as a tiny girl. '*Elle était un enfant très tranquil. Très reposé. Toujours calm. C'est tout.*'

How far the Rosenberg children were made aware of their Jewishness in these early years remains unclear. Siegfried had written that in Kassel the family observed Jewish rituals and holidays but were not ultra-religious and were quite opposed to the Zionist movement of the time. 'Although we were Jewish with Jewish beliefs we felt German.' Certainly Max and Hilda's young family would not have been brought up as devout Jews, but Teresina said they would probably have observed the Jewish Sabbath and attended synagogue on high days and holidays.

Anti-Semitism, though not at that time a serious concern to upper-class Jews in Romania, was clearly prevalent enough to persuade a man like Max Rosenberg that it made sense to emphasise his German rather than his Jewish origins. To be German in Romania in those days was to be highly respected.

Jews of their standing had little to do with lower-class Jews, said Teresina. Would they have been accepted by the elite in Romanian society? 'Acceptance in Romanian society was certainly possible,' she said, 'though not automatic.' As time went by, and certainly between the wars, Hilda let those around her begin to question whether she was a Jew at all. It was said that she had once converted to Catholicism but immediately suffered a leg injury and, taking this as a punishment from on high for deserting her faith, converted straight back. Hilda was remembered as a simple soul; 'somewhat childlike', in Teresina's words. Teresina Mendl was one of only two people I found who had any memory at all of Vera's father. Like Vera, Max was 'very calm', she recalled.

By 1910 the Rosenberg business was growing fast. The German headquarters of Gebrüder Rosenberg Handlung had moved from Kassel to Cologne, from where Simeon Rosenberg that year sent a postcard to his grandchildren, '*Lieber Vera und Ralph*', showing a photograph of the family's new apartment on one of the city's most fashionable rings.

Also that year, the Rosenbergs and the Mendls cemented their business partnership by forming a global shipping company called Dunarea, which was notarised in London. The company had a fleet of vessels and among its eight dredgers was one named *Vera*, which busily plied the Danube clearing silt.

In 1911, the year when Vera's brother Wilfred was born, the family's prospects continued to look excellent. The little Rosenbergs had new cousins now to play with: Nina Rosenberg gave birth to twin boys, George and Hans, and also in 1911, Cousin Fritz was born, in that same house in Domneasca Street. The very young Rosenbergs and their cousins were now raised together in Braila and Galatz in a rarefied atmosphere, rocked on verandas to the sound of clinking china tea cups and pushed along the Danube by nannies in starched pinafores, who, in the case of Vera, Wilfred and Ralph, would certainly have been English.

Meanwhile, Max Rosenberg, who had already fought his way back from bankruptcy, had become one of wealthiest Jewish businessmen on the Danube.

In 1910 Galatz had eighteen synagogues and a yeshiva, or Talmudic college. At the back of wasteland on the edge of the Jewish quarter, we found the only remaining synagogue, surrounded by iron bars. Mr Goldenberg, president of the Jewish community, was in his adjoining office and willingly heaved hefty volumes on to his desk to scan lists for the name Rosenberg. He looked through Jewish burial records and a tome listing Jews transported from Galatz to Transnistra, territory in Russia, occupied by Romanian and German forces in 1941, where Romanian Jews were worked to death in labour camps. There were Rosenbergs here – Rifka, Liuba, Soloma – but none I knew. 'Was Max buried here?' Mr Goldenberg asked. I had no idea, so he suggested it might be worth my looking in the Jewish graveyard. 'We have our own Association for Victims of the Holocaust,' he said. 'Our Holocaust here in Galatz. We are trying to account for as many as we can. We are getting new information all the time.'

Then he fixed me with a look and said: 'We have even buried soap, you know.'

I said nothing.

'*RIF! RIF!*' he exclaimed. 'You have heard of that?' And he kept saying, '*RIF!*' again and again because I didn't understand. Then he got a photograph of a gravestone. On the stone were carved the letters '*R.I.F.*' and underneath was an inscription in Hebrew which Mr Goldenberg translated. 'Here rest the bodies of our brothers turned into *R.I.F.* soap by the criminal Hitlerites during the Second World War.' The letters '*R.I.F.*' stood for '*Reichstelle Industrielle Fett*' said Mr Goldenberg. 'The Nazis called it "clean Jewish fat". It was on sale here in the central market – right over there. People bought it as soap. They didn't know what they were doing, of course. After the war they gave it back to us and we buried it, here in the graveyard.' Notwithstanding Mr Goldenberg's certainty, stories that the Nazis used fat from Jewish corpses to make soap have never been proven.

We left the synagogue and made our way up to the Jewish graveyard, high above the town. The graveyard looked down over the Sidex steelworks. An old crippled woman, dressed in rags, struggled to unlock the padlock on the gate. Yes, she said, she thought she had a Rosenberg gravestone here, but she didn't know where to find it.

There were grand avenues of graves, all overgrown, and we walked up and down reading all the names we could manage before it got too dark. Below us orange flames from one corner of the Sidex plant were now lighting up the contours of that hideous creation and marking out the clean black lines of the delta.

11

CRASNA

It was quite possible we might not be allowed across the Ukrainian border, Ion announced the next morning as we left Galatz behind. He had been unable to get his passport renewed in time for our journey, though an official had told him he might be able to negotiate a day pass at the border. I said we would talk them into it. Ion shrugged. 'If we get "*un type soviétique*" we have no chance.'

Of all the places in her life, Vera had well and truly closed the book on Crasna.

It was only thanks to Annie Samuelli that I had heard the name at all, though Uncle Siegfried also mentioned Max's '6000-acre estate' but without giving any clue as to where it was. With the package from Canada, however, I had also received a photograph album which included pictures of Vera at a large, elegant house. One showed Vera as a child with long, blonde plaits cradling a dog in front of a large stable; others as a young woman striking poses on a veranda. But, again, there was nothing to say where the house was.

'Krasno' is the Russian form of 'Crasna' and 'Illshi' is the name of one of the old boyar, or noble, families who owned the land around this part of northern Bukovina in the eighteenth and nineteenth centuries. Northern Bukovina changed hands several times in the twentieth century. In the early years of the century it was still a part of the Austro-Hungarian Empire, but with the empire's dissolution at the end of the First World War, it was given to Romania. Then, in June 1940, when Germany, the Soviet Union and Hungary were all vying for slices of Romania, northern Bukovina was taken by the Soviet Union. Today northern Bukovina is in Ukraine.

While it was almost impossible for Jews in Romania to own land in the early years of the century, on these isolated eastern marches of the Austro-Hungarian Empire, a wealthy German Jew might gain acceptance as a landowner. And it was when Crasna was part of Austro-Hungary that Max purchased the estate, paying for it with the riches accumulated in Galatz.

Acquiring Crasna must have been the achievement of a lifetime for Max Rosenberg. He had become a boyar himself – a feudal landowner and a de facto nobleman. And yet, no sooner had he bought the place than he was forced to abandon it for several years, because in 1914 he was called up to fight for Germany.

Vera's earliest memory, or at least the earliest she ever avowed, was of the outbreak of the First World War. It was another story she told only to her Home Office interviewer. Vera was six when war broke out in the summer of 1914. At the time her family, apparently oblivious to the possibility of war, were planning a holiday on the Dutch coast, a good place for the various branches of this cosmopolitan tribe to come together.

While Max stayed behind in Romania, or perhaps at Crasna, Vera, her mother and Wilfred, then just three, travelled west from Galatz, taking the train to Berlin. The idea, Vera said, was to break the journey in Berlin, where Ralph, who had been brought over from his English prep school, was to join them for the last leg.

Taking up the narrative, the immigration officer then wrote: 'Miss Atkins says that her family had just arrived in Berlin when the outbreak of war was announced', but his dry tone quite failed to disguise what must have been the panic of that moment: Hilda and her young family stepped off the Orient Express in Berlin on 1 August 1914, looking forward to a family holiday, only to hear the news that their entire world had fallen apart and all the Great Powers were at war. No longer could Hilda continue west to Holland, nor could she return easily to the east, as armies would be gathering in that direction.

Her mother's horror at her position must have made an impression on six-year-old Vera. For, on top of everything, Hilda now found she was physically trapped in Germany, which for her was the enemy.

Her sister May and her husband Anthony were already ensconced in England, in a new house they had bought on the Sussex coast at Winchelsea. Two of her brothers, Montague and Arthur Atkins, were volunteering to fight for the Imperial forces, and May would soon be working for British postal censorship. Yet Hilda's German husband and his brothers were sure to be called up to fight for Germany, where she would now have to stay for the duration of the war.

Her only recourse was to take refuge with her husband's German relatives, and she continued on to Cologne. The immigration interviewer, summarising Vera's words, put it like this: 'The outbreak of war naturally changed their plans and they then travelled to Cologne to join her father's parents and remained there throughout the war.'

Stories about wartime in Cologne circulated among the family in later years. Ralph joked about how his mother used to hang a Union Jack in his bedroom in case he should forget whose side he was really on. Wilfrid, presented with swede to eat in Cornwall, protested that it reminded him of the gruel they lived on in wartime Cologne. Hilda's children had the company of their cousins, Gert and Klaus, also growing up in Cologne, and saw as much as possible of their cousins Trude, Aenne and Hilde, daughters of Max's sister Bertha, who lived in Hanover. But they saw almost nothing of their father, who was now serving on the Eastern Front. Of the Rosenberg brothers, Uncle Siegfried recorded, at least two won the Iron Cross in the First World War.

For Hilda this was a miserable period, as Vera's immigration officer's report confirmed: 'Miss Atkins told me that although she was only a child at the time she remembers the unhappy atmosphere of strain in the house, where her father's people naturally had the German point of view and her mother, an Englishwoman, had quite other sympathies. Later they left the grandparents and went to live on their own in Cologne where they were taught by a governess who was a refugee from Belgium.'

Ion said we were now closing in on Romania's border with Ukraine. Everyone was wearing peaked woolly hats. Horses and carts outnumbered cars and giant rusty pipes curled up out of fields and over roads. The first dirty snow appeared on the roadside and we passed tourist signs for painted monasteries.

Suddenly I couldn't see anything but thick fog, wet on my face. We had been talking so much we hadn't noticed the steam rise from under our feet. Ion pulled up. We both jumped out and he lifted the bonnet. The car was boiling over. Geese squawked at us. My greatest fear now was that the Mercedes wasn't going to make it to the border, but Ion said he had driven across the whole of Europe when Ceauşescu fell. The Merc wouldn't let us down.

By dusk we had reached Radautz, a town right on the border, and we decided to try our luck with Ion's papers first thing in the morning.

I asked Ion if he thought there was any chance we would find the Rosenbergs' house. He said he thought it unlikely but not impossible. A few of the grander houses had been used by the communists as schools or sanatoria and today some old families from '*la belle époque*' were even trying to get their houses back. Ion himself was one of them. 'We are called "*nostalgiques*",' he said. Vera was not a 'nostalgic', I replied.

Why Vera's father and her two uncles had chosen to return to Romania after the First World War was not at first clear from Siegfried's memoir. Much of what the brothers had built up here before the war had now been destroyed – the shipyards on the Danube and the timber mills were all obliterated.

For Max, returning here meant starting again from nothing at the age of nearly fifty. Perhaps he had simply fallen in love with the place, and looking from my tiny hotel bedroom across the undulating, forested landscape, framed by snow-tipped mountains, it was easy to see why. Crasna was now only about 25 miles away.

The next morning we found the frontier policeman at Radautz sitting at a desk inside a wooden box, his bullet-shaped head bent over a large, filthy ledger, a big thumb tracing down a line as he laboriously filled in numbers, names and dates in columns.

Another uniformed figure was slowly tearing off little slips of paper with serrated edges and giving them to people in a long queue.

Our man looked up eventually. He looked at Ion. Ion said something and the man stared hard at me, then jerked his chin at Ion as if to say: Why are you wasting my time? Ion showed his papers and explained what we wanted, but the answer was: *Niet*. We had landed '*un type soviétique*'.

Not only was it impossible for Ion to get a day pass at this border, the man said, but I could not pass into Ukraine here – even with a visa. Crossing at this post was only for locals. We would have to go to the main north–south border post, at nearby Siret, and even then Ion would not be allowed across. I would have to go alone.

Trucks were lined up on the tarmac at the Siret border post; they weren't moving. I was now sitting in a yellow Trabant. It was unbelievably small and I was hunched next to a man named Constantin, who wore a shiny black leather jacket, had dark-red cheeks and smelled strongly of aftershave. Outside the temperature was plummeting, and a storm from Siberia was forecast.

Ion and I had found Constantin in the car park at the border, and I agreed to pay him $50 to take me to Krasno'illshi. He told Ion that he knew exactly where it was and that he spoke French. Ion and I exchanged mobile telephone numbers. He insisted I be back by nightfall. Constantin was now talking to me in very fast Romanian with the odd French word thrown in and he seemed to think I understood.

Soon several tall Romanian border guards were standing around the car, then bending double, their large, frying-pan faces staring in through the windscreen. They were all wearing long, green overcoats that looked like they weighed a ton. Despite the freezing cold their sheepskin earflaps were tied up on top of their caps. Outside, scores of women with children wrapped up in thick wool scarves clutched little pieces of paper with serrated edges. Contents of suitcases were tipped out and rifled through by great big hands as large Alsatians sniffed around them.

This entire frontier, carving northern Bukovina from Romania, was slapped down in a matter of hours in June 1940, when Russia issued an ultimatum. Families living here had to take split-second decisions which would affect their entire lives. Anyone in the north who could rushed over to the south to be in Romania before the line was drawn. Those who didn't make it were trapped in the Soviet Union. For the next fifty years members of the same families, fellow Romanians, would grow up in different countries, visiting one another occasionally by crossing this hellish checkpoint.

Now it was the turn of the Ukrainian guards. 'A book!' exclaimed one, asking me what my business was. 'About a woman from

Krasno'illshi? This is interesting to you?' He tilted his head.
Eventually the border post spat us out the other side.

Constantin was chattering away again as we drove north into
Ukraine towards the town of Czernovitz. Did he know where he was
going? We turned sharp left, then stopped and took in an elderly
couple loaded with baskets. At a place called Liborca the higher
peaks of the Carpathians were suddenly visible and we stopped
again, where more rusting pipes looped over the road, and picked up
an old man with a mouthful of gold teeth and suddenly everyone in
the car kept saying 'Krasno'illshi'. We were trailing slowly behind a
cart full of plump women sitting on logs, chewing gum.

Back across the River Siret again, we began to climb through
woods and soon we were winding through the streets of a wretched
place called Ciudin, which I had found on my map. 'Krasno'illshi 23
kilometres,' said a sign, but suddenly, about 2 kilometres further
on, we were there.

'School, school, *école, école*.' I was trying to explain to Constantin that
we must find the village school because it was my only hope of finding somebody who spoke French or English. We tried a senior
school, where we were greeted by a thousand staring eyes, but here
nobody spoke anything but Russian. Krasno'illshi was a sizeable
little town of plain houses lining muddy zigzagging streets, but I
hardly noticed it, too busy looking for a large mansion with a lake
and stables. Instead we passed a huge decaying pile of iron – a factory of some sort, with conveyor belts suspended in the air on what
looked like pulleys ready to tumble any moment. We passed a large
onion-domed church, newly painted pale blue and gold. And then
we saw a mass of pretty bobble hats and plaits and little girls playing
hopscotch. It was the junior school. Zinovia Iliut spoke French, they
told me. She was the history teacher. She was sent for.

A round-faced woman with intelligent, dancing eyes and nut-
brown skin, wearing a green sweater and long skirt, Zinovia appeared,
half-smiling, half-suspicious. I explained I was a writer trying to find
out about somebody who once lived at Crasna. Did she know the history of the town? Did the name Rosenberg mean anything to her?

She looked quite blank and still nervous. No, she said emphatically. History here had been wiped out. '*Avec le communisme, c'était
coupée*,' she told me, making a chopping gesture with her hands.

Then Zinovia looked at me more closely. Where had I come from? How did I get here? '*De Anglia*,' piped up Constantin as if he had personally brought me all the way from '*Anglia*'.

'*De Anglia?*' she said, wide-eyed. 'It is a miracle.' She looked at Constantin again for confirmation. He nodded smugly.

'*Pas possible*,' said Zinovia, and laughed. She took us through to a teachers' common room and, sitting down, explained that when this part of Bukovina was cut off from the southern part everyone was told to forget their past. It was forbidden to teach the children about Romania for many years and they did not learn their own language. They learned Russian. 'We are a forgotten community. We have learned not to ask questions about the past.'

I asked: 'Is there a large house here in Krasno'illshi – an old estate of any kind?'

'No! No, not at all. Nothing like that,' Zinovia said, and glancing anxiously at Constantin and then at a group of other teachers, she led me alone into another room.

Zinovia then told me she knew of a little booklet about Krasno'illshi; a kind of history. She said she had a friend who had a copy.

While we waited for her friend to bring the booklet I tried to probe Zinovia further. Were there Jews in the town? There were once many, she said. In Ciudin there was a school for Jews and a synagogue. But they left. Where did they go? 'We do not know. It is better not to ask these things.'

At that moment her friend arrived and swiftly pulled a little white booklet from her bag and passed it to Zinni. (She had asked me to call her Zinni.) She read the title. The booklet was in memory of a local poet, Ile Motrescu, who disappeared from Krasno'illshi. How did he disappear? 'We don't know. We do not ask.'

Zinni got up to shut the door. Children were now lining up outside the window ready to leave at the end of their day. She sat down again and started to translate the Romanian into French for me, apparently intrigued.

'In 1613 the community at Crasna was attached to the monastery at Putnah and the forests that surrounded the town were rich and famous and bought by the local boyar, Alexander Illshi, who built the church,' she read. 'During the Austrian period the factory making wood was built and became the biggest in Bukovina. It was made by the Austrian boyar Rosenberg in the first years of the century. He built a railway from Ciudin to Crasna 6 kilometres long to transport the wood.'

I looked up.

'Rosenberg. Yes, it says here Rosenberg,' Zinni said. 'So you were right.' She was now quite excited and read on.

'There was a château in Crasna built by Alexander Illshi in 1750. Many famous people lived here – the Starcea family, Rosenberg and Nicholas Mavrocodat.'

'So there was a château?' I said. Was she quite sure there were no remains of such a château here in the town today?

'No. It no longer exists. That is for sure. It has disappeared since those days.'

She continued: 'Krasno'illshi had the forests and Crasna Putnah was connected to the monastery. The Russians united the two parts and called it Krasno'illshi. The château was surrounded by beautiful parks with trees of different types and in 1949 it was designated a sanatorium.'

I looked up again. Zinni paused and reflected.

'Is there a sanatorium here today?' I asked.

'Yes. It is just here.'

'Where?'

'Just over the road from this school. You must have driven past it. It is behind the trees.'

'Could it be the château?'

The idea had never occurred to Zinni.

'Can we go and look?' I asked.

'I suppose we can,' she said.

I rose and picked up my bag. 'Can we go right now?' I said. It seemed to me there was absolutely nothing to stop us walking over the road that second and straight back into Vera's past.

Across the road were two elegant stone gateposts which opened on to a drive. By the time we reached the gateway we had collected Constantin once again and a gaggle of new guides, including the school's mathematics teacher and his friend.

My new guides looked at me and agreed that it was a 'miracle' that I had come all the way from '*Anglia*'. Then we started to walk up the drive together, stopping periodically as they turned to look at me again, as if I was not quite real.

We kicked up dust and leaves as we went, and a figure passed by pushing a wheelbarrow. To our left was a pile of fallen masonry – a building constructed by the Russians, I was told – and another hideous rusting pipe. We climbed over debris strewn around and I smelled a stench of decay and then a strong scent of pine. We continued further and walked into an opening. A large structure came into view, not suddenly but gradually, as if it had been lurking there, shabby among the trees.

I walked round quickly to the front and stood back to look. The château was encased in blistering paint, but had lost none of its grandeur. The distinctive portico was instantly recognisable from one of the photographs I had with me – six stout pillars holding up a large balcony. Max had been photographed standing up there on the balcony and on horseback in the drive behind me.

An old man was now walking towards us, picking his way across wet grass and melting snow. He wore a black, pointed woollen hat and was very thin, with a stubbly face that seemed silvery grey. He was carrying something flat, like a large photograph. My new friends greeted him and called him over. This was Yaroslav, they said; he would know everything. 'He is the historian of Crasna,' they chorused.

I saw that what Yaroslav was carrying was an X-ray. The plastic sheet was flapping in the breeze. It seemed to be of somebody's chest as I could make out a rib cage. The old man was the radiologist at the sanatorium, the maths teacher explained. Yaroslav had a pixie face and was quizzing me with his eyes.

'Where would you like to see first?' asked the maths teacher. Outside perhaps? The stables or the tennis court? Yaroslav wanted me to come inside straight away so that I could see his papers on the history of the house, but the maths teacher insisted I follow him while there was some light. We looked at the stables and I imagined where the photograph of Vera cradling the dog had been taken. She was perhaps twelve in that picture. Wilfred by then had followed his brother Ralph to prep school in England and would soon go on to Radley College, while Vera was left behind alone in Romania, to be educated by governesses. It seems that it was Max who opposed the idea of sending Vera away at a young age, perhaps because he wanted to keep her close. 'My father definitely had a dislike of the practice of English girls' public schools,' she once said.

Though Vera spent the winter months in Bucharest with her mother – who, according to Annie Samuelli, hated Crasna – she visited her father at Crasna as often as she could and spent all her summers here, riding, picnicking with friends and running around with the schnauzers over the vast grounds. Her brothers returned for summer holidays. In front of the stables was where another of Uncle Siegfried's photographs had been taken – one with Siegfried grinning, riding in a sleigh 'with curly bits on', his niece and nephews behind him. I had also seen a picture taken of Wilfred and Vera sitting in a pony and trap on the drive.

I was beginning to understand another reason why Max had chosen to return to Crasna. Here he could try to recreate the happy family home he knew in Kassel, with animals and space for children to play. In Kassel the Rosenbergs were raised 'in a very free way', wrote Siegfried, 'but if we did something wrong our father talked to us very seriously. He was very strict when it was about the truth. And we could always tell our parents everything without being afraid.'

I had a sense that Max might have taken a similar attitude. Vera certainly adored her father, as she had told friends in her older years. 'It was her mother who was the problem,' Zenna had told me. 'My father said Hilda always wanted Vera all to herself. And when men came along she stood in the way every time.'

And here, at the back of the house, was a large mossy patch where the ornamental lake once was. I had seen a picture of a priest in robes standing on a tiny bridge that crossed the lake. Max acquired a papal medal while he was at Crasna, apparently for helping to build a nearby Catholic church. Attempts to bury the Rosenbergs' Jewish roots had already begun.

But, however much she loved to be at Crasna, Vera too would be sent away to be educated. She rarely talked about her education and when she did she was dismissive, saying she had had no real education. 'It was a long time ago when many parents, including mine, felt a girl's education was not of particular interest or value. Girls were educated for life in general – for social life, languages and other little essentials.' Vera was not, however, quite truthful when she said she had had 'no real education'. At fifteen she was sent to Switzerland, to one of the most exclusive finishing schools in Lausanne. At Le Manoir, where the extras cost more than the fees, the 'little essentials' she learned were perhaps not what she would have chosen to study but nevertheless left a very distinctive mark on her character.

Thanks to Le Manoir, she would never be at a loss as to how to lay the most elegant dinner table, preserve a pheasant or prepare the most luxurious linen for a perfectly turned bed. And Vera's articulated English was undoubtedly acquired in her diction classes – reciting Byron, say, or Swinburne.

She went on to a further finishing school, Montmorency in Paris, also attended by her friend Annie Samuelli. Here the curriculum included a course on French culture, which, though taught at the Sorbonne, did not have the status of a degree.

When Vera completed her finishing schools at sixteen, Max felt the time had come for her to have a little independence. As she once told a neighbour in Winchelsea, he had visited her when she was taking her final exams in Lausanne and promised that if she passed he would grant her three wishes. She chose a puppy, a flight to England and to have her long hair cut. The exams were passed with flying colours, the puppy ruined the hotel bedroom, a flight to England was arranged and her hair was cut, much to her mother's fury. Hilda didn't want Vera to lose her plaits so young.

'It is a wonder, is it not?' said the mathematics teacher, pointing to the 'tennis court' – another muddy bog. 'Imagine,' and he flicked his wrist as if in a backhand. My guides continued to point out the archaeology of the gardens with ever more enthusiasm but the thin sun was starting to go down. We climbed back up the long flight of steps from the bottom of the garden to the veranda on the east side of the house, where the carcass of a rotting animal lay next to a pile of plastic bottles. Many portraits of Vera had been taken on this veranda. By now in her late teens, alluring in flowing silk and chiffon, she was always shown in these stylised pictures turning her eyes away from the camera, as if not quite comfortable as a debutante, with her fashionable new twenties bob.

The pictures of Vera here on the veranda had obviously been taken after her finishing-school days, at the time when her parents considered her ready to be launched into society. In this corner of the former Austro-Hungarian empire 'society' was a curious mishmash of Romanian, German, Austrian and even Russian landowners and aristocrats: a place where a German-Jewish boyar's daughter might well be accepted, if not in all circles, at least in some. After all, Max himself employed a White Russian prince as his estate manager. Prince Peter zu Sayn-Wittgenstein, whose father was killed in the Russian Revolution, had fled Russia in 1918, crossing the Dniester River with his mother, brothers and sisters to the safety of Romania, where he found himself in need of work. At Crasna he grew fond of Vera. In her old age Vera had, as I already knew, talked affectionately of Peter Wittgenstein, reminiscing about how he had once offered her a set of his family's jewels.

Before leaving Bucharest on this expedition, I had spent time hunting down survivors of '*la belle époque*' who might remember Crasna, the Rosenbergs or even Peter Wittgenstein.

In the Romanian capital I found Mona Lalu, a member of what was once one of the richest Romanian noble families, sitting in a dark, one-bedroom basement flat under the Hungarian embassy. Her family had once owned the whole building.

Mona Lalu's mother's family, the Grigorceas, had a large estate in northern Bukovina, she said. 'Yes, I remember Crasna very well. My cousin Nicholas Mavrocodat bought it from the Rosenbergs in 1932.'

And then she got out old family trees and old maps. 'But these roads have probably all gone now. We used to come down to Bucharest on the sleeper. The trains were excellent in those days.'

'Did you go there often?'

'Oh, yes, I went there many times for parties or gatherings. It was a very old house – from the seventeenth century. I remember the hallway was dark and vaulted, with a big stone staircase up to the first floor. There were ornate murals on the walls and beautiful paintings.'

A woman who still exuded faded grandeur, with her grey hair swept up in a jewelled comb, Mona Lalu spoke of a 'most pleasant existence in Bukovina in those days'. 'You were invited to stay as guests in grand houses in the summer. You played bridge and tennis and made expeditions. There was a large staff and at the parties there was music and dancing. We had a gramophone and we danced the foxtrot, the Charleston, and then the South American cha-cha-cha came in.

'Czernovitz was a most elegant town. There was a national theatre and music that came from Bucharest. The train to Munich was fast and quick. You took the train to the Polish border and then on to Breslau.'

In huge tower blocks built by Ceauşescu, I found other elegant old ladies in tiny flats who pulled out enormous family trees and showed me photographs of grand houses they had once lived in.

Princess Ileana Sturdza disappeared into her miniature kitchen to serve an exquisite lunch of goat's cheese and beetroot salad which we ate on our laps as she told me how her grandmother and mother had been ladies-in-waiting to Queen Marie. All young girls – not just Vera – in those days had an English nanny or governess. There was a Miss Stork and a Miss Collins and then there was Alice Goose (from Norwich), Blanch Snordell and a Miss Phyllis Parrat and Miss Michael. All took their charges for walks along the chaussée each afternoon and then took tea in the country club.

Now Princess Ileana was tending her snowdrops on a narrow balcony as she talked of the time of her imprisonment. 'The communists just came and seized our forests.' She was locked up and put in a cell with no windows. Her family lost everything except a crate of furniture, which was stored in the ice cellar. 'For years we children were told nothing of our past. It was better we didn't know.'

I found Stanu Marescu along another dark walkway above a large neon sign. Stanu too had cleverly fashioned a new life in her little box of an apartment, where she chain-smoked, popping ash into a silver pot. When I asked what she remembered of life before the war, she replied in a husky voice: 'Which war?'

Then she said, 'It was a good time,' and showed me a picture of her family's mansion at Botoshan. 'But you know what? I don't care that it has all gone. Seven years my father was in prison for being an enemy of the people.'

'Why?'

'For being opulent.'

More family trees came out and the names were starting to sound familiar, many having intermarried. I wondered how much Vera had really wanted to appear in one of these family trees and what good these roots would have done her anyway. Her own family were to be scattered to the four winds before long, but so were all of these people. Stanu Marescu had ended all the way up here, on the twenty-second floor, above a flashing Samsung sign.

I asked all of these ladies if they remembered Prince Peter

Wittgenstein or had heard about a love affair with Vera? Mona Lalu remembered him well. He was certainly manager at Crasna when she knew him, she said.

What was he like?

'Oh, he was very big and solid and passionate about hunting. He was a very gay man. He had a big, round face – no hair. But he had a certain . . .' She paused. 'A certain style.'

Did she remember anything about a love affair between Vera and Peter Wittgenstein? 'No,' she replied. I said that Vera told stories late in life that Wittgenstein had fallen in love with her and offered her diamonds and amethysts.

Mona Lalu raised a carefully plucked eyebrow.

'Even if it were true, it would not have been possible,' she said. 'It didn't matter that she was a Jew. That is not what I mean. My mother's family had many Jewish friends. It is true that there were many rich Jews who were not liked at that time. The managers of estates, you know, were often Jews and they were not popular. But the Rosenbergs owned Crasna. That was different. And they had many friends. I had many friends who were Jews. And, of course, the Jews were persecuted during the war. I saw them myself sent out to shovel snow.'

'But would families like yours have married Jews?'

'Marry Jews – no, that was not so often,' she said.

Would Peter Wittgenstein have married Vera? Would he have married a Jew?

'No,' said Mona Lalu emphatically. 'He had come from the pogroms in Russia. He had a coat of arms. I don't think he would have considered marrying a Jew.'

We rushed now to look inside the house because it was getting dark and Yaroslav announced there was no electricity. We entered the gloomy vaulted hallway, where a nurse in white overalls was shuffling through a doorway. The hall smelled cold and damp, like a dungeon.

Yaroslav gestured to us to go upstairs. It was hard to see but I seemed to be brushing past another nurse in white carrying a bucket.

'There are patients in these rooms?' I asked and my voice echoed.

'Yes,' said Yaroslav. And he slapped his chest. We were in a TB hospital. 'Come, come,' he said. He seemed excited.

At the top of the stone stairs we turned into a room that was completely dark. Yaroslav threw open the shutters to draw in as much of the fading light as he possibly could. He looked more like a pixie than ever. Strange shapes appeared; in the gloom they looked like reclining sculptures. They were large lumps of metal with levers and dials. We were in Max's salon, now Yaroslav's radiography room. This was where patients were once X-rayed, he explained, but now there was no power to operate the machines. Yaroslav disappeared a moment before reappearing with a little folder, which he laid down on the X-ray table and opened up. He had been collecting information about the house for years, he said. 'History is my hobby.' Now he was pulling out black-and-white photographs of fine mural paintings and he pointed up to the roof showing where they once were. The house, he said, was more than three hundred years old. Many of the murals dated back to Ottoman times. But they were all lost in a fire in the 1960s.

He walked over to a giant stone and wrought-iron stove in one corner of the room. This was the original stove. It still worked if lit, and he pointed at the long, black chimney flue running up to the ceiling. He opened the door of the furnace and told us the stove was here when the boyar Illshi owned Crasna. Several dynasties had owned the place. Max Rosenberg bought Crasna before the First World War, he thought.

Was it true that Rosenberg built the railway and the timber factory? Everyone around the X-ray table looked at Yaroslav. 'Yes,' he said. I told him that this made sense, because two of Max's brothers had first started timber mills and built railways not far away from here in the Maramures. At this Zinni suddenly exclaimed: 'The Maramures, you say. *Mon Dieu!* In the Maramures? Well, that explains everything.'

'Why?' we all asked.

'I have always wondered why the young men of Crasna dance in the style of the Maramures. It is so different from dances of the other villages round here,' said Zinni, and danced a little to show us. '*C'est une danse très excitée.*' The Rosenberg workers from the Maramures must have come to work in the mill at Crasna, we all agreed, and brought their dance with them.

'When did Rosenberg leave Crasna?' I asked Yaroslav.

He didn't know exactly. 'Rosenberg borrowed a lot of money from the bank in Switzerland to build the factory and he could not pay it back. He lost everything. He had to sell the place to Nicholas Mavrocodat sometime in the early 1930s.'

What happened to him? Yaroslav did not know. He proudly laid out more and more pictures of coats of arms and Ottoman carvings but now there was only the weakest of evening light coming in from the window with which to summon up the past.

I suggested we leave, as I wanted to look around the village. Zinni said she knew of a man who might be old enough to have worked in Rosenberg's factory.

We were outside again, and we paused to look at trees. Rosenberg loved to plant trees, said Yaroslav, and I showed him a photograph of Vera and her Aunt May standing next to a new sapling in front of the house. As we left, the mathematics teacher raised his glass to Rosenberg up on the balcony. 'Would you care for a schnapps?' he said with a laugh.

By now I was nervous about the time. Ion would be waiting back at the border and I was told there was no way to call him except from the post office, which would just have closed, but when we arrived there a woman in long skirts and a sheepskin hat agreed to open up. She asked what number I wanted and wrote it down. Then she tore the paper off at the serrated edge, put a carbon copy on a spike, dialled a number and listened into a heavy brown earpiece.

'Moment. Moment,' she said. '*Niet, niet*.' Then, 'Moment,' and she held a finger up to me and fixed me with a look that said be patient. She was quite young and pretty.

'Now,' she suddenly said in English. 'Where is it? In England?'

'No,' I said. 'It is a mobile telephone number and the person is just across the border at Siret.'

'*Niet, niet*,' she tutted again. Not possible. But she was thinking. 'Not possible from Krasno'illshi.' But then, 'Moment, moment,' and she suggested that perhaps the connection could be made via Kiev. So she held up a finger again and dialled, seconds later talking to Kiev very fast. Kiev seemed to agree it was possible and she suggested I speak to Kiev myself. I took the earpiece. Kiev sounded a long way away and there was a ringing noise on the line. I said to Kiev that I wanted to ring a mobile phone, which was 20 kilometres from where I was standing. 'Moment, moment,' said Kiev and I

heard a long, modulating, whirring sound and then, after an inter-
minable wait, I heard a faint, familiar, gravelly French voice. It was
Ion. He would wait, he said.

We piled back in the Trabant and drove down past Max's timber
mill, its arching and bowing limbs now silhouetted against the setting sun. We left the main street, branched off up a hill and
immediately began skidding in mud and slush, the steering wheel
spinning in Constantin's hands. The houses were getting smaller
and smaller and soon were little more than shacks. We got out into
ankle-deep mud and dirty snow reddened by the sunset, and
trudged along a track in single file behind Zinni. She stopped outside a shed-like building on stilts. A pair of stiff leather boots,
encased in mud, stood neatly beside the door.

Zinni knocked. As if he had been waiting for us, the old man
came to the door, stepped forward, turned to look down at us,
nodded and listened to Zinni, who explained our purpose. He was in
stockinged feet, standing next to his boots, wearing woollen trousers
and a thick brown leather belt with lots of hooks and straps for tools,
fastened over a woollen jacket also held together across his chest by
a large safety pin. His face was scored deep like bark. His name was
Petrov Tadaodyk and he was born in 1917.

As Zinni explained why we had come, the old man's expression
did not change, but when she mentioned the name Rosenberg he
suddenly began talking. Zinni became so interested in what he was
saying, she forgot to translate for me. I had to remind her I didn't
want to miss a word.

Of course he remembered Rosenberg. He worked for him. The
factory was built by Rosenberg, he said, and Petrov pointed towards
the mill, which was now pumping out smoke down the valley. He
started working there in 1930 when he was thirteen years old. He
had to learn his trade, of course, and it was hard. His job was to cut
the wood to length and shave it down. The wood was exported by
train to Leningrad and also to England. They made panels that
measured 2.3 metres by 90 centimetres, and he held out his fingers
to show the width.

What did he remember of Rosenberg?

'He was rich – an important man. He was a good employer. Good
to his workers. The salary was paid once a month but you could get
an advance if you ran short.'

They made the very best wood in Bukovina. Everyone was proud to work there, he said.

Did he remember the Rosenberg family at all? Did he remember a young woman perhaps?

'No, no', he said. The workers had nothing to do with the family. Rosenberg didn't mix with people in the town. They had a car. There were big parties at the house. Grand people came and went.

Did he remember a Prince Wittgenstein, by any chance?

'Wittgenstein?' he said, looking at me as if I had mentioned a ghost. 'Yes, of course. He was my boss. Yes, he was a Russian prince. He managed the estate and the factory. He had a house right in the town, where the senior school is now. But he had a big house in Czernovitz too.'

I asked Mr Tadaodyk when Rosenberg left, and he could not recall exactly but did remember the 'bad time'. Rosenberg went bankrupt. Everyone knew about it. We worried for our jobs, he told me, but then the factory was sold.

Were there many Jews living here in Crasna at that time?

Yes, he said, there were many.

Did he think Rosenberg was a Jew?

'Rosenberg? A Jew? He was a German or Austrian, was he not? He was a boyar.' No. Rosenberg didn't have anything to do with the Jews in the town. The Jews were the merchants, the shopkeepers – not the boyars. And he started to list some of the Jewish names of those who had lived here: Goldstein, Zonestine, Himner, Moses and so on. And then he pointed to a house across the street and started talking faster and gesticulating.

Zinni had again stopped translating and was simply saying, 'Oh', her face expressing disbelief and dismay. Something shocking from the past was spilling out here in the dusk and Zinni thought I should not know about it.

'What is he saying?' I asked.

'Oh, just bad things.'

I told her I wanted to hear exactly what he was saying.

'He said the fascists took all the Jews of Crasna away. They killed them in the town nearby.' Then she looked at the mathematics teacher as if she was concerned that she should not be saying what she was saying.

Petrov Tadaodyk went on. 'They took them to Ciudin, where

there was a prison. And all the ones that were put in prison were shot. And then they dug a great big hole and threw the bodies in.'

He paused a minute and we all shifted in the mud, watching him. Zinni looked quite horrified by what she was hearing. He started talking again and he pointed down the road, raising his voice a little, then swinging around at the hips as if he were shooting a gun. Zinni was once again transfixed and forgot to translate.

'What did he say?'

'He is talking of a family he knew. The Besnar family. They were Jews. The mother was a widow and there were two sons. They owned a shop. They lived just over there,' said Zinni, pointing down the road.

'He says he remembers that one day the fascists came for them and shouted and ordered them into a truck. One of the boys refused to get in. He was shot right there, where he was standing.' We all looked down the street to the spot where we imagined the boy was shot.

Then the old man said: 'Besnar. Eti Besnar.' We learned that Eti Besnar was the mother's name and that she had a grocery store. 'They were all thrown in a hole in the middle of the night.'

It was the Germans, of course, Zinni said to me, but Mr Tadaodyk heard what she said and understood, interrupting and wagging a finger: 'No, no. It was the Romanian fascists,' he said. Then they discussed how, when Romania entered the war on the Nazi side in 1941, Romanian fascists poured into northern Bukovina and Bessarabia to join the German advance on Russia, butchering as many as thirty-three thousand Jews on the way. More than 150,000 Romanian Jews, living in areas such as northern Bukovina, which had been annexed by the Soviet Union just a year before, were then deemed to have been 'Bolshevised' and were transported to labour and extermination camps. This, however, was years after Rosenberg and his family had gone. They had left Crasna well before the war.

We were leaving now as it was almost dark. Everyone was quite sombre. Zinni pleaded with me to stay a little longer and meet the schoolchildren. I took her details and promised to write.

It was quite black by the time we reached Ciudin – too black to look for graves. After a long time white floodlights appeared and frying-pan faces were soon staring at my papers again. A young

Romanian guard looked up from under his cap and smiled cheekily.
'*De Anglia?*'

'Yes,' I said.

'Busy as a bee, busy as a bee,' he said.

I asked: 'You speak English?'

He grinned again. 'Busy as a bee, busy as a bee.'

I was back. Ion was hunched up in the Merc waiting for me. Over
eggs and bread in the warm café we wondered if Petrov Tadaodyk
was the only witness to Eti Besnar's death. Had the story of what
happened to Eti and her boys ever been told before?

When I tried to phone Zinni the next day to thank her, I could not
get through. When I wrote I got no answer. I have still not had an
answer.

12

A MOUNTAIN PICNIC

Ion turned the car south and Crasna sank back into obscurity. Striking into the heart of the high mountains, along the valley of the River Trotus, we were closing in on the border with Transylvania, looking for the place where, one weekend in May 1932, Vera had come for a Whitsun gathering. I had with me the photograph of the gathering – the one I had shown to Vera's Romanian friend Annie Samuelli, picturing Vera, Annie and others on horseback. I now also knew from Uncle Siegfried's memoir that the place I was looking for was called Vallea Uzului.

Vallea Uzului was where Vera's uncles Siegfried and Arthur had made their home in the 1920s and built a thriving timber mill. In the early 1930s it became Vera's second home. Every Whitsun weekend the brothers held an extravagant picnic to mark a spring festival. The guests were lavishly entertained: they stalked deer, hunted wild boar, fished in the trout streams and ate and drank. The weekend was also an opportunity for Vera's uncles to entertain important contacts.

On the guest list for the picnic in 1932 were several influential names, including the German ambassador to Bucharest, Count Friedrich Werner von der Schulenburg. Vera did not want to miss the weekend, not least because the German ambassador had been paying her much attention of late. What Vera could not have known as she rushed to catch the train north from Bucharest was that this Whitsun picnic was going to be the last of its kind. A year later

Hitler's accession to power was to unsettle even those living in this remote corner of the Carpathians. Vera's personal life was already undergoing dramatic change.

Sometime in 1932 Max Rosenberg again went bankrupt and was forced to sell Crasna. The world financial crash must have precipitated his plight, but his brothers had not been so badly affected and there was a certain mystery about Max's latest bankruptcy. Perhaps he simply ran up higher debts than his brothers, possibly by taking more risks.

At the same time, Max had fallen seriously ill and by early 1932 he had no money to pay for care in any of Vienna's famously lavish sanatoria. Instead he was consigned to the shabby Purkersdorf Sanatorium in the Vienna Woods, where, as I finally established after months of further research, he died on 3 October that year.

Like his bankruptcy, Max's final illness was something of a mystery to everyone. No doubt brought on in part by his financial worries, his illness and death became a taboo subject and his family rarely spoke about him again. Only in later years would Vera sometimes fondly recall her father's loving kindness – for example, the present he gave her on her twenty-first birthday: that luxury trip on a steamship to Alexandria.

A schoolgirl named Ann Rogers, the daughter of an oil manager in Bucharest, caught a glimpse of the dying Max when she visited the Rosenberg family in an apartment in Vienna in 1932, on her way back to school in England. 'I saw Vera's father lying on a bed of some sort, quite covered up in bandages. He was wrapped from head to toe, all white. I could only see his face.' According to the Purkersdorf Sanatorium records, Max suffered arteriosclerosis and died of a pulmonary embolism. There was nothing shameful in such a death. Yet the records showed that not one member of his family ever visited him there. Perhaps Max's death was taken as the moment to bury and obliterate their German-Jewish roots for good. His father gone, Wilfred for one, hastily changed his name by deed poll from Wilfred Rosenberg to Guy Atkins, acquiring his British naturalisation just one year later, in 1933. Yet the taboo about Max's death and bankruptcy still seemed unexplained.

What was clear, however, was that with Max's death the dreams the family had begun to see realised at Crasna were now shattered. Any prospect Vera had of marrying a man like Prince Wittgenstein –

had she ever wished to – fell away. Harsher realities now suddenly had to be faced.

The family were not left destitute. Vera's mother, Hilda, always had her own money, provided by her wealthy father, Henry Atkins, in South Africa. Money was still available in 1931 to send Vera to London for a shorthand–typing course at the fashionable Triangle Secretarial College (where she learned to type to 'Tiptoe through the Tulips') and, the following year, to send Guy to Oxford.

Nevertheless, on returning to Romania from her training in London, Vera immediately looked for work, finding a post as a sec-retary with the Polish representative of a small American-owned oil company, Vacuum Oil. And by the early 1930s she and her mother were living modestly in an apartment in Bucharest.

The young woman who was heading to the Whitsun picnic in Vallea Uzului in 1932 was therefore very different from the girl in the debu-tante pictures at Crasna. Although still only twenty-three, Vera had turned herself almost overnight into a self-reliant working woman who would endeavour never to depend on another's money or patronage again – a trait which was remarked upon throughout her later life. 'There was something strange about Vera,' a South African cousin, Barbara Horak, recalled. 'She never wanted anything that she had not chosen herself. She once told me she had sixteen ball gowns in her wardrobe and she never wore them because each was chosen by her mother. I think she reacted against this.'

Vera was enjoying her new-found independence. In Bucharest she was no longer chaperoned around, but chose her own networks of friends. And for their part, Vera's uncles considered their niece quite mature enough to play the lady of the house in Vallea Uzului (Arthur's wife was seriously ill and Siegfried was unmarried), where she could not only choose the menu but also ski, fish, ride and, no doubt, stalk deer alongside the men.

Vera, however, nearly didn't make it to the picnic that Whitsun weekend, as Annie Samuelli had told me. Vera had invited Annie, also by then a working girl, to join her for the weekend and the two had arranged to leave their offices early and meet at Bucharest sta-tion in time for the last train north. 'We were to leave late on Friday morning and to meet on the platform. I was ten minutes late. Vera didn't lose her temper often, though she could often be extremely cutting. But on this occasion she was in a rage. As soon as she saw me she said, "Get your stumps moving or we'll miss the train." But I was too slow and we missed it.'

The last connecting train had left without them. Not to be thwarted, Vera marched off with Annie to the office of Bill Rogers, manager of Steaua Romana, the father of her friend Ann, and, using her already considerable powers of persuasion, managed to secure from him a car and driver which she ordered to catch up with the train before Darmanesti, where a tiny valley train was to carry the party up a single-gauge railway to the house.

As Ion stopped the car outside Darmanesti station it was easy to see how, if they had not caught that valley train, Vera and Annie would have been in trouble. For the two of us there was no way at all of getting further. The Rosenbergs' rail track had long since disintegrated. A tarmac road running through the valley had been built by foresters some years earlier but we were told that potholes now made it impassable. Ion did not want to risk the Merc, especially as locals said they knew nothing of a house or a timber mill up at the end of the valley. When I took my photograph out to show them, they just shook their heads unhelpfully. Then a teenage boy came out of a house and said he climbed on old ruins further up the valley. Ion looked interested.

Somehow the bigger potholes were easier to get across than the smaller ones: the Merc just tipped its nose down into them as if descending a moon crater and then climbed out of the other side. With the stream of the Uzu running below us, the forest gradually thickened into anaemic greys and browns. In the spring, when Annie and Vera came here, the valley would have been bursting into colour.

We passed a little shrine to the Virgin Mary and then the valley opened out wide, its slopes still forested. Arthur and Siegfried must have celebrated on finding this valley and within a short time they had brought workers here, built a house and timber mill and established an entirely self-sufficient community, connected to the world beyond by the railway.

The Rosenbergs' home in Vallea Uzului was not a château like Crasna but a luxurious mountain chalet with pitched roofs and verandas on every floor, rooms for countless visitors, a large and diverse library, paintings, tapestries, linen imported from Antwerp and a large wine cellar. The house was run by a housekeeper, usually brought in from a high-class German household, and staffed mostly by local girls who also served the sexual appetites of the 'wicked uncles', as they were known in the family, as well as their three sons, Hans, George and Fritz. The sexual promiscuity of Rosenberg men was legendary, as I had heard from several people, among them Annie Samuelli. 'That first night Vera came to my bedroom and said: "Lock the door, because, you know, Fritz is a man who likes girls and he will certainly make a pass at you." And afterwards I realised that Fritz was making love to Karen, who was the housekeeper.'

We drove on until Ion stopped, climbed down and signalled to me to come and look. Below the road were four large, man-made caves, built, he said, as charcoal-burning ovens. Above them was an inscription: 'S 1932 R', which obviously stood for Siegfried Rosenberg 1932. So, as late as 1932, the brothers were not only hosting parties but also investing in the future.

Of course, Arthur and Siegfried knew as well as anyone that fascism was now inexorably on the rise across mainland Europe. The family had relatives in Hanover and Berlin who were already starting to consider leaving Germany should Hitler come to power. Closer to home, in Romania, the popularity of the fascists was spreading. Corneliu Codreanu, leader of Iasi's League of Christian National Defence, had recently formed the Legion of the Archangel St Michael, popularly known as the Iron Guard.

Even so, the brothers saw no reason to believe their own lives would be affected. Arthur had by now been baptised a Catholic, taking Franciscus as a middle name. All his sons were similarly baptised and none was circumcised. Their security, they believed, was assured by excellent political and diplomatic contacts in Berlin and other capitals of central Europe.

Ironically, so elevated were the Rosenbergs' connections thought to be that in Vallea Uzului in the late 1930s their workers believed that Arthur and Siegfried were related to the influential Nazi ideologist Alfred Rosenberg.

In a crisis the brothers knew that they could depend on friends like their guest this weekend, Count Friedrich Werner von der Schulenburg, a German diplomat of considerable stature to whom National Socialism was personally abhorrent.

But the purpose of the gathering was not to discuss politics but to fish, hunt and eat. And the young women were also expected to play a part in a spring ritual: the sacrifice of the lambs.

Annie Samuelli had described to me what happened in tones of horror. She and Vera and the other women had spent the morning fishing for trout in the streams, while the men went off hunting boar in the woods. Afterwards they all rode back up through the woods on their mountain ponies for a meal laid out on tables with white tablecloths under large awnings.

Before the meal, however, the young women were taken to an enclosure to look at the newest lambs. 'They asked us each to choose one. We didn't know why we were choosing them and didn't ask, I remember, and we chose the ones we thought the cutest. We were enjoying ourselves. It was a lovely spring day. Then we rode back slowly down the hill but about halfway down the field to the house we heard the most terrible piercing screaming. It went on and on and on. It wouldn't stop and was the most awful sound I have ever heard. Vera was horrified too. She said: "Come on, let's go." It was as if the screams echoed through the whole mountains. We learned later, of course, what it was. They were carrying out a ritual slaughter of the lambs. I have never ever forgotten that noise,' said Annie, trembling now in her Paris flat at the memory. She told me she had heard a similar ritual was performed in Morocco.

'What was it exactly?' I asked.

'Let's not talk about it. It's too horrible.'

She said that it was after that, before they sat down to eat, that the photograph was taken, somewhere near the house.

Annie had then helped me identify the picnickers in the picture. There was Mr Pow, an elderly man, manager of the Bank of Romania, and next to him was his deputy, an Englishman named Charles Robinson, who later became commercial attaché at the British legation and was 'in intelligence'. Mrs Pow was there and next to her was Arthur Rosenberg – fair, unlike his brothers – whose pony was pulling at the reins, and then came Count Friedrich Werner von der Schulenburg, balding, with closely cropped hair and a moustache, looking distinguished, with a large overcoat spread over the rump of his horse. And here was Vera in tweed riding jacket, holding her mount steady, and a tall, good-looking boy whom at first Annie did not recognise. Then she identified him as one of Arthur's twin sons. Arthur had three boys: twins, George and

Hans, and then Fritz. George and Hans were identical, she said. The next young man, small and dark, was Fritz. Annie was beside him, looking pert and nervous at the end of the line.

I said that the ambassador looked a little old for Vera and Charles Robinson looked more eligible, but Annie told me I was quite wrong. Schulenburg had far greater stature than Robinson, who was just a deputy in a bank. Vera was much more interested in the ambassador, who was unattached. Schulenburg had divorced years earlier after a brief marriage, and often sought out attractive women to act as hostess at his embassy functions. After noticing Vera's impeccable manners and grace, he requested that she take this role, which she had agreed to do at lunches but not at dinner, as she felt this would be compromising.

In any case, said Annie, Schulenburg was attractive to women not so much for his appearance as for his kind nature and attentiveness. 'He was a charming man. Not patronising. He listened and was highly intelligent. He respected Vera and vice versa. I think there was a mutual attraction.'

The ambassador was evidently a marvellous escort for Vera. At the very least, being taken around Bucharest in the German ambassador's chauffeur-driven car (as long as the swastika was not flying) must have been something of a thrill for a young shorthand secretary. And for a young woman keen to build new networks, as Vera was, Schulenburg also offered an immediate entrée to the highest level of Romania's diplomatic society. Anyone regularly invited to the German embassy was in demand by diplomats all over town, each of them eager to find out what the Führer was up to in Berlin.

If Vera had felt deeply for Schulenburg, however, why did she not accompany him to Moscow when he left Bucharest? Vera confided in her friend Barbara Worcester, many decades later, that he had invited her to go with him to Moscow when he was appointed ambassador there in 1934. Perhaps Vera sensed that Schulenburg would only ever want an elegant and intelligent 'hostess' at his beck and call. But then she also told Barbara that it was the greatest regret of her life that she did not go.

It was not clear to Vera or anyone else at the time the photograph was taken just how closely the fate of the Rosenbergs pictured in it would be linked to Count von der Schulenburg just a few years later. As Germany's ambassador to Moscow, Schulenburg was much acclaimed for drafting the 1939 agreement between Moscow and Berlin known as the Molotov–Ribbentrop pact. It was this agreement which began the dismemberment of Romania and led to the disastrous transfer of northern Transylvania to Hungary in 1940 and the consequent expulsion of the Rosenbergs from this very piece of land. Still German ambassador in Moscow in 1940, Schulenburg would try to help his former hosts in Vallea Uzului, who, after expulsion, faced the prospect of deportation to concentration camps.

As the war progressed, Schulenburg grew more and more dismayed by the Nazi aggression that he was being asked to help enact. He was particularly shocked by the invasion of Poland – a country he loved – and horrified by the slaughter of the Jews. By the summer of 1944 he had joined the conspiracy to kill Hitler with his cousin, Hans Dietloff von der Schulenburg, and he was one of two men who might have become Foreign Minister had the plot succeeded. On 20 July 1944 the coup failed spectacularly and Schulenburg, along with many others, was hanged.

Annie continued looking at the picture. She thought the Rosenberg twin she could not identify was probably George. Hans, she now recalled, had suffered from a mental illness or breakdown of some kind and might already have been in hospital or an asylum. She believed the breakdown happened while he was a student in Munich. He never fully recovered. She was not sure what became of him, but she had heard a suggestion that he might have been gassed during the Nazis' programme of euthanasia killings.

I said I had not heard Hans's story before. None of the family had ever mentioned it. It was not surprising, said Annie. 'Mental illness was something to hide. And for the Rosenbergs to be Jewish was a matter of shame. Hans would have been seen as a double shame. The Rosenbergs wanted nobody to know that they had mental illness in the family or that they were Jewish, so they would want nobody to know that they had relatives who died in the Holocaust.'

Along the valley floor Ion and I were looking up and still trying to identify the site of the photograph when a woman in bright scarves appeared from one of the two tumbledown cottages there and said excitedly that we should talk to her mother. She pointed to a shack and we walked towards it across a field, scattering a flock of early lambs. The roof of the little one-room building appeared to have half slipped off; it was held in place by a few plants.

We peered in the door and there a thin little lady, very old, was sitting all alone, in her neatly ironed apron. She turned and smiled. It was as if history had thoughtfully left her behind to talk to us. The scrubbed house had nothing in it except a wooden bench, which was also the bed, a bucket, a small table and a warm wood-burning stove with an iron sitting on it. One saucepan hung from a nail in the wall. The woman was wearing very thick glasses. Her name was Maria Novac and she was ninety-two, she told us. I noticed a different dialect and Ion explained that she was speaking a variant of Hungarian. He talked to her gently and learned that she had been born in the valley. Her husband worked as the cobbler when the Rosenbergs ran the factory. What did she remember of the family?

'Arthur and Siegfried,' she said immediately. 'I remember their names.'

Did she remember what they looked like at all?

'No. Except that Arthur had red hair.' All the village was made by the Rosenbergs, she said. There were about three hundred people living here, she added proudly.

Did she remember the spring festival?

Yes, she did, and many people came in those times. She took us out to the front door to point to where the big house was, just up the hill a little. 'It was all destroyed in the war so nobody could come back,' she said.

'Where had everyone gone?'

She didn't know where the Rosenbergs went, but the villagers all fled over the mountains when the area was given back to Hungary. Gradually one or two came back. She had returned with her husband.

'Why did you come back?' I asked.

'It was my home.'

We wandered back to the site of the house and found the foundations and the remains of what had been a wine cellar, but there was nothing more.

Driving back, I read a passage of Siegfried's diary to Ion. He was describing what happened at another dinner held here the following year, when other important guests, mostly Germans, were being entertained:

> One evening in 1933 we had many guests for dinner, including lots of Germans, and we heard the Reichstag was on fire. Goebbels said they had already found out who lit the fire, but I said in my opinion it could only have been started by the Nazis themselves, as it would be crazy for the socialists to do such a thing. Especially now that the Nazis were so powerful, it would have been suicide for socialists to have started the fire.
>
> So all the Germans left the house, and my brother said it was my fault as I should not mention these opinions of mine. During this debate my nephew, my brother's son, Fritz, said you are absolutely right, you can't have any other opinion when you hear what Goebbels says.

13

SPY GENTS

A young British diplomat arriving in Bucharest in 1934 wrote home to his parents about his trip to Romania:

> My journey was on the whole comfortable except that as we
> jolted through the continent the food got worse and worse
> reaching its nadir at dinnertime in Poland. My impression of
> Poland was deplorable, it rained solidly all through Germany
> and Poland and the Silesian district is like County Durham at
> its worst. The train was filled, corridors and all, with the most
> incredible Polish Jews about 4 feet high with immense black
> beards and greasy curls, who gibbered like monkeys and
> stank like badgers.

Romania was a refreshing change, he said.

John Coulson had left Cambridge with a double first just eighteen months before being catapulted from Whitehall to the edge of the Orient. Once he arrived in Bucharest, he was entranced by the European mêlée he found there: quasi-royals, diplomats, business-men, journalists, hangers-on and spies.

'On Tuesday night there was a dinner at the legation where I met a nice girl with the ghastly name of Vera Rosenberg,' wrote Coulson a few days after arriving. And in a letter a few weeks later he told his parents:

> People I meet a lot here, and who I have not I think described,
> are two sisters Mrs Mendl and Mrs Rosenberg, both of whom
> (as is obvious) have married Jews. They are fair themselves –
> about 45 I suppose – and I simply cannot tell whether they are

Jewesses or not. On the one hand they look so essentially
Aryan; on the other, it seems strange that both should marry
Jews. Mrs Rosenberg is a widow, and has one daughter, who,
strangely enough, is also fair, but obviously a Jewess. All these
women have attractive – extremely attractive – voices.

I had found it puzzling why Vera stayed on in Bucharest after her
father's death. Having completed her secretarial course in London in
1931, she could easily have found work in London and sought
British citizenship, like her brother Guy; yet she returned to
Romania for six more years.

John Coulson's letters home gave one possible answer. Vera was
enjoying herself in Bucharest and for some time she flitted gaily in and
out of Coulson's prose. A curious replacement for Count Schulenburg,
this gauche young diplomat became Vera's new escort about town. She
in turn became Coulson's guide as he muddled through streets
smelling of raw sheepskin and full of jostling hawkers to reach the
seductive ambience of the Capsa or the Melody Bar. 'I met 50 people
last night, and haven't been to bed before 4am for days,' he wrote to
his parents and, a little later in the same letter: 'On Wednesday I
dined with the Rosenbergs and played bridge until a late hour.'
If Coulson was not accompanying his minister to the Danube 'to
watch him miss some duck and to drift about in his new motor boat
all over the Delta', he was rushing to bridge or golf or tennis at the
Bucharest Country Club, where Vera Rosenberg was to be found, or to
a lecture on 'An Englishman's View of the World' at the Anglo-
Romanian Society, where Vera and her mother might be, although
Vera was just as likely to be found at the bar of the Athenée Palace.

Vera's detachment from political change as these years passed
seemed unreal. In 1935 her own relatives in Germany became subject to the anti-Semitic Nuremberg Laws, whereby German
citizenship could belong only to a 'national of German or kindred
blood'. Vera's uncles Arthur and Siegfried, still in Romania, could no
longer export to their own company in Cologne. Vera could perhaps
ignore the daily jibes that a 'Jewess' attracted even in polite society.
But as time went by it could not have been easy to ignore mass
demonstrations in Bucharest in support of the Iron Guard. Vera
could see for herself the desperate wish of other Jews to flee each
time she visited the Black Sea port of Constanza, from where many

were already leaving for Palestine, among them Vera's own friends and relatives. 'Vera and I to Constanza, saw M off to Palestine,' noted her mother in a pocket diary on one such occasion.

Yet in Vera's privileged circle the threat still seemed distant. Far from feeling afraid about her future, the Vera Rosenberg Coulson encountered was at ease in this bustling, cosmopolitan world of pre-war Bucharest. She had her influential patrons, such as Bill Rogers, the doyen of the expatriate community here. The long-time manager of Steaua Romana in Bucharest, 'Uncle Bill' was an admirer of Vera's. His daughter Ann Eagle, who knew Vera at this time, said: 'Daddy was one of the only people who could tease Vera and say: "How are your co-religionists?" Mummy was not so sure. People used to ask her why she had so much to do with those awful Jews. And when Daddy let them send their furniture back to England in one of his tankers, Mummy was furious.'

Searching for more of Vera in Coulson's letters, I noticed that her name had suddenly vanished. But, flicking through Hilda's pocket diaries, I saw that the moment Vera disappeared from his world he started appearing in hers. In his letters home Coulson was now disguising Vera's presence in his life, but the initials 'J.C.' appeared frequently in Hilda's diaries: 'Vera to dinner J.C.'; 'Vera to club with J.C.'. Hilda noted down her own appointments with sad monotony: 'Morning massage; tea Gladys; evening film.' If she did anything of interest it was with Vera: 'Vera to supper. Very nice.' Occasionally others, including Siegfried and Arthur, popped into Hilda's life, and Hilda reported: 'Wilfred [Guy] leaves Oxford' and 'Ralph leaves for Istanbul via Sophia.' But more regularly came entries such as: 'Vera for drive with J.C.' and 'Vera to concert with J.C.'.

If I wanted more detail of Vera's outings I could check by referring to Coulson's letters to his parents. For example, after the concert he had written to them to say that he had enjoyed a performance by the director of the Berlin Opera. Hilda wrote on another day: 'Vera to ball at Athenée Palace' and Coulson told his parents, without mentioning Vera's name, that 'there were five hundred for dinner and we danced till four in the morning'. He added that there had been 15–20 degrees of frost as the Crivat wind was blowing down from the Russian steppes.

When Vera went away Hilda's life was empty. 'Supper alone', 'film alone', she wrote. Then, for days on end, it could be: 'Vera away.' Where was she? For Hilda it was: 'Morning massage. Afternoon film alone, *Scarlet Pimpernel*. Tea at Samuellis'.' Then, 'V returned with J.C.'

In counterpoint, Coulson's letters and Hilda's diaries provided some of the texture of Vera's life. They also contained names of all the many friends and contacts who now peopled Vera's busy world. Reading on, I became familiar with those names – Kendrick, Boxshall, Gibson, Humphreys, Chidson – and began to recognise individuals from Vera's later papers and even from official files. They were businessmen, diplomats or journalists and many of them were also spies. My material showed that Vera met them all at dinners, dances or on skiing trips. A regular contact was the commercial attaché in Bucharest and also an MI6 man, Leslie Humphreys. Humphreys was referred to by Coulson as 'the Hump' and 'a bit grim'. One of his colleagues described him to me: 'A funny chap. A homosexual. You wouldn't recognise him from one day to another. No extrovert character at all.'

'The Hump' seemed an unlikely companion for Vera, but she was evidently at ease with such shadowy figures and they enjoyed her charms. Montague 'Monty' Chidson, another MI6 man in Bucharest, was another fervent admirer of Vera's and in later years he related how he had once proposed to her in a Bucharest bar in the small hours.

The 'spy gents', as they were known, certainly enjoyed the revelry of Bucharest as much as anyone, as was evident from several photographs, including one I had acquired which showed Leslie Humphreys, his sister Dot, Montague Chidson, John Coulson, Vera and other revellers on a stage at the Targul Mosilor, a market in Bucharest, with a famous puppet theatre.

But there was good reason to suppose that Vera's contacts with the intelligence world were already more than social, and they may even have been the most important reason she chose to stay on in Romania in the 1930s. In 1934, now aged twenty-six, she acquired a more responsible job, as a 'foreign correspondent' with the Pallas Oil Company, which involved working as an interpreter and intermediary dealing with foreign clients. The job gave Vera access to useful information about the oil industry and required her to travel widely, so that she was now in a good position to pass on titbits to a man like Humphreys. At the time Humphreys's task was to provide the

Department of Trade in London with intelligence reports on German economic policy throughout the region, and of paramount interest was Germany's policy towards Romania's large oil reserves. Vera's access to the German embassy of Count Schulenburg certainly would not have gone unnoticed by the British intelligence community in Bucharest or anyone else who had interests in the region.

And providing intelligence to the British was already a Rosenberg and Atkins family tradition: names listed among Vera's referees on her Home Office naturalisation papers revealed as much. She had four referees, all contacts she had made in Romania. The first two names were familiar to me: Arthur Coverley-Price had been a diplomat in the legation in Bucharest in the early 1930s and George Swire de Moleyns Rogers was Bill Rogers. The third and fourth referees were at first more difficult to place. There was a Lieutenant-Colonel Thomas Joseph Kendrick, who said on his testimonial that he had known Vera and both her parents (until her father's death) for fifteen years, but he gave no indication of how or where.

The fourth was a Major Reginald George Pearson, who stated he had known Vera for twenty-two years. 'I have known Miss Vera Atkins since she was a little girl and have no hesitation in stating that she is in every way suitable for naturalisation. She is British to the core as are and were also her parents and grandparents – all of whom I knew well for many years in South Africa and here.'

Both Kendrick and Pearson turned out to have been spies. Reginald Pearson had indeed known Vera's grandparents in South Africa in the early years of the century and it seemed highly likely that this contact came about through intelligence circles. From the earliest days of the Boer War, British intelligence officers were building up wide networks of informers in South Africa, and even the famous Claude Dansey, later deputy head of MI6, cut his teeth as a spy in Africa in the early part of the century. Henry Atkins, a staunch British patriot, one-time owner of the Lace Diamond Mine and a powerful figure in the Cape, would have been a useful person for any British intelligence officer to know.

Perhaps Vera's father also made himself useful to British intelligence during his period in South Africa. Max Rosenberg was certainly a source for British spies once he established himself in Romania in the 1920s, where, coincidentally, Claude Dansey was operating, particularly in the Danube ports. Max was by then a German businessman of international standing and came to the attention of Thomas Kendrick, the second spy on Vera's list of referees. It was Kendrick who forged the strongest links with Max and his family.

Kendrick was MI6 station chief in Vienna in the 1920s and 1930s. Vera kept several cuttings about him in her papers, as well as photographs of him as a youngish man. In Vienna, Kendrick was in a pivotal position for gathering intelligence on the Nazis, who, during the time he was there, were developing the defunct Austrian secret service into a major branch of the Abwehr. Max Rosenberg had highly placed Austrian and German contacts, travelled widely, often taking Vera with him as interpreter, and so was exactly the kind of contact Kendrick needed. Furthermore, Vera's elder brother, Ralph, was, by the late 1920s, based in Smyrna and then in Istanbul, where he was a manager for Steaua Romana. Ralph was also 'loosely connected' to the consulates in these two cities – code for an intelligence source.

In her later years, if ever pressed about her father's occupation in Romania, Vera liked to give the impression that he was involved in some sort of diplomatic work, and she sometimes said he was a member of the International Commission of the Danube, a powerful body which regulated shipping on the river. I could find no trace of Max Rosenberg's name on any Danube Commission lists, but any association he had with this body would have brought him to the attention of the spies. German policy towards the waterway was always carefully monitored, and such was the Danube's strategic value that in 1940 the British sent saboteurs on an abortive mission to blow up the Iron Gates, a narrow channel through which all river traffic passed.

In fact the Rosenbergs and their wide European networks offered British intelligence a fund of information between the wars. Vera's relatives the Mendls effectively ran the shipping on the Danube and themselves had long-standing intelligence ties. Sir Charles Mendl was knighted in the First World War for services to British intelligence and throughout the 1920s and 1930s was press attaché at the British embassy in Paris, another MI6 cover. Sir Charles had links to many other networks. He and his wife, the American actress Else de Wolfe, were famous for throwing lavish parties at their villa near Versailles, where Vera often dined when in Paris. Here Sir Charles gathered many a famous British spy around him – and quite a few infamous ones too. He briefed all young war correspondents who came to Paris and certainly knew Kim Philby. Vera's uncle also knew a young Reuters correspondent named Nicholas Bodington, who would later join SOE and work closely with Vera in F Section. Curiously, it was Sir Charles Mendl, in his role as press attaché, who in April 1940 had to negotiate the withdrawal of Bodington's accreditation as a war correspondent in France. The French considered the Reuters man to have '*un mauvais esprit*' and refused to work with him.

Whatever Vera's connections to these broader intelligence networks before the war, she was probably on MI6's books only as a 'local recruit' or 'stringer' and London may never have known her name. Nevertheless, providing freelance intelligence would have given Vera a useful extra income. 'Vera was the kind of person who knew about money, and she liked money and would not have passed up the chance of getting some more,' said Annie Samuelli, who also considered Vera ideally suited to a clandestine life. 'You knew if you told Vera something and said it was a secret it would be secret. It was always like that with Vera. And she was extremely resourceful – always. She knew how to fix things. I don't know how she knew but she did. She knew the right people. I think you are just born that way – you have a knowledge that you are right and what you are going to do is right. You know things before other people do.'

Sometime in 1937 Vera knew – probably before he did – that John Coulson was not going to marry her. That summer he wrote to his parents: 'It has been the most heavenly week you can possibly imagine. The temperature has been 70 almost every day and hearts are fairly sizzling with joy.' According to Ann Rogers (now Eagle), it was about this time that Coulson asked her father, Bill Rogers, whether he should marry Vera. 'Daddy thought that if Coulson was asking him the question he was obviously in two minds. Anyway it would have been quite impossible for a diplomat like Coulson at that time to have married a local Jew. I think there were rules about it.'

Annie Samuelli said: 'It may not have been like that. She may have rejected him – pre-empted him in a way. She may have feared that if she got too close she would have to admit to being a Jew. And then he would recoil. This might have been her greatest fear: that she would repel the person and that would spoil everything.'

It may not have been like that either. Mavis Coulson, John Coulson's widow, recalled her husband talking of Romania but understood that he and Vera were simply good friends. 'He certainly had a marvellous time there. It was his private world and I was not allowed into it, but I don't believe there was a romantic attachment – I don't think there was. But I must admit that when I met Vera after the war she always made me feel uneasy. I felt she wanted to be invited to our house as a special friend and I feel guilty that we never did.'

What Vera knew for sure in early 1937 was that it was time to leave for London. Even the most privileged Romanian Jews were now being ostracised. 'It came very suddenly,' said Annie Samuelli. 'Many of the young in our social circle suddenly joined up with the Iron Guard. Close friends of mine told me quite frankly they could not go on seeing me because I was a Jew. It was a horrible time. But I think it was even worse for Vera in some ways. Her family were cultured and wealthy German Jews who had been immune from anti-Semitism for so long. The ghettos were in Poland, not in Germany. So when the tables turned it was worse for them than for anyone else. They had not expected it.'

Mass demonstrations at the funerals of two members of the Iron Guard, killed fighting for Franco, had won new sympathisers for the movement throughout Romania and regulations against 'non pure-blooded Romanians' were being tightened. The left in Vienna was crushed and few now doubted that Hitler would march on Austria at any time. Fresh from completing his PhD in Prague, Guy had seen at the closest quarters Hitler's aggressive manoeuvring, and was pleading with his sister and mother to leave for England.

Even Coulson now seemed to be reporting some 'alarms and excursions', referring to the 'monster funerals' of the two Iron Guard members.

The first hint of a decision to leave Romania was barely noticeable from Hilda's diaries. On Friday 12 March 1937 she wrote: 'Spent morning sorting things. Afternoon people came to look over our furniture. Dinner with Rogers.' Life then continued: 'Vera dinner at John C' and 'Vera at country club.' And on 12 May Hilda notes: 'Coronation.'

Then, on 9 September, 'furniture man came with estimates' before, on Saturday 25 September, 'our furniture was taken away to be packed. We sorted some things and dined with Mrs Rogers.'

Sunday, noted Hilda, was a 'dreadful day sorting things'. So was Monday: 'Awful day packing. Vera went to look at packed furniture.'

On Friday 1 October: 'Our things left for Constanza docks.' Then, on Wednesday 20 October, Hilda and Vera left Bucharest for the last time. Hilda's words were: 'Vera hair washed. Mrs Rogers 7.30 at Station. Siegfried.'

The following day Hilda noted: 'Arrived in Vienna', where they were met by Rosenberg relatives, with whom they stayed. On Friday 22 October: 'We unpacked, Norah drove us to crematorium,' Hilda wrote of a visit to her husband's grave, and in the evening 'dined at Kendricks', a reference to the MI6 man. Vera and her mother stayed a week in Vienna and then, on Thursday 28 October, 'We packed and left Vienna at 3.15 for England.'

The following day they had, Hilda noted, a 'Wonderful crossing'. Then: 'Wilfred came to see us here'. She didn't say where 'here' was, but her diary notes for the following days suggested clearly that it was somewhere in London.

By Saturday morning Hilda's life appeared miraculously to be resuming a familiar pattern. There were even old friends from Bucharest to greet them. 'Morning went out, evening went for drinks with Humphreys,' she wrote. Then it was Guy's birthday and they 'went to show at Palladium then drink at Café Royal'. Within a week or so Hilda was writing once again: 'Massage morning, hair washed. Film. Alone.' Vera continued to come and go. It was as if they had transplanted their lives but nothing had really changed.

A young woman named Mary Williams, Guy's girlfriend at the time, recalled their arrival in England differently. 'It was as if they had just escaped from some very great danger,' said Mary, who had been taken by Guy to meet his mother and sister just after they disembarked. 'I remember it very well. They were in a single room in an apartment. It was dark and they were dressed in black. It was like a bedsitting room. The furniture was old and not theirs. And I think they had arrived with just their hand luggage.

'They talked about some terrible trouble they had had getting away. They had packed everything they could possibly carry into suitcases. Then they had been stopped on the platform by the police or some kind of patrol and people on the platform were being questioned. It was an awful moment when they thought they might not get away. They had been afraid of something, I sensed that. And they were terribly pleased to be here. I remember that Vera went out almost straight away and came back with a hat. It was a sort of pill-box hat with a veil and she put it on and said to us: "Very Mayfair, don't you think?" I didn't really know what "very Mayfair" was.'

At first it was hard to fill in the story of Vera's first three years of life in England. She had been obliged to give certain details herself for her Home Office naturalisation applications, but without the help I received from Mary Williams this period of Vera's life would have remained largely blank. The well-educated daughter of a northern mill owner, Mary had met Guy when she answered his advertisement for German lessons before the war. They became engaged and when Hilda arrived in England she viewed Mary as the perfect English daughter-in-law. But Mary later called off the engagement.

'Mrs Atkins was so anxious I should accept them and I could not understand why she was so anxious as they seemed perfectly acceptable,' she told me. 'She seemed to know everything about England and gave the impression that she had always lived here and that Romania had just been a temporary thing.'

'How did she give that impression?'

'Oh, by saying if I talked of places: "Oh, yes, we've been there" or: "We know that." She was very patriotic and I remember she said with great feeling when war broke out: "We must all do our little bit." They were all very Empire- and Commonwealth-minded, I thought. And Mrs Atkins was also very anxious that Vera should be accepted too.'

For Vera these were difficult times. Unlike her mother and her brothers, she had no claim to British citizenship. Guy had secured his British naturalisation in 1933, when times were easier, and Hilda, being British-born, regained British naturalisation automatically. Ralph had been born in colonial South Africa and so also had a right to naturalisation. But Vera, born in Romania, only had Romanian citizenship and one of her first acts on arriving in London was to go to Bow Street police station, where she was obliged to line up with scores of other refugees, to secure an Aliens Registration Certificate.

As war approached, her sense of insecurity intensified. In September 1939 several of the family's German friends who had come to England as refugees were interned, including a woman friend of Guy's who was locked up in Holloway Prison. Britain did not declare war on Romania until 7 December 1941, and so Romanian refugees were not strictly classed as enemy aliens until that time. But Vera knew her German roots could have brought her under suspicion.

'I remember one terrible occasion when somebody had arrived unexpectedly at the door and she was very frightened that her moment had come. "I thought it was my turn. I was off to Holloway," she told us later.' Even to trusted friends the whole family remained totally secretive about their background. 'Wilfred [Guy] once said that he didn't tell me about his family because he was afraid that he would lose my friendship,' said Mary.

How Vera passed her time during this period was difficult to know. She could not work, owing to restrictions on the employment of foreigners, and, according to Mary, the family had little money to spare. Vera spent as much time as she could with her mother's sister, Auntie May Mendl, who was now living at Winchelsea. May and Vera understood each other well and shared something of the same aura. An elegant, intelligent woman, only thirteen years older than Vera, May was perhaps as much an elder sister as an aunt, and was said to be the only person in the family who was able to put Vera in her place.

For a while Vera also lodged in Kensington with a divorcee who was a contact from Vienna. An acquaintance of the divorcee recalled that Vera and the woman used to 'play bridge all day'.

All this time, as Mary observed, Vera was adapting. The black clothes that she and her mother had arrived in were soon cast off and Vera acquired a brilliant cyclamen coat, while her mother took to wearing colourful floral silks. Vera liked to be invited to Mary's parties and was always 'most beautifully mannered', Mary told me. 'But she was not quite like us. And I remember feeling that she wanted to be liked, particularly by any young man who was there. She had absolutely no taste and attached herself to the most impossible characters. I recall one occasion when a surgeon captain – she liked high-ranking people – said he had to go and she said: "I must go too," so that he could give her a lift. We all knew he was a middle-aged playboy.'

Surprisingly, given her alien status, Vera was still willing to travel. And she cannot have been so very short of money, because her Home Office papers showed two trips to Switzerland; the first, for three weeks up to 10 January 1939, was for 'winter sports'. A companion on the trip, Mimi Rocke, recalled two things about Vera: she always skied with the men and she won the hotel's fancy-dress contest. Vera's skiing prowess was no surprise, for the young ladies of Le Manoir finishing school in Lausanne skied throughout the winter at St Moritz. 'What was her disguise for the fancy-dress contest?' I asked Mimi, knowing also that Vera had excelled at costume design at Le Manoir. 'Bluebeard,' came the reply. 'And she knitted the beard herself.'

Two months later Vera was in Switzerland again, this time, according to her Home Office papers, 'for thirty-nine days'. Given the turmoil in Europe by the spring of 1939, such a long trip abroad seemed surprising. In March came the German invasion of Czechoslovakia, which appeared to be the cause of a rare exclamation from Hilda. 'Goodness how sad,' she wrote in her diary on 11 March, just before the invasion; then: 'Vera rang from mountains.' She was evidently skiing again.

In fact, I already had photographs of Vera on this second trip to Switzerland. They were the pictures rescued from a bin by Christine Franklin, Vera's cleaner, and showed Vera in the mountains, blissfully happy with Dick Ketton-Cremer. At first it had been hard to tell when or where those photographs were taken. But, in one of the photos Christine had shown me, a second, unidentified man (who presumably had taken most of the pictures) was shading his face with a copy of *Life*. On the front cover was the actress Tallulah Bankhead, the magazine's cover girl in March 1939.

In the first half of 1939 Vera had evidently spent a great deal of time with Dick Ketton-Cremer. In July, just after Dick had joined up, she even took this eligible Norfolk aristocrat to meet her mother at Winchelsea. For Vera to bring a young man to meet her mother was obviously an event of some significance, as Mary Williams, who was also in Winchelsea at the time, with Guy, was able to observe. 'Vera's friend was an airman and was in uniform. He was tall and fair, I believe, and quite quiet. Vera was evidently anxious about introducing him to her mother, I remember. It was obvious that he was important or she would not have brought him down.

'It was a gorgeous weekend and we all went for blissful walks. We all stayed in the pub in Winchelsea and I also remember Wilfred [Guy] was very rude to Vera's friend at breakfast. He refused to acknowledge him in any way.'

Mary did not see Vera's airman again and Vera never spoke further of him. However, Mary did hear, quite coincidentally, after the war, that Vera had been engaged and that her fiancé had been killed. I asked how she heard. Did Vera tell her?

'Neither Vera nor anyone in the family spoke of it. I never saw an engagement ring. But I heard in an odd kind of way. I happened to know somebody who had worked with Vera during the war and Vera told her. I met this person later and she said to me: "Isn't it terrible about Vera's fiancé? She was engaged to an airman and he has been killed." I assumed it must have been the man she brought to Winchelsea. When I asked Wilfred if Vera had been engaged he said: "Rubbish! If she were I would have known about it." Far from ever expressing a wish that Vera should marry, I thought Wilfred was quite glad to have an unattached sister. There was a bond between Wilfred and Vera.'

Mary's recollections of Vera's 'engagement' to Dick were contradictory, just as all my other discoveries so far about this relationship had been. After Christine Franklin had first showed me photographs of the couple, and the letter from the RAF Standing Committee, which dealt with personal effects, notifying Vera that Dick was missing, I applied to see his RAF casualty file. Given that an RAF committee had informed Vera when he went missing, I presumed Dick had officially named her along with his next of kin as someone to be notified; this would certainly have proved the seriousness of the relationship. The casualty file, however, showed Dick had named only his brother Wyndham and his local vicar in Norfolk. There was no reference here to Vera. RAF experts, however, cautioned that this might not, after all, prove anything.

It was not uncommon, I was told, for servicemen anticipating death to conceal the identities of certain loved ones from the official files, perhaps fearing disapproval from family or friends. If discretion were needed, directions of a more private nature could be left by a serviceman or -woman in a letter with personal effects, asking for a person who was important to be privately notified should they die. Perhaps Dick, for reasons of his own, had been unwilling to make public his relationship with Vera, even in the event of his death.

I tried to find Dick's relatives to learn more. There were none to ask. Dick's brother, Wyndham, a noted scholar and the last 'squire' of Felbrigg Hall, the family home, died in 1968 and had never married. A friend and former neighbour of the Ketton-Cremers, Lady Wilhelmine Harrod, however, gave me some indication of why Dick's relationship with Vera might have had to be kept secret.

The Norfolk landed gentry, she suggested, were a particularly insular group and she implied that it would have been unusual for somebody outside the county – particularly a foreigner – to have married into such a family. Dick's brother and mother, Emily, also were wary of any claims on Dick's inheritance. It had been tacitly understood that Dick would inherit Felbrigg one day, as his elder brother would not produce an heir, owing to illness in his youth.

And there had been many women in Dick's life. 'He was good-looking and athletic – all the things his older brother wasn't,' said Lady Wilhelmine. 'Women were attracted to him.' Dick's mother doted on both her boys, but despaired of Dick's womanising and his constant travelling. If there had been any serious relationship between Dick and a woman he had met abroad, Emily Ketton-Cremer certainly would have disapproved. 'The mother would have been the problem in this case,' said Lady Wilhelmine. When I pressed her as to why, she considered for some moments and said: 'I just feel it instinctively to have been so.'

Then I visited Felbrigg Hall hoping to find more clues there. Now owned by the National Trust, the house lies 2 miles inland from Cromer, on the north Norfolk coast, its imposing mullioned façade looking out over rich, wooded parkland. On the wet December day when I visited, the house was closed, but two volunteer guides, Joan Chapman and Mari Chalk, had offered to show me around. Everywhere were large, bulging shapes under white dustsheets.

From a drawer in the west corridor, Mari pulled Dick's old firearms certificate, dance cards and other records of his social life. Here also were his flying goggles, found in a desk in the cabinet room, off another corridor, and a membership card of the Norfolk and Norwich Aeronautical Club. Joan found postcards Dick had sent to his mother when he was skiing, and I looked carefully at these. They were postmarked 1939 but there was no clue as to whom he was with.

We entered the morning room, which was completely dark.

Electricity was not allowed, explained Joan, and she threw open shutters to let in some drizzly light, revealing portraits all around. Dick's photograph albums were here, in another desk drawer, and she got them out. There were numerous pictures of Dick cradling cats, donkeys and dogs. Now Dick was in the mountains skiing again. And again I looked hard for Vera. 'Curling with Nancy and Phil.' 'Self on luge.' Vera wasn't here.

On another page Dick was off on tour on the Continent with 'Fluff', his Ford. There had been attempts to get him to work in the City, Joan and Mari had heard, but he preferred to travel. Here was Dick standing on a steamship with two smiling girls; and in Bali in multicoloured shorts. And here was a picture of his plane, which appeared to have landed on the lawn at Felbrigg. Dick was sitting astride it, clutching a glamorous, dark-haired girl. But there was not one photograph of Vera. It was as if she had been blotted out.

Then, just as I was giving up, I turned another page and saw a picture of a familiar-looking church. Underneath it somebody had written, 'Winchelsea Church'. There was no explanation as to why a picture of Winchelsea church should be stuck here amid more pictures of Dick and Fluff, Dick skiing and Dick with more glamorous girls.

Before I left Felbrigg, Joan and Mari led me to the very top of the house. They carried torches and seemed quite excited about what we were going to see next. We climbed up and up and then stopped on a half-landing under the eaves. Joan pushed at a wooden door, which opened inwards on to blackness. She shone a torch on shapes piled up – leather suitcases and old trunks. These were Dick's trunks, she said; from his travels. I climbed into the attic room with Joan, her torch picking up labels in the darkness.

She read out the names of places on the labels: Marseille, Bali, Shanghai, Alexandria. I asked her to pull out the trunk with the Alexandria label. According to her friend Barbara Worcester, Vera first met her 'English pilot' when she went on the travels which began with her twenty-first birthday present from her father – the trip to Alexandria. Barbara thought the pilot was Vera's true love.

The trunk was dragged out, sending up more clouds of dust. 'Dollar Steamships' said the sticker; 'SS *President Van Buren*'. And there was a picture of a large, white luxury cruise ship with tall funnels bearing dollar signs. 'Mr Ketton-Cremer. Cabin to Alexandria, 4 July,' it read, but the year was hard to make out. We all took turns to guess what it was – either 1930 or 1935, we thought, although it could have been any of the years in between.

We forced open the thick steel hinges of the trunk, but there was nothing inside. The light had faded now and we could look at nothing more. On leaving I took a copy of Dick's handwriting to compare with the love letter I had found among Vera's papers in the shed in Zennor, the one with no signature, the address snipped off and just a curious dollar sign at the bottom. 'My Sweet, my Lovely, my Darling.'

Vera was still in Winchelsea when war was declared on 3 September 1939. 'Owing to her nationality', as she told her Home Office immigration interviewer, she had been rejected for work with the Land Army, the British Red Cross and Postal Censorship, but at least in Winchelsea she was able to 'do her bit' by helping care for children evacuated from the East End of London. In a rare expression of sentiment, Vera later described in great detail the deprivation of the poor, malnourished evacuees, saying 'nothing the war produced subsequently could equal the shock of seeing those children'. The words seemed inappropriate, given the horrors that the war later produced for her.

By June 1940, with German forces just across the Channel, Vera had moved back to London to live with her mother in a small two-room apartment in Nell Gwynne House, a block of well-appointed flats in Sloane Avenue. The local Air Raid Precautions group, which met in the basement, was already practising for the Blitz and accepted Vera as a member. A woman named Pat Holbeton, also in the Chelsea ARP, remembered meeting Vera in her boiler suit as they patrolled the streets. 'She was always very cagey,' said Pat, 'and I never really knew anything about her.' Pat was a friend of Elizabeth Norman, the SOE secretary at whose bridge party Vera had appeared in February 1941 when Pat had taken her along to make up a four.

It was at about the time that she joined the Chelsea ARP, Vera told her immigration officer, that she was approached by SOE. The interviewer wrote: 'Miss Atkins heard that a friend of the family, a Major Humphreys, had put forward her name for a post in the War

Office for certain special confidential work. She was interviewed in March 1941 and appointed immediately.'

Major Humphreys was Leslie Humphreys, 'the Hump', whom Vera had known in Bucharest and for whom she had already worked gathering intelligence. Nothing in her papers suggested she had maintained contact in England with the 'spy gents', but evidently she had. At the outbreak of war Humphreys was working in a new department within MI6, Section D, which had begun to plan for sabotage operations behind enemy lines. By the summer of 1940 Section D had been absorbed into the newly formed SOE and Humphreys was the first head of SOE's French Section.

The invitation to an interview for 'special confidential work' engineered by Humphreys marked an extraordinary turn of events in Vera's life. Since arriving in England she had been treated as an alien and had been refused any form of regular employment or war service. Now she was to be interviewed for a job at the heart of Britain's newest and most secret of organisations: the Special Operations Executive.

Vera had kept a copy of the letter. Sent from 'Inter Services Research Bureau, 64 Baker Street, London W1' and addressed to 'Dear Miss Atkins', it read: 'Could you please get in touch with me as soon as possible, as I would like you to come and see an officer here as I think we have found a vacancy for you?' The letter was signed by a Mrs Stanier, a popular woman nicknamed 'Naps', who was in charge of SOE's secretarial staff.

Yet Vera's own account of the job offer made out it was a matter of no great interest: 'I received an anodyne little letter out of the blue telling me to come for an interview. I went to see a woman I did not much like. She would not say exactly what it was one would be doing. I said I would give it a month and if I liked it I would stay.'

PART III
GERMANY

14

A WOMAN IN BLUE

Major Anghais Fyffe left Bad Oeynhausen at 8am on Saturday 1 December 1945, to be in Berlin on time to meet Vera in the Hotel am Zoo at 2pm. For Major Fyffe, Vera's sudden arrival in Germany had come at an inconvenient moment – he had been up all night dancing 'Strip the Willow' at the St Andrew's Night dance in the officers' mess.

The town of Bad Oeynhausen, a sprawling nineteenth-century health resort in Westphalia, had been taken over by the British lock, stock and barrel within weeks of the German surrender in May 1945 and was now the headquarters of the British Army of the Rhine.

At the centre of the British-occupied zone of Germany, Bad Oeynhausen had emerged from the war untouched by bombs and had a large supply of spacious villas and hotels from which the residents were expelled to make way for five thousand British soldiers, intelligence staff and civilians. A barbed-wire fence was strung around the British requisitioned area and only Germans working for British forces – as cooks, labourers or translators – were allowed in. The policy of 'non-fraternisation' imposed a ban on contact with the Germans and most of the new occupants of Bad Oeynhausen hardly noticed those on the other side of the fence as they went about transforming this most Germanic of spa towns into a model British military encampment. British Army signs went up on all buildings and hotels were transformed into messes. On Sundays the church was filled with khaki instead of frock coats. Everywhere soldiers walked briskly along walkways, although when the writer Stephen Spender arrived here one day at teatime he found nobody around. The Germans beyond the fence 'do not look at one', he noted, 'or if they do, it is without expression. It is like watching them behind a glass screen.'

Despite the devastation which lay beyond the perimeter fence, and the crises facing the politicians trying to manage a shattered Germany, the atmosphere in the British camp was positive. Young servicemen transferred from fighting at the front relished the freedoms and the spoils of victory on offer in every mess and bar. Junior officers were given a car and a driver to get around the British and other occupied zones; the car was taken from a pool of requisitioned German vehicles, though it was the Americans who got the first pick of the SS Mercedes. Wives were not allowed to join the husbands in the occupied zone, but the supply of single young women was constantly being replenished. Hundreds of typists were needed to process the vast number of permits and orders allowing people to move between zones, as well as the countless directives aimed at instilling order on chaos. The British zone included some of the greatest devastation of all: the blasted wasteland of the Ruhr, once Germany's industrial heartland. In autumn 1945 millions of displaced people were still on the move, mostly pouring in from the east.

For the Americans the priority was to ensure total denazification by interning hundreds of thousands of German males in camps for screening. The British element of the Allied Control Commission, the central body administering occupied Germany, was more concerned with how to get the Ruhr mines working again and feed the swollen, shattered population.

Winter – predicted to be a bad one – was approaching, as Anghais Fyffe was well aware as he set out for Berlin in his fifteen-hundredweight truck. The road he had to follow took him across several pontoon bridges, which could freeze over in minutes and were often clogged with German convoys returning home. Bad Oeynhausen to Berlin could take more than eight hours if heavy rain swamped the craters in the roads. But Fyffe sped through the British zone at the regulation speed of 50 mph, stopping only at the petrol dump at Helmstedt to put two jerrycans' worth of fuel in his tank. For a change, there was no delay at checkpoints into the Russian zone.

A sinewy, sharp young Scot, Fyffe, formerly of SOE's security directorate, had been posted to a small mission sent out to the British zone to start searching for SOE agents. Until the summer of 1945 his boss had been Commander John Senter, but in more recent weeks Flight Officer Vera Atkins had been sending him instructions from London. Vera was one of very few SOE staff officers still in post in the autumn of 1945. Senter was back at the Bar, prosecuting a case against the Anti-Vivisection League. And, as Buckmaster had returned to the Ford Motor Company as its public relations manager, Vera had now acquired the symbol 'F'.

For Fyffe the first sign that Vera was in charge came in September when he received a teleprint containing a long list of desiderata in respect of F Section's missing men and women. Vera's questions demanded instant answers. For example, could Fyffe get 'confirmation' from the Russians that Cicely Lefort was gassed in the *Jugendlager* at Ravensbrück? Could he arrange for interrogation of the Kommandant of Ravensbrück? And could he recheck the nominal rolls at Belsen for the name Yvonne Rudellat? Vera still could not believe that Yvonne could have simply disappeared, given that records showed she was alive on the day of liberation.

Fyffe considered Vera's requests showed an ignorance of reality on the ground and he signalled back that it would take weeks to secure an answer on Ravensbrück from the Russians, who were refusing access to their zone. Most of the internment camps were guarded by Germans and suspects were escaping all the time. Indeed Ravensbrück's Kommandant, Fritz Suhren, had just escaped from a US-run camp. Finding people in Germany's bombed-out cities was almost impossible as most streets were now piles of rubble. And the latest figures from Belsen showed that as many as fifteen thousand inmates had died – most of starvation or typhoid – within days of the liberation; each impossible to identify, the bodies thrown into mass graves.

———

Anghais Fyffe told me that he knew of Vera's reputation as a 'conniving woman' well before the end of the war. Buckmaster and she ran F Section 'like an ivory tower'. We were talking over mint-pea soup at Anghais's home in Cupar, Scotland. A copy of Mrs Beeton's *Book of Household Management* lay close by, as well as Anghais's war diaries, hundreds of pages of detailed daily reporting, all typed out by Anghais himself on an Imperial typewriter that went everywhere he went.

After the war, however, Anghais had come to like and admire Vera. He described her in exactly the way Pat Holbeton had – 'cagey', he told me, but he respected her determination to find her agents. 'They were her "bairns", if you like. And, after all, she knew she had sent them to their deaths.'

———

Despite the urgency of her questions from London, Fyffe had not expected that Vera might soon be coming out to the British zone in person to get her own answers, although she had long been campaigning for the authority to take over the investigation in Germany. As by far the largest number of the missing were F Section agents, it should be an F Section staff officer who went to look for them, she insisted. Men like Fyffe, she argued, though assiduous, knew nothing of the individuals they were being asked to trace; his people had failed to uncover a single piece of new evidence. At first Vera's superiors in London rejected her request, but before long several factors shifted Whitehall opinion in her favour.

First, confirmation of further SOE deaths at Dachau, Flossenburg and Mauthausen had dispelled lingering hopes that men and women might still just 'turn up', as Buckmaster had prophesied back in January of that year. Several of the men once thought to have been in the Russian zone were found to have been murdered at these three camps, among them Gilbert Norman, hanged at Mauthausen, and Jack Agazarian, hanged at Flossenburg. 'Agazarian was the last to go,' wrote Vera in a report on what she had learned about the Flossenburg deaths. 'He tapped on his wall: "It's my turn next. Send my love to my wife."'

Furthermore, as the Foreign Office was well aware, if any missing people were still stranded in the Russian zone, there was no time to waste in the search for them as relations with the Russians were worsening every day.

A further help to Vera's case was, as she put it, the new 'market' for war crimes. At the end of the war prosecution of Nazi war crimes focused on the trial of men identified as the 'major' Nazi war criminals – Goering, Hess and Ribbentrop among them – which began at Nuremberg on 20 November 1945. But, as the facts of the Nazis' atrocities began to sink in, public demand for wider justice could not be ignored. At Nuremberg a map was produced showing more than three hundred concentration camps and sub-camps scattered across Europe.

The Allies began scouring Germany for every suspect war criminal, and by autumn 1945 the four occupying powers – Britain, the USA, France and Russia – had become responsible for trying crimes committed in their respective zones and a Central Registry of War Criminals and Security Suspects (CROWCASS) had been formed.

It was, however, quite another development that really began to shift official opinion in favour of Vera's search. Charles Bushell, a second-hand car dealer in Brixton, south London, had been agitating for news of his daughter, Violette Szabo. Bushell was angry that he had been told nothing about Violette's whereabouts. In June 1945, a year after her disappearance, he approached the Red Cross, only to be referred back to the War Office, which, by November, still had no news. Bushell then raised the matter with his MP.

To date it had been kept largely secret that British women had been deployed behind enemy lines. Most of the families of the missing had obeyed instructions and kept quiet about their missing loved ones, agreeing not to make enquiries of their own. But now Charles Bushell, for one, appeared set on making sure everyone got to know about the women's secret missions, particularly Violette's. If the matter were raised in the House of Commons, the government would be hard put to explain how the deployment of women was legally authorised and questions would certainly be asked about whether it was morally justified. A defence would be even harder to mount if the government also stood accused of showing disregard for the fate of these women. Perhaps, some suggested, there was a use for Vera Atkins's mission after all.

Even now, however, Vera secured permission to go to Germany on no more than an exploratory trip. On this first mission, in early December 1945, she was given just four days to demonstrate that she, better than anyone else, could achieve results.

When Fyffe arrived at the Hotel am Zoo, raided the previous night by Russians looking for Red Army deserters, he found Vera waiting for him. She had spent the morning picking up souvenirs around the destroyed ministries of the Reich Chancellery, after persuading a Russian sentry to give her a guided tour. As soon as Fyffe turned up she announced that she would like to go straight away to Buch, a small town just north of Berlin, to look for the grave of a man named Jumeau. An F Section agent, twice dropped into France and twice captured, Clément-Marc Jumeau had caught TB in a German jail and was the only agent, as far as Vera knew, to have died in a hospital. His case should therefore be simpler than others to clear up and would help her prove she could get things done. Fyffe, however, told Vera that it would be impossible to reach Buch as it was inside the Russian zone, and it would take days, if not weeks, to get the paperwork. Without a permit, Vera would not be allowed through the checkpoints and would be treated just as another '*blau Angezogen*', or 'woman in blue'. Undeterred, she said she was quite sure they could manage without the papers and by early afternoon she and Fyffe were heading towards the Prenzlauer Allee in the Russian sector of Berlin.

They lost their way and moved cautiously, wary of robbers and looters. As they went, Fyffe briefed Vera fully on security, warning her that to stop by the roadside always meant attracting hordes of refugees, mostly children, clamouring for food and firewood. But they saw little to worry them that afternoon. Tramcars were running, children were playing in the streets and there was hardly a Russian to be seen.

Approaching their first Russian checkpoint, Fyffe spoke first. The sentry spoke no German and Fyffe no Russian. '*Franzeski?*' the Russian asked, and Fyffe replied that they were British military. '*Ah, Angleski,*' said the sentry, looking bemused. To Fyffe's astonishment, Vera then uttered a few words in Russian and showed her new WAAF identity card. The sentry cleared his throat, took the card and stared at it. Then suddenly he took a step back, saluted smartly and waved the truck on. Within another hour Vera and Fyffe had located Buch and found a hospital close to the Russian headquarters. From hospital staff they learned the most likely location of Jumeau's grave and, although it was impossible to locate the grave itself, they were given the name of an official who would send the required information on in writing the following week.

By the time Vera and Fyffe arrived back at the Hotel am Zoo, she, not surprisingly, was in excellent spirits. She had cleared up her first case and already had a success to report back home. In addition she seemed pleased by the arrival of a major from the War Office's public relations department, Jerrard Tickell, a good-looking and engaging young man who was in Berlin to start researching a biography of Odette Sansom on which Vera was advising. Also here to greet Vera was Francis Cammaerts, now working with the Allied Control Commission.

Fyffe observed that Vera and Cammaerts were 'very close' and had the impression that Vera was seeking Cammaerts's advice on securing work herself with the Control Commission. Vera, Cammaerts and Tickell were then driven off by Fyffe through the rubble to drink gin at the infamous black-market Royal Club – frequented by Russian, American and British officers, as well as wealthy

Vera with her brothers
Guy and Ralph.
[courtesy of K. Rosenberg]

Vera (with plaits) and
friend at Crasna, early
1920s. [Atkins papers]

Vera (with plaits) at a
wedding at Crasna, early
1920s. [Atkins papers]

Vera with her brothers in
pony and trap at Crasna,
early 1920s. [Atkins papers]

Vera's father Max at the front of the house at Crasna, 1920s. [Atkins papers]

The rear of the house at Crasna. [Atkins papers]

Vera in her teens. [K. Rosenberg]

Vera (seated) with her mother Hilda, Uncle Siegfried and father Max on the rear veranda at Crasna. [K. Rosenberg]

Mountain picnic guests at Vallea Uzului, 1932. Riders (from left): Siegfried Rosenberg (second); Count von der Schulenburg (third); Charles Robinson, commercial attaché, (fifth); Vera (sixth); Vera's cousin (one of the twins Hans or George Rosenberg) (seventh); Fritz Rosenberg (ninth); Annie Samuelli (end). [Atkins Papers]

Vera at Crasna before a ball.
[K. Rosenberg]

Targul Mosilor (theatre), Bucharest, mid-1930s. Vera, back row, centre; John Coulson, middle row, far left; Montague Chidson middle row, second left; Leslie Humphreys, middle row, far right. [courtesy of Valerie Chidson]

Vera (second left) as Bluebeard, Samedan, near St Moritz, Switzerland, 1938.
[courtesy Mimi Rocke]

Vera with Dick
Ketton-Cremer in
the Swiss Alps,
1939.

Vera as WAAF
squadron officer, 1946.
[Atkins papers]

Sonia Olschanesky, descriptions
of whom led Vera to think she
was Nora. [Special Forces Club]

Nora Inayat Khan
(alias Madeleine).
[Atkins papers]

◁ Diana Rowden.
[Courtesy of Special Forces club]

▷ Vera Leigh.
[Special Forces Club]

◁ Andrée Borell (alias Denise).
[Special Forces Club]

▷ Yvonne Rudellat.
[Special Forces Club]

◁ Violette Szabo.
[Atkins papers]

▷ Lilian Rolfe.
[Special Forces Club]

Denise Bloch.
[National Archive]

Cicely Lefort.
[National Archive]

Madeleine
Damerment
(alias Martine).
[Atkins papers]

Yolande Beekman
(alias Yvonne).
[Atkins papers]

Eliane Plewman.
[Special Forces Club]

Odette Hallowes
(formerly Churchill,
formerly Sansom).
[Special Forces Club]

◁
Yvonne Baseden.
[Atkins papers]

▷
Eileen Nearne.
[Special Forces Club]

Francis Suttill
(alias Prosper)
with his wife
Margaret, 1935.
[courtesy of
Anthony Suttill]

◁
Francis Suttill in
lieutenant's
uniform.
[Anthony Suttill]

▷
Gilbert Norman
(alias
Archambaud).
[National Archive]

◁ France Antelme.
[courtesy of Alain Antelme]

▷ Jack Agazarian.
[Special Forces Club]

◁ Frank Pickersgill.
[National Archive]

▷ Henri Dericourt (alias Gilbert).

◁ Maurice Buckmaster.
[National Archive]

▷ Nicholas Bodington.
[National Archive]

Buckmaster (centre) on tour – the Judex Mission – in liberated France, 1944.

The Judex Mission: Vera, centre; Buckmaster, far right.

Vera in office with war crimes investigators, including Stephen Stewart (back right), Bad Oeynhausen, 1946.
[Atkins papers]

Vera with Tony Somerhough, Germany, 1946. [Atkins papers]

War crimes investigators at Bad Oeynhausen break for lunch, 1946: Somerhough, far left; Vera, second left. [courtesy of Jane Hamlyn]

Vera on investigations in Germany, 1946. [Courtesy of John da Cunha]

Vera with John da Cunha in Hamburg during the Ravensbrück trial, December 1946. [John da Cunha]

Sturmbannführer Hans Kieffer at his desk in Avenue Foch. [Courtesy of Kieffer family]

Horst Kopkow, SS counter-intelligence chief in Berlin. [Berlin Document Centre]

Fritz Suhren, Kommandant of Ravensbrück concentration camp [Atkins papers]

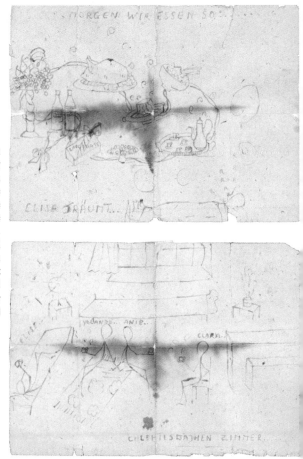

The drawings in blood made by Yolande Beekman in her cell at Karlsruhe prison, 1944. The captions read: 'Elise dreams . . . Tomorrow we will eat . . .' and (though the German is not perfect) 'The bad girl's room'. [Courtesy of Erich Johe]

Natzweiler concentration camp on the Struthof Mountain, Alsace. [Wiener Library]

A coat worn by a Natzweiler prisoner designated *N+N* (*Nacht und Nebel*).
[Atkins papers]

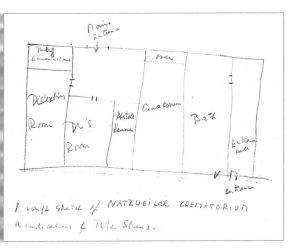

Vera's sketch of the crematorium building at Natzweiler, 1946.
[Imperial War Museum]

Brian Stonehouse's sketches of women prisoners walking down the *Lagerstrasse* at Natzweiler. [Imperial War Museum]

The Natzweiler defendants in the dock at the 1946 trial held at Wuppertal. Right to left: Zeuss, Straub, Meier, Wochner, Hartjenstein, Berg, Rohde, Bruttel and Aus dem Bruch. [Wiener Library]

Vera (left) with Odette (right) and Hedwig Rosenberg, Vera's sister-in-law, at the time of the London opening of *Odette*, 1950. [Atkins papers]

Vera with Virginia McKenna and Paul Scofield during filming of *Carve Her Name With Pride* at Pinewood Studios. [Atkins papers]

Vera walking with Buckmaster in the garden of his retirement home in East Sussex, late 1980s. [Mike Champion/ Champion Photographic]

Vera at memorial service at Ravensbrück concentration camp, Germany, 1993.
[Atkins papers]

Berliners – before returning to the Hotel am Zoo to dine. The following day, a Sunday, Vera intended to spend with Cammaerts at the Yacht Club at Gatow, just west of Berlin. And on Monday, she informed Fyffe, her plan was to interrogate the Kommandants of two concentration camps. Would he please collect her early, so they could drive to Bad Oeynhausen, and make plans for the interrogations?

Fritz Suhren had been the Kommandant at Ravensbrück and Anton Kaindl at Sachsenhausen, and both were now in British custody, as Vera had discovered before leaving London. Suhren, who had been recaptured after his earlier escape, would, Vera very much hoped, be able to tell her what had become of Violette Szabo, Lilian Rolfe and Denise Bloch, of whom there was still no trace. Kaindl, she hoped, would know the fate of Francis Suttill (Prosper), last heard of at Sachsenhausen.

So, on the third day of Vera's visit to Germany, Fyffe drove her to Bad Oeynhausen, where she sought out the head of the war crimes unit, Group Captain Tony Somerhough, whom she would have to win over to secure permission to interrogate Suhren and Kaindl. Although momentarily taken aback by the WAAF officer who breezed into his office unannounced, Somerhough was instantly impressed by Vera's knowledge of the concentration camps and judged her mission to be of the utmost seriousness. He cautioned only that she should not go straight away to interrogate the men as the camps where they were held would be hard to find and it was already dark. Vera, however, said she had no time to lose, so Somerhough sent along one of his officers, Captain Arribert Volmar, as a guide.

———

During my visit Fyffe would not let his Germany diaries out of his sight, but after lunch he offered to read extracts to me. He said he had not picked up the diaries himself for more than fifty years. Sitting beside his gas fire, he read aloud what happened as he, Vera and Volmar set off first to find Anton Kaindl, at a British internment camp for suspect war criminals near Paderborn. 'We travelled over the moors until we came to a road that I thought led to the Paderborn camp. We turned this way and after a mile or two we saw the beams of searchlights in the air; that was the internment camp all right, but the difficulty was to find our way to it. We circled round

and round, now making for the beams, now from them. It was raining now, very hard, and it was difficult to see our road.' Eventually
the three reached the camp: 'a huge place holding various types of
prisoners – SS, camp guards, Nazi bad hats and other kinds of sinister Germans and it is swept from dusk to dawn by a battery of
searchlights to keep the place bathed in a cold blue light.'

On their arrival Vera, Volmar and Fyffe were told that Kaindl was
waiting to see them and they were led by an adjutant down a muddy
path through trees to a hut. 'We walked into a small room and finding Kaindl was already there took us back a little, for it would have
been much better if we had been sitting there waiting for him, rather
than that he should have been there waiting for us. There were
three chairs in the room; one was behind the desk and Vera sat herself on that one as she was prepared to carry out the interrogation.
Kaindl of all people was given a chair by this small adjutant fellow,
while he himself took the third chair, leaving Volmar and myself to
hang around the walls.

'This Kaindl fellow', continued Fyffe, smiling to himself as he
recalled the Kommandant, 'was a very small man, just five feet, if that.
He had a high forehead, with sandy hair that was cropped short. He
had high cheekbones over which a red-veined shiny skin was drawn
tight. He had a kind of ferret face, and wore glasses; his hands were
well kept, and he looked a bit of a dandy. I believe that he wore top
boots that had specially high heels, and a peaked cap with a high
crown, so that he might give the impression of being taller than he was.'

Vera's interrogation got nowhere, read Fyffe. She learned nothing
about Suttill or any of the others. 'She thought she was doing nicely,
as she told us afterwards, trying to show that she had nearly tricked
Kaindl, but we were no further forward than we were when we
started.'

Reading on, Fyffe recounted how, the next morning, he, Vera and
Volmar made an early start to get to the other internment camp, at
Recklinghausen, where they were to interrogate Fritz Suhren, 'erst-
while full colonel in the SS and ex-Kommandant of the notorious
annihilation camp at Ravensbrück, where thousands of women died
of hunger or were put to death by hanging, gassing or shooting'.

Once again they got lost looking for the camp and stopped to ask
where the *Internierungslager* was, but this reference to an internment
camp brought no response from locals. Then a small boy asked if they

were looking for the *Konzentratsionslager*. Evidently, Fyffe had recorded, this internment camp had formerly been a concentration camp. 'Now we got precise instructions how to reach the concentration camp.'

Fyffe had noted down that there were different kinds of Germans in Recklinghausen. 'There were well-dressed ones who had had enough time to bring decent clothes with them; there were others who had either been seized whilst a fugitive, or had been arrested suddenly without warning and had had no time to collect anything other than the clothes they stood in. As we drove through every German took off his hat or cap and stood there clasping it in front of him in an attitude which was meant to portray abject humility.'

The three English officers were shown into a room and Suhren was brought in. 'He stood to attention. He was a youngish-looking man of probably forty or so, with a fairish complexion topped by red-dish fair hair that was well kept. His face was round and seemed intelligent. He wore only socks, breeches and shirt.'

Vera handled the interrogation better this time, wrote Fyffe, but Suhren denied any knowledge of Englishwomen in Ravensbrück. She asked him about Odette Churchill (the surname Odette Sansom had given on her arrest) 'and he admitted that she was a special prisoner for whom he was held personally responsible, probably because it was thought that she was a niece of Winston Churchill, which was quite untrue'.

Suhren continued to admit nothing and they sent him out in order to interrogate two women guards from Ravensbrück who were also being held. The first, read Fyffe, was a middle-aged woman of 'very low mentality' and the second 'looked half silly' but did reveal there were English girls in the camp and they wore red triangles on their shoulders with the letter 'E'.

They confronted Suhren with her admissions 'but he still insisted he knew nothing of the gas chamber or the hangings or the English prisoners'. Fyffe said that Suhren did 'start slightly' when Vera mentioned the crematorium. 'But he recovered himself quickly; he gave no reaction when mention was made of the gas chamber.'

By this time it was dark and the cell was lit by a fluorescent strip light in which Suhren looked a sickly colour. Fyffe then described how they left the interrogation room, hungry and tired, to find the car, only to discover that somebody – probably a hungry German child – had stolen their sandwiches. Vera was quite peeved but 'brightened visibly' when they were offered doughnuts filled with cream in the Red Shield Club, the canteen used by 'other ranks'.

Putting the diary aside for a moment, Fyffe told me how the next day he saw Vera off from Bückeburg airfield and a few days later received a letter from her which he had kept all these years, and he produced it for me to see. In the letter Vera thanked him for all his help, saying she had been 'dazed with the experiences of the last few days'. She added that she had had a rather bumpy return flight and had been sick 'but discreetly so'. Fyffe chuckled as he pointed out Vera's signature: 'the *Blau Angezogen*'.

———

After arriving back in London from her four-day trip Vera lobbied to return to Germany on a long-term basis, but many obstacles remained. As anticipated, SOE was to be closed for good at the end of the year, and no government department would henceforth have any responsibility at all for SOE affairs. Officials pointed out therefore that even if Vera's mission were deemed worthwhile, there was nobody to 'carry' her – in other words, to pay for her mission. And there was considerable objection still to the very principle of a woman carrying out such a task. But then the evidence of a young intelligence officer named Prince Yurka Galitzine swiftly changed minds.

Just as signals intelligence had, from the start of the war, uncovered far more about Nazi atrocities than anyone had been told, so much intelligence about war crimes gathered after D-Day was also kept secret. As Allied armies began to push through France in August 1944, SHAEF had sent specialist officers to gather 'political intelligence' about the German occupation of France and in particular about war crimes. One of these officers was Yurka Galitzine, a twenty-five-year-old captain, son of a former military attaché at the Imperial Russian embassy in London, and his English wife.

Appalled by much of what he found as he progressed through France, Galitzine was most horrified by the ghastly remains of the little concentration camp of Natzweiler, hidden away among the spectacular Vosges Mountains in Alsace.

Natzweiler, as Galitzine discovered, was specifically designated as a camp for prisoners who were to disappear under the '*Nacht und Nebel*' order. Galitzine immediately sent an official report on Natzweiler to SHAEF, anticipating an outcry. He expected an outraged reaction in

London in particular, because his report had uncovered the death of at least one British woman at the camp. He had few details but he had gathered enough evidence to write that 'one day three women spies were brought to the camp and shot in the sandpit. They were described as being one Englishwoman and two Frenchwomen.'

But Galitzine's report was buried. Outraged by the official silence, Galitzine, a former journalist on the *Daily Express*, leaked the story. By autumn 1945 word of his findings reached a charismatic young SAS intelligence officer named Major Eric 'Bill' Barkworth, who had men missing after two operations in the Vosges in September 1944. Armed with Galitzine's report, Barkworth immediately set off for Germany with a team of investigators. He promised to signal any findings to Galitzine's office in Eaton Square, London, where, under the eaves, Galitzine had installed signallers, including a man named Freddie Oakes, to receive Barkworth's reports.

———

In a letter to Vera in 1985, Oakes said he had never been able to forget taking those signals. He had kept a diary, which his son, William Oakes, showed me:

> We established ourselves in an attic room and ran an aerial
> between some chimneys. The traffic we handled was quite
> traumatic. In one incident eight members of the SAS
> regiment, who had been held and interrogated for several
> months, were manacled and driven in a lorry into a large wood.
> Here a hole had been scraped – not more than a couple of feet
> deep. One at a time they were unchained, stripped, taken to
> the edge of the hole and shot in the back of the head. After
> the first one had been shot subsequent victims could see the
> bodies of their friends for a moment before they too were
> shot. The German driver of the lorry stated that none of the
> men showed any fear and none trembled even though it was a
> cold day in October. None spoke except the last man – a
> signaller I knew – who told the SS squad they were 'bastards'
> and would be hounded down for what they were doing.

Oakes also recalled receiving the signal about the women who died at Natzweiler. 'Evidence showed', he wrote, 'that one of the women woke up as she was about to be put in the oven and scratched the face of the camp doctor who was carrying out the murders.'

————

One day in early December 1945 Vera paid a visit to Yurka Galitzine. She found a striking figure, at least 6 feet 4 inches tall, with dark good looks and impeccable English public school manners. Galitzine was surprised to discover a WAAF officer knocking at his door. She did not say how she had heard about him but he thought she might have seen a story about his report on Natzweiler in the *Daily Express*. She asked directly about the report. 'I believe you have evidence of the death of young women at Natzweiler?' Galitzine could help her little with identities except to say he had heard the women might have been brought to Natzweiler from Karlsruhe.

Galitzine had heard of at least two British men who had been imprisoned at Natzweiler, one of whom, rumour had it, had drawn sketches of inmates. The sketches were signed 'J.B. Stonehouse'. Galitzine had no idea who J.B. Stonehouse was, but Vera most certainly did. Her own agent Brian Stonehouse had been in Natzweiler and in civilian life had been a graphic artist for *Vogue*.

Vera now wrote to Stonehouse, asking him to think back to Natzweiler and enclosing photographs of her missing girls to jog his memory. She also arranged for photos of her missing women to be sent to Bill Barkworth in Germany so that the SAS major could show them to any witnesses from Natzweiler he might trace. Before the end of December Galitzine was back in touch with Vera to say Barkworth had signalled from Germany that he had tracked down an important witness to the women's deaths at Natzweiler. The witness was a man named Franz Berg, who had worked in the camp. Galitzine already had a summary of Berg's statement, which had been signalled to Eaton Square; the full text was delivered by courier a little later.

I Franz Berg of Block 1.7 No. 29, 3rd Floor, Mannheim, Germany, make oath and say as follows: I am a waiter by trade living in Mannheim. During my life I have received so far as I can remember twenty-two sentences of imprisonment. I cannot remember what they were all for but I can recall two cases of theft, several of obstructing the police and of causing bodily injury, and the last sentence of two years which I received for procuration.

Berg went on to state that he had been transferred from prison to prison and found himself sent to work in the quarry at Natzweiler in 1942. The following year he was given a job as a stoker in the camp crematorium, which had just been built.

'The first crematorium outside the camp used to work on Wednesdays and Saturdays but when the new crematorium was opened we used to burn bodies about three times a week. Peter Straub was in charge of the crematorium.'

He then described an incident in which women were killed at the camp:

In June 1943 I can remember having been told by an *Unterscharführer* that four Jewesses had been given injections by the SS medical orderly of the SS camp hospital.

Peter Straub was present as he was at all executions that took place at Natzweiler.

Next morning in the course of my duties I had to clear the ashes out of the crematorium oven. I found a pink woman's stocking garter on the floor near the oven.

Berg then stated that near by he had also found empty glass ampoules of a drug called Evipan on top of a pile of coffins.

Vera read on as Berg described the arrival of four women at Natzweiler in July 1944.

The next women to be killed by injection as opposed to gassing were two English and two French women. These were brought to the cells in the crematorium building one afternoon in July 1944.

Peter Straub told me about 6 o'clock on the evening of the day on which these women arrived to have the crematorium oven heated to its maximum by 9.30pm and then to disappear. He told me also that the doctor was going to come down and give some injections. I knew what this meant.

Berg then went to his cell, which, his statement suggested, was actually inside the crematorium building. He and his two cellmates were then locked in and saw no more of what happened that evening. But Berg and the other two men – Alex, a Russian from

Leningrad, and a prisoner named Georg Fuhrmann – all heard what
happened. And Fuhrmann even managed to catch glimpses.

> Fuhrmann, who occupied the highest bunk, was able to look
> through the fanlight without standing up. He whispered to me
> that 'they' were bringing a woman along the corridor. We
> heard low voices in the next room and then the noise of a
> body being dragged along the floor, and Fuhrmann whispered
> to me that he could see people dragging something on the
> floor, which was below his angle of vision through the fanlight.
>   At the same time that this body was brought past we heard
> the noise of heavy breathing and low groaning combined.
>   The next two women were also seen by Fuhrmann and
> again we heard the same noises and regular groans as
> insensible women were dragged away.
>   The fourth, however, resisted in the corridor. I heard her
> say: '*Pourquoi?*'

Berg said he then heard a voice, which he recognised as that of
one of the camp doctors, say: '*Pour typhus.*'

'We then heard the noise of a struggle and muffled cries of the
woman. I assumed that somebody held a hand over her mouth. I
heard this woman being dragged away too. She was groaning louder
than the others.'

Berg's cell was close enough to the oven room to allow him to hear
the oven doors being closed. 'From the noise of the crematorium oven
doors which I heard, I can state definitely that in each case the groaning women were placed immediately in the crematorium oven.'

When all the senior camp staff had gone away and the building
was quiet again, Berg, Alex and Fuhrmann came out of their cell.
'We went to the crematorium oven, opened the door and saw that
there were four blackened bodies within.'

The statement ended:

> From the photographs shown to me I can state with the
> utmost certainty that one of the women who I saw when
> brought to the camp in the afternoon at 3.30 as I have
> described was the same as that shown to me whose
> photograph is marked Vera Leigh. I believe that another was

the same as that whose photograph has been shown to me marked Inayat Khan. I remember also that a third was dark-haired and fatter than the others.

Vera took Berg's statement to her superiors, who needed no more convincing that her search in Germany must begin immediately. If this evidence that British women agents had been burned alive in a concentration camp turned out to be true, it would be impossible to keep quiet. Somebody, it was agreed, should be given the task of finding out exactly who these blackened bodies were. The person chosen should be competent but, above all, discreet.

Within days of the arrival of the new evidence it was agreed that Vera should return to Germany, funded by MI6. Once in post she should write a monthly report to Major Norman Mott, formerly of SOE's security directorate and now appointed to handle any residual SOE affairs while the office was closing down. For operational purposes, however, Vera would be attached in Germany to the war crimes unit of the Judge Advocate General's department at the British Army HQ in Bad Oeynhausen, under Group Captain Tony Somerhough. Within a few days it was also agreed that Vera should be promoted from Flight Officer to Squadron Officer to give her the extra authority she would need to get things done in the occupied zones.

Before leaving London Vera handed over all her F Section files containing details of next of kin to Norman Mott's staff. Every family now received a terse round robin informing them that 'the office' was 'ceasing to exist' and giving a new War Office address for enquiries. Vera found time to write a more personal letter to the families of the Karlsruhe girls, saying they were last seen alive at the jail but giving little more information and not mentioning that she was investigating whether any of them might have died at a camp named Natzweiler. She then emptied her store cupboard, sending photographs and other personal items of the agents to their families. A brown paper parcel containing Violette's camel-hair coat was sent to her mother, Mrs Bushell, along with a brief note from Vera saying: 'We are unfortunately still without further news.'

Vera left Baker Street for the last time on 8 January 1946 with a list of fifty-two missing SOE agents, of which most were from F Section. Twelve of the F Section agents still missing were women. She had been given three months in which to discover their fate.

15

FOLLOWING TRACKS

United States War Crimes Liaison Detachment. Headquarters British Army of the Rhine. European Theater. The following British Military personnel is proceeding to Frankfurt, Wiesbaden, Karlsruhe, Baden Baden (French Zone) and Munich on an important mission in connection with war crimes.

'Squadron Officer V M Atkins 9913. On completion of your mission you will proceed to your proper station. No per diem is authorised.'

Whether she liked it or not, Vera's life was now to be governed by movement orders. Pieces of paper allowed her to cross between zones, to enter the internment camps and to speak to CROWCASS. Signed chits even granted access to billets, or a meal – important if, as in Vera's case, orders excluded a per diem.

On 9 January 1946, when Vera arrived in Bad Oeynhausen to take up her post, she was shown to her billet, a bare and extremely cold room in a villa, and then to her office in a similar house near by. The office had a chair and a desk, on which were an angle-poise lamp and an upturned foil tin for an ashtray. On the wall was a large map of Germany. The ration cigarettes on offer were not to Vera's taste (she smoked Senior Service) and she had brought too few warm clothes. But at last she was in the place she needed to be for her investigation.

Vera spent her first few days becoming acquainted with the war crimes legal staff and the all-important Haystack men. Haystack was the name of a group of highly motivated Nazi hunters, mostly volunteer German or Austrian exiles, usually Jewish, who were capable of 'finding a needle in a haystack' by tracking Nazi war crimes suspects hiding out in the German hills or mountains or, just as likely, amid the rubble of bombed cities.

Few of the young officers Vera met at Bad Oeynhausen knew much about her secret mission and fewer had heard of SOE. Some were put out that a woman had arrived to pull rank, while others were simply bemused by the sudden appearance in their midst of this self-assured, mysterious WAAF officer.

Then, as soon as Vera had secured the paperwork to enter the US zone, she acquired a driver and car from the pool and headed south. She spent a day in the visitors' gallery of the Nuremberg courthouse, and took a tour of Dachau concentration camp, which had already been converted by the Americans into a museum with waxwork figures for SS guards. Vera was now eager to start work. She asked her driver, Corporal Job Trenter, to press on to Karlsruhe. It was snowing.

After she had read the evidence of Franz Berg, Vera's priority on arriving in Germany had never been in question: it was to find out which, if any, of her girls might have been among those murdered in the crematorium at Natzweiler. She had known since May 1945 that several SOE women travelled from Paris to Germany on 11 May 1944 and were first interned in Karlsruhe. Odette Sansom, who was on the transport and the only one to make it home, had identified Andrée Borrel, Madeleine Damerment, Vera Leigh, Eliane Plewman, Diana Rowden, Yvonne Beekman and one other female agent. Although Odette had failed to identify the seventh woman, Vera had come to believe that she could have been Nora Inayat Khan. According to Odette, some of these women were, like her, then taken east, possibly even to Poland or Russia. Vera believed that if this was true, those women might still be alive. Before leaving for Germany, however, she had received her long-awaited reply from Brian Stonehouse, which contained startling new information on the women held at Natzweiler.

Brian Stonehouse had survived four concentration camps: Neuengamme, Mauthausen, Natzweiler and Dachau. This in itself was remarkable, but given that he was a Jew, his survival was astonishing. Since his return in May 1945, Stonehouse had passed much useful information on to Vera. He had told her, for example, about a dead British airman whose body he saw one day lying naked outside the crematorium, apparently brought into the camp in an SS car and dumped. Stonehouse decided to draw the body before it was burned. He had subsequently lost the sketch but he described the dead man to Vera – typical English face, fair hair and small nose – and she had passed the information to the Air Ministry.

But Stonehouse had certainly never spoken about women arriving at Natzweiler. Now, after all this time, and only after Vera's urgent prompting, he had at last recalled that he did see some English girls – three, he thought – enter the camp in July 1944 and walk right past him on the way to the crematorium. Not only had Stonehouse suddenly dug up this long-buried memory, but he had managed to summon up what they looked like, and out of the same letter had tumbled two artist's sketches – one of a girl whom Vera recognised and one of a girl she did not.

Posted in Belgium, where he was now working with the Allied Control Commission, Stonehouse's letter began: 'Dear Vera, My sincerest apologies for this shocking delay but since my return from Brussels I have been laid up in bed with flu (who?), you know, GRIPPE! Anyway Vera a Happy and Prosperous Year.' He went on: 'I have been thinking hard about your corpses . . . I have been jogging my memory to try and picture your missing girls.'

He then gave descriptions of two he remembered and matched the descriptions to the two drawings.

'No. 1,' he wrote on the top-left-hand corner of the first sketch and underlined it. The girl in the drawing looked conventionally English. A schoolteacher, perhaps, or a secretary, she was smart and had a purposeful, leggy stride with head held high. She was carrying a suitcase and had a distinctive bow in her hair at the back. Vera knew immediately who it was. She had last seen Diana Rowden on 13 June 1943, when she took her to Tangmere airfield with Nora. She had last heard from her just before she was captured at Clairvaux in November of that year.

Without ever naming her – because he had never met any of these girls and knew none of their real names – Stonehouse had also described Diana to perfection.

No. 1 was middle height, a little older I should say than I was

then (25) with short blonde mousy hair tied with what I took to
be a piece of Scottish tartan silk ribbon, wearing a light grey
flannel suit – the coat a shortish swagger model – obviously
English, as was her face with a good humoured, kindly
expression and a defiant look, which included that pathetic
piece of gay silk in her hair – she had obviously been in jail quite
a while – as she had no lipstick – and her face was rather pale.

Diana was the most English-looking of all the agents. Vera's photographs of her showed her pleasant, toothy smile, blue eyes and
bobbed, light-brown hair, set off against the khaki of her FANY uniform. And, had there been any doubt at all as to whether this was
Diana, here was the bow. She always wore a bow in her hair.
Stonehouse had never met Diana and knew nothing about her, yet
he had captured her on paper.

As recently as Christmas Vera had written to Mrs Rowden at her
home at Alton, in Hampshire, telling her the news that Diana had
last been seen alive in the prison in Karlsruhe and still holding out
hope of finding her alive. But here was this drawing showing Diana
striding directly to her death, more than eighteen months ago.

Then came Stonehouse's sketch of No. 2. When Vera first turned
to this second drawing she was expecting to recognise this girl also.
But she was taken aback; she did not know who it was.

She looked for the description. 'As for No. 2,' wrote Stonehouse,
'the sketch describes her. She was I believe perhaps a little younger
than No. 1 – smaller – with dyed blonde hair . . . only it had not been
retouched for a long time as there were several inches of hair from
the roots of the hair line which were dark.' His description went on:
'She wore wooden soled shoes, a black coat, carried a fur coat of not
very good fur – some sort of dyed rabbit – rather chocolat au lait.'
Looking again at the sketch, Vera could see that the roots of the girl's
dyed blonde hair had indeed been sketched in. Perhaps it was
somebody she knew, she thought, but with dyed hair, so that she was
hard to recognise.

Like No. 1, the second girl was smartly dressed. In the drawing it
looked as if her dress was striped. She had a coat slung over her
right arm and a bag in her left. She was more stylish than No. 1. In
fact she was 'quite different', Stonehouse wrote. 'No. 2 was obviously continental – maybe Jewish.'

Vera had hoped for more sketches. There were none. As for No. 3, Stonehouse said, he could remember too little to draw her. She was 'nondescript' with very black hair – a brown tweed suit and shortish. But she had made so little impression that he had retained no more detail and confessed to Vera: 'I can't remember anything else about her.' The visions he had summoned up nine months after he first came home had suddenly faded.

Next Stonehouse addressed himself to the photographs Vera had sent him of the missing women, and he marked the photograph of Diana Rowden as the match for No. 1. As for No. 2, he could not be sure. He, like Vera, must have seen that she did not obviously match any of Vera's 'corpses', so he marked two as possibles: Yolande Beekman and Nora Inayat Khan. At first he seemed confident of being able to identify No. 2 as Yolande. 'Her hairstyle and type of face correspond exactly with No. 2 photo.' But then he seemed to hesitate as if something was not Yolande, after all, and added: 'The silhouette anyway.'

He made no comment about why he had seen a similarity between the sketch of No. 2 and the photograph of Nora, and Vera could see none. And yet the written description he gave could have been of Nora. It was quite possible that she would have dyed her hair and that her clothes had been part of a deliberate disguise, purchased in Paris while she was on the run. She had an Eastern, possibly Jewish, look. And who could say what months in captivity might have done to her appearance? Furthermore, Diana's story had been to an extent entwined with Nora's. They had left for France together. They had been imprisoned together at Avenue Foch. Their names had been carved alongside each other on the wall in the cell. Perhaps, at the very end, fate had thrown the two young women together.

Stonehouse's letter was invaluable to Vera's investigation. When this was taken with Franz Berg's deposition, it now seemed likely that at least two of her girls were among those who had died at Natzweiler. Berg had confidently identified Vera Leigh and Stonehouse had clearly identified Diana Rowden. However, there was no certainty about who the other girls were, or even if in total there were three or perhaps four. Vera's only hope was to gather more evidence in Karlsruhe, at the prison in which the women were first held. In particular she hoped to find the chief wardress, whom Odette had named as Fräulein Beger, a Quaker and most 'correct'.

*

The car was now making good time towards Karlsruhe. The snow had eased and on the road there were just a few horses and carts and the odd military vehicle. The roads here were also clear of refugees, as few had come as far west as Baden Baden. Tented camps near Karlsruhe were mostly filled with the city's homeless. Passing through pine forests, Corporal Trenter pulled up beside a large *Schloss* on top of a hill to look over the city. Heaps of reddish masonry dusted with snow stretched to the horizon. Down below, filth lay all around in oily pools. Trenter was worried about how they were to reach the city centre.

Vera's instructions from US liaison were to check in, on arriving in Karlsruhe, with the representative of OMGUS (Office of the Military Government of the United States for Germany), which was quartered in the main post office in the city's central square. Trying to follow the line of what had once been a railway, Trenter eventually steered the car into the square. On one side not a single building was standing and figures clambering on heaps of stone and metal girders passed stones to one another. They were mostly women and old men trying to clear the rubble. The air stank of sewage spilling from holes which had once been drains. On the other side of the square, buildings were intact, including the main post office, where Vera found the American Town Major, who was the local military governor, and his Public Safety Officer, Captain Truxhall. She wanted to find Fräulein Beger of the city's women's prison, she told them, but Truxhall was not hopeful. The prison was empty now, he said. Any public building left standing had been gutted by the French before the Americans arrived.

A complete list of Karlsruhe residents had survived from pre-war police files but the chances of finding anyone was remote: 70 per cent of the city had been bombed. Some people had stayed put, living in basements or tents near their homes, waiting for their men to return from the front. But many had left, some going into the country to find food. People were afraid to talk.

Truxhall showed Vera his rogues' gallery of Nazi war criminals, circulated in each city and updated daily. Vera noted certain names, for example of men who had joined the local *Werwolfgruppe*, one of the gangs of Gestapo diehards who vowed to fight on and 'come back from the dead'. Truxhall said his staff had little time for catching war criminals; they were swamped by denazification work and were dealing with 200,000 forms, filled in by every adult in Karlsruhe, answering questions about their Nazi past. Vera then scanned

Truxhall's residents' lists. She found no Beger but a Fräulein Theresia Becker lived at Eisenlohrstrasse 10. After noting other useful addresses Vera left to see if Becker was a prison wardress.

Most streets on the way there were flattened or, if houses had been left standing, these were often just burned-out shells. But Trenter and Vera found Eisenlohrstrasse largely intact. A woman came to the door of number 10. Fräulein Becker was not in; she was at the women's prison. She had never left her post. Fräulein Becker was an excellent wardress, said the woman. She was 'very humane and very fair'.

The *Frauengefängnis*, the women's prison, at Akademiestrasse 11, was almost empty in January 1946. It had been hit in the bombing and most of the windows were boarded up. Arriving at a large double door that opened directly on to the street, Vera reached for a huge bell rope and pulled at it. There was no sound, but it must have rung somewhere inside the building, because in a few moments a woman appeared. Fräulein Theresia Becker, the chief wardress, was tall and thin, aged about fifty, with a sparrow's face, and wore a light-blue overall faded with washing. Observing Vera's uniform, she ushered her indoors.

She showed Vera into a small room and they sat. Another woman now came in, who was as round as Theresia Becker was thin. The second woman, whom Fräulein Becker introduced as her deputy, Fräulein Hager, greeted Vera with a broad smile. Vera explained she was looking for missing women who had been held in the prison in 1944. Fräulein Becker nodded and gave Vera a short speech, saying she had worked at the women's prison for twenty-eight years and had been chief wardress for the past eight. She explained a little of the workings of the prison, which during the war had been divided into two: the main part here in Akademiestrasse and a second part, for female political prisoners, in a wing of Gefängnis 11, the men's jail in Riefstahlstrasse. It was in Riefstahlstrasse that the British and French women had been held. In May 1944, when they arrived, the main women's prison was very overcrowded, as many prisoners had been transferred there from France, ahead of the German retreat.

Vera now asked Fräulein Becker if she could identify the women, showing her photographs of all those who Odette Sansom had said were on the train to Karlsruhe, and including one of Nora Inayat Khan. Becker looked at the pictures and said that they had all been in the prison. Was she quite sure that she recognised the photo of

Nora? 'Quite sure,' answered the wardress. Then Vera asked if she remembered the women's names. She recalled only one: Martine. This was an alias used by Madeleine Damerment.

When Vera asked Becker to describe the girls, she said she could not recall them in any detail, although one, perhaps the one they called Martine, had a red pullover. 'What else do you remember about them?' Vera asked. 'About how they looked?' Becker said she could remember very little else, except that one – again she thought it was Martine – had arrived carrying a New Testament.

'And their admission to the prison was, of course, most irregular,' added the wardress, who now explained that the women had been admitted under the 'protective custody' order, which applied to political prisoners and spies. 'I had no authority to take such prisoners into a civilian jail. It was highly unusual. It was against the rules,' she said. She had protested to her seniors, and it was agreed that she should only have to keep the women for a maximum of two weeks. It meant a lot of extra work keeping such prisoners, said Becker, as they had to be exercised separately and the prison was short-staffed. Protective custody prisoners could not associate with one another and therefore could not be taken to the basement during air raids.

After two weeks the women were still here, Becker said, so she called the prison governor to ask what was to be done. The governor said he would speak to other authorities but still nothing happened. Becker called again a few weeks later. 'It was as if they had been forgotten,' she said. But eventually somebody took notice of her protests and came to take the women away.

'When were they taken?' asked Vera.

'Mrs Churchill left alone in July 1944 and the rest left soon after,' said Becker, suddenly remembering Odette's name. When Vera pressed her further, she said she was sure all the other women, apart from Mrs Churchill, had left together in one group, sometime in August. But she had no other memory at all of the circumstances of the women's departure. However, Vera might like to talk to a man named Stuhl, the gatekeeper. Vera asked to see the prison records, but Becker said they had all been destroyed by the French. When Vera expressed surprise that the French had destroyed prison records, Becker insisted this is what had happened. They had made a fire.

Fräulein Becker had not told the whole truth, of that Vera was quite sure, although she was certainly 'very correct', just as Odette had said. Becker was a bureaucrat who always obeyed the rules. And it was evident to Vera that, had Becker not been such a stickler for the rules, her agents might have stayed here safely in the wardress's custody – entirely forgotten until the end of the war. It was only because, according to the rules, Becker was not supposed to hold prisoners of their category that she had protested and asked to be relieved of them.

'I interrogated staff at the women's jail at Akademiestrasse,' noted Vera in her report on the meeting. 'While they are all very anxious to be helpful, their information cannot be relied upon.'

————

I had not expected to find many traces of Vera's investigation in Karlsruhe. There is no prison in Akademiestrasse today, and I was told there never had been. When I asked ordinary people about the period they all looked blank and said: 'Go to the archives.' In Karlsruhe's main archives I found some files on OMGUS, given to the city by the US in the 1980s. The files were indexed in such a complex way that it was almost impossible to look at anything in sequence.

Karlsruhe's pre-war police files were here too, so I looked up Hans Kieffer, the counter-intelligence chief in Paris, who, I had read, came from Karlsruhe. His file stated: 'Hans Josef Kieffer, born in 1901 in Offenburg [south of Karlsruhe].' But it was just a record of his police pay until he left Karlsruhe for Paris, along with notes of the remuneration he received to keep his children in college here while he was away. The note gave their names, Hans, Gretel and Hildegard, and dates of birth.

Then, as I walked past the main post office, I spotted Zum Goldenen Kreuz, the bar Vera identified in one of her 1946 interrogation reports as a haunt of the Karlsruhe *Werwolfgruppe*.

————

After interrogating Fräulein Becker, Vera headed for Baden Baden, the nearby headquarters of the French zone, where she had secured a billet during her stay. The French war crimes team were based in the city's luxury Badischer Hof hotel, as were British liaison officers, whose job was to ensure communications between the different zones, but off-duty they were having the time of their lives. The French had ensured all manner of entertainment for military and civilians seconded here, including a casino, horse shows and even hunting in the surrounding countryside. Vera found much in common with a bullish Grenadier guardsman based in Baden Baden named Peter Davies, who after the war ran a nightclub in Park Lane. And she developed a close friendship with a Haystack investigator, also based in Baden Baden, named Charles Kaiser, a colourful Austrian never seen without his vast Great Dane, Lord. Parachuted into Austria by SOE just before the end of the war, when he found that his father had been deported to Auschwitz, Kaiser was much acclaimed for his success in getting suspects to talk, which some put down to the fact that Lord accompanied him to interrogations.

Vera also made the acquaintance of General Furby on this visit, head of the French war crimes group. A fervent Anglophile, who spoke English with a cockney accent, Furby took a shine to Vera and she dined at his table at the Badischer Hof for the duration of her stay.

Back in Karlsruhe over the following days Vera saw a number of further witnesses. The most useful to her was a young German woman, Hedwig Müller, who had been held in the women's prison. Vera had found the woman's name by pure chance in a letter she had sent nine months previously to a Catholic convent in Hertfordshire and addressed to 'Madame Martine Dussantry, c/o Réverende Mère Superior, French Convent, Verulem Road, Hitchin, Herts, England'.

Chère Madame, I was given this address by your daughter Martine (she never told me her real name). I knew Martine in June 1944 in the prison at Karlsruhe. The Gestapo kept me there for three months for political reasons. Martine and I shared a cell. I learnt to love her as she deserved. I once said to Martine: 'I cannot understand how you can be a spy.' Her reply was: 'I love my country. I would do anything for England. I am an officer.' I came out of prison on 6 September 1944. From 15 June until 6 September 1944 when I was in prison I saw eight English women, among whom were Mrs Audette or Odette Churchill and one Eliane . . . Every now and then some of these English women were taken away . . . we didn't know where to.

The letter, dated June 1945, had been intercepted by Britain's

Postal Censorship and after many months had found its way into Vera's hands. She saw at once that it concerned Madeleine Damerment, whose alias, misspelled by the letter writer, was Martine Dussautoy. Vera hoped Fräulein Müller might know more about her girls, when they left the jail and where they went.

The small woman wearing spectacles who answered the door of Im Grun 28 appeared nervous when she first saw Vera standing on her doorstep. Hedwig Müller, aged twenty-nine, a nurse, had been arrested by the Gestapo in May 1944 for loose talk to her boyfriend about the Führer. As soon as she saw the letter Vera was holding in her hand, however, she offered to help. She had loved Martine 'as a sister', she said, repeating this many times.

'When were you arrested?' Vera asked her, in order to pinpoint the exact chronology of her imprisonment.

'It was on a Pentecost Saturday evening,' said Müller, because she recalled going for a walk with her boyfriend, a Frenchman, who had been brought to Germany as a labourer. 'My boyfriend, Henri, said that the Germans would never beat England and America. "They are too powerful and strong. Hitler is pursuing murder on Germany and the rest of the world," he said. I said I feared this was so, then I told him a loud joke to show him what the German people thought about the Führer. We didn't notice that a woman passer-by had called a policeman. A few days later I was imprisoned by the Gestapo. The charge was that I had made a joke to a foreigner.'

Vera and Müller then established that in 1944 Pentecost had fallen on 4 June. From the other information Vera now had, she knew that all her girls were still in the prison in Karlsruhe on 4 June. This meant that Müller might have encountered all of them.

'Which was your cell?' Vera asked.

'It was cell number 17.'

'Who was in the next cell?'

'There was another Englishwoman, Eliane, in cell number 16.' Müller added that she never saw Eliane. The political prisoners were not allowed to mix. She just knew she was there, because Martine had told her. Eliane and Martine spoke to each other through the walls, tapping with plates or spoons in Morse code. Eliane was obviously Eliane Plewman, another of the women on the Karlsruhe transport.

There was a woman called Lisa Graf in cell 18, said Müller. This was not a name that Vera knew. Lisa Graf was another political prisoner, a Frenchwoman from Strasbourg, said Müller. Graf had tried to help American spies escape and was a very clever woman, very beautiful and very strong. And in cell 25 was another 'political': Elise Johe, a German from Karlsruhe, who was imprisoned because she was a Jehovah's Witness.

'What of the other Englishwomen?' asked Vera. Müller said she had heard there had been others – she thought seven in total at one time – but she could not name any more – except Odette Churchill. Odette had left alone. The rest left in two different groups. One group left in July, soon after she herself arrived, and the second in September.

Müller's recollection that after Odette's departure the other women left in two separate groups contradicted what the chief wardress had said. Fräulein Becker insisted that the remaining seven girls left in one group. Müller's evidence fitted, though, with Brian Stonehouse's recollection that three women only arrived at Natzweiler sometime in July.

It was now imperative that Vera learn which three women left Karlsruhe in the first group, in July. They must have been Stonehouse's Nos. 1, 2 and 3, whom he had seen walking to the Natzweiler crematorium.

In the first group, said Müller, there had been a girl called Diana. She had only heard the name. And there was another, 'a dark southerner', who had left in the first group, and there was also an older woman. The older woman was more stocky in appearance, she thought, and now she recalled that she was named Simone. Vera Leigh's alias was Simone, so Müller was probably talking of her. Berg, the crematorium stoker, had identified Vera Leigh at Natzweiler from a photograph.

After this first interrogation of Hedwig Müller, Vera felt close to identifying No. 1 and No. 3 of the Natzweiler dead. No. 2, however – Müller's 'dark southerner'– remained a mystery. And then Müller suddenly complicated the picture by saying there might have been a fourth. But she could not identify the fourth in any way at all.

Vera now tried to solve the problem in a different way. She asked Müller which of the seven women stayed behind after July. Müller said she herself had left the prison by the time the second group departed, in September. But she knew from a friend, another political prisoner, Fräulein Else Sauer, who stayed on longer, that Martine

and Eliane had left in the second group for sure. And then suddenly
she remembered another girl whom she had known in the prison
named Yvonne. Yvonne did not leave her cell much because she
suffered badly with her legs, Müller said. But she did see Yvonne
from time to time and remembered that she was blonde. Yolande
Beekman's alias was Yvonne.

'Was her hair dyed blonde or naturally blonde?' came Vera's question. Stonehouse had said that No. 2 at Natzweiler had dyed blonde
hair. From photographs Yolande had been identified by
Stonehouse – along with Nora – as one of the two possible matches
for No. 2. Perhaps Müller was now going to confirm that No. 2 was
therefore Yolande and not Nora, after all. 'It was dyed blonde,' she
said with certainty. But then she added that she didn't think Yvonne
left in the first group. Was she sure? Vera insisted. Hedwig was not
sure. She would check with her friend Else Sauer.

By the time Vera wrote up her notes on her interrogation of
Hedwig Müller she had gathered a few more details from the young
nurse and, as a result, had formed the firm view that Yolande
(Yvonne) had indeed stayed behind in the jail until September and
therefore she could not have been No. 2 in Stonehouse's drawings.
By a process of elimination, Müller's evidence had, in Vera's opinion,
added strength to the case for saying Nora must indeed have been
No. 2.

But the story was still confused and by the time Vera wrote to Lisa
Graf, the French political prisoner in cell 18, she was once again
seeking confirmation of No. 2's identity.

And now she was also considering the identity of a fourth girl
who might have gone to Natzweiler. She asked Lisa Graf: 'Have you
heard the name Andrée – or Denise – Borrel?' She stressed: 'The
smallest details would be of interest to me and could prove vital, for
example descriptions of clothes, of hair, and approximate dates of
various little events that might have taken place.'

Before Vera left Karlsruhe she tried to find one more witness.
Hedwig Müller had given her the name and address of Elise Johe,
the Jehovah's Witness, who had shared a cell with Yolande Beekman.
But when Vera and Corporal Trenter found the house it had been
destroyed by a bomb.

———

'My mother talked a lot about Yolande when she came out of jail,' Erich Johe, Elise's son, told me. 'There were four in the cell, which was made for one. My mother was the eldest. There was a German woman named Nina Hagen who was jailed for selling food on the black market. And Clara Frank, who had slaughtered a cow on the family farm. And Yolande told the others that she was with an English circuit in France. She was transmitting by wireless from a farmhouse when the Germans found her. My mother loved Yolande. She was very young and my mother took pity on her. Yolande was very scared, especially during the bombing when they could not go to the shelters. My mother said she cried a lot all the time. She used to ask: 'Are they going to execute me?' My mother thought they probably were because she knew about many Jehovah's Witnesses who were executed. She tried to comfort Yolande but I think she knew she would probably die.'

As we spoke in Erich's flat, his wife served tea and raspberry cakes with dollops of whipped cream. 'They got very little food in prison and were always hungry,' he told me. 'They made jokes about what they would like to eat if they were back at home. My mother said Yolande loved to embroider and to draw. She lay on her bed embroidering for the chief wardress and sometimes she would take a needle out and prick a finger until blood came out and then she used the blood to draw little sketches on the toilet paper – because she had no pencils and no paper.

'Once she drew a picture of the cell. It showed all four of them, and another showed a plate of food. They were all imagining something nice to eat and words described what they were thinking of. She gave the pictures to my mother on the day my mother left the prison.'

I asked what happened to the pictures, and Erich said he had them right there. He reached up to the table from where he was sitting and passed two flimsy pieces of paper to me.

On one paper was what appeared to be a sketch in brown ink, which was obviously the blood. At first it was hard to make out what it showed, but then I saw the outline of the cell with the window high up the wall and an iron bed underneath it. On a bed a girl was lying and there was a name: Yolande. Three more figures were sketched in and in the middle of the cell was what looked like a plate piled high with grapes, joints of meat and bread. The names of the prisoners were written here, also in Yolande's blood: Clara, Elise, Nina and Yolande.

I said I was surprised I had not found any statements from Elise in Vera's papers. Did Erich know if his mother had been interviewed by Vera about Yolande? He didn't know, but as soon as his mother had been released in September 1944 the family house was hit by a bomb and they had to move away. His mother always talked of Yolande and never learned what became of her, though she tried to find out.

After we had finished talking Erich said he wanted to show me where his mother had been imprisoned. He walked me to Riefstahlstrasse and I realised I had earlier been looking for the wrong prison entirely. This was a massive jail constructed in granite around a central courtyard. I rang at the gate and eventually a youngish man came to the door. He was friendly enough but said I was in the wrong place. There had never been women in the jail. This was a high-security jail and had recently held a number of suspected Al Qaeda terrorists.

I pulled out some old prison records with the words 'Gefängnis 11' written on them. The records were copies of the original prison records and gave the list of names of prisoners admitted to Prison No. 11 in May 1944 and the dates when they left. 'Well, yes,' he said, 'we are Gefängnis 11.' Now he remembered there had once been a women's wing, a long time ago. I also showed him a deposition, made by Ida Hager, the deputy chief wardress, giving a detailed description of the prison in 1944. He said not much had changed. Would I like to look around? He was called Heinrich Graf.

We mounted stone steps to the right of the gatehouse to reach a first-floor corridor. The women's wing, said my guide, had been on the east side of the courtyard but to reach it we had to walk anti-clockwise around the three sides of the rectangle, past all the first-floor male cells. This had always been the case, he said, and the women would have walked this way in the past. I mentioned points of interest from the 1946 deposition. The cells with their tiny portals were still here; they closed with little shutters and had tiny shelves for putting a cup on. And the floors were original, my guide said, as his feet clicked on the brown and black tiles. The prison was full of echoes – banging doors, shouting male voices, keys clanging. There was a smell of disinfectant and stale food.

When we had walked the full three sides, Ida Hager's description said we would arrive at a big white gate outside cell 26. And here it was. Herr Graf now showed me a room which was still used as a warders' office and then we peered into cell 25. The door was so low we had to stoop.

The cell was exactly as Yolande had drawn it, with a tiny meshed window very high up under a sloping buttress so that all you could see without climbing up was the sky. I told Herr Graf about the picture and he was intrigued and asked if he could have a copy for the files.

We walked back to Herr Graf's office and he laid Yolande Beekman's drawing of cell 25 on the desk. Would I mind if he scanned it into the prison computer? The drawing was private and I was reluctant. But within moments the paper was being sucked into the scanner, which almost instantly began to read the picture of the four women. Herr Graf and all his office staff were leaning forward, staring at the machine as the images began to appear. 'Super,' said Herr Graf, delighted with the results. The picture drawn in blood by Yolande in her cell across the courtyard had now been reproduced on the Karlsruhe prison computer screen.

16

INTO THE WILDERNESS

Known affectionately as 'the Gruppenführer' to his war crimes staff at the British HQ at Bad Oeynhausen, Tony Somerhough, a barrister by training, was a big, jolly man with a razor-sharp intellect and a cynical wit. Formerly Deputy Judge Advocate General, RAF, in the Middle East, he was also something of a father figure to his team in Germany and thought nothing of getting up in the small hours to cook an omelette for a hungry investigator back late from an interrogation.

After an exhausting time in Karlsruhe, Vera was content to be back at Bad Oeynhausen in the company of Somerhough and other new colleagues. In March 1946 time was already running out for her mission and she still had much to do. She was pressing the Russians for information on the Ravitsch prisoners, who she now believed had been marched to Dresden. In addition she was busy interrogating new suspects, picked up by the Haystack men and held at a small British prison in the woods near Minden called Tomato, an anagram combining two investigators' names. Anton Kaindl, the Kommandant of Sachsenhausen, had been transferred to Tomato by February 1946, but he was still claiming to have no knowledge of any British prisoners. Investigations into the fate of Francis Suttill, last heard of at Sachsenhausen, therefore remained stalled.

A handful of Somerhough's men, among them Alan Nightingale, head of the Haystack intelligence unit, Gerald Draper, a qualified solicitor who was later to become a leading human rights jurist, had become hardened to war crimes by 1946, having already prosecuted the Belsen case. But most of the team were under twenty-five, had little knowledge of law and probably had been seconded to war crimes work for no other reason than that they spoke a little German (although several did not) and were kicking their heels waiting to be demobbed. By contrast, Vera's maturity and aptitude for war crimes work deeply impressed Somerhough. Her task, he said, writing after the war, involved 'negotiating with numerous different ministries of justice and police, military headquarters and governments' and called for 'the highest qualities of tact, patient research, recording and cross referencing'. She was able to 'evolve her own systems as she proceeded', her judgements were 'unbiased and detatched' and she 'never flapped'. Somerhough also observed that Vera 'could deal sympathetically with the most peculiar people, and was at her best with foreigners who happened to be a little odd'. Vera's young colleagues also observed in her an unusually steady nerve, and it wasn't long before she had won them over. At work they found her a calming influence. In the mess they discovered she was also excellent company. Not matronly, as she had seemed to begin with, Vera liked nothing more than to carouse until the small hours and even enjoyed playing the black market when the opportunity arose. She won over many of the women staff too, particularly a lively young Norwegian secretary named Sara Jensen, who quickly became a fast friend. One colleague wrote of Vera:

> Sitting in her office just above waist deep in files
> Midst Arribert and Stephen is our Vera, wreathed in smiles.
> In office hours she doesn't look as if she liked a frolic,
> But just sit next to her when she's a little alcoholic.

On her return from Karlsruhe Vera also spent much time answering correspondence. Norman Mott, who was supervising affairs for her in London, wrote regularly with comments on her 'peregrinations' and she kept him up to date on her progress 'tracing our chaps', complaining that 'one spends much time chasing around the countryside' and often asking him for news of 'the old firm', particularly with regard to honours and awards. Whatever bad news might be uncovered in Germany, Vera was keen that SOE's successes should be the main news back home.

Many letters came from next of kin. In March, Christian Rowden wrote to say she had not given up hope and was starting her own search. 'I should like to know what name Diana was going under as that may help my search for her. A friend of a cousin of mine, who went out with Mrs Churchill to Russia, wanted to get information from Russia for me from either Stalin or Molotov, who she knew personally!'

Madeleine Damerment's mother had also written and thanked Vera for a photograph of her daughter. 'It was with great pain that I found the face of my beloved Madeleine in these photographs you sent me. I don't believe any more in the return of my daughter Madeleine. Perhaps you know some details of the situation of Madeleine in England? In what condition did she come to France and where was she? In fact I want to know so very many things – and I don't know who to ask.'

There was also a letter from a FANY officer in London filling Vera in on the latest salvos from Violette Szabo's father, Charles Bushell, which had appeared in the Sunday newspapers. Mr Bushell was now telling the papers that he 'needed funds' to provide for Violette's baby, but Vera was told the baby, who was in the care of Violette's chosen guardian, had been visited and was 'perfectly happy'. Vera was sent a newspaper cutting. 'Wondering she gazes at a picture of her missing mother,' said a picture caption below a photograph of Tania, now aged three.

Since interrogating Fritz Suhren, Kommandant of Ravensbrück, in December 1945, Vera had heard nothing definitive about the fate of Violette Szabo, Lilian Rolfe or Denise Bloch, although in her hunt for them she had filled her files with descriptions of every imaginable atrocity.

She had even hunted down a Polish survivor named Danuta Kowalewska, who, she had heard, had kept notes while in the camp. Kowalewska provided a wealth of new details about as yet unidentified prisoners and Vera scanned this material for anything new, even spotting a reference to a 'British major' in the small male subcamp of Ravensbrück identified, oddly, as 'Frank of Upway 282'. The 'major' turned out to be Frank Chamier, one of Vera's 'special cases', who used the telephone number at his home near Weymouth as a kind of alias. Shortly before Vera had left for Germany, MI6 had suddenly decided she could search for their 'bodies' too; among them was Chamier, the first British secret agent to be parachuted into Germany, where he went missing, presumed captured.

While she was alerting colleagues to the Chamier lead, Vera's own attention still focused on her girls. What had happened to Violette, Denise and Lilian after they returned to the main camp at Ravensbrück from a work commando in January 1945? Several witnesses had seen the three women when they returned from the commando. One said of Violette: 'She always had such strength and never complained', although Lilian was desperately ill. Others had passed on stories about what happened next. One former prisoner said that on 25 January 1945 all US and British prisoners had been summoned by Suhren and it was thought they were going to be repatriated but instead they were 'all hanged'. Another woman said she too had heard that the three were hanged. But Vera rejected these stories out of hand as 'too vague'. Other reports suggested Violette was seen alive in the camp as late as March. Nor had Vera forgotten the words of the Ravensbrück escapee Eileen Nearne, who said that two English girls were also rumoured to have escaped.

Moreover, many prisoners had suffered memory loss and extreme psychological damage, and in the chaos of the liberation some had been mistakenly repatriated to the wrong country or had been so incapacitated they were unable to identify themselves to the authorities. Vera had even heard tantalising stories of a woman answering Violette's description being seen among repatriated women in France. So far she had failed to verify the story but had certainly not given up hope, even at this late stage, of finding one or other of the Ravensbrück girls alive.

When arrests of Ravensbrück camp staff began, more information flowed in which Vera hoped would reveal what really happened; but it only added to her confusion. There appeared to have been in the camp two Szabos, three Blochs and several Leforts. In desperation, Vera sent out a ten-point 'questionnaire' to all survivors she could trace in various countries, including survivors of the men's sub-camp at Ravensbrück, asking them to recall details of any executions.

The replies inundated Vera with more and more horrific stories: French priests were made to hang a fellow prisoner, wrote one survivor; other concentration camp inmates were forced to 'eat their dysentery'; and sick women were cremated alive. But none of this information was any use.

––––

'And you might be interviewing somebody and they may be telling you about a grotesque crime, but you are thinking I have heard this before, and what I want is for this woman to tell me something I have not heard,' said John da Cunha, one of Somerhough's war crimes staff. Now a retired circuit court judge, da Cunha was just twenty-three when he was seconded to Bad Oeynhausen.

Sitting in the kitchen of his Somerset house, he had spread out his old war crimes papers on the table. He told me he was nearly physically sick when he opened his first Ravensbrück file. He had never spoken of his war crimes work to his family.

Clipped to the papers with rusty pins, photographs fell out showing women in skirts and jackets with their hair pinned up, hanging limp from a crude wooden gallows. 'I don't want to shock you,' he said. I asked if Vera ever seemed shocked at Bad Oeynhausen. 'No,' he said. 'Vera was always composed.'

I looked through Vera's own accounts, written later in life, for a sense of what she felt behind that composed façade. I was disappointed; her attention seemed focused only on the procedure of a particular crime, rather than on the human beings involved.

Occasionally, however, Vera's writing caused an unexpectedly violent shock. It was precisely her attention to technical detail, her concentration on how something had happened, that sometimes made her – accidentally almost – draw the reader face to face with the horror of the situation. On one occasion Vera assisted at the interrogation of a man named Gustav Moll, who was in charge of the gassing operation at Auschwitz. The interrogation came during preparation of a British case against the German industrialist Bruno Tesch, who made a 'killing solid' in the form of a solidified poisonous gas for the gas chambers. Recalling the occasion many years later, Vera wrote:

> The gas chambers were built of cement with long pipes, rather like those in a wash house, running along the low ceiling. In these pipes were sprinklers, not unlike those in a harmless watering can. The tins of crystallised gas supplied by Tesch were rammed into the apertures in the roof where they fitted exactly. A plunger then punctured them so that the gas was released. For a moment, nothing happened. Then the warmth and heat of the packed human beings below gasified the killing solid.

I had to read the sentence twice to understand that the packed human beings were mentioned in this sentence only in a passive sense – in order to explain the process of killing. 'The procedure took just over twenty minutes and after a safe interval the doors could be opened and the bodies removed to the crematorium.'

At other times Vera recounted her war crimes work in a tone designed to convey the ordinariness of it all, even when the circumstances had been as extraordinary as the interrogation of Rudolf Höss, the Kommandant of Auschwitz. In an interview she gave in 1986 for the Imperial War Museum's sound archives, Vera told the dramatic tale of how one day Höss was arrested by Gerald Draper after a tip-off was given to a Haystack investigator that he was working on a farm. Precise details of Höss's arrest and interrogation are much disputed, but, according to the story Vera told, he was picked up overnight on the pretence that he was suspected of stealing a bicycle, and taken to the British prison Tomato.

> One morning I came into the office, late as usual, and Group Captain Somerhough said to me: "You've kept us all waiting." I was rather surprised, and he said: "Well, we thought it'd be nice for you to interview Rudolf Höss with Gerald Draper and act as his interpreter."
>
> I said: "Delighted." So I went off with Gerald to our little jail in Minden. And there was this little room, which had a window on to a small interior courtyard and they brought in Rudolf Höss, who was in a normal sort of suit, had great white moustaches and was very relaxed.
>
> Gerald started off by saying: "Your name is so-and-so", using his false name – and he said: "Yes." "And you lived at this farm?" said Gerald, naming the farm where Höss had been picked up.
>
> "Yes."
>
> "And you did an absolutely dastardly thing, you stole a bicycle from a poor Polish foreign worker?" And he said: "No. I never did such a thing. Oh, no, that's a mistake. That was nothing to do with me." Gerald Draper then said: "We think you are Rudolf Höss, ex-camp Kommandant of Auschwitz." Well, this knocked him back a little, and he denied this. So we said: "Well, all right, think about it," and we pressed the bell for

a sergeant to come in. Gerald said: "Remove this gentleman's moustaches." And he was taken into the courtyard – and I'll never forget this, because it was such an incredible scene. We all knew who he was and the sergeant held him gently by the nose, and removed his moustaches and brought him back.

You know, you often hear of people's knees knocking, but it is the only time when in actual fact I've seen a man with his knees knocking. That was the great Rudolf Höss.

And he very quickly admitted it because we had photographs of him and everything that was necessary for proof. And so he spoke very freely, really, of his tenure there. We weren't going into great details but we were concerned with the number of people gassed during his period, and as usual you prepare yourself for this kind of thing by trying to keep a record of the convoys who went there, and so forth.

We reckoned that it was probably in the region of about one and a half million people and we put it to him and he said: "Oh, no, 2,345,000" or whatever it was, and corrected it upwards to an alarming degree. And I remember at this point Gerald looking at him and saying: "There is no reason really to boast, you have no cause to boast. In any case, you are by far and away the greatest murderer, including Nero of antique fame. So why do you say this number?"

He replied: "Because when I took over the number was so-and-so, and when I left the number was so-and-so. So I know." And Gerald said: "Well, you are prepared for this statement to be taken down?" And he said: "Yes" and we wrote it down and he signed it.

After a short pause, and the inevitable inhalation of smoke, Vera added: 'All between breakfast and lunch.'

———

On 11 March 1946 Vera walked into her office in Bad Oeynhausen to be told by Somerhough that an SS man named Johann Schwarzhuber had been brought in and was being held at Tomato. Vera took a car out to the prison. She knew Schwarzhuber from the Ravensbrück lists: he was the camp overseer and was more likely than anyone, other than Suhren, to know the fate of her three girls.

When Vera arrived at Tomato, Schwarzhuber was marched into the small interview room and immediately declared he was ready to talk. Within minutes he had positively identified two of the three girls as Lilian Rolfe and Denise Bloch. He not only recognised the third girl from the photograph, but also remembered that 'she had the name of Violette'.

After just a few brief questions from Vera he recalled all the details of the deaths of these three British agents. Vera had no cause whatsoever to doubt the SS man's evidence. He was there when it happened, he said. 'All three were taken to the crematorium building of the camp and one by one they were shot.'

On returning to Bad Oeynhausen, Vera immediately wrote out a detailed report to Norman Mott in London.

Today I have heard the full story from one of the few eye witnesses, SS Obersturmbannführer J. Schwarzhuber, who held the post of Schutzhaftlagerführer [camp overseer] in Ravensbrück and who is now under arrest. I attach three copies of the translation of a statement which I took from him, which will enable you to obtain death certificates. In short, he states that the girls' names figured on a list drawn up by the Gestapo in Berlin of persons to be executed. They were recalled from the work camp to the main camp and shot one evening under arrangements made by the Camp Commandant Suhren. Their bodies were cremated.

Vera added: 'No doubt you will take immediate casualty action,' and she listed precise file references containing details of next of kin for each of the dead girls.

With the Ravensbrück case closed, Vera knew she must turn back immediately to the question of the Karlsruhe women. By mid-March 1946 new letters had arrived from Hedwig Müller, the German nurse who had been imprisoned in Karlsruhe.

Müller's first letter, six pages of closely typed script, provided more details of daily life in Karlsruhe, which Vera scrutinised for new information. 'On the first day I could not eat the prison food. It was impossible. Martine said: "You will eat when you are hungry." Her prophecy became true. In the first days Martine was somewhat mistrustful of me. But as I explained to her why I was in prison she began to trust me. We knocked on the walls in conversation with the girls in the other cells. Other cell inmates watched in guard to make sure the warders did not come. We transferred letters. We were all a conspiratorial society.'

Martine became anaemic, said Müller, but got no medicine and became quite fat. 'Dear kind lady, It would make me happy if I could receive a piece of news from you.' Vera noted that Martine had put on weight, and replied to Müller with more specific questions, such as: 'Are you sure of the colour of Yolande's hair?'

Then, soon after the correspondence from Hedwig Müller, came the letter Vera had been hoping for, from Lisa Graf in Paris. Lisa was the French political prisoner, held in Karlsruhe, mentioned by Müller. At first Lisa also seemed to have information only about Martine and the second group. But when Vera read on she found new details about the first group of girls.

'I came to know Martine Dussautoy in Karlsruhe prison,' wrote Lisa Graf. 'Her cell was next to mine and we spoke to each other in Morse through walls during the night. She described her other companions to me whom I was then able to recognise in the corridor or the courtyard and with whom I exchanged a few words. I had the chance to speak to Madame Odette Churchill and to Eliane, Yvonne and Denise [all four names were underlined] and others whose names I no longer remember.' The mention of Denise was clearly a reference to Andrée Borrel, and the first sighting of her from any of the Karlsruhe witnesses.

'Towards 5 July [1944] four of them left in the morning in a transport for an unknown destination.' Lisa underlined 'four' and, like Stonehouse, numbered the women. There were no drawings this time, but the descriptions were even more acute. Lisa's No. 2 was almost identical to Stonehouse's No. 2, and Lisa's No. 3 was again Diana Rowden. Lisa wrote:

They were
1) Denise, a young woman with black hair, blue eyes, pale skin, wearing a grey coat and short blue socks, with navy-blue shoes that had rubber soles.
2) A young pretty blonde woman, with black eyes who people said was a Jewish dancer. If my memory is right people called her Dany. She was wearing a dark green, stripy dress and

white espadrilles and must have been about 20 years old.
3) A young woman about 30 years old, fair, with blue eyes,
dressed in beige and in her hair she wore a little green ribbon.
4) Somebody aged about 25 with blond-red hair and grey eyes
and she was wearing a grey coat with white espadrilles. Those
who stayed behind were Odette Churchill, Martine
Dussautoy, Eliane and Yvonne, who suffered with her legs.

P.S. Before I left the prison Martine gave me a picture of a
saint on which she wrote a sweet dedication.

Taking what Lisa had said with the other evidence, Vera was now in
no doubt that four, not three, women left together in a group in July
and that it was these four who arrived at Natzweiler. And, of the identities of three, she was now quite sure. They were Vera Leigh, Andrée
Borrel and Diana Rowden. But Vera was still not sure about the fourth.
Lisa had corroborated Hedwig Müller's assertion that Yvonne stayed
behind with Martine and Eliane. Logic therefore suggested that the
fourth girl at Natzweiler was Nora Inayat Khan. On the other hand,
Lisa Graf had described No. 2 – the one with the green striped dress –
as a Jewish dancer who she thought went by the name Dany. Vera now
felt she was going round and round in circles, because Nora was not a
dancer and never went by the name Dany. And yet again, as Vera had
always acknowledged, Nora had often been mistaken for a Jew. But it
was surprising that Nora, so unique in many ways, who everyone had
always said would be so conspicuous, so hard to hide, had left no
stronger impression on any witnesses.

Vera wrote back to Lisa and this time sent her photographs of each
of the girls, trying to pin down Nora's identity by making sure beyond
doubt that she could not have been confused after all with Yolande.

'If', wrote Vera, thinking aloud, 'Eliane, Martine and Yvonne
stayed, those who must have gone were Denise (Andrée Borrel),
Simone (Vera Leigh), Diana Rowden and Nora – alias Madeleine.

'Nora, alias Madeleine, had chestnut hair (if she did not dye it)
and very fine features. You could have thought her a Jew although
she was not. You have fairly well described her "*en disant Dany*" but
she was certainly not blonde.'

And then she implored Lisa to examine the enclosed photographs
with care: 'It is therefore important to know first if you are absolutely

sure that Yvonne was with Eliane and Martine. I must be able to identify these women definitively and without any doubt.'

Then Vera decided to return to Karlsruhe. If Nora had really been held in Karlsruhe, somebody there must remember her. Vera was determined now to interrogate more prison staff. And she would reinterrogate Fräulein Becker, who so obviously had lied.

———

Franz Becker told me he remembered listening to his aunt, Theresia Becker, chatting to his father about the war. Theresia – a devout Catholic and not a Quaker – had started out in life in her father's tailoring and laundry business, which handled all the Karlsruhe prison's laundry and mending. 'Sometimes prisoners helped with sewing and ironing. They got privileges for this,' said Franz, adding that he himself had some handkerchiefs which had been beautifully embroidered by a prisoner. Yolande Beekman did beautiful embroidery, I told him, and I asked if I could see his handkerchiefs, but he looked embarrassed, saying he didn't know where they were.

I spoke to Franz Becker at his home in the village of Untergrombach, near Karlsruhe, as we sat in a conservatory surrounded by tropical plants. One story used to come up regularly when his aunt and father talked of the war, and it had stuck in his mind. 'I remember the story about the girls who had gone up the chimney,' he said.

'What was the story?'

'Well, it began with my aunt saying that one day these girls, who were spies, were brought to the prison. Then they were suddenly taken away from the prison and had left behind clothes and some other little personal possessions. My aunt always kept the prisoners' personal possessions in her office on the women's wing. It was routine in the prison that everything was written down: when given and when given back. Well, in the case of these girls, lots of possessions were left behind. She was worried about what should be done with them. She liked to do things by the book. She wanted to send the things on to the girls but she didn't know where they had been taken. So she called up the chief and said these things should be sent on to the girls. But she was told it was no good. They had gone up the chimney.'

A strange grimace broke out on Franz Becker's face when he said 'gone up the chimney'. I asked him if he thought this news had shocked his aunt. He considered for a moment. 'I think it had an impact on her, yes. It was something, you could say, something she could not step over later in life. It was working in her mind all these years.'

Had he heard that his aunt was interrogated by the British? He said he had heard something of it. I said it appeared she had not told the full story to Vera Atkins and perhaps this was because she feared she might be blamed in some way. 'She certainly would not have liked any criticism,' Franz agreed. 'And, you see, it would have worried her that the correct procedure was not carried out in respect of the clothes. Everything was always handed over and carefully looked after and then ticked off when it was given back. She would have worried that if anyone found out this had not happened she might be criticised.'

Did he know what happened to the clothes which could not be returned? He did not remember.

———

Back in Karlsruhe, Vera retraced much old ground, but she also collected several new statements. She spoke to the guards who booked in the prisoners and she even memorised the shifts of night watchmen to find the guards who might have seen them leave. One guard thought he recalled the women leaving in a green car 'that looked like a hearse'. It was dawn, he remembered, because he had just removed the prison blackout curtains. Vera spoke to the female guard who exercised the girls in the courtyard and to those who supervised their showers. She learned every detail of the prison routine and the layout with each cell's precise location.

Vera also discovered that it was one of Theresia Becker's hallowed rules that men were never allowed into the women's wing of the prison and that only she and her deputy, Fräulein Hager, held the keys to the women's wing and nobody left unless accompanied by one of them.

So, when Vera arrived to be guided around the women's section in Riefstahlstrasse by Becker herself, the prison seemed quite familiar. From the gatehouse she knew that straight ahead was the courtyard where the girls exercised singly, by walking up and down. She knew that if she looked up to the left she would see the cell windows, high, barred and covered with metal mesh.

To reach the women's section, Becker led her up stone steps on the right of the gatehouse, then down a corridor and round three sides of the courtyard anti-clockwise, passing line after line of male cells. The white gate leading into the women's section was just where she had been told it would be, by cell 26, and there was the warder's office where Becker kept the prisoners' possessions. Vera looked in the empty lockers. She walked the corridor where Hedwig Müller had told her the girls lined up peeling potatoes. She saw the bathroom where, as Lisa Graf had told her, every three weeks the twelve women were escorted for showers. She inspected the cells, first entering cell 17, where Martine had played hairdresser, putting bright things in people's hair while Yolande next door did darning, patching and embroidery for Becker. And she saw where, during the bombing, Martine had stood in a corner holding her rosary, while Yolande, in the adjacent cell, cried. Lisa Graf had told her that sometime in July she had climbed up the sloping buttress to the window's edge and seen Andrée Borrel in the courtyard below. Andrée had suddenly turned her face up towards Lisa's window and signalled 'goodbye'.

The walls between the cells were of solid granite one foot thick, as Vera could now see. Yet through these walls the women had 'chatted' with their forks and spoons. The scratches where they had done this were still there on the whitewashed walls.

Vera had learned how the girls had forged deep friendships in Becker's prison. Sometimes, perhaps, they had even felt safe under Becker's lock and key. But, for all her new enquiries on her second trip to Karlsruhe, Vera learned nothing more to confirm who left when. Theresia Becker had stubbornly stuck to the same story she had always told.

———

I asked Lisa Graf if the girls might have stayed safely in the jail until the end of the war had Becker not so rigorously observed the rules. 'Maybe,' she said, with a shrug. 'Maybe not.' I had long been sure that Lisa must be dead. But I was sitting talking to her in Paris at a long table covered with Indian fabrics and pots stuffed with pencils, and papers everywhere. All around were artefacts – elephants and storks – and vases brimming with orchids.

'So, who are you?' she exclaimed, staring at me wide-eyed. 'What have you brought me here from my past?' Striking still at eighty-two, Lisa had shining green eyes. I showed her the letters she wrote to

Vera in February and March 1946. 'Yes, yes. That's me,' she said, and laughed.

Lisa was nineteen when war broke out. One day she saw a German walk up the drive at her home in Alsace, so she reached for a shotgun and tried to shoot him. Later, while in the resistance, she tried to rescue an imprisoned American spy but was caught and locked up in Karlsruhe.

'Yes, Martine was in a cell next to me for about a year. One day I went to empty my pot outside the door – you know, the pot for dirty water to wash and so on – and the door opened next door, and I was bending down and I looked around and this woman was bending down and she turned to me and she smiled and I smiled and when I went back in my cell I thought, She's French. So I tapped in Morse: "You are French." And she tapped back: "Yes."' Lisa had learned Morse as a girl scout.

'We couldn't talk, you see, as there were three guards standing by the door. I remember she had brown eyes and a nice smiling face, a little round with dark hair, big lips. She had a pleasant face. Not pretty.

'Then we began our conversations in Morse, which carried on for hours every night. So I used to tap the point of the fork for the short sound and scratch with the prongs for the long sounds. Our conversations took a long time, you understand, but we had a long time. She told me her name and about her family. She told me she was not married and I told her I was not married. She was arrested with other people and denounced, like me, by a Frenchman.

'Then we talked of politics, the landings, that Germany had lost the war. We had such lovely conversations. We were both *en secret* [in solitary confinement] at that time.'

Lisa read on through her letters to Vera, nodding. 'I have a great visual memory, you see – this is my métier,' said Lisa, who after the war had become a comedienne. 'And I thought at the time when I saw these girls, They are not going to come back. And so, I thought, I will fix them all, now, in my mind.'

'How did you survive?' I asked.

'You know, I never knew. But one day they took me to see a Gestapo man. He was nice and gave me food. I didn't know why he was being nice and then one day, when the door opened, I saw somebody come in the outer room who looked just like me. It was his daughter. She could have been my twin. So I knew why he was so kind.'

I asked Lisa what Theresia Becker was like. 'Madame Becker?' she exclaimed, as if surprised to hear herself voice the name all these years later. 'Madame Becker. We got on fine. I was not a whore or a murderer, so she liked me well enough. *Enfin*, she was severe! But she could be kind. And when you left she saw you off and you collected your belongings from her. I had a little valise and collected it when I left.

'One day she put in the prison an enormous bag of potatoes and told me to peel them. I said: "You think I am going to peel potatoes. *Je ne suis pas condamnée, je suis prisonnière politique!* I do not peel potatoes for the Germans!" And you know what? – she never asked me again. I said I would like to iron. They gave me an iron, so I ironed the clothes of the priests from the church. I could turn the iron over and reheat my soup.'

'How did you get to know the other girls?'

'Martine told me about them. We were all *copines* [pals], she said. When they were in the courtyard below I was at the window and Madame Greiner, one of the guards, would come and tell me the name of each and everything they were wearing and when they were leaving. I told Madame Greiner: "You know, Fräulein, Germany has lost the war and you must help me," and she did!

'Then I caught glimpses of them sometimes. In the shower, perhaps. I had a few words with Odette in the shower, I remember. She told me some girls were leaving. I remember her face.

'If I think now, I do not see the faces of the others, you know.'

I asked Lisa if she had known somebody named Noor, or Nora, who might have used the alias Madeleine. 'I saw her,' she said, and turned to look at me as if she were not certain.

'Are you quite sure?' I said.

'I think so. I saw her in the courtyard, didn't I? I didn't know her name. She was not called Nora. Yes, I saw her. At least I thought it was Nora – later when I saw the photograph that the British officer sent me.

'She was called Suzanne. She had black hair, brown eyes and the skin a little dark. She could have been Jewish. She was a dancer.'

I told Lisa that Nora wasn't a dancer. 'Well, perhaps I didn't see her after all,' she said.

17

THE VILLA DEGLER

The Villa Degler in Gaggenau, a small town near Karlsruhe, on the edge of the Black Forest, was an unlikely place to interrogate war criminals. The stylish house caught the eye of the young SAS intelligence officer Major Eric 'Bill' Barkworth when he drove through the wreckage of Gaggenau in the summer of 1945. He was looking for a base from where to search for missing SAS soldiers.

A centre of the brewing industry, the town had also been home to an important Mercedes-Benz factory, and in 1944 RAF bombers growled down the river valley here, depositing their loads on the factory. But many of the bombs missed their target, flattening 70 per cent of the town. The Villa Degler, however, remained intact, for it was sturdily built in the Bauhaus style and set back far enough from the river to escape the bombs.

When Barkworth's jeep pulled up outside the villa he found it occupied by Herr Herman Degler, owner of one of the biggest breweries in the area. The brewer and his family were turfed out in under an hour, and Barkworth, with about twelve NCOs, moved in. Frau Degler and her daughter were asked to come by each day to cook and clean for Barkworth's men.

Gaggenau was exactly where Barkworth needed to be to scour the countryside for SAS soldiers who had gone missing on operations. More than twenty SAS men were believed to have been captured after being dropped behind enemy lines just after D-Day. Yurka Galitzine's 1944 investigation into Natzweiler concentration camp had provided Barkworth with his first important clues as to the whereabouts of his missing soldiers.

By early 1946 Barkworth had rounded up and interrogated many of the Natzweiler camp staff, including the crematorium stoker, Franz Berg. Vera came to Gaggenau to interrogate Berg in early April. The statement taken from Berg had already proved vital to her research; first by alerting her to the possibility that some of her women died at Natzweiler. It was Berg who claimed that the women might still have been alive when they were burned. And crucially for Vera, it was Berg who, by studying photographs, had first identified Nora as one of the women.

The trial of the Natzweiler staff had been set for the end of May, just weeks away, and Vera wanted to be certain of her evidence in good time. Her strong view now was that Nora must have been 'No. 2', but doubts had been awakened once again by a further letter from Lisa Graf. After examining the photographs Vera sent her, Lisa wrote back: 'The only one I have difficulty recognising is the one you call Nora and I called Dany because when I saw her she had very long hair – more blonde.' Berg was to be a vital witness at the trial and Vera now wanted to see him for herself to judge if he was credible.

Berg was brought up from the cellar of the villa by one of Barkworth's team. The cellar had been converted into makeshift cells by Barkworth, who often got his prisoners to help a little around the house by serving drinks or shining shoes. Barkworth spoke fluent German and even hired a German secretary from Karlsruhe, whom he later married.

Vera was already seated in what had once been the Deglers' dining room when Berg was led in. Next to her was a row of shelves containing a cut-glass bowl and an ornamental clock, left behind by the Deglers. Through the glass doors dividing the dining room from the living area came the sound of male voices as Barkworth's team played cards. On the table in front of Vera lay Berg's deposition, Yurka Galitzine's report on Natzweiler, a pen and two blank sheets of paper.

By now Vera knew Berg's background. A common criminal, he had made himself useful to the SS and been given a comfortable job in return: stoking the crematorium oven at Natzweiler. He had also become the head prisoner, or *Kapo*, of the *Zellenbau*, the prison block. Unlike most *Kapos*, Berg was not detested. He was the camp gossip, the prisoners' eyes and ears, as well as the SS's dogsbody. Everybody knew Kapo Berg, which was why Barkworth's men had found him easy to trace. After the war he had simply made his way home to Mannheim.

Vera explained to Berg, a small, dark-haired man with a broad, square jaw, that she wanted him to describe in more detail what he had already explained to Major Barkworth.

'You started work in the crematorium, you say, in February 1943. What was your job exactly?'

'Burning bodies.'

'Bodies that had been executed?'

'Yes. Or bodies which had died by other means.'

'By injection?'

'No,' he said. He had never burned a body that had died by injection, though others had. 'I mean, I burned the bodies who had just died in the camp. You know, in the quarry and other places.'

Vera knew all about the 'bodies' in the quarry from Galitzine's evidence. Men were sent to the quarry to be worked to death. The prisoners returning to the camp each night carried the bloody and emaciated corpses of those who did not survive the day. And she had familiarised herself with the names of the sadists who flogged the prisoners to death – Zeuss, Nietsch, Ermenstraub – all of them listed in Galitzine's report.

'And the executed ones,' Berg elaborated. 'The shot or the hanged ones.'

Vera knew all about these dead bodies too. Shot bodies were stacked roof high in the cellar, awash with blood, below the furnace room. And the hangings she had heard about in person from the executioner, Peter Straub. Some weeks previously she had interrogated Straub. Berg and others had said that he was the person who had pushed the four women into the ovens. And people had said that one of the women had revived on being pushed into the oven and lashed out, scratching Straub's face. Straub, however, had denied all involvement with the killings, saying he was away from the camp that day.

———

Just as Vera's accounts of her investigations, written years later, were dry and distant, so the depositions she took at the time were mostly devoid of interesting detail. Her casual jotted notes were much more revealing, but, in the formal statements she took, her subjects disappeared off the page as she honed their words. It was as if she wanted to draw inside herself any emotion or texture in what was said, and not communicate it. The statement Vera took from Peter Straub, the man who pushed her four women agents into the oven at Natzweiler, was only five lines long.

I had, however, found another account of the interrogation of Straub. Gerald Draper, the war crimes lawyer, was with Vera at the time and remembered the occasion well. Like others, Draper considered Vera 'unflappable'. He said she was 'a quiet person who conveyed great reserves of mental energy and purpose'. But, during the Straub interrogation, her behaviour was a little different.

Draper said it had been of importance to Vera to establish from Straub what exactly had happened to her girls: 'whether they had been injected before they were thrown in the furnace or not at all'. Then, after efforts to secure an admission from Straub in relation to the girls had failed, the questions moved on to other executions he had carried out, by hanging. 'We discussed the height of the stool on which the wretched victim stood before it was kicked away,' said Draper. 'And he was not sufficiently intelligent, this man, to realise the drift of my questioning until he realised that I was establishing that he had let them die by slow strangulation as opposed to a prolonged drop to break the neck. At the end of this interview, he referred to the number of "pieces" he had disposed of in a day, and with that I said: "You leave this room on your hands and knees like an animal." At that stage, I seem to recall, was the first and only and last time I ever saw Vera Atkins show the slightest form of distress.'

———

Vera took Berg through the early part of the evidence he had given to Barkworth, then asked about the others he had worked with. At first, he said, he had worked with a man named Jehle, who was arrested for black-marketeering. Then he worked with Fuhrmann. 'But Fuhrmann caught an infection of the arm from one of the bodies being cut up in the mortuary, so he was replaced by Ziegler and a gypsy named Mettback. Peter Straub was in charge of the crematorium. He counted the bodies.'

Vera then asked Berg for every detail he could recall about her girls, from the moment they arrived at the camp.

'They were carrying suitcases and coats over their arms and I think one had a travelling rug. At first I thought it was a party inspecting the camp,' he said.

'Where were the women when you saw them?'

'On the Lagerstrasse,' he replied, then explained that this was the path that ran from the top to the bottom of the camp.

Vera asked Berg to explain the camp layout and as he talked she drew a rough sketch.

The camp was built in a clearing at the top of the mountain, he explained, at about 3000 metres. It consisted of fifteen barrack huts built in three rows of five on terraces cut out of the mountain. At the very bottom of the terraces was the *Zellenbau*, along with the disinfestation hut and the crematorium. Vera sketched the terraces and the huts and the steep path down which the girls would have walked.

At first the women were placed all together in a single cell in the *Zellenbau*, and later in solitary confinement, said Berg. What were the numbers of the separate cells? Vera asked him. 'Eleven, twelve, thirteen and fourteen,' he said, and she marked these also on her sketch. Berg had told Barkworth that at 6pm he had been ordered by Peter Straub to heat the oven to a maximum temperature by 9.30 and then disappear. Now Vera asked him exactly what happened next. 'Franz Berg was present when they were moved into separate cells at about 7pm after Nietsch had given them food,' she noted.

Vera knew the name Nietsch from Galitzine's report. He was an SS *Scharführer* who had participated in numerous sadistic acts. And Ermenstraub was there that evening also, Berg said. SS *Unterscharführer* Ermenstraub had also been picked out by Galitzine as a torturer. Witnesses had described how he had once strung prisoners up by chains tied behind their backs and whipped them to death.

Then one of the women asked for a pillow, Berg said. 'When was that?' asked Vera. 'Sometime after 7pm.'

Berg kept talking and Vera jotted scraps of what he said: '9.30 Berg still stoking the oven. Straub: "Everything all right?" Answer, "Yes." The doctor from Auschwitz told him to "disappear". Went to cell.'

Vera now pulled out another piece of paper and asked Berg to draw a plan of the crematorium building.

———

When I visited Natzweiler, on the occasion of the annual memorial service, I took with me the maps Vera and Berg had drawn, but everything was clearly signposted. The road wound up and up and round and round the Struthof Mountain until it levelled out where a sign said: '*Chambre de gaz à 1500 metres*'. Then the road went on some more. The mountain views were breathtaking. Outside the camp were more signs, one requesting '*une tenue décente*' (respectable dress).

A large man in shorts and vest emerged from a camper van. A former prisoner here, Robert Salmon attended the ceremony every year. I asked him if he'd seen the four women arrive in July 1944.

'Of course. We all saw them. They were very well dressed,' he told me. Then he led me into the camp, under the entrance gate bearing a vast sign saying, 'Konzentratsionslager Natzweiler Struthof', to show me where he was standing when the women passed by. They walked down the *Lagerstrasse* to the crematorium, he said, indicating a squat building at the bottom of the camp.

When I reached the crematorium building there were more signs explaining the washing room and the dissecting room, and in one room urns were lined up on shelves. In the oven room itself, there was a large black metal construction with several pipes running off it. A sign explained: 'The body was placed in the metal transporter located at the entrance of the furnace and pushed into it and there it burned like a torch.'

———

Berg explained to Vera that the first room on entering the crematorium was the oven room. To the right was a large washing room used by the SS, with water supplied by pipes running off the oven. Vera marked that room 'Bath'. On the other side of the oven room was a short corridor with small rooms off it. One of these was used to hold urns full of human ashes. At the end of the corridor was the dissecting room. Berg's cell was beside the dissecting room.

Vera now asked Berg to repeat everything he had told Major Barkworth of what he had heard through his cell door and what his cellmate had seen through the fanlight. As he talked she drew out of him new details and noted them down:

Two SS orderlies in white coats, names unknown, took
women swiftly from the *Zellenbau* to the crematorium past
Berg's door to next room. Women undressed as ready for bed.

No words spoken and no resistance from three but fourth
woman resisted loudly and was shut up and forcibly dragged
into room. Berg heard groans.

Women were only for minutes next door then dragged along
corridor to crematorium. Fuhrmann said dragged by hair, but in
any case dragged not carried. Fourth woman placed on bed
next door asked, '*Pourquoi?*' Answer: '*Pour typhus.*'

Vera also noted:

Stoutish one who resisted . . . Heard oven doors. After
injections higher ups left and Straub remained. Half an hour
after noises heard in crematorium – i.e. after bodies placed in
oven – Straub came and unlocked Berg's door and said it was
all over. They waited for Straub to disappear and then Berg,
Georg Fuhrmann and Alex went to room, opened door and
looked in. Saw four blackened bodies.

When Berg had completed his account Vera pulled out a separate
piece of paper to summarise her notes. She then asked him to describe
in detail each of the women he had seen. She wrote down something
but crossed it out. Then she wrote something else and crossed that out
too. She could not make sense of the words she was writing.

Then, on another page, in clearer words, she wrote:

First, dark blond hair. 1.64 m abt 30/32.
All killed. Undressed. Clothes and bags put into cell 11.
They were in cells 11, 12, 13, 14 in Zellenbau.
Vera Leigh. Quite certain spoke about pillow.
Second, slim. Believed to be Nora.
Two dark, two fair. One dark and stouter.
Clothes later placed in Dienststelle [office] until
evacuation. Seen by Berg shortly before evacuation Sept 44.
Untersturmführer Otto later Adjutant in Dachau and Nietsch
locked clothes up. Doctor small, dark, slim in civilian clothes.

Berg seemed to think that Vera Leigh, 'the stout one who asked for
the pillow', was the woman who resisted. And he believed the second,
who was 'slim', was Nora. He had not changed his story about the girls

being burned alive. He had not changed his identification of Nora Inayat Khan and Vera Leigh. He was consistent and credible. At last Vera could make up her mind that Nora was Stonehouse's No. 2. After Barkworth's men had taken Berg away, Vera drafted a note for Norman Mott: 'It has now been definitely established that the above mentioned women (Vera Leigh, Diana Rowden, Andrée Borrel and Nora Inayat Khan) were killed in the camp of Natzweiler on 6 July 1944. It appears that at least one of them was still alive when she was pushed in the furnace.' On 15 April 1946 the note was sent to Mott, along with draft letters for the women's next of kin.

———

Among Vera's papers I had found a diary of sorts. Notes of events during one week of her investigation were jotted on a single page which had been torn out of – or become detached from – the whole. 'Friday. Charles to Wiesbaden. I to Gaggenau in 4x4. Lunch at Gaggenau and then Karlsruhe. Get dossiers on girls. Inspect prison. Return to Gaggenau with papers. Merc towed in. (Galitzine).'

Events recorded were mostly mundane. One day she went to a 'Belgian horse show'; another, the 'Merc disintegrated'. But 'Get dossiers on girls' was interesting. Theresia Becker had said the prison records were all destroyed. Eventually, piecing together the sequence of events mentioned during the week, I established the date that Vera must have got the dossiers on her girls. I then took the diary to show Yurka Galitzine in his Chelsea flat. According to Vera's diary, Galitzine was there in Gaggenau the day they acquired the dossiers.

Galitzine was frail, his voice so weak that a tape recorder hardly picked it up. Slowly, though, he was able to explain. First, he said, I had to understand about Bill Barkworth, who was 'totally driven . . . totally dedicated to finding his men'. Vera was similar and they understood each other very well – as hunters they were perhaps even rivals. But Barkworth was 'almost a mystic in a way', said Galitzine. 'He played planchette to find his men.' One night when Galitzine was at the Villa Degler, Barkworth seemed at a loss as to where to look next for his bodies. The men were sitting around as usual playing cards. Suddenly Barkworth had the idea of a séance – of calling up the spirits of the dead so they could say for themselves where their corpses lay. Galitzine, Barkworth and four others set up a Ouija board in the living room. They placed an upturned glass in the middle of the table and laid out pieces of paper with numbers on them and others with letters of the alphabet and a 'yes' and a 'no'. Each man then placed a finger on the glass and as they began to ask questions the glass moved and spelled out numbers and names and places. The glass spelled out a name nobody knew and then gave the man's rank and number and the number of his Lancaster bomber, which had crashed. The glass spelled out: 'Killed at Cirey in the Vosges.'

Barkworth and his men jumped into jeeps and in the early hours went to Cirey, on the other side of the Rhine. They found three unmarked graves in a churchyard and over the next few days pieced together the story of the crash, in which three airmen had died.

Galitzine said that something of the same mystic sense caused Barkworth suddenly to charge off one day to hunt for the prison records relating to Vera's girls. Vera was cock-a-hoop at finding them, he recalled.

———

A fortnight after her interrogation of Berg, Vera was back at the Villa Degler. It was Friday, 27 April 1946 and Yurka Galitzine had come to Gaggenau to brief Barkworth and Vera on preparations for the Natzweiler trial, to begin on 29 May. They assembled in the dining room to talk. Galitzine explained that there was now great pressure from the War Office to expedite all war crimes investigations and so the Natzweiler trial was being rushed through even though not all the accused had yet been traced. A young trainee solicitor, Major Anthony Hunt, had been appointed to prosecute the case.

Vera asked about tactics. The women, she said, could be rightly classified as 'spies' since there was 'no other category for military persons operating in civilian clothes in enemy occupied territory'. But she was determined that the defence should not therefore claim lawful execution.

It was her firm view that the trial should be kept out of the papers. If this was not possible, the names of victims should be suppressed.

Galitzine asked Vera and Barkworth about the state of the prosecution evidence. Was Vera quite satisfied that the identities of the victims were finalised? The defence was sure to seize on any weakness in identification to undermine the prosecution's case. Vera admitted there had been doubts about the identity of one of the girls, but she was now satisfied that it was Nora Inayat Khan. There was, unfortunately, still no documentary evidence. The chief wardress at Karlsruhe had claimed that women's prison records had been destroyed, although, Vera said, she wasn't to be trusted.

At this moment Barkworth stood up and announced that the records had quite obviously not been destroyed. Vera was right: Theresia Becker had been lying and the records must be hidden – perhaps in the women's prison itself in Akademiestrasse, or in the chief wardress's own house. What fools they had been not to look before! With that they all rose and Barkworth ordered everyone to pile into the jeeps, then off they sped down the hill from the Villa Degler and across the river in their hunt for the records of the Karlsruhe women's prison.

Barkworth said he would start the search at Becker's house, and taking one of his men with him, he left Vera, Galitzine and the others to search the prison. The prison was searched and all the staff lined up and questioned, but nothing was found. Then Barkworth's jeep pulled up again outside the front of the building. The back of the vehicle was piled high with boxes – records for women prisoners for every year of the war, he announced. He was beaming. There was no sense in inspecting the papers there at the prison, under the eyes of its inquisitive staff, so the group hurried back to the villa.

The records were spread out on the dining table. Every entry and exit from the prison was marked here. Hunting for May 1944, the date of the girls' arrival at the prison, Vera saw five columns. In the first column were prisoners' numbers, then their names. Here was 'Churchill, Odette' and, running a finger further down, Vera found 'Plewman, Eliane', 'Leigh, Vera', 'Rowden, Diana', 'Beekman, Yolande'. But then came a name she didn't know: 'Olschanesky, Sonia'. Vera passed over this name and found two more she did know: 'Borrel, Denise' and 'Dussautoy, Martine'. Then the names of her agents ceased and there were others she did not know. She turned the page, still looking for one more name. Nora was not here. After searching throughout the register for June, Vera went back to May, then to February and January 1944 and even December 1943. Then she went forward to July. There was no sign of Nora Inayat Khan or Nora Baker. Vera looked back at the entry for Sonia Olschanesky. Sonia had been admitted on exactly the same date as the other seven girls. She was obviously one of the group. Nora had changed her aliases several times. She might have given an alias to the prison, just as Madeleine Damerment had given 'Martine Dussautoy'. Nora might well have chosen a Russian-sounding name: she was born in Moscow. 'Sonia Olschanesky' could well have been an alias for Nora.

Now Vera looked for other registers, which would say where the girls were taken. She saw the column 'taken to'. Against the name Diana Rowden it said she had been taken to '*einem KZ*', shorthand for *Konzentratsionslager*. All the four girls, including Sonia Olschanesky, had been taken to '*einem KZ*'. That concentration camp, as everyone now knew, was Natzweiler.

Vera turned several pages and scanned the same register for the second group of women, who left on the night of 11–12 September 1944. If Yolande Beekman was here, this was Vera's final proof that Yolande could not have been Stonehouse's No. 2 at Natzweiler. Here were the three names: Eliane Plewman left on 11 September 1944, as did Martine Dussautoy and Yolande Beekman. The record for these three gave no indication of where they had gone. Under 'taken to' it said '*abgeholt nach*': 'no destination'. Under another entry was written '*Fr fuss*', meaning literally that they went 'freely on foot', or were set free.

Barkworth and his men were pulling out more and more files, containing various sorts of registers. There was one loose slip showing Diana Rowden's next of kin: '*Mutter*. Christian Rowden. Cornwall Mews West, London SW7'. Another slip showed Eliane Plewman had handed in no money on the day of her arrival and she was given no money back. Eliane had signed the slip, as had Fräulein Becker. And here were records of clothes handed in. Eliane handed in one pair of shoes, one pair of stockings, one shirt, one pair of trousers, one winter coat and three rings 'of no value'. Again Theresia Becker had signed the form.

There were many more forms here, giving much the same information but in a different way.

Though it remained a mystery where the second group had gone, these records made it quite clear to Vera that, wherever it was, Yolande Beekman was with them and not with the first group that left for Natzweiler. So Nora must, as Vera had already concluded, have been Stonehouse's No. 2. Sonia Olschanesky was clearly an alias for Nora. There could be no other explanation and Vera saw nothing in these records to make her change her conclusion, which had already been communicated to the War Office. And letters confirming the deaths of the girls at Natzweiler had already gone to next of kin, including Nora's mother.

18

NATZWEILER

The road to Natzweiler took Vera deep into the Vosges Mountains, through the pretty, red-granite town of Schirmeck and on to the little village of Rothau. Sometime in early May 1946 she chose to visit Natzweiler concentration camp before the trial to be held at the end of the month.

The question of identity was now settled in Vera's mind and the task of informing next of kin was complete. Christian Rowden, replying to the junior officer who had signed Vera's draft letter containing the news, said, 'Mrs Rowden thanks the Junior Commander Prudence Gwynne for her letter of 29 April telling her the grim details of her daughter's fate. She thanks her and her staff for the sympathy expressed and is trying to find consolation in what she has learned.'

Now Vera was focusing not on who died at Natzweiler, but on how precisely the four women had met their deaths. She had travelled as far afield as Belgium and Luxembourg taking statements, in order to be sure whether all or some of the women were still alive when they were burned. Before giving evidence, Vera now felt she needed to see the layout of the camp for herself.

Under the steep, forested slopes of the Struthof Mountain, Vera's driver suddenly switched the jeep sharply left and seemed to head straight up through the trees. The mountain track was built by prisoners when the camp at the top first opened. German geologists came to Rothau in the spring of 1941 prospecting for red Alsatian granite to face the party's buildings in Nuremberg. The stone was located on an upper ledge of the mountain behind Rothau, very near the Hotel Struthof, which had been a small skiing centre. When the desired granite was found, a local stonemason's firm was conscripted to work a quarry. Inhabitants of the area were turned out of their homes, SS staff moved in and more and more prisoners were transported here, both as slave labour for the quarry and to build the concentration camp. Set above the tiny village of Natzweiler, in a clearing on the mountain's summit, it was to be the only Nazi concentration camp on French soil. Prisoners were brought by train to Rothau's small station, and villagers watched as they were marched 8 kilometres up the hill.

Both Barkworth and Galitzine had spoken to the locals about the atrocities at the camp. Some evidently had openly collaborated with the Nazis, providing food or shelter. Others felt tarnished – even guilty – simply because they lived on the same mountain while the atrocities were taking place.

Now the jeep was moving up slowly through the foliage, revving hard. For about the first 6 kilometres the track ran almost straight up the hill. The jeep passed near the Hotel Struthof, with alongside it the small brick structure which had served as the camp's gas chamber.

Near to the summit a low wall appeared on the left-hand side and behind it was a large house with a swimming pool – the SS officers' mess, as Berg had described. Then the road turned in a sharp dogleg to the left and, up ahead, Vera was suddenly staring at bright, open skies. As her eyes adjusted to the glare she saw, silhouetted against the white light, two massive wooden structures – giant watchtowers – and arching between them was an enormous sign over a gate smothered in thick razor wire. Black letters painted on white on the sign announced that this was the entrance to Konzentratsionslager Natzweiler Struthof. The gate, at least 20 feet high, was what the prisoners called 'Das Tor'. As Vera's evidence now showed, four of her girls, Andrée Borrel, Vera Leigh, Diana Rowden and Nora Inayat Khan, had left Karlsruhe prison at dawn on the morning of 6 July 1944. How they travelled to Natzweiler, and with whom they travelled, was still unclear. But Vera knew for sure that at about 3pm on that afternoon they had passed through these vast and ugly gates.

The jeep emerged into the open, kicking up dust and stones behind it, and the noise of the engine was echoing right across the valley and then back across the empty wooden barracks of the deserted camp, which now lay at Vera's feet, here on the mountain's uppermost slope.

When the engine was turned off there was silence, broken only by birdsong. The camp was overlooked by nothing except the wide, open sky in the daytime and the stars at night. Nobody passed by. Nobody came here, unless they had business with the camp. In summer the slopes were exposed to glaring heat. But in winter, 3000 metres up, the temperature sometimes dropped to −30 degrees Centigrade and the camp was almost always shrouded in freezing fog. What better place to make people disappear into *Nacht und Nebel*.

Barkworth and Vera had by now uncovered a mass of new evidence about the Nazis' notorious 'Night and Fog' order. Given that the whole purpose of this order was that nobody would be told where the prisoner had been sent and the prisoner would have no contact with the outside world, this was the perfect place. The idea of making people 'disappear' had come from a decree issued by Hitler's chief of staff, Field Marshal Wilhelm Keitel, on 12 December 1941. It was intended to deal with civilian resisters – either in Germany or in German-occupied countries. The aim was to deter others by treating '*N+N*' prisoners abominably and then killing them off so nobody would know anything about what had happened to them. Some SS chiefs chose to apply the decree to spies and foreign commandos. Some did not. But by the end of the war hundreds of thousands of '*N+N*' prisoners had indeed 'disappeared' in specially designated secret camps. Natzweiler was one of the best-kept secrets of all.

Only hand-picked SS men who could be relied on not to talk were allowed to work at Natzweiler. And nobody was allowed to say anything about what happened inside the crematorium. If anyone was going to witness crimes committed here it was only the other inmates. And, from the evidence Vera had gathered so far, it seemed as if every single prisoner in the camp had witnessed something of the crime which happened on 6 July 1944.

As Vera stood beside Das Tor, looking down over the barrack roofs, it was obvious to her why so many of the other inmates witnessed what happened: this was a place where everything could be hidden – and nothing at all could be hidden. The camp was laid out like a massive amphitheatre, with the low wooden barracks stepped up one behind the other on terraces, looking down towards a 'stage' at the bottom of the camp: the *Zellenbau*, with its punishment cells, and the crematorium, both cradled by pine trees.

So, when several of the camp's senior SS staff denied that the women were here on 6 July 1944, hundreds of pairs of eyes were able to say that they were. The Kommandant himself, Fritz Hartjenstein, told Vera that he knew nothing about the case at all. Yet Hartjenstein had personally collected the four women from the bottom of the hill in his car. A Belgian prisoner, Albert Guérisse, later awarded a GC for his bravery in the resistance, had seen the car arrive and watched as Hartjenstein took the car on a curious lap of honour around the camp.

Guérisse, a prisoner in Barrack 7, told Vera that Hartjenstein's car carrying the new prisoners drove in through the gates at about 3.30pm. The car drove along the inside of the perimeter, following three sides of the square, so that Guérisse, from his barrack at the bottom of the camp, had seen it pass. 'In view of the fact that vehicles were rarely seen inside the wire its presence caused a good deal of interest.'

So, before anyone even knew that the car carried women – for nobody could see who was in the back – the camp's interest had been excited. And when female figures stepped from the car, gossip spread like wildfire from barrack to barrack. It was almost unheard of for women to enter the camp. The rumour that these women were English and French intensified the inmates' curiosity.

The women's first minutes in the camp were witnessed close-up by just a few members of staff, who caught sight of them as they were ushered into the SS offices beside Das Tor. A Luxembourger named Marcel Rauson who was passing by on an errand saw them standing outside the camp's political office, where the SS political officer, Magnus Wochner, was sitting. Rauson supposed they were there to fill in reception papers. Under interrogation, Wochner told Vera that he had first seen the women in the office of his colleague Wolfgang Zeuss. Wochner too supposed that they were dealing with paperwork.

Then a man from the Karlsruhe Gestapo, who had accompanied the women, walked into Wochner's office and explained that there were orders from Berlin to execute the women immediately. Wochner disputed this 'unorthodox' procedure, saying that such orders usually arrived in Zeuss's office by secret teleprint, or by letter direct from Berlin to the Kommandant of the camp. A carbon copy was always immediately made of such an order and sent to the Kommandant. But the Karlsruhe Gestapo man said the women's names should not be entered in any records at all. Wochner claimed he then said he wanted nothing to do with it. Other witnesses, however, suggested he was simply lying and that the camp executioner, Peter Straub, was never authorised to kill a prisoner without Wochner's order. In any event, the women's arrival had clearly caught the senior SS staff off guard. They were busy preparing for a big leaving party to be held that evening for the camp doctor, Dr Plaza. Dr Plaza was one of a large number of officers transferred to Natzweiler from Auschwitz, including his replacement, Dr Werner Rohde.

While the procedural dispute was going on, others saw the women sitting waiting. They were 'very quiet', according to a Polish prisoner, Walter Schultz, who was working in the political office as an interpreter. 'One was smoking a cigarette.' When the women eventually emerged into the open, escorted by four SS men, every inmate in the camp strained to look at them.

Among the prisoners were Danes, Norwegians, Frenchmen, Luxembourgers, Dutchmen, Belgians – nearly all of them resisters. There were large numbers of Russians and a whole village of Poles who had infected the entire camp with typhus. There were a few Greek, Italian and Yugoslav partisans too. There were priests, doctors, scientists and ordinary criminals; and there were hundreds of Jews, although Natzweiler was not a camp for Jews. And there were two English SOE agents: Brian Stonehouse and Robert Sheppard, both from F Section. Every man in the camp was labelled: a blue triangle for homosexuals, green for felons, black for work dodgers, violet for Jehovah's Witnesses, yellow for Jews and so on. Those designated to disappear as 'N+N' prisoners wore over their heart a round, yellow label with three concentric black circles. They were walking targets and could be shot at any time. They were not allowed any communication with other prisoners. Many of the resisters were designated 'N+N' and large letters were written on the backs of their jackets to confirm this.

But, as Vera knew, the four women would have been quite unable to identify any individual in the camp by name or nationality. Had they looked around at the thousands of men now staring at them they would have seen only a sea of identical emaciated faces, with identical shaved heads and skeletal bodies.

The evidence suggested, however, that the women did not look around. Stonehouse portrayed them in his descriptions and sketches stepping out, looking ahead, holding their heads high as they carried their little cases and packages down the *Lagerstrasse*, almost as if they had come to stay just for the night. The trail running down the centre of the camp was steep and very long.

The women had made their appearance at a time of day when the largest number of prisoners was certain to be present to watch. By 4pm the work commandos were returning from the granite quarry, marching to the order of ranks of SS guards, dogs all around. Some prisoners were preparing for evening roll-call outside the barracks. Others were carrying out tasks inside the fence. One of these was Stonehouse. He had been laying pipes just inside the wire on the east side of the fence when the women came past.

Descending the steps a little, Vera soon reached the point where Stonehouse must have first seen the women. She stopped momentarily and adjusted the diagram, based on Berg's description, that she had brought with her, altering a directional arrow here or the position of a watchtower there. Everyone who had noticed the girls pass by saw something slightly different. Some said there were three and some said four. Some said they passed at 3pm and some at 5pm. Some said one carried a rug, others that one had a coat. One said they were all carrying boxes, another that they were suitcases. Some said June, some July. But every single witness Vera spoke to had, like Berg and Stonehouse before them, said that the women were well dressed.

'One could see from their appearance that they hadn't come from a camp,' wrote Roger Linet, a French prisoner, who was working in the kitchens when they passed by. 'They seemed young, they were fairly well groomed, the clothes were not rubbish, their hair was brushed and each had a case in her hand.'

And yet although many remarked upon their clothes, no one was able to help Vera with a description of the women's faces.

Stonehouse got closer than anyone else. Vera had had the chance to talk to him in person since he sent his sketches, and gradually he had remembered more. He now timed the arrival of the women by the news of the attempt on Hitler's life, which he remembered spread around the camp shortly after the women arrived. One of those accompanying the women was an SS NCO whom he and other prisoners had nicknamed 'Fernandel', because he looked like the French actor. Ferndandel's real name was Ermenstraub.

'The whole party moved down the path on which I was working and passed me within a few feet, so that I was able to observe them very closely,' Stonehouse said. But even he did not observe them close enough for Vera. She wrote in her notes at the time that the women had been seen by many people, including fellow SOE prisoners. 'But none saw them at sufficiently close range to identify them from photographs, but gave descriptions of their colour of hair and clothes etc.'

Along with their clothes, witnesses noticed the women's general bearing. There was no doubt they were 'first class', said Major Van Lanschot, a Dutch resistance leader. Van Lanschot wrote to Vera that he was working with other potato peelers when he saw the girls going down in the direction of the bunker. 'It was the first time we saw women in Natzweiler and everybody was interested in the reason for which they were brought in. The general opinion was they were too good to start a Puff [a brothel] with.'

Rumours naturally spread about the real intentions of the SS guards. Walter Schultz, the Polish prisoner and camp interpreter, had been told that the women were to be 'employed in the officers' mess'. And when a new rumour flashed around that beds were being prepared for them in a room in the crematorium, there was more talk of a brothel.

But by the time the women moved down the final flight of steps all the prisoners knew the real intention of the SS: to kill the four women, right there that night. The only people in the whole concentration camp who did not know this were the women themselves. Was this why their story was so deeply scored into every witness's mind – prisoner and SS alike? These four women, alone of all the people brought to Natzweiler, had no idea of the possible fate in store for them. They were not taken to their deaths already emaciated and half-dead. They were healthy and smartly dressed and might have walked in off any London or Paris street. And nobody could warn them, still less help. The six thousand men imprisoned in the camp, many of the bravest resisters in Europe, could do nothing that afternoon but watch as these young women walked past on their way to certain and horrific death.

Even before the women had reached the bottom of the camp a dispute had broken out among the senior SS staff, including the camp doctors, about how to kill them. Vera had heard differing accounts of this dispute. Dr Rohde said he had been resting on his bed in the SS officers' mess when Dr Plaza, Otto and Straub rushed into his room to tell him about the arrival of the women 'spies'. They were all as surprised as anyone.

According to Dr Rohde, his three colleagues told him that the women had been condemned to death and were therefore to be hanged. Straub had objected, saying that to hang women – Englishwomen and Frenchwomen – would lead to a great 'to-do'. 'He said it would cause "*ein grosses Theater*" and we would have to find another way,' said Dr Rohde, who was surprised, as Straub usually enjoyed such spectacles. The other way proposed by the doctors was to inject the women with a lethal substance, but they were not sure if they had the necessary quantities in stock.

Emil Brüttel, a medical orderly with the junior rank of *Unterscharführer*, was in the dispensary, near the crematorium, at the time these discussions were taking place. Under interrogation he recalled receiving a phone call in the early evening from Dr Plaza, who was dining in the officers' mess, outside the perimeter fence. 'He told me to look in medical stores and see how many capsules of Evipan there were. I told him there were just enough for the normal requirements of the operating theatre. Then Plaza rang down again. He said: "Look and see if we have any phenol and how much there is." I reported back that we had about 80cc. Then he called and told me and Eugen Forster to be ready for duty and to bring the phenol and a 10cc syringe and one or two larger-gauge needles.'

The evidence taken by both Vera and Barkworth suggested that a timetable for the killings had been drawn up by the time the women reached the bottom of the steps of the *Lagerstrasse* at about 5pm. The women were first led round the back of the prison block, entering from the rear entrance, which faced the forest, and down the mountain. They were then locked in cells.

Since the women's arrival at the camp, Franz Berg had been busy making sure everyone knew as much as possible about them. It was he who passed the word right down to the barracks on the lower terraces that there were British women among the group. Hearing this, one prisoner, Georges Boogaerts, decided to try to get a word to the women when the guards were distracted, by calling across to them in their cells.

Boogaerts, like Albert Guérisse, was a Belgian doctor, and had been placed in charge of the prisoners' hospital. The windows of the hospital block looked directly on to the prison block – a distance, as Vera could now see as she stepped down the last step, of about 25 yards. Choosing his moment carefully, Boogaerts made a first attempt to contact the girls. He managed to get the attention of two, who appeared to be in the same cell, by whistling and whispering as loudly as he dared.

The women then opened their window. A few hurried words were passed between Boogaerts and the girls and he managed to get a glimpse of one of them, and even a name. He told Vera: 'I remember one of the women was dark and that she called herself Denise.' Then, miraculously, he was able to throw some cigarettes at her window. 'In gratitude for this she sent me, through Franz Berg, a small tobacco pouch.' Boogaerts still had Andrée (Denise) Borrel's tobacco pouch in his possession when Vera saw him in Brussels in early April 1946.

Having found out that the girls were English and French, Boogaerts was determined to tell his friend Guérisse. Boogaerts knew that, given Guérisse's connections with the English, he would want to try to talk to them too. Guérisse, better known in resistance circles by his alias 'Pat O'Leary', was already something of a resistance legend. Evacuated from Dunkirk, he was back in France by 1941, where he ran one of the most successful British escape lines, the 'Pat' line, along which numerous British airmen travelled to get back home.

Emile Hoffmann, a Luxembourger and a military musician, was in Guérisse's barrack and remembered that as soon as Guérisse heard the women were English he was determined to make contact and 'took a great risk' to get close to the prison block. He had to scramble through two barracks and across the gap between them to reach Boogaerts in the hospital block.

Guérisse's account of what happened next was as follows:

Boogaerts came to see me after he had first made contact
with the women, saying he had managed to get them some
cigarettes and he suggested that I should come to his block at
7pm in order to talk to them and find out who they were,
from the window of his block, which was within speaking
distance.

And I went to his block and by looking through the
window and whistling I could see the head and shoulders of a
woman appear in the window of the cell opposite in the
prison block and I noticed that she had dark hair but it was
not possible to observe more.

He said he had started shouting in English: 'Hello, hello, are you
English girls?' And all of a sudden a girl's face appeared behind the
bars. 'Yes, we are English and French,' a voice said. 'Well, why are
you here?' asked Guérisse, and then the face disappeared, but he
managed to shout back: 'I am a British officer.' Vera asked if
Guérisse had managed to identify the girls in any way. At first he said
he had not, and that this was the last sight he had of them. Later, in
other interviews, he said that he had recognised the girl with dark
hair as Andrée Borrel. Guérisse had known Andrée Borrel in France
early in the war. Before escaping to England and joining SOE,
Andrée had worked on the 'Pat' line in France. Everyone who had
worked with Andrée had been impressed by her steely nerve,
including Guérisse, who had relied on her on many occasions as
Allied airmen were hidden in safe houses, and moved to safety.

Talking to Vera at this stage, however, Guérisse did not recall that
the girl was Andrée. He recalled only that, whoever she was, he had
been unable to help her escape or help any of them in any way at all.
This was because, as soon as he had made the contact, a warning was
whispered down the barracks that the SS were present. Guérisse
had to give up. As he told Vera, he would have been shot on sight if
overheard. There was nothing more he could do. There was nothing
anyone in the camp could do. He was entirely impotent; but he had
done his best. 'As I well knew, any conversation with people in the
prison cells would lead to the most serious consequences. I was
obliged to desist.'

The timing of what happened from now on was also easy to verify
because, soon after Guérisse's conversation with the girls, the

prisoners were all given strict orders to be in their barracks early that evening, which made an impression on all of them as it had never happened before. They were told to stay indoors, close the shutters and curtains and not look out. They were told they would be shot immediately if they looked out.

'I remember that on the evening of this day prisoners had to be inside their barracks by 8pm. This was unusual because generally the prisoners were allowed to be outside until 8.30pm and need not close their windows or draw their curtains,' said Marcel Rauson, the Luxembourger. At the same time another rumour went around the barracks that the women were from the prison in Fresnes, near Paris. They were definitely to be executed that evening.

As Dr Boogaerts told Vera, the curfew order did nothing to hide what was about to take place. From the hospital, so close to the crematorium, it became particularly obvious: 'Towards the evening we all observed the usual preparation for an execution, that is to say – much coming and going among the SS and the lighting of the crematorium furnace.'

Standing in front of the little red-brick prison block now, Vera further refined her sketch. She scribbled '25 metres' above an arrow from Guérisse's Barrack 7 to the hospital block – the distance Guérisse had had to scramble to reach Boogaerts's window without detection. And she scribbled '10 metres' on the arrow from the hospital to the prison cells, showing the distance their voices had to carry to be heard by the girls.

It was Berg who had first sketched for Vera the layout inside the prison block, when he was telling her how it was that he had brought four portions of food – thin soup and bread – for the women's last meal, down from the kitchen at the top of the camp. The other prisoners saw Berg do this. Major Van Lanschot had told Vera: 'The *Kapo* of the bunker, his name was Berg, if I remember well, was the one who was to fetch personally food for the people he had in his bunker. So we always knew by him if there were people to be executed.' But on this occasion Berg was not allowed inside the cell to distribute the food; this was done, according to Berg, by the senior *Blockführer*, Nietsch. Entering the prison block through the back, Vera could easily identify which cell the girls had been in at this stage, as there was only one room large enough to hold all four.

Shortly after their meal the women were moved into the single cells, so it must have been just before this, when they were still all together, that Berg was asked for a pillow by one of them. This, as he told Vera, he had provided, and he was sure the request had come from Vera Leigh. By the time Walter Schultz arrived in the bunker, the women had been moved into separate cells – small, airless cubes with low ceilings where it was impossible to stand. Schultz, who had first seen the women sitting quietly in the political office on their arrival, now wanted a second glimpse of them. A Russian speaker, he had been called to the prison block to speak to a Russian prisoner and as he walked down the prison block corridor he opened the traps to get a glimpse of the women inside the cells. Straub, who was there at the time, said to Schultz: 'Pretty things, aren't they?' Schultz soon left, and this was when Peter Straub turned to Berg and told him to heat the crematorium to maximum heat by 9.30 that evening.

Until about 9pm there was little further activity in the main part of the camp. Dr Boogaerts recalled that at one point an SS medical orderly came into the hospital block to borrow a syringe, but it caused him no surprise as by then the rumour had spread that they were likely to be killed by injection. The prisoner, Rauson, said he heard that injection was to be used from the *Kapo* in his own barrack, a man named Duchanek, who had heard it from Berg. By 8pm, as ordered, all the prisoners were in their barracks, shutters closed. The night sentries were on guard in the watchtowers. And the only movement was inside the crematorium, where Berg, as instructed, was stoking the oven.

To see the exact position of Berg's room, Vera had to enter the crematorium building, and she went in as the girls had done, through the door at the rear. Thanks to Berg's earlier description, Vera felt well prepared to find her way about, although there was very little light inside the first room and it was not clear to her at first that the squat, black iron structure, consisting of a large cylinder about 7 feet long and 2 feet in diameter with pipes running from the top and sides, was the oven.

She looked to her right and saw the various tools: shovels and pans and long forks and a stretcher, shaped just like a hospital stretcher but made of iron (Berg had called it a 'transporter') leaning up against a wall. Beside it was a pulley mechanism fixed above a trap door. Looking ahead again, as her eyes adjusted to the light she could see that the metal structure was indeed the oven. Its round door at the front end of the cylinder was clamped shut.

Moving to the other side of the room and turning again to face the metal structure, she saw that attached to the other side of the oven cylinder was the furnace, which was connected to the ceiling by a chimney. Stepping back a little towards the tiny window and still looking upwards, she saw a line of large metal hooks.

Pipes led from the furnace to the room on her left. These apparently fed hot water to what Berg had said was the bathroom, used by camp staff. The corridor leading off the room to her right was the way to Berg's cell. At the end of the corridor Vera could now see, through an open door, the corner of a gleaming white ceramic slab. She was looking into the dissecting room at the end of the corridor; it was lighter than anywhere else in the building. Passing on down that way, she looked into a small room on the right where lines of small ochre clay urns were lined up on dusty wooden shelves extending from floor to ceiling. Berg's cell, as he had described it, lay just along the corridor from here, but it was hard to judge exactly which it was from his description as there were more small rooms than he had mentioned and the distances seemed much less than he had led Vera to believe.

Although the camp was silent by the time dusk fell, every pris-oner in the barracks outside was straining to look through curtains and shutters to see what would happen next. Sometime just before 9pm, and certainly before it was completely dark, the medical order-lies, Emil Brüttel and Eugen Forster, received an order telling them to walk up the *Lagerstrasse* to just outside the camp gates, where they were to meet up with other staff who would be coming from the offi-cers' mess in the trees beyond. Brüttel described to Vera what had happened: 'I took the phenol with me about which I knew nothing. It was contained in a dark brown bottle with a glass stopper. Forster took charge of the syringe and needles and then we reported to the place to which we had been ordered. There we met Dr Plaza, Dr Rohde, the adjutant *Obersturmbannführer*, Ganninger, and some *Blockführers*, among them Nietsch and Ermenstraub. Ganninger insisted on speed and the whole party entered the camp and the gate was shut behind us.'

The party then began their procession down the *Lagerstrasse* to the bottom of the camp. 'One of the *Blockführers* went in front with the oil lantern which was normally banned for safety reasons,' said Brüttel. 'I had the impression that the doctors did not wish to carry the necessary material themselves to the place of execution, and that they wished, by the presence of the greater number of staff, to increase their courage and self confidence for an action which was obviously extremely unpleasant for them. It was apparent for those reasons we had all to go with them.' He added: 'There was no way for Forster and me to turn back since we had no safety lamp with which to walk through the darkened camp, and to walk without a lamp would have been the same as suicide since the sentries would have fired immediately.'

The group was now observed as it made its way down the *Lagerstrasse*, exactly the same path the women had followed earlier that day. Albert Guérisse, peering between curtains, observed the group carrying their torch on the way down and among them he identified the two SS doctors – one in uniform and one in civilian clothes, and several other SS staff and officers.

At 9.30 Straub made his way back to the crematorium building and, as Berg had said, checked that all was well with the furnace, before sending Berg to his room with orders not to come out again. The doctors' group, which had been processing down the *Lagerstrasse*, now arrived inside the building. Brüttel said that when he entered the crematorium building with them, the light in the furnace room was switched off, so that anyone who didn't know already would not be able to determine what the room was really for.

Berg was found still stoking the furnace and was ordered away a second time. He himself had said that it was the doctor in uniform who chased him out of the furnace room and this was when he went into his cell along the corridor and pretended to be asleep. From that moment on Berg's knowledge of what happened was limited to what Fuhrmann had been able to see through the fanlight along one tiny piece of corridor outside. Others, however, since interrogated by Vera, had now filled in parts of the rest of the picture, although several of those present – Nietsch, Ermenstraub and Plaza – had still not yet been traced and so there were gaps in the accounts of what happened next. According to Brüttel, the execution squad then went along the short corridor to a small room just before Berg's cell, where several beds were standing.

Here Ganninger addressed the execution squad and explained the plan. The two *Blockführers* Nietsch and Ermenstraub, were to be sent off to fetch the women, one at a time, from the *Zellenbau*, the prison block, adjacent to the hospital. The women would then be brought into this room, where they would be injected by the doctors.

The fetching of the women from the cells was witnessed by several prisoners. Maurice Bruyninckx, another Belgian prisoner, who was in Barrack 15, had been 'looking through a small peep-hole in the shutters' when he saw two SS men enter the prison block. 'They came away with one of the four women I had previously seen on their arrival in the camp. These same two returned to fetch the second, third and fourth at about fifteen-minute intervals to take them to the crematorium building.'

Guérisse had seen the same ritual through his curtains, picking out SS faces by torchlight.

It was important for Vera to understand precisely how the sequence of events then unfolded. Brüttel, who had seen what had happened in the injection room, along with Berg, who had heard, via Fuhrmann's running commentary through the fanlight, provided the best evidence. Brüttel said that the plan had been that once a woman had been brought into the injection room she would be made to lie on a bed and a doctor would then administer an intravenous injection in her arm.

In each case 10cc of phenol was used. Brüttel said that it was Dr Plaza who gave the injections, but others said it was Dr Rohde. Dr Rohde himself said that he did give the first injection but was so upset by having to perform the task that Dr Plaza had to take over. Others said that Dr Rohde gave two injections and Dr Plaza the other two, to share the responsibility. Dr Plaza was to be replaced as camp doctor by Dr Rohde the following day and there was some discussion about the fact that this would be his last duty in the camp.

As the injecting began, Berg had said he heard 'low voices' in the next-door room 'and then the noise of a body being dragged along the floor'. Brüttel recalled that one of the women asked a question immediately before her injection and one of the doctors said: '*Pour typhus*.' Berg had also heard the woman's question: '*Pourquoi?*' And then the answer, '*Pour typhus*', was given in a voice which he recognised as that of the doctor in civilian clothes. He said the woman who asked the question was the fourth woman and that this woman also struggled. 'We then heard the noise of a struggle and the muffled cries of the woman. I assumed that somebody held a hand over her mouth. I heard this woman being dragged away too. She was groaning louder than the others.'

Brüttel said that after receiving an injection, each of the drugged women was then taken to the next room. He said they were carried, not dragged – by Nietsch or Ermenstraub – and there they were laid down and on the order of Otto 'nearly completely undressed'. Brüttel also said that at this time he had heard the noise of speaking in a room where the 'prisoner stokers' were locked.

According to Walter Schultz, the events unfolded slightly differently. He said that Straub told him the following day that what had happened was as follows. When the four women were brought from the cells they were first made to sit on a bench in the corridor which led from the oven to the dissecting room. They were told by Ganninger, who spoke a little French, to undress for medical examination. This they refused to do unless a woman doctor was called. They were also told they would be given injections against illness. The first woman was then taken by Straub into the room where the doctors were and injected in the upper arm. Straub then helped the first woman back to the bench, where she sat down next to the others who were still waiting. The same procedure was followed with the second woman. When Straub arrived back with the second woman after she had been injected, he found that the first was sitting 'stiff and stupefied'. The process continued until all four had been injected and were sitting in a stupefied condition. It was then, according to Schultz, that they were taken to the room next to the crematorium. Here they were laid down and their clothes were taken off by Nietsch and Ermenstraub.

Dr Rohde had said that, after the injection, three of the women were easily undressed. However, the SS *Scharführer* had difficulty undressing the fourth woman as rigor mortis had already set in. He was therefore unable to take off the pullover she was wearing and had to 'tear it open'. Rohde said: 'I then yelled at him and told him that the bodies would have to be undressed in a decent manner.'

All the witnesses were agreed that, once undressed, the women were dragged along the remaining length of the corridor to the oven. They were then placed inside it. The usual practice was to place a body on a transporter and then push it into the oven. Normally bodies were laid out alternately: the first went in feet first and the next head first.

When Vera had interrogated Franz Berg at the Villa Degler he had been quite clear that at least one woman was conscious when she was put in the oven. Berg said that once the women had been dragged through he could hear, 'from the noise of the crematorium doors', that each woman was placed immediately in the crematorium oven. He said each was 'groaning'.

More than one witness talked of a struggle when the fourth woman was shoved into the fire. Brüttel described what happened: 'As the last body was being placed in the oven a mistake appeared to have occurred, since the body threatened to slide out of the oven again. The possibility of death not having occurred appears completely out of the question.' He said that as far as he could tell, after the injections, 'death occurred within five seconds with the accompaniment of twitching'.

But Schultz's account of what Straub told him was as follows: 'When the last woman was half way in the oven (she had been put in feet first) she had come to her senses and struggled. As there were sufficient men there they were able to push her into the oven, but not before she had resisted and scratched Straub's face. Straub also said she had shouted: "*Vive la France.*"' Emile Hoffmann, the military musician from Luxembourg, testified to having heard the same cry. And Rauson said the whole camp was listening and watching, peeping through gaps in curtains, as these things were happening. 'That evening we were listening carefully as we suspected foul play. I myself heard some screams and I now suppose that the women, still unconscious from the injection but alive, when put in the oven must have recovered consciousness and screamed.'

In any event, the bodies were burned, as all the camp witnessed. They could see the flames rising from the chimney. Guérisse said: 'It should be stated that whenever the oven doors of the crematorium were opened, an increased draught caused the flames to come out of the top of the chimney and this was clearly visible to the whole camp. It was common knowledge in the camp that whenever flames were seen to come out of the top of the chimney a body had been put into the crematorium. On this particular night, at intervals of about 15 minutes, I observed the flames coming out of the top of the chimney on four different occasions.'

After the bodies were burned, the SS doctors went away almost immediately. Emil Brüttel, who walked with the doctors back up to the officers' mess, said the doctors discussed what had happened over and over again, saying that they had intended to use the drug Evipan but because of the small amounts in stock they had used phenol. They repeatedly told each other that the reason the women had been killed was because they were spies. And they described their method of killing as more humane than shooting or hanging.

When everyone was gone, Berg, Fuhrmann and Alex emerged from their cell and went into the furnace room to look around. This was when they pulled at the handle of the oven door, opened it and saw the four blackened bodies. Dr Boogaerts said the bodies were still there the next morning. As he had access to the crematorium he went and opened the oven doors the following day and saw 'the charred bodies of women and an unburned woman's shoe'.

Rumours about what had happened spread rapidly the following day. 'Some people said that the women had been hanged after being raped by the SS, while others just said they had been injected by the SS doctor,' said the Frenchman Roger Linet. Walter Schultz was in the camp's political office at work again the next day and noticed that Magnus Wochner, the political officer, seemed very shocked by what had happened the night before. Peter Straub, however, was still drunk the next morning as the officers and doctors had drunk until late at Dr Plaza's leaving party in the officers' mess.

Schultz said: 'Straub told me: "I have been in Auschwitz for a long time, in my time about four million people have gone up the chimney, but I have never experienced anything like this before. I am finished." And I noticed that Straub's face had been severely scratched.' The next day Van Lanschot remarked to Berg that there were four fewer portions of food and Berg said that four prisoners had been burned that night in the crematorium.

Emil Brüttel was sitting at his desk in Dr Plaza's room the next morning when a man came over from the *Kommandantur* and handed the doctor an envelope marked 'secret'. Dr Plaza opened it and found that it contained the execution protocols for the four women. Stonehouse said that a few days later he saw 'Fernandel' 'walking up the steps in the middle of the camp, carrying a fur coat'.

19

'FREELY ON FOOT'

Vera had learned a lot in recent months about the men who gathered at Zum Goldenen Kreuz, the noisy bar on the corner of Karlsruhe's central square. Close to the town hall and the Nazi party offices, it was a favourite haunt of the city's Gestapo men, who came here to pick up gossip from the many bureaucrats and politicians in town.

There was, for example, Otto Preis, who was one of the landlord's closest friends. Preis's job with the Gestapo was to watch over foreign workers brought to Karlsruhe as forced labourers. He saw to it that they were horsewhipped for laziness and killed for any more serious misdemeanour. Preis was also called on when any 'dirty work' was needed, any quick killing – of a spy, an escaping airman, a Jew. His speciality was the *Genickschuss*, a shot from a 7.65mm pistol to the base of the skull, followed by a shot to the heart. In Zum Goldenen Kreuz they heard Preis boast about his prowess with the pistol.

Vera had also learned about Hermann Rösner. His department of the Gestapo picked up escaped prisoners heading for the French border close by, or hunted down infiltrators, commandos or parachutists. His boast at the bar was that he once took a tank into the Warsaw Ghetto at the height of the uprising.

Having cleared up the case at Natzweiler, Vera was now concentrating all her energies on tracing the second group of women, who left Karlsruhe prison in September 1944. Vera had learned that this group were picked up from the jail by the Karlsruhe Gestapo. She was looking in particular for Preis and Rösner, who might know where they went.

It had taken Vera several further interrogations in Karlsruhe itself to establish for sure that it was the local Gestapo who took away Madeleine Damerment, Yolande Beekman and Eliane Plewman. Her first clues had come from Else Sauer, Hedwig Müller's friend, who had shared a cell with Madeleine Damerment in her final days in the Karlsruhe jail. Else had given Vera a detailed account of Madeleine's departure.

During the daytime on 11 September, Madeleine had been taken by Fräulein Becker to collect a little case containing her belongings, which had been taken from her on arrival. Then Madeleine was returned to the cell. In the small hours of the next morning Else, Madeleine and a third cellmate, Frau Wipfler, heard a man's footsteps stop outside cell 16. Else recalled: '"Get up, Plewman," said a voice. Then a knock came to our door and a man opened the hatch. "Get up, Dussautoy." Then the footsteps disappeared along the corridor in the direction of cell 25, where Yolande was. The man came back and called out: "Get out, Plewman." Then he came to our door. He opened the door and I could see through a crack a girl whom I recognised to be Eliane Plewman. He called out, "Get out, Dussautoy." Frau Wipfler then said, *"Wie spät ist es, Herr Spät?"* ["What time is it, Mr Spät?"] and he answered, "One-thirty."'

Frau Wipfler had recognised the man as an official from the male prison, 'small, shrunken and grey-looking'. The group then left. 'Frau Wipfler and I were listening carefully and heard the heavy footsteps of Spät echo down the corridor,' said Else. 'Suddenly there was complete silence, we both said that it was as if the earth had swallowed them up.'

Else's evidence had led Vera to Herr Spät, an elderly night-watchman, who revealed that three Karlsruhe Gestapo men had taken the women away. He didn't know who the men were, but with Spät's help Vera established whose orders they were under. Gestapo cases were always 'special cases', said Spät, which meant the destination of departing prisoners could not be recorded in the register. Sometimes the Gestapo just ordered the gatekeepers to write '*Einem KZ*'. But often the words written were deliberately meaningless. A man named Hermann Rösner always told the jailers to write in the register: '*fr fuss*'. As Vera knew now from the records, which she had inspected at Gaggenau, the words '*fr fuss*' were used to describe the manner in which these three women left the prison, and this link led her to suspect the order was from Rösner.

Vera's suspicion that Otto Preis was also involved was purely instinctive. After months of fruitless enquiries in Poland, Russia and throughout Germany, she began to suspect that these three women were never taken east, as witnesses had first suggested, but were killed very close to Karlsruhe. In this case Preis was the most likely executioner; he had carried out scores of executions, including that of an escaped British airman whose case Vera had helped with. The airman, who had been impossible to identify, was being taken to Natzweiler for execution but Preis finished him off with a *Genickschuss* on the way. It happened on the edge of a wood and afterwards Preis wrapped the body in a piece of canvas and dumped it outside the crematorium, stopping only to give the camp office the *Sonderbefehl*, or order for 'special' treatment.

'I think Otto Preis was the professional bumper off and may have been involved in the killing of the three women whose fate is still unknown,' Vera wrote in a note at the time.

Finding Gestapo officers, however, was not easy. At its height the Karlsruhe Gestapo numbered 350 men. Run by a committed Nazi ideologue, Joseph Gmeiner, it was such an efficient operation that early in the war the Karlsruhe region was declared the first to have cleansed itself of Jews. Just days before the city of Karlsruhe was taken by the Allies, the lower ranks of the Karlsruhe Gestapo were ordered to form into a *Werwolfgruppe*, retreating to a camp deep in the Black Forest. More senior men transferred to new offices further behind the lines, at Freiburg, Offenburg, Rosenfeld and Moosbach. When defeat looked certain these senior officers went to ground, usually in the American zone – in rural areas or in the foothills of the Bavarian Alps. If they were to be caught, they wanted to be sure to fall into American hands and not into the vengeful hands of the French.

Vera hoped eventually that the top men who issued the orders would be brought to book, but her enquiries could not wait for them to be found. Their foot soldiers, who carried out those orders, she hoped would be quicker to trace. In March her three-month stint in

Germany had been extended for another three months. She had been given until June to solve this case, but it was already the middle of May.

Five months after her arrival in Germany, Vera had achieved a great deal. As well as gathering evidence for trials at Flossenburg, where fifteen F Section men were now known to have died, and Mauthausen, where nine were killed, she had cleared up the deaths at Ravensbrück and preparations for the Natzweiler trial were now well advanced. In London Vera's work had been winning high praise. As Norman Mott wrote in a letter, her results had been most satisfactory, especially given the 'skimpy catch as you can conditions' in which she was operating. Even the head of SOE, Colin Gubbins, now a major-general, had written an effusive testimonial, and thanks to a further testimonial from Tony Somerhough, Mott had let Vera know unofficially that she was more than likely to secure an OBE.

Within Whitehall there was also satisfaction that Vera's results were defusing criticism about missing women agents. As Mott wrote to her, there had been 'a fair amount of stir in the press recently, mainly arising out of Szabo's case and apparently engineered by her father. This has led to enquiries in some quarters about what action had been taken and we have luckily been in a position to make an effective reply.'

There was, nevertheless, much still to do. Vera was not only battling with bureaucracy in the Allied zones, but with British bureaucracy too. A frustrating task was clearing up the affairs of the dead and in particular producing evidence for death certificates for the FANY women. Because they had no military status they had to be certified dead under civilian rules, requiring independent witnesses of death, which in these cases were hard to come by. In the case of the Natzweiler girls Vera had even had to ask Dr Rohde, the camp doctor, who had administered lethal injections, to sign death certificates before he was hanged. Had the girls had any military status, such regulations would have been overridden, as they always were for service personnel in time of war. Such matters, as Vera complained to Mott, were 'taking a considerable amount of time'. Meanwhile there were no new leads on the Karlsruhe Gestapo.

Then, at last, came a breakthrough. Haystack reported that the French had picked up a Gestapo man named Helmuth Späth, a character 'of the worst possible kind', according to the liaison officer, Peter Davies. A veteran of the *Einsatzgruppen*, the elite Nazi murder squads who swept east with the invasion of Russia in June 1941, Späth was said to have the blood of at least two hundred Jews on his hands, all killed at Rawa Rusha in Ukraine. Charles Kaiser, the Haystack man, had already been up to Reutlingen to interrogate Späth, and the SS officer was talking.

Späth knew nothing himself about the Englishwomen but he knew who did, and Haystack were already acting on his leads. One senior Karlsruhe Gestapo officer had been traced to his home but his wife had not seen him for six months, although she had heard from neighbours that he had been arrested on the Danish border. Her neighbours heard the news listening to a German radio broadcast giving locations and fates of German PoWs. Another Gestapo man had disappeared after 'seeking employment with the Americans', according to one of his friends. And several names given to the Americans for checking against their rogues' gallery had come back 'rogues not met'.

But, thanks to Kaiser's interrogations of Späth, Vera secured vital descriptions, including one for Hermann Rösner, who had a broad face with bulging eyes and was aged about forty-five. A check with the search bureau suggested he might be in US Camp 75, but the central locator of Camp 75 came back: 'no trace'. Vera had a description for Preis too: he was said to look like a butcher and speak the regional dialect.

At the end of the month Vera had made significant progress and ten suspects were to be extradited from the US zone.

Thanks to Späth, Vera also now had her first significant clue as to the whereabouts of Hans Kieffer, of the Sicherheitsdienst in Paris, whom she very much wanted to interrogate. Kieffer, as she had by now established, was himself a member of the Karlsruhe Gestapo before he moved to Paris. His connections with Karlsruhe obviously explained the curious decision to send the SOE women to a prison in that city. Presumably, the arrangement simply suited Kieffer as he could easily reinterrogate them on visits home.

Späth, who had known Kieffer, said he had probably retreated to Offenburg and might now be in the Bodensee area, but he refused to say more. Vera put an urgent new search order out for a Hans Josef Kieffer. The accompanying description stated that he was thought to have a roundish face and dark, curly hair. He sometimes wore glasses and was of medium height and athletic build. He had two daughters and a son, also called Hans Kieffer, serving in the Waffen-SS, and a search order was also put out for his son.

––––

Hildegard Kieffer told me that by the summer of 1946 her father was hiding out in Garmisch Partenkirchen, in the Bavarian Alps.

It had taken me more than a year to track down Hans, Gretel and Hildegard Kieffer. Had I not found their names and dates of birth in the Karlsruhe archives they would have been impossible to locate.

Hildegard, the youngest daughter, now aged seventy-one, explained that after the German retreat from Paris, in August 1944, Hans Kieffer first stayed briefly in Strasbourg then moved back across the German border to Offenburg, and in early 1945 he set up an office in Rosenfeld, in southern Baden. The Kieffers' family home in Karlsruhe had been destroyed by a bomb so they went to Rosenfeld to join their father. His wife, Margarete, was dying of cancer. Then, when the German collapse was imminent, Kieffer retreated further. 'He just came to us one day to say goodbye,' said Hildegard. 'We didn't know where he was going. It was, of course, a painful goodbye.' Hildegard, though, was determined to find out where her father was and heard a few months later that he was in hiding in Garmisch Partenkirchen with a colleague, Karl Haug. Kieffer and Haug had been members of the same gymnastics club as boys, and Haug had worked for Kieffer in Paris.

'I hitched a lift to Garmisch with the Americans. I found him working in a hotel as a cleaner and stayed with him for two weeks. I think he expected to be caught by then. He was a little worried because his friend, Karl Haug, had left to go home.' Hildegard explained that Haug, who was her godfather, had five children and felt he must get back to them. 'I know my father was worried that Haug would be caught and then perhaps he would be made to talk.'

––––

Many of the Gestapo men now rounded up were found in Karlsruhe itself. Local men, they had been drawn home to their families, hoping that with the swollen population they would not be noticed. All had said they were acting on orders and, by meticulously piecing together their stories, Vera now understood the complex Gestapo command structure right up to the Reich Security Head Office in Berlin. Orders, even for everyday matters, always came direct from Berlin and were then marked for appropriate departments: foreign workers; Marxist and reactionary groups; Jews; or counter-espionage. Any orders concerning spies came from the desk in Berlin of a man named Horst Kopkow. It would be Kopkow, Vera learned, who ordered every *Sonderbehandlung*, or 'special treatment', and who signed every protective custody order used for spies. Kopkow was fastidious and always required 'receipts' for bodies when executions had taken place, except when the cases were '*N+N*', in which case special secret procedures were enforced. Even the smallest decisions appeared to spring from Kopkow in Berlin – for example, whether a prisoner should be given a 'harsh interrogation'. This, as ordered by Kopkow, meant twelve strokes with a horsewhip, which, as one captive put it, 'naturally referred to the number of strokes which could be given in succession and not their repetition'. Vera also learned that Kopkow's department had a *Nachrichtendienst*, or secret section, which handled matters about which nobody was to know.

From these latest interrogations Vera heard several times that the Karlsruhe Gestapo always handled women's cases with 'special care'. If women were to be sent anywhere the chief, Joseph Gmeiner, would send one of his women office staff along on the transport, to deal with the female prisoners' 'special needs'.

Vera therefore arranged to see the Gestapo's women typists and clerks. Lili Simon, a Gestapo secretary, said she had indeed gone on such transports to care for the women, but not in September 1944. She had gone on an earlier journey with women prisoners to Natzweiler, with a colleague named Max Wassmer, who was in charge of transport. Quite unintentionally, therefore, Vera found herself returning to the Natzweiler story. She had never established how the four women had reached the camp, but now Lili Simon filled in this missing chapter.

'I met the four prisoners and their luggage in the hall of the station in Karlsruhe. They were handcuffed two together. We took the express train as far as Strasbourg and then got a local train. During the journey the prisoners asked where they were going and Wassmer said they were being taken to a camp and that they would be expected to work. They talked about how they would be glad to get away from peeling potatoes now they had left Karlsruhe prison. The surrounding country was lovely and the women enjoyed it and looked forward to working.' Lili said she was ordered to leave the train at Schirmeck and return to Karlsruhe. 'I did not know they were being taken to a camp in order to be executed.'

Not only had Lili Simon described the journey to Natzweiler, she had also given Vera another lead in her hunt for the second group of women. If Max Wassmer accompanied the first group, perhaps he also accompanied the second group, whose destination was still unknown.

Before Vera could follow any new leads, however, she had to take a complete break from her ongoing investigation to give evidence at the Natzweiler trial itself, which was to be held at the Zoological Gardens in Wuppertal, starting on 29 May 1946. On the eve of the trial Vera's anxiety about publicity was intense. Everything had been done in London to try to keep 'this disgusting business', as Norman Mott put it, out of the papers. Now it was up to Vera to dampen publicity once the trial had begun.

Vera was the first witness to take the stand and she named each of the four victims: Vera Leigh, Diana Rowden, Andrée Borrel and Nora Inayat Khan. But before she did so, she had secured the agreement of the court that the names of the dead be withheld from publication, on the grounds that this would spare the anguish of their next of kin. The claim that withholding names was to spare such feelings was, however, to say the least, disingenuous on Vera's part. The families themselves had no objection to publicising the names. Mrs Rowden had written to say Diana's name could be publicised. 'My pain is too deep and my loss too great to mind seeing it in print. I am convinced that the only possible further pain I could suffer would be if the camp officials are let off.' Vera Leigh's half-brother had actually stated he thought it 'preferable' for the full story to be published. Furthermore, suppressing names in news reports could not possibly spare the families pain, as each of them knew by now that their daughters, sisters or fiancées had died at Natzweiler. The official letters they had received had glossed over the brutal facts, but when these facts appeared in newspaper reports and when they saw the camp named in the reports as Natzweiler, they knew only too well that it was their loved ones that were being referred to.

The only real purpose served by suppressing names was to curb any detailed press interest in the cases of the individual women, and thereby reduce the unwelcome questions about their recruitment and deployment by SOE. And, from the point of view of the 'old firm', the publicity was not 'too averse', as Mott observed to Vera in a letter summarising the coverage.

'British women burned alive' was a headline in the *Daily Telegraph* on 30 May 1946, but the story did not make front pages, and careful briefing of journalists, arranged by Vera at Wuppertal, meant SOE itself was not exposed to any close scrutiny as a result of the case.

The German defence lawyer, Dr Grobel, had, as anticipated, argued in court that international law allowed for the execution of irregular combatants and he invited the court to 'consider this case from the point of view that it was a normal and simple execution of spies'.

Dr Grobel's words, however, were barely reported in the press. Instead, a 'WAAF officer' (Vera's name was also withheld) was quoted as saying 'the women were not spies'.

Mott did, however, point out to Vera one piece of unfortunate coverage: a gossip columnist writing in the *Star* had reported comments of 'your old friend Mr Bushell'. Mott wrote: 'The gist of which was that Mr B noticed that the names of the four girls had not been published at the behest of "officialdom" which had felt that it would be distressing to the relatives. He went on to say that as father of Violette Szabo he was sure that this was not a correct decision and he felt that the utmost publicity should be given to those who carried out duties of this nature and whose sacrifices, as far as he could see, were not being recognised by the War Office.'

The leniency of the sentences also caused a stir. Only the camp doctor, Werner Rohde, received a death sentence. Franz Berg was sentenced to five years in prison. Peter Straub, the executioner, was sentenced to thirteen years in prison. Fritz Hartjenstein, the Kommandant, received a life sentence.

On the sentencing, Vera pointed out to Mott: 'I was at Wuppertal during the entire time of the trial and I am satisfied that the sentences were perfectly fair. It should be borne in mind that the people in the dock were not all directly concerned with the killing and a number of those directly concerned with the killing were not in the dock.' Furthermore, many of the accused would be tried on other counts, when their sentences would almost certainly be death, she said – an observation which was soon borne out.

On her return to Bad Oeynhausen Vera found more notes from Hedwig Müller pleading for news of 'her Martine' and enclosing little stencilled drawings and gifts, and a letter from Tom Plewman, Eliane's husband, asking if he should go to Poland in person to search for his wife. Vera also had to deal with an awkward letter from Cicely Lefort's husband. Witnesses had told Vera that Cicely received a letter in Ravensbrück from her husband, seeking a divorce, just before she was gassed. Vera had made her views of Dr Lefort's behaviour known to him, and now he was pleading for her understanding.

Here also was a statement from American investigators, taken from a Karlsruhe Gestapo man named Christian Ott. In the very first lines of his statement Ott revealed where Madeleine Damerment, Yolande Beekman and Eliane Plewman were taken after they left Karlsruhe prison, and what he said was not at all what Vera had expected: 'Statement of Christian Ott; born 23.10.1886 in Blaubeuren, living in Stuttgart: "It became known that a transport was to leave Karlsruhe for Dachau."'

By mid-1946 each Nazi concentration camp had given its own version of horror. Dachau, opened in 1933, largely for German communists, was the first such camp. As a prototype of barbarity, it had long held a special resonance; positioned on the edge of Munich in the heart of Bavaria, not hidden away, like Natzweiler, it was there for all to see.

Vera had visited Dachau when she first arrived in Germany, when she found it had already been turned into a macabre waxwork museum, before its story had yet been told. Never had she imagined that she might return there to look for her girls. She had been mentally prepared to accept that Otto Preis's anonymous murder might have brought about their end. But she was not prepared for Dachau.

And yet, from the moment Vera started reading Ott's statement, her agonised speculation of recent weeks was suddenly all set aside. Packed with authentic detail which only an eyewitness could provide, Ott's evidence gave no reason to doubt what he was saying. Even the reason he gave for remembering what happened sounded authentic. He volunteered to accompany the transport to Dachau so that on the way back he could stop off at Stuttgart and visit his family.

There was one detail in Ott's statement which jarred as Vera read it. Throughout his evidence he talked of transporting 'four' prisoners, whereas Vera was concerned with only the three who had remained at Karlsruhe. Ott appeared to suggest that the fourth prisoner had been held at Pforzheim prison, close by, and had been brought to join the other three before the transport to Dachau. But this inconsistency did not, in Vera's view, lessen the overall credibility of his story and she swiftly read on.

'On 23.8.44 towards 2 o'clock in the morning I drove from my office, 28 Ritterstrasse, with a light van and two officials to the prison to fetch the four prisoners. The person on night duty brought the four prisoners into the reception room,' said Ott.

'In the reception room of the prison I saw the four prisoners for the first time. They were four women in civilian clothes aged between 24 and 32 and all were well dressed.' He said he could not remember their names. Before departure they were given all their personal effects and it became evident to Ott that 'they must have come from better origin. One of the prisoners – the oldest – spoke good German. Through questioning them I came to know that two of the prisoners were English, a third was French born and a fourth was Dutch through marriage.

'The four prisoners met for the first time again in the reception room and said that they had now been in solitary confinement for nine months. When they greeted one another they were delighted and surprised by how well they looked.'

Vera then read about how Ott had handcuffed the prisoners together. 'It was mentioned that the greatest care would have to be taken with this transport,' he said and a colleague named Kriminal Sekretär Wassmer was placed in charge. Vera carefully underlined the name Wassmer. As she had suspected, Wassmer had supervised the second transport as well as the transport to Natzweiler.

Allied bombing had already disturbed railway traffic, said Ott, so it was agreed that the prisoners should be taken by car from Karlsruhe to Bruchsal, where they would catch the train south. This arrangement suited Wassmer because his family lived in Bruchsal. He took the opportunity to leave the office the previous day in order to see his family, and then met up with the group at Bruchsal station at 2.30am, when they all caught the train to Stuttgart.

As planned, Wassmer arrived at the station and had already bought the tickets, stated Ott. 'At Stuttgart we had about one hour's wait. We got out and remained on the platform until we continued the journey. The prisoners stood a little aside and chatted together.'

Waiting on the station platform, Ott expressed surprise to Wassmer that women were being sent to Dachau. He understood that Dachau was a camp for men only. He asked Wassmer 'several times' whether Dachau was now taking women. 'Wassmer, at last tired of my repeated question, showed me a telegram from the RSHA, Berlin, and told me to read it.'

The telegram Ott read said the women were to be 'executed at Dachau' and was signed by Ernst Kaltenbrunner, head of the RSHA.

Ott said he recalled that Wassmer had told him 'this must be an important case since the telegram had been signed personally by "Ernst" – that is to say, Dr Kaltenbrunner'. At this point Ott claimed he had begun to regret coming on the transport 'as the four prisoners had made a good impression on me and I regretted their fate'.

Vera then read how Ott had chatted to the girls on the next stage of the journey. He spoke in particular to the Englishwoman who spoke a little German.

I did not tell them of the fate in store for them, on the contrary I tried to keep them in a happy mood. They wanted to know where they were being taken. Wassmer told them that they were being taken to a camp where much farming was done. They were not told that they were going to Dachau.

The Englishwoman told me that all four were officers in the women's auxiliary forces. She said she had the rank of major and that one of her companions was a captain and two were lieutenants. On closer questioning she told me that she had been dropped by parachute in France and had worked in the secret service. One or two of them had been caught as they jumped in France for the third time. In France she said they had only spoken French in order not to be recognised as English.

The train arrived in Munich and from Munich they travelled on to Dachau, arriving after dark, at about 10pm. 'We then walked to the camp of Dachau and handed in the prisoners. After about fifteen minutes the prisoners were taken over by the camp officials.' Their possessions were handed over again, this time to the SS. There were comments, Ott recalled, about 'pretty watches and jewellery, rings with sapphire stones and gold bangles'. This was the last that Ott saw of the women. He slept in the building above the camp gate and when he awoke Wassmer had already left and gone into the camp. When Wassmer returned he told Ott he had seen the Kommandant and that the execution would take place at 9am. It was then about 8.30am. 'Wassmer then left again as he had to report to the Kommandant once more. At about 10.30am Wassmer returned again and said everything was finished. The four prisoners had been shot. He himself had read the death sentence to the prisoners.'

Ott's statement continued:

About the shooting itself Wassmer said the following: 'The four prisoners had come from the barrack in the camp, where they had spent the night, into the yard where the shooting was to be done. Here he [Wassmer] had announced the death sentence to them. Only the Lagerkommandant and two SS men had been present. The German-speaking Englishwoman (the major) had told her companion of this death sentence. All four had grown very pale and wept; the major asked whether they could protest against the sentence. The Kommandant declared that no protest could be made against the sentence. The major had then asked to see a priest. The camp Kommandant refused this on the grounds that there was no priest in the camp.

The four prisoners now had to kneel down with their heads towards a small mound of earth and were killed by the two SS, one after another by a shot through the back of the neck. During the shooting the two Englishwomen held hands and the two Frenchwomen likewise. For three of the prisoners the first shot caused death, but for the German-speaking Englishwoman a second shot had to be fired as she still showed signs of life after the first shot.

After the shooting of these prisoners the Lagerkommandant said to the two SS men that he took a personal interest in the jewellery of the women and that this should be taken into his office.

Vera then read that four prisoners had loaded the bodies on to a handcart. 'Wassmer could not say what happened further with these bodies but he thought that they had most probably been burned.' This was the end of Wassmer's account of the deaths, as reported by Ott, who went on to say that he had noted down the details of each woman on the back of an envelope which he kept for a long time with the intention of notifying their next of kin, but he had later destroyed it 'as I myself was not very certain of the Gestapo'. He remembered the German-speaking Englishwoman well enough to describe her: she was about thirty-two with a full figure (she herself said she had gained 30 pounds in prison) with a pale, round face, full lips and dark hair. He was describing Madeleine Damerment.

———

'For me there was no doubt that Martine was already dead as soon as the war was over,' said Lisa Graf, at our meeting in her Paris flat. 'Anyone who was not back by July 1945 was not coming back, that was certain. But, you know, the curtain had come down on that period of my life. Those who did not close the curtain suffered badly.'

I told Lisa how Vera kept hoping for several months after the end of the war. Lisa said Vera would not have hoped if she herself had been deported and seen the way things were.

'But your Vera was Jewish, you say? Well, she went to look for them not because she had hope but because she wanted to see for herself how it had all happened and to understand. And when you are responsible like she was you are responsible to yourself in front of yourself. She needed to know.'

Then Lisa paused a moment. 'But, you see, I knew that Martine was dead way before the end of the war. If I tell you this, you will not believe it, but I knew even before she was dead. You know, when you are in prison you are alone with your soul. So I made myself some playing cards out of old papers and every Sunday I played them – to see what they might tell me. At first I saw nothing and then I started to see things. I saw that I would leave the prison and go to a court and then, when Becker came to my cell and said: "You are leaving prison and going to a court," I said: "I know." She said: "How did you know?" So I said: "I know." I was lucky. I had that guardian angel in the girl who looked like me.

'Then, before I left, I wanted to play the cards for Martine. I did the cards and I saw nothing. I played the cards again and I saw something unclear. I played the cards a third time and I saw this road and then death and when I left Karlsruhe I cried as I knew I would never see her again.'

What exactly did you see? I asked.

'I saw a road and a death at the end.'

'What was the death?'

'The end. *La noirceur* – blackness. Horror. *La chute*. It was a road with a darkness and a hole at the end. *Terminé*. For me it was death – a terrible death. What it was I can't say, but in the end it was horrible.

'I saw that the day before I left Karlsruhe. We spoke through the wall. I said: "*Je t'embrasse, je t'embrasse très fort*." I did not tell her, of course. Would it serve any purpose to tell her? You cannot tell somebody: "You are going to die." It is not possible.'

Yolande Beekman's mother also knew that her daughter was dead, long before Vera ever told her. When I returned to London from Karlsruhe I went to see Diana Farmiloe, Yolande's sister. She had promised to look out letters of Yolande's sent on to their mother by Vera, and I wanted to give Diana the picture, drawn by Yolande in prison, with her own blood.

Diana's flat was in Kensington. It was a cold day and Diana, at her front door, shivered and seemed anxious; builders had just discovered dry rot, she said, and she showed me where plaster had been removed in her living room to reveal underlying brickwork and timbers. She had had to cover everything with dust sheets and she pulled back a cloth from a photograph of Yolande, with oval face, dark, shining eyes and the palest complexion.

I told Diana I had brought pictures drawn by Yolande for her to see. I explained that they had been drawn sometime early in 1944, when she was in prison in Karlsruhe. She had no ink. So she pricked her fingers and drew the pictures with her own blood.

'Yolande loved to draw,' said Diana, and I put the picture down on the table next to Yolande's photograph while we began our search in Diana's bedroom for the letters.

Using an aluminium stepladder, I reached up into a tiny cupboard full of Diana's possessions, all neatly packed and labelled: stockings and linen, along with papers in bundles.

'Something is stopping me finding these letters,' said Diana and she then went to the other side of her bed and bent over, looking through some more promising plastic bags. Here she found Yolande's baptism papers. Yolande was baptised and married just before she went to France. Here were some old postcards. Diana showed me a photograph of herself and Yolande on a summer holiday at the YWCA on the Isle of Wight.

Yolande's summer frock was nipped in around her tiny waist and had a sailor's collar. 'Our mother sent us on our holidays to the YWCA because it was safe for girls,' Diana told me. 'My mother was very protective of Yolande. She kept her working with her, making children's clothes. She embroidered beautifully. She was her first child. I think it was natural. It often happens that mothers of first-born feel attached like that.' Her mother's protectiveness might have explained why Yolande didn't marry earlier, Diana said. Yolande met her husband, Jap Beekman, a Dutchman, at an SOE training school.

I asked Diana what their mother thought when Yolande went to work with SOE.

'We knew she had joined something she couldn't talk about, but we thought it was translation or something. My mother worried, but she was happy if Yolande was happy. That was the most important thing for her. Then Vera Atkins sent these letters on from Yolande saying she was happy and sending her love – that sort of thing.' Diana was thinking back. 'I remember it was that word "shot" we could not take. That was the end, completely. So final.

'And later, when eventually we worked it all out, I saw Vera Atkins and I almost accused her. I said: "So you knew all along that she was captured and you sent these letters all that time." She said, "Yes, but you must understand, I could not say."' Diana looked up. 'I always thought there was something in Vera Atkins – what it was I do not know – something that would not let out. And the terrible thing was that my mother always blamed herself for being too protective with Yolande when she was growing up. She said, "I wish I had not kept her so close." My mother felt that if she had let her see more of the world, perhaps she would not have had the need to go off. Yolande so much wanted to do brave things.'

Then Diana pulled out an old discoloured exercise book with handwriting in ink. She started reading from it. 'Ah, this is my mother's diary written from when Yolande went missing,' said Diana. 'You are probably not interested in that.' She started reading it a little. 'What's this?' she said . . . "Do not avenge me I will avenge myself . . ."' She seemed to sigh and her shoulders slumped.

'It's in French,' she said. 'Can you read French?'

I took the diary and went to the living room, sitting next to the table where I had placed Yolande's drawing. I could still see Diana through the door, sitting on her bed with her back to me, moving things around in plastic bags.

I started to read the diary. 'In the spring of 1944 I dreamed that my dear Yolande was lying on a bed of iron, flat on her stomach and crying and writing painfully with a bleeding finger.' The words were written in an almost childlike hand across the squares of this old exercise book. 'And on the wall under the small table was the word: "*Maman*" and a voice said: "Yes, there are those who write with their blood."'

I read the paragraph again: '. . . Yolande was lying on a bed of iron, flat on her stomach and crying and writing painfully with a bleeding finger.' I looked up to where Diana was sitting, still shuffling through papers, and I tried to say how extraordinary it was that their mother had dreamed about Yolande, lying on an iron bed, writing in blood at exactly the time that Yolande was writing in blood on her iron bed in her prison cell. The pictures which I had found by chance in an elderly man's home in Germany, only two weeks earlier, were now lying on the table next to me. But when I tried to speak to Diana I found for a moment I couldn't. She turned and saw me and came over straight away and took the diary and read it herself and said: 'Yes, my dear, I know it is so terrible, it is, I know, my dear. You see, I am so glad you see how terrible it all is.'

And then, for the first time, Diana looked at Yolande's drawings. 'But it is not possible my mother could have known that she was writing in blood at this time. It is not possible she could have known,' she said over and over again.

We carried on reading the rest of the diary, which described more dreams. In September, the month that Yolande died, her mother wrote: 'I dreamed that Yolande was in a camp and policemen were looking at her with their hands in their pockets, and she was sitting down and started putting on her stockings and she told me: "Do not take revenge. I will avenge myself."'

And there was a description of another dream: 'Yolande is on a bed. She is very thin. She is crying and screaming. I am holding her very, very tight.'

On another page she wrote: 'The one who reads this do not laugh at me. I observe my dreams and I try to see what it means. Anyway I am very happy when I dream about my daughter each time I see she is happy.'

———

As soon as Vera had finished reading the statement of Christian Ott, she intensified her hunt for Max Wassmer. She soon located him in an internment camp and, under interrogation, he confirmed most of Ott's story. Vera then wrote a report to Norman Mott saying the case had been 'cleared up' and attaching, as always, draft letters to next of kin. The first paragraph of the letters was the same for all three girls, with blanks for names left for the London official to fill in.

It is with deepest regret that I have to inform you that your — was killed in the early hours of 13 September 1944 in the Camp of Dachau. According to what is believed to be a reliable report she was shot through the back of the head and death was immediate. The body was cremated in the Camp Crematorium.

The second paragraph of Vera's draft continued: 'As we have already informed you — was captured on or about — at — after many months of success and very gallant work.' On one of the letters Vera noted in brackets: 'This passage will have to be modified in the case of Madeleine Damerment who unhappily was captured on landing.' Vera then devised a form of words to disguise the fact that Madeleine had been dropped by F Section direct into German hands. Instead of saying Madeleine was captured 'after many months of success and very gallant work', the Damerment letter should say she was captured 'when she had volunteered to return to France on a special mission in the company of two British officers'.

Then this letter would continue the same way as the others, concluding with the consolation that 'until the end they were cheerful and of good faith'.

20

DR GOETZ

In early October 1946 Vera had returned from Germany and was on the road to Colchester, in Essex. The bulk of her war crimes work concluded, she was glad to be back in England. Her honorary commission in the WAAF would expire at the end of November and her mission in Germany could not be extended further.

There were still unsolved cases, but these largely lay in the Russian zone, which by the autumn of 1946 had been almost entirely closed off to the Western allies. Even Vera could not break through the new Iron Curtain.

Francis Suttill's trail – along with those of the Ravitsch boys and the MI6 man Frank Chamier (Frank of Upway 282) – were among those Vera had been forced to abandon as the remaining evidence lay in the Russian zone. Before she left Germany she had found a Sachsen-hausen orderly who said Francis Suttill was executed, but the witness had only glimpsed what happened through a chink in a cell door. Suttill was hanged, not shot, he said, but his only proof was that there was no blood on his clothes, which he had the job of collecting.

The Russians were planning to hold a trial of the Sachsenhausen camp staff, but Vera had been unable to find out when, and she knew there was little hope that any news of the trial would reach the West.

———

I discovered that Vera did, however, receive news of the Sachsenhausen trial shortly after it took place in October 1947, thanks only to a resourceful young Haystack investigator and a British journalist who defected to Moscow. The story was recounted to me by the Haystack man, Sacha Smith, now living in Devon. Smith worked for the British war crimes unit in Berlin as liaison officer with the Russians, although by 1947 almost no information was coming through from his Soviet counterparts.

'One day I was in the officers' club in Berlin when I was told there was a call for me from a man called Peter Burchett,' said Smith. Burchett had worked in Berlin for the *Daily Mail* and been friendly with Smith, often covering war crimes cases, until he surprised everyone by defecting. He was calling his old friend from somewhere in the Russian zone.

'I had to take the call from Burchett in a cupboard with no light bulb, so I couldn't see what I was writing and the line was bad, so I couldn't hear well,' Smith told me. 'Even though he had chosen to go over to the other side, he was calling as a favour, because he knew I would want to know about the Sachsenhausen trial and we wouldn't get to hear otherwise. I had to scratch down what I could in the dark. I just got that people were convicted but certainly no details and nothing about Suttill. But I was able to pass on what I had to Tony Somerhough, who I am sure told Vera.' Six months later, during the Berlin airlift, Smith became the last British officer to leave Berlin by road. The Cold War had now begun.

———

Nevertheless, by the time she left Germany, Vera had achieved much of what she set out to do: the fate of all the women had been settled, as had the fate of the majority of the men imprisoned in camps liberated by Americans or British. Now she hoped she could put the tragedies behind her and devote her time to helping survivors, securing honours and awards and promoting positive memories of SOE.

And yet Vera's enquiries were not quite over. Although her investigation into the fate of the missing appeared to have run its course, her investigation into how agents were captured was certainly not complete. Vera was still hoping that certain senior German officers, particularly those responsible for rounding up her people, would be tracked down. On 11 September 1946 she had issued a note to the Haystack team passing on new intelligence as to where these men –

Horst Kopkow, the Berlin counter-intelligence chief, and Hans Kieffer, of the Paris Sicherheitsdienst – might be found. As she admitted in that note: 'It seems impossible to stop this game of War Crimes once you have begun.'

And even now Vera was making her way across Essex to another interrogation. Along with thousands of German internees and suspect war criminals, Dr Josef Goetz, the radio mastermind at Avenue Foch, had been brought to England for investigation and was being held in a disused army barracks at Colchester now serving as a camp for prisoners of war.

Vera was already seated at a table when Dr Goetz was led in. She didn't offer him a seat, but simply observed him. She already knew a fair amount about him. Dr Goetz was a schoolteacher from Hamburg who had been selected for the Sicherheitsdienst because of his facility with languages. She saw now that he was a tall man with a high-domed cranium, brown eyes and glasses. His hair was white but he could not have been more than forty.

Dr Goetz also observed Vera, then he pulled up a chair and sat down opposite her. She was annoyed at this impudence but said nothing and took out a cigarette, as did he. She lit her cigarette without offering him a light, so he asked her for one. He had a deep bass voice. She paused, looked at him again and offered him the light. Then Vera laughed, and she signalled to the attending corporal that he could leave the room and wait outside the door.

Vera's discussions with Dr Goetz were to be conducted on quite different terms to her earlier interrogations of SS concentration camp staff in Germany. Those meetings had been held to establish how and where her agents were killed. Dr Goetz had not been hired to kill. He had been hired to outwit the British by playing back the radios of captured agents. He then pretended to be those agents, talking by Morse signal directly to London. Vera had not only spent the last months piecing together how her people died, she had also been slowly piecing together how they were caught, and on that subject Dr Goetz would be able to tell her more than any German officer she had seen so far.

'How did it begin?' asked Vera.

'It began with Bishop,' said Goetz, and Vera nodded. They were going to understand each other well. In a sense they had met before – or at least communicated – as Vera herself had sent messages to Dr Goetz, believing him at different times to be Gilbert

Norman, Marcel Rousset, Nora Inayat Khan, Lionel Lee or one of the other dozen or so captured signallers whose radios he had operated. She had also received his messages back.

And in a sense they also had a lot in common. Dr Goetz was probably the only person in the world who knew the French Section agents – their aliases, their codes, their messages – as well as Vera. Vera had helped create their cover stories, but Dr Goetz had had to learn every last detail about these people in order to imitate them when playing back their radios. So both Vera and Dr Goetz knew that 'Bishop' was the alias for a radio operator named Marcus Bloom, a gutsy and flamboyant north London Jewish businessman, infiltrated France by boat in November 1942 to work with the Pimento circuit, headed by Tony Brooks. On his return to England after the war Brooks claimed to Vera and others that Bloom had arrived in Toulouse in a loud check coat, smoking a pipe and looking as though he had stepped off a train from Victoria. Nearly blowing Brooks's cover, Bloom greeted him with the words ''Ow are ya, mate', so Brooks decided to have nothing more to do with him. Vera had established that Marcus Bloom was shot at Mauthausen.

When Bishop was arrested, said Dr Goetz, his radio was found with all his codes. This gave Goetz's boss, Hans Kieffer, his first chance to play back a captured radio. He told Dr Goetz to experiment, so he sent a few messages. But it didn't work well. He needed more practice.

Vera remembered the worries in the late spring of 1943 when Bloom's strange messages came in, but the worries had not lasted. Though F Section had been duped before by enemy radio deception, staff officers in early 1943 were confident that they could prevent it happening again.

And nothing was known in F Section at that time about the systematic way such deception had already been worked on other SOE sections. Only since the end of the war had Vera learned the full story of how, the year before Bloom was captured, the Germans had been playing the *Funkspiel*, or 'radio game', to devastating effect against SOE's Dutch and Belgian sections (N and T sections). As a result of that deception almost every SOE agent parachuted into the Low Countries had been dropped into German hands.

———

In 2003 a raft of secret wartime documents were finally made public in the National Archives, showing that senior figures in MI5, MI6 and SOE knew a great deal about the disaster in the Low Countries as early as spring 1943, yet Maurice Buckmaster and his staff were never warned that they might face the same threat in France.

The danger of the enemy 'turning' SOE and SIS agents was 'by no means hypothetical', wrote Dick White, an assistant director of MI5 in March 1943, later head of MI5 and then MI6. 'Perhaps the most important [example] of all is that of the SOE organisation in Belgium which ran for many months without SOE realising that it was almost completely under the control of the Germans. It is impossible even now to say how much damage was done by this,' wrote White, setting out plans for an 'early warning system' to prevent a recurrence. Yet the same newly released files revealed that White's proposals for ensuring the deception did not recur were never acted on. There was no definitive explanation in the files as to why the warnings were ignored, but there was overwhelming evidence of self-serving, inter-agency wrangling involving SOE, MI5, MI6 and the Foreign Office, in the midst of which White's proposals were most probably buried.

Why SOE's own senior staff – Colin Gubbins and his European directors – failed to alert Buckmaster to the dangers exposed by the Low Countries disaster remains a mystery. One retrospective report by security staff found a ready explanation for Buckmaster's own misjudgements, saying that country sections 'were always full of understandable optimism and a natural unwillingness to regard an agent as lost, particularly if they liked or had befriended them'.

As SOE's official historian, Michael Foot, pointed out, however, those above Buckmaster in the hierarchy had no such excuse as they hardly knew the agents at all. 'Yet they [the senior staff] were necessarily remote from the day to day business of running operations in progress and this hindered them from noticing anything was going astray in France,' wrote Foot.

Although F Section was never officially informed, rumours of the Low Countries disaster did reach F Section's floor in Norgeby House. As I had heard from Vera's friend and former colleague, Nancy Roberts, gossip about N and T section was exchanged in the Ladies' on the half-landing. Staff, however, carried on regardless because they knew they were 'not supposed to know'.

——

Although the Bishop playback in early 1943 had not worked, continued Dr Goetz, Kieffer was determined to persist. Kieffer was a competitive man and wanted to pull off the same coup as his rival Hermann Giskes, the Abwehr officer who captured numerous British agents in the Low Countries by playing the *Funkspiel*. But to achieve anything like the success of Giskes, Kieffer needed to capture more radio operators. As Vera now knew, this was exactly what Kieffer then did. In June 1943 Frank Pickersgill and his wireless operator, John Macalister, were captured and three days later Francis Suttill was caught, followed by his radio operator, Gilbert Norman.

'I remember the arrest of Prosper [Suttill] very well as I was away on leave in Germany,' Dr Goetz said. 'My wife was having a baby. I was called back and ordered to return just after the baby was born, which was 25 June. My wife wept but I had to go back. I was loyal to Kieffer.' When Dr Goetz reached Avenue Foch on 26 June he found the place in a state of excitement over the arrest of Prosper. But Kieffer was equally excited about the capture of Gilbert Norman [Archambaud], the radio operator, because he had his radio and crystals as well. The radio – with back messages – was seized when he was captured and Gilbert Norman's crystals, with details of frequencies, had been found in a package brought to France by Pickersgill and Macalister, conveniently labelled by HQ in London. Using Norman's previous messages, therefore, Dr Goetz's men set to work figuring out his codes, transmission times and security check.

Kieffer's men brought Gilbert Norman to Dr Goetz's room to see if he would help with a transmission, but Dr Goetz got nothing out of him at first. Dr Goetz's first message to London as Gilbert Norman (call-sign 'Butcher') announced Prosper's arrest. But Dr Goetz was nervous and feared that London would not believe the message to be genuine. And Kieffer was nervous too. He kept going to Dr Goetz's room to see what was happening. 'The reply I got from the first message was quite unexpected,' said Dr Goetz. 'The message I got back said: "You have forgotten your 'true' security check. Take more care."'

Immediately Dr Goetz realised that Norman had been concealing the fact that he had a second security check. The absence of the check in his message should have warned London that he was caught. Dr Goetz showed the reply to Norman almost straight away and Norman was naturally astonished at London's reaction and went into a fury. He soon began to behave differently.

———

Among the secret files now placed in the National Archives were the SOE personal files, which I had first seen two years earlier on the SOE adviser's desk, awaiting declassification. The files were numerous but it was pot luck if papers on a particular agent or a particular episode had survived.

Vera herself had been responsible for 'weeding' many F Section files before SOE closed down. A fire in Norman Mott's office was also said to have destroyed files, although a note written by Mott to Vera on 8 March 1946, mentioning the fire, said that 'nothing much of historical importance was lost'.

Even where files survived, crucial paragraphs or whole pages were often blanked out under secrecy legislation. Among the reasons for these omissions, I was told, were 'unsubstantiated accusations of treachery' or 'personal sensitivities'. Yet slurs abounded, like the comment made by Roger de Wesselow, head of an F Section training school, who, in an official training report, called Marcus Bloom 'this pink yid'. And 'unsubstantiated allegations of treachery' were printed here with gay abandon – as in the case of Gilbert Norman, who was hanged at Mauthausen. A note appeared on Norman's casualty report, signed by Buckmaster in 1945, saying: 'Probably fell for a Gestapo trap. Nothing ever proven against him.'

After a while I became familiar with certain voices in these files – like the voice of a distraught father battling tirelessly to clear his dead son's name. Mr Maurice Norman, a prominent chartered accountant working in Paris, had been first angered by the failure of SOE to tell him, until nine months after Gilbert's capture, that his son was missing. His wife fell critically ill from grief and never recovered.

In the months after the end of the war Gilbert Norman, along with Francis Suttill, was accused in France of making a 'pact' with the Germans and selling out the Prosper network. Maurice Norman refused to allow his son to become a scapegoat and called on the British government to stand up for him. It was Vera who advised on how to handle Mr Norman, and her responses were often chilling. She had evidence by now that Norman had given away information to the Gestapo. But she also knew better than anyone what exactly led him to break down: Buckmaster had blown the agent's cover by revealing the existence of a second security check.

But when asked for her views on the Norman case, Vera simply stated that he 'probably fell for the German trick of you play fair by us and we'll play fair by you'. Of Norman's father, she said: 'He is an awkward customer who for some reason has a grudge against SOE.'

———

Once Dr Goetz had trapped London into revealing the existence of Gilbert Norman's second security check, his task of playing back Norman's radio became much easier, he told Vera. And Norman began to talk. Norman gave Dr Goetz his first insight into the French Section and 'had been quite helpful especially as regards the moral effect his appearance on apparently good terms with his captors had on agents later'.

Dr Goetz paused again and observed Vera. He found her 'haughty' but also beautiful.

'Go on,' said Vera.

'And once they [the agents] could see how much we already knew about their organisation they saw the sense in talking. They realised there was a traitor. You see,' said Dr Goetz, 'it was mostly down to the mail.'

Vera asked him to explain.

'Kieffer had copies of all the agents' mail, which was sent back to London,' said Dr Goetz. He had their letters home, their reports to headquarters – everything. When captured agents were shown their mail the effect on them was quite dramatic.

Vera had heard this story about the captured mail many times before, and always it was Henri Déricourt (Gilbert) who was accused of passing the mail to the Germans, but no SOE or MI5 investigation to date had found evidence strong enough to charge him. One theory, put about by Déricourt's defenders, including Buckmaster, was that the Gestapo had deliberately blackened his name to unsettle fellow agents or to divert attention from a genuine German double agent.

'Where had Kieffer got the mail?' Vera then asked Dr Goetz.

Goetz said it came from an agent called Gilbert who worked for Karl Boemelburg, Kieffer's commanding officer. Boemelburg handed the mail to Kieffer but Kieffer himself never encountered Gilbert. He didn't wish to meet him, said Dr Goetz. Kieffer didn't trust Gilbert. 'He thought he was a double. But he found him useful.'

But on occasion Dr Goetz himself had encountered Gilbert. Kieffer wanted Dr Goetz to be present at meetings between Boemelburg and Gilbert in case any information emerged which would help him with his radio deception. Gilbert had 'dark blond wavy hair and a sportive figure', he said. Vera then showed Dr Goetz a photograph of Déricourt and Dr Goetz recognised him as Gilbert. He also said that all the photostats – prints derived from photographs of the agents' mail – carried the marking 'BOE 48', which he understood to refer to the fact that Gilbert was Boemelburg's forty-eighth agent.

Vera asked Dr Goetz when exactly the mail was first used in interrogations. Dr Goetz had heard that the mail had been used in the Prosper interrogation, carried out by another German officer who was now dead. Dr Goetz himself first used the mail in the case of Gilbert Norman. Kieffer had produced for Dr Goetz copies of Norman's own detailed reports back to London, in which he gave names of circuits and addresses of recruits as well as plans for parachute drops. 'He could see we knew everything already,' said Dr Goetz. 'It was not then hard to convince him that the best course for him was to save as many lives as possible by helping us.'

Even so, at first the Norman transmissions had been of only limited use, said Dr Goetz. Mostly London just sent questions back asking about Prosper: 'Where is Prosper? Where has he been taken? What news of Prosper?' and so on. And then, he said, a request came through for a rendezvous address in Paris. London said that two officers were coming over from London and wanted a safe house for a meeting with Gilbert Norman. 'I sent a message back with a rendezvous address at rue de Rome,' said Dr Goetz. 'We set up surveillance at the place for days, waiting for these officers to turn up. Eventually one did.'

It was obvious to Vera that Dr Goetz was now referring to the decision to send out Nicholas Bodington to Paris to investigate the extent of the Prosper disaster. There was debate in Baker Street in July 1943 about the wisdom of sending into the field such a senior staff officer as Major Bodington. Furthermore, there were questions about whether it was wise to arrange a rendezvous with Norman over his own radio if there was a risk he was already captured. But Bodington had insisted on going, and took with him the radio operator Jack Agazarian. Dr Goetz was now confirming what Vera had known since the end of the war: that the rendezvous was made direct with the enemy. On arriving Bodington suddenly decided not to go himself to the meeting, sending Agazarian along instead.

Bodington said on his return to England that he and Agazarian tossed a coin over who was to go and Agazarian lost. Vera had traced Agazarian to Flossenburg, where he was hanged.

———

'But even that explanation never made any sense, however you look at it,' the SOE agent Tony Brooks told me. 'Even if they did toss a coin, everyone knows in those circumstances what you do: you arrange for a signal at the window, like placing a pot of flowers in a certain position to show the rendezvous is safe and if the signal isn't there, don't go. Or else before you go up there you give a small boy a coin and say: run and give a message to my girlfriend on the third floor. If he comes back and says, "There is no girl but a couple of men," you scarper.'

What was Bodington like? I asked.

'A crook,' said Brooks, but neither he nor anyone else knew what sort of crook. SOE colleagues all said he was profoundly dislikeable – 'a shifty little cove' – and never had any money on him. His former Reuters colleagues called him something of a 'romancer', or fantasist, who was always asking for pay rises.

When the new files appeared in the National Archives I hoped they would throw light on the affair of Déricourt, as well as the question of Bodington. The files spilled over with evidence showing Déricourt's various dealings with the Germans. They also revealed that at one point investigators seriously considered whether both Déricourt and Bodington were traitors, in part because the two men seemed to be protecting each other. The various episodes led the MI5 man handling the case to say: 'this leads one to wonder whether Bodington was himself an agent in the pay of the Germans'.

Particular suspicions arose directly out of Bodington's trip to Paris in the summer of 1943, during which several puzzling things had happened, including the capture of Agazarian.

It had emerged at the time of the trip, through the mysterious intervention of an Abwehr officer, known then only as Colonel Heinrich, that the Gestapo knew all along of Bodington's presence in Paris but had not arrested him. Colonel Heinrich had made this startling claim at the time to an SOE agent in Paris called Henri Frager, who passed it on to Bodington himself. Frager took the German's claim most seriously, he said, because he believed Colonel Heinrich to be an anti-Nazi who could be trusted. Reporting on the matter later to Buckmaster, however, Bodington gave only the skimpiest details of Colonel Heinrich's allegations and then dismissed them as 'obviously untrue'. This same Colonel Heinrich turned out to be Hugo Bleicher, the Abwehr's counter-intelligence sleuth.

The MI5 interrogations of Bleicher, now released for public view, ran to several pages, revealing, in mind-boggling complexity, his early penetration of British networks, including the story of how he turned a young Frenchwoman named Mathilde Carré, known as 'the Cat', who had worked for one of the earliest spy networks in France, run jointly by MI6 and Polish exiles. Carré became Bleicher's mistress and by early 1942 she had betrayed every member of the British organisation, also putting Bleicher in touch with SOE circuits. When Carré was finally brought to London for investigation in February 1942, Vera was entrusted by MI6 with the task of watching over the Frenchwoman, which gave her a very direct and early insight into German methods of penetration.

Bleicher was particularly closely questioned by MI5 about events in Paris in the summer of 1943. By that time, Bleicher explained, it was Hans Kieffer of the Sicherheitsdienst who was largely responsible for rounding up British agents, with the Abwehr now forced to take a secondary role. Kieffer, nevertheless, still found his old adversary Bleicher useful, and they spoke from time to time. On one occasion Kieffer let Bleicher know that Bodington was in Paris. It happened like this, according to the MI5 interrogation report: 'He [Bleicher] was informed of Bodington's arrival by Kieffer who personally told Bleicher that he had been informed of it by Gilbert.' The interrogator wrote: 'According to Bleicher, Gilbert handed over many of our officers to the SD ... he had, however, some scruple in regard to Bodington, and although he gave away his arrival said he did not know his address. Kieffer telephoned Bleicher in the hope he might know the address. And it was then that Bleicher warned Frager.' During the same interrogation Bleicher said he had also warned Frager in the summer of 1943 that several British wirelesses were being run by Kieffer, telling him that 'ultimately there were about a dozen'.

Within MI5, Bleicher's account obviously provoked intense suspicion, both of Déricourt and, by implication, of Bodington. What precisely Bleicher's own motives were in the affair, especially regarding giving information to SOE's Henri Frager, was, of course, far from clear. Dr Goetz, speaking after the war, suggested that Bleicher was simply shopping Gilbert out of jealousy that such a valuable agent should be working for the Sicherheitsdienst and not for him. Certainly Frager's claim that Bleicher could be trusted – simply because he was an anti-Nazi – was just another example of F Section's tragic wishful thinking: in June 1944 Bleicher personally arrested Frager, who was later shot at Buchenwald.

In their interrogation of Bleicher, MI5 then tackled the odd circumstances surrounding the arrest of Jack Agazarian, who attended the fatal rendezvous set up, supposedly, with Gilbert Norman. The interrogator asked Bodington the important question: why had he sent Agazarian, his wireless operator, to the rendezvous and not gone himself? Bodington's standard answer – that they tossed a coin – was not deemed satisfactory, but he offered no other.

Why then did either go, if there was thought to be a risk? Bodington was asked.

He told his interrogator: 'They had, after all, to take some chances, otherwise they would have got nowhere with their mission.'

One possibility MI5 evidently then considered was that Bodington had been warned by Déricourt that the Germans would be there, but Bodington could not possibly say he had been warned as that would disclose his source. So he sent Agazarian along instead.

Suspicions of Bodington deepened when it emerged that among his many peculiar pre-war acquaintances was Henri Déricourt.

When MI5 asked Bodington why it was that Déricourt always seemed to have so much money, Bodington replied that Déricourt had been a highly paid 'trick aviator' before the war. In fact, as soon emerged, the two men regularly met at flying shows and dirt-track racing near Paris in the 1930s, when Bodington worked in Paris as a journalist.

Even more suspicion was aroused when Bodington was asked how he thought the Germans knew of his presence in Paris in the summer of 1943. The unexpected and dismissive reply was that the German secret police had known about him since 1934, 'when owing to certain journalistic activities of his, he had come to their notice'.

One of the German secret policemen Bodington was referring to was almost certainly Karl Boemelburg. British intelligence had long held a file on Boemelburg. The most senior Sicherheitsdienst officer in Paris for much of the war, he had been based at the German embassy in

Paris in the early 1930s as a quasi-diplomat. 'Appearance of a Prussian officer. Speaks good French; homosexual,' said a note in the Boemelberg file. Boemelburg, also met Déricourt and Bodington at the dirt-track racing, as Déricourt himself would later reveal.

Rather than reach any conclusion from this plethora of incriminating evidence, MI5 appeared simply to give up, and brought no charges against Déricourt or Bodington. So interwoven were the allegations of treachery involving SOE that the British security service men simply could not decide whom or what to believe – a state of affairs which may well have suited the former staff officers of SOE.

All these years later it was still hard to know what to believe, not least because of the 'weeding' of the files. What was clear, however, was first that Henri Déricourt was not only a traitor but also a brilliant conman. No sooner had the British acquitted him of treachery for a second time than he was arrested at Croydon airport in 1946, on his way to pilot a plane carrying a large amount of gold and platinum to France. The magistrate, in view of his 'excellent war record', let him off with a £500 fine.

Second, it was clear that Bodington went out of his way to protect Déricourt. Déricourt had some sort of hold over Bodington, perhaps dating back to their pre-war liaison, though what that hold was – financial, sexual or something else – was anyone's guess.

What was also clear from the files was Vera's own deafening silence on the question of Déricourt. She appeared not to have given her views – or her evidence – on him to the British inquiries at any stage, yet she had gathered more incriminating evidence against him than any other investigator. This reticence to speak out officially was in stark contrast to the way Vera made her abhorrence and distrust of Déricourt known unofficially. Anyone who broached the subject of Déricourt privately with Vera after the war was given a rundown on his treachery.

'She had a feminine intuition he was a rotten apple. I was completely conned by him,' said Hugh Verity, the head of Lysander operations.

Vera herself even told me when I met her at Winchelsea: 'I knew he was rotten from the very start', and as she spoke she suddenly raised her voice a little as if the very mention of the name had stirred long-buried anger. 'When he came to us, the men were all thrilled to bits with the fellow, but I gave him one look and said I would not trust him across the road. They were furious with me. He seemed to do a very good job for a while. But he was motivated by money and intrigue.'

'How did you know?' I asked, surprised by these forthright observations.

'Instinct,' she said, and blew one of those chimneys of smoke above her head. 'Some people's instincts serve them well. Mine have always served me well.'

————

Continuing her interrogation of Dr Goetz, Vera now asked about the deception that was carried out in the north of France. Dr Goetz said that Kieffer had instructed a second officer, Joseph Placke, to operate a captured wireless near Sedan, in the Ardennes, and by August 1943 the second deception scheme was successful.

As Vera knew, Dr Goetz was referring to the radio of John Macalister, Frank Pickersgill's wireless operator. Vera had traced the victims of this fiasco to several concentration camps. Bodington had warned Buckmaster that the Ardennes circuit 'should be considered lost' in his report about the Prosper disaster, on his return from Paris in August 1943. But the Ardennes circuit then began to work well, so the warning was ignored.

Dr Goetz explained that the Ardennes circuit had been created from scratch by Kieffer. The French resistance in that area did not know the two new arrivals from London, so when the Canadians, captured just after landing, were impersonated by Kieffer's men, nobody knew the difference. Arms poured in from London to the new circuit, as did agents. Placke and Kieffer then drew up all sorts of plans for sabotage, which were approved by London.

It was evident that by this time the German double-cross system had become a highly complex affair, as phoney plans were developed for each phoney circuit, all coordinated and planned so that London did not guess what was happening. Dr Goetz even developed his own set of code words and radio plans to mirror the real ones. He would send messages asking for arms or arranging a landing and London would reply with the details. The message on the BBC would come over signalling that all was ready to go ahead. Kieffer's men then charged off to the landing fields and formed reception committees. Dr Goetz even set up his own letterboxes for his 'agents' and sent the details to London. On occasion Dr Goetz and Placke were asked by London to fix up meetings with agents who were still operating freely in the field.

In August 1943 a message was received from London, intended for Pickersgill and Macalister, telling the two Canadians to meet up with Nora Inayat Khan (Madeleine), who was then still operating freely as a radio operator in Paris. The message told Pickersgill and Macalister to go to the basement of the Café Colisée in the Champs-Elysées, where they should make themselves known to the cloakroom attendant, who would then ensure they met Madeleine. Vera recalled the message. It was sent by Buckmaster, who wanted Madeleine to pass on contacts to the two Canadians.

Kieffer had been keen to locate Madeleine for some time, said Dr Goetz, but although his men had been closely on her trail she always got away. Now there was a chance for Kieffer to lure her right into the hands of two of his best men. Placke, whose English was fluent, was to be Macalister. To pose as Pickersgill, Kieffer chose another Gestapo officer, Karl Holdorf, who had a transatlantic accent from his time working on an ocean liner. It was assumed that Madeleine had never met Pickersgill or Macalister before, and so would not guess the two men who met her were Gestapo officers.

Now Vera learned what she had long suspected: that Madeleine had been sent by Buckmaster direct into Gestapo hands. But why, Vera now asked Dr Goetz, did Kieffer not follow Madeleine after the meeting and arrest her? This, said Dr Goetz, was another question for Kieffer and not for him. He supposed it suited Kieffer to have her run around a little longer.

In the end, said Dr Goetz, Madeleine was arrested after a denunciation. A woman had called up Avenue Foch offering to tell them the whereabouts of a female British agent in return for money. It was a story of jealousy. The woman who denounced Nora was Renée Garry, the sister of Nora's organiser, Emile Garry. When Nora arrived in Paris in June 1943 Renée was already in love with France Antelme, but during those terrifying weeks Antelme gave not only his protection but also his affection to Nora. In the autumn of 1943 Renée Garry 'sold' Nora to the Germans in revenge.

What Vera was more interested to know from Dr Goetz was when exactly Nora's arrest had taken place. Dr Goetz thought it must have been in September or October 1943. It was certainly early in the

autumn, because he was already very busy with several 'decoy transmissions', as he called his 'radio game', and then he had to learn to
play yet another radio – Madeleine's.

————

I hunted through the new files for the original telegrams from Dr
Goetz to see just how he had tricked London, but almost none had
survived. There was one interesting message, however, in Nora's file.
It came from an agent named Jacques and was sent from Berne on 1
October 1943. In it he told London that, according to a source called
Sonja ('Sonja' was garbled in transmission), Madeleine had had 'a
serious accident' and was 'in hospital' – code for captured or in serious
trouble. The telegram also mentioned a suspect agent named Maurice
Barde, who worked with another agent whose alias was Ernest.

CIPHER TEL FROM BERNE. DESP 13.57 1.10.43. REC 1820
2.10.43
    IMMEDIATE
    FOLLOWING FROM JACQUES.
    SONJ?A RETURNED FROM PARIS 25TH REPORTS ERNEST
MAURICE AND MADELEINE HAD SERIOUS ACCIDENT AND IN
HOSPITAL?. MAURICE IS BARDE. MADELEINE IS W/T OPERATOR.
    IF YOU GO AHEAD ON PICK UP PLAN I COULD TELL ON
RECEIPT OF PHOTOGRAPH WHETHER GENUINE OR GESTAPO
MAURICE.
    AM TRYING TO ?GET FURTHER INFORMATION VIA SONJ?A.

On the telegram were scrawled various initials showing that it
was sent to 'F' – Buckmaster. He replied to Berne the same day,
saying: 'Have had apparently genuine messages from Madeleine
since 25th therefore regard Sonja's news with some doubt. Can you
give us estimate Sonja's reliability?' Whether Buckmaster got such
an estimate was not recorded.

The 'Sonja' message was an extraordinary revelation. It showed
that London had received a serious warning of Nora's capture as early
as 1 October 1943 and that there was reason therefore at least to suspect that her radio was in enemy hands from that date. Yet the warning
was ignored. Perhaps Buckmaster simply dismissed the information
because it came from a local recruit – Sonja was hired in Paris – and

local recruits were never valued as much as London-trained agents. But Jacques, who sent the message, was Jacques Weil, a valued radio operator with a small Jewish SOE circuit known as Juggler operating near Paris. Weil, who had escaped to Berne after the Prosper collapse, had provided reliable reports before. Buckmaster's refusal to follow up this clear warning of Nora's capture was yet another stunning example of the tragic incompetence that littered these files.

It was, however, the identity of Sonja herself which made this telegram particularly remarkable. Sonja was in fact Sonia Olschanesky, a Jewish Russian-born dancer who had worked as a courier for the Juggler circuit. She was also Weil's fiancée. Unknown to London, Sonia had refused to follow Weil to the safety of Berne, and remained in place after the collapse of Prosper, taking immense risks by running messages between different SOE groups. She was herself captured in February 1944 and sent to Karlsruhe prison in the same convoy as Odette Sansom and the other British SOE women. She was then sent to Natzweiler, along with Diana Rowden, Andrée Borrel and Vera Leigh. It was, in fact, Sonia Olschanesky who was the woman drawn by Brian Stonehouse as No. 2 on the *Lagerstrasse*. Vera did not recognise her from Stonehouse's drawing because she had never met her. It was also Sonia's name that Vera had found in the prison records at Karlsruhe. She did not recognise the name because, as Sonia was a local recruit, she had never heard it before. Having already decided that Nora had died at Natzweiler, Vera had assumed that Sonia Olschanesky was an alias for Nora. As Vera was to discover some time later, however, it was Sonia Olschanesky who died at Natzweiler and not Nora Inayat Khan.

What this message showed for the first time was that the fates of Sonia and Nora were even more inextricably entwined than that. Thanks to the bravery of Sonia Olschanesky, London was first warned of Nora's capture on 1 October 1943, but Sonia was ignored. Had Sonia's warning been heeded at that time, Dr Goetz's 'radio game' would have been exposed and probably halted there and then, saving countless SOE lives. Sonia Olschanesky herself, arrested when another Prosper sub-circuit was penetrated in February 1944, would probably not have been captured.

————

Dr Goetz said that very soon after Madeleine was caught he was instructed to begin working her radio. She gave no help. 'But we needed none,' said Dr Goetz. Nora, he explained, was quite simple to impersonate because German signals staff had been intercepting her traffic for a long time. Furthermore, she had written all her letters to London *en clair* – that is, not in code – so they had been able to acquire all details of her signal plan and of her style through the usual method, 'the mail' handed in by the agent BOE 48. Dr Goetz had also been given a notebook belonging to Nora, found in a drawer in her apartment. The notebook contained all her back messages carefully written out. 'From that we could work out her code and all her security checks.' Dr Goetz set up an entire fake circuit for Nora, and gave her his own alias, Diana, for use within Avenue Foch.

'When was Nora sent to Germany?' asked Vera.

'I could not say. But she was one of the first to go,' said Dr Goetz, who recalled that Nora was removed from Avenue Foch and sent on to Germany soon after being captured and certainly well before Christmas 1943. 'I told Kieffer I didn't need her to work her radio.' Now Vera was hearing something entirely new. Her investigations into Nora's fate had concluded that Nora had been sent to Germany with Odette Sansom and the other six women on the transport from Paris to Karlsruhe in May 1944. But Dr Goetz was telling her that Nora had been sent to Germany alone, probably in October or November 1943, and certainly many months before the other women. He did not know where Madeleine was sent, but it cannot have been too far away, he thought, because there had been a need to reinterrogate her at Christmas. At Christmas Dr Goetz received a message for Madeleine from London, which was obviously designed to test her, so Kieffer sent a man to Germany to get the answers. The message Dr Goetz was now referring to was composed by Vera and asked for certain information about Nora's family. Vera had received the replies from Dr Goetz and judged them authentic.

Madeleine, however, was as usual uncooperative, said Dr Goetz, so he had had to guess the answers himself, relying on his wits. And though Nora refused to assist at all while at Avenue Foch, she had inadvertently passed on certain personal details which proved useful, said Dr Goetz.

———

Evidence from the newly opened files showed that at the end of the war as many as one-third of F Section circuits were penetrated as a result of radio deception alone. But the actual penetration of F Section was, of course, far wider, thanks to Henri Déricourt. A total of fifty-four British agents who landed in France passed through his hands. All were potentially contaminated, as were any other agents they contacted, as each one of them could have been trailed. The true extent of the penetration of F Section circuits on the eve of D-Day was therefore incalculable and clearly concerned MI5's counter-intelligence experts when they considered the disaster after the war.

MI5's own T.A. Robertson, known as TAR, who helped run the much-acclaimed British double-cross system, under which German agents captured in Britain were 'turned', commented in August 1945 on how SOE had failed to use properly 'wireless finger printing', whereby the agent's messages could be checked against an electronic trace. Had they done so, he said, 'they would surely have been able to discover that their own agents were not operating the sets'.

Robertson's MI5 colleague Guy Liddell, head of counter-intelligence, gave an indication of how London was duped in his wartime diaries, released in 2002. It had come to Liddell's attention shortly before D-Day that a sub-circuit of SOE's Ardennes group (Archdeacon) was 'operating near the north coast of Brittany', which, from a study of the traffic, 'appeared to suggest the possibility of German control'. Given the utmost importance of keeping the chosen place and date for landings secret, this development was deeply worrying, said Liddell, who then referred to the decision by an F Section officer to test the circuit by means of an S phone, which allowed him to speak in person to the organiser on the ground.

'He reported on his return that the voice of the latter individual had sounded extremely guttural, and that he spoke neither fluent French nor English.'

Buckmaster, however, still refused to believe that Pickersgill or Macalister was caught, Liddell noted.

————

After Christmas Dr Goetz was worried that London had not been taken in by his reply to the Christmas questions over Nora's radio. 'At this time my own impression was that although London were answering my messages they were not really deceived. At one reception for example we had asked for twelve containers but only one was dropped. This strengthened my view that they had guessed.'

Then London seemed convinced again. 'At the next reception for which we asked for 500,000 francs we received precisely this amount. I therefore changed my opinion and continued to work the set and ask for large receptions. In the early months of 1944 we received not only a great deal of material but also agents.' He remembered arranging over Nora's radio for three agents to drop in February, and among them came France Antelme, as well as a woman. Antelme was in a 'towering rage' when he realised what had happened but Kieffer was very excited when Antelme landed, as he knew he was an important agent, not least because Dr Goetz received a message, meant for Antelme, congratulating him on his OBE. Kieffer even hoped he would know the date of D-Day. Antelme, however, gave nothing away. To prevent London guessing from Antelme's silence that he had been caught, thereby throwing suspicion on Madeleine's radio, Dr Goetz then had to construct a cover story about his capture. He devised a series of complicated medical reports about an 'accident' on landing.

By March 1944 Kieffer was obviously revelling in his conjuring trick and began to think that he might match the success of his Abwehr colleague, Hermann Giskes, in Holland.

———

The extent to which F Section was deceived by Kieffer and his radio mastermind was best illustrated by two further pieces of paper I found in Nora's personal file. Many months before the end of the war in France, Buckmaster and Vera had been busy preparing citations for gallantry awards for more than two hundred F Section agents. On 24 February 1944 Buckmaster submitted a citation for Nora Inayat Khan to receive a George Medal, a gallantry award granted to civilians.

In the citation Buckmaster wrote that as a result of Nora's bravery the Prosper group had been 'reinforced and reconstructed and today is in perfect order'. Apparently convinced that Nora was still free and operating, he wrote: 'It is unique in the annals of this organisation for a circuit to be so completely disintegrated and yet to be rebuilt because, regardless of personal danger, this young woman remained on her post, at times alone, and always under threat of arrest.' In fact, at the time he wrote this, Nora had been in German hands for at least three months and the Prosper circuit had been largely destroyed.

Perhaps Buckmaster believed much of what he said in this absurd document. Or perhaps it was written by others and handed to him to sign. One element, though, he must have simply fabricated. Nora, he said, 'has also been instrumental in facilitating the escape of thirty Allied airmen shot down in France'. Such an escape never happened.

Another apparent fabrication also crept into the citation. Buckmaster claimed that Nora had been 'instructed' to return home after the collapse of the Prosper network in July 1943 'because of the dangers she faced'. He said she 'pleaded' to remain and was therefore allowed to do so. He wrote 'subsequently events have fully justified this course of action'.

It was quite possible that Nora was offered the chance to return home and it was quite possible that she preferred to stay, as she appeared to have been exhilarated by her work. But there was no evidence that Nora was ever 'instructed' to return. Had she been instructed she would have been obliged to obey. Buckmaster needed a radio link between Paris and London and she was more than willing to fulfil the role. Now he was attempting to justify his decision to leave her in the field.

———

By May 1944 Dr Goetz realised that London really was suspicious of his transmissions as supplies of arms and men slowed down. As Vera knew, though, there was one circuit which Buckmaster refused to accept had been penetrated until the very end, and this was Archdeacon. Gerry Morel, the operations officer, had decided to test out the circuit by arranging to talk to Frank Pickersgill by S phone from the air.

When London proposed talking to Pickersgill by this means, Kieffer had a dilemma, said Dr Goetz. If a German tried to imitate Pickersgill's voice to a London desk officer the deception would be exposed. So, with the permission of Horst Kopkow at head office in Berlin, Kieffer brought Pickersgill back from his jail at Ravitsch with the intention of forcing him to talk. Pickersgill, however, had refused to cooperate. He even tried to escape from the Gestapo prison in Place des Etats Unis and was shot and badly injured. Eventually he was sent back to Germany. Vera had established Pickersgill's fate: he was hanged at Buchenwald.

Dr Goetz said Kieffer then asked Bob Starr, still based in Avenue Foch, and still favoured by Kieffer, to do the talking for him. Starr at first agreed and Kieffer was happy. But, at the last minute, Starr changed his mind, perhaps because he realised that by refusing so late he would cause Kieffer the greatest difficulty. Kieffer would now have no choice but to use one of his own people even though a German accent would be noticed. This was clearly what happened, said Dr Goetz, because the plane quickly flew away.

Dr Goetz's 'radio game' was then effectively over. On D-Day the Führer himself had the idea of sending a message thanking London for all the agents and the arms. 'I thought this unnecessary and argued against it but Hitler was determined. He thought it would frighten you and would damage morale. So I arranged for the message to be sent. He then changed his mind. But it was too late.'

Finally, Vera asked Dr Goetz where she would find Kieffer. Only Kieffer would know about the capture of Francis Suttill. And only Kieffer would be able to confirm, once and for all, whether Henri Déricourt was a traitor. Dr Goetz said he had last heard that Kieffer 'was moving towards Munich'.

21

RAVENSBRÜCK

When Vera returned to London in November 1946 after interrogating Dr Goetz, she had expected to spend a few days closing down her affairs before resuming a civilian life. Her allotted time on the war crimes investigation was about to expire for good and she had no desire to remain under military orders.

A letter, addressed to a Labour peer named Lord Walkden and redirected to Vera, persuaded her to change her plans. The letter was signed by Yolande Lagrave – a name that meant nothing to Vera.

Monsieur, I don't know if you remember me and Monsieur Dujour who organised an excursion to St Emilion in August 1933. I worked as a secretary at the information bureau in the city. I found your letter and the photo taken of that trip along with your kind words.

Alas 13 years has passed and what tragic events have taken place. Mr Dujour and I were arrested by the Gestapo – he in February 1943 and me four months after, that is to say in June 1943. He was part of the resistance. I helped him but it will take too long to explain all of that. The result was that he is dead. He was deported and sent to Natzweiler Struthof and then to Dachau, where he died after torture.

As for me: I was deported to Pforzheim prison and I was lucky to get back. I was the only returnee of my group. Everyone else in the prison with me was massacred. It is in relation to all of this, Monsieur, that I ask you to remember me, and I ask you to come to my assistance. At Pforzheim, where I was imprisoned in a cell, I was able to correspond with an English parachutist who was locked up there also. She was very unhappy. Her hands and feet were chained and she was never allowed out. I heard the blows which she received from prison guards.

She was taken away from Pforzheim in September 1944. Before she left she had been able to send me – not her name because it was too dangerous – but her alias and she also wrote down her address for me. It was this: Nora Baker, Radio Centre Officers Service RAF, 4 Taviston [sic] Street, London. I kept the address on a paper sewn into my hem.

I wrote to this address but the letter came back 'not known at this address'.

I was astonished that the Service RAF Radio Centre Officers [sic] was unknown and couldn't believe that the postal service could not find a way to find them.

I cannot believe that the RAF would be indifferent to knowing the fate of a devoted officer, who had suffered as she had for her country and for the victory of the Allies. I know that intelligence services are very secret. I even tried myself to make contact at the British Embassy when last in Paris but it was a Saturday and everything was closed – the English week!

I hope, Monsieur, that you will be able to help, both as a favour to one of your compatriots and to somebody who knew you 13 years ago. Luckily I had kept your letter and photograph in my box of souvenirs.

Lord Walkden passed the letter to the Air Ministry, which eventually passed it on to the office of Norman Mott, who was still handling SOE affairs, and he passed it to Vera. Though the letter had arrived in a roundabout way, its authenticity was evident. Nora Baker was obviously Nora Inayat Khan and 4 Taviton Street had once been her family's address in London, but since Nora's disappearance her mother had gone to stay with friends and the house had been rented out, which was why the letter had been returned to Bordeaux marked 'not known'.

The implications of the letter were far-reaching. Quite simply, if Nora was in Pforzheim prison in September 1944, as Yolande Lagrave said, she could not have died at Natzweiler three months earlier, as Vera had concluded in April the previous year. Vera's doubts about Nora's fate had already been reawakened by Dr Goetz, who told her that 'Madeleine' left Paris in autumn of 1943, and not in May 1944 as she had thought. Now, with Yolande Lagrave's new evidence, the investigation into Nora's death would have to be reopened.

Mott drafted a very carefully worded reply to the Air Ministry thanking them for 'the sight' of the Nora Baker folder. 'Nora Baker is one of our agents who was captured and incarcerated in various concentration camps . . . Enquiries have shown she is identical to Inayat Khan WAAF.'

He did not draw the Ministry's attention to the fact that this matter had been 'cleared up' by Squadron Officer Atkins six months earlier.

Vera's return to Germany, however, was by this time no simple matter. Her honorary commission in the WAAF had been resigned, so she could acquire none of the necessary 'movement orders' for further travel. And her inability to travel was compounded by the fact that, despite her naturalisation nearly two years previously, the necessary time had still not elapsed for her to receive a British passport.

Then Vera received a timely request from her own former war crimes colleagues asking her to return to Germany to join the prosecution team in the Ravensbrück trial, to be held in Hamburg in three weeks' time.

Writing on behalf of his commanding officer, Captain Michael Raymond told Vera:

> Lt Col A.J.M. Harris has asked me to write to you to find out whether you would be prepared to arrive in Hamburg before the other witnesses who arrive on 28, 29, 30 November to act as a sort of marshal. The sudden arrival in Hamburg of about 16 women of about 10 nationalities will present many problems; it was thought that you, having met many of them and speaking their languages, would be able to deal with them more tactfully than anybody else. HQ Hamburg would be most grateful if you would help them in this way.

Although Vera had not intended to attend the trial, it was entirely appropriate that she should be present at the Ravensbrück proceedings, not least because her early investigations had first exposed the truth about the camp. Vera had returned only recently from a tour of Sweden, Denmark and Norway interviewing witnesses. It was also in large part due to the deaths at Ravensbrück of Vera's women agents that it fell to the British to investigate and try the case. Otherwise the case, Ravensbrück being in the Soviet zone, would have been tried by the Russians. As with the Sachsenhausen trial, the details might then never have been known.

The request for Vera to join the prosecution team was therefore not unwelcome and it also solved her travel problems. In view of the summons the Air Ministry immediately agreed to extend Vera's honorary commission and gave her authority to return to Germany for the trial, during which time she hoped also to investigate the new leads about Nora's death. Her first obligation, however, was to the Ravensbrück case.

When Vera arrived in Hamburg on 21 November 1946 her immediate task of marshalling witnesses was daunting. Temperatures in the city were –20 degrees, which made the logistics of shepherding female witnesses all the harder. Finding suitable accommodation was itself not easy in a city that had been so badly flattened. Many witnesses arrived in a state of acute anxiety, knowing they would have to confront in the dock, among others, Dorothea Binz, the arch-sadist SS camp overseer, as well as Vera Salvequart, a prisoner 'nurse' who sent her 'patients' on their way to the gas chambers, and Carmen Mory, the *Blockführer* in charge of Ravensbrück's punishment block. The Kommandant himself, Fritz Suhren, would not, however, be on trial as he had escaped for a second time, this time from British custody.

For all involved the case was also one of vast complexity. The simple fact that Ravensbrück was a concentration camp for women had placed the trial in a category of its own. Many of the crimes committed here were crimes not so much against humanity as very specifically against women: gynaecological experiments, forced sterilisations, forced abortions, to name but three. Moreover, as the court would hear, the whole concept of Ravensbrück was specifically designed by Nazi ideologues as a crime against women. Most of the women held at the camp were brought here not to answer for anything they had done, but to punish the men and the families they had been taken from, in order to deter resisters to Nazi occupation. 'All of these women were brought here', the prosecution would declare, 'as part of an organised attack on the life of womanhood to intimidate men.' And the fact that many of the accused from Ravensbrück were also women only contributed further to the macabre nature of the case.

Nevertheless, despite the stress of getting ready for the trial, Vera found that the atmosphere in Hamburg was not altogether bleak. Though the central station had been obliterated, the station hotel was still standing and served as a comfortable base for the prosecution team. The chief prosecutor, Stephen Stewart, and John da Cunha, his junior, both good friends of Vera's from Bad Oeynhausen, were at the Hotel Bahnhof, as were a team of secretaries, including Vera's close Norwegian friend from Bad Oeynhausen, Sara Jensen.

Vera was allotted Room 50, on the fifth floor, and close by, in Room 56, was Odette Sansom. Odette, who six months previously had become the first woman ever to be awarded a George Cross and was already a household name at home, was to be the prosecution's star witness. And also here in Hamburg, arriving with extra duffel coats and whisky for Vera and her colleagues, was Jerrard Tickell, Odette's biographer, who, when he wasn't researching his book, kept the 'chaps and chapesses', as he called the prosecution team, perpetually entertained. Vera he cheered along at every opportunity with witty notes. 'Riddle of the Girl "Vera" – Nobody Knew Her' was a newspaper headline he brought out to Hamburg for her. The cutting had nothing to do with Vera Atkins, but underneath Tickell had written: 'and I thought to myself how true and how sad'.

Finding time to scribble a postcard to her mother on the eve of the trial, Vera wrote: 'Have had a very lively two days as people are arriving every few minutes and as we get nearer to the opening date (tomorrow morning) so tempers get short and the excitement increases. It is no mean thing to have 20 highly strung women waiting about with nothing to do. I shall be glad when we start to get going.'

'May it please the court,' began Major Stewart, starting his opening speech in calm and almost conversational tones. Born Stefan Strauss in Vienna, Stephen Stewart fled Austria in 1938, just after the Anschluss, when he discovered his name was on a Nazi hit list, and was later called to the Bar in London. 'In Mecklenburg, about 50 miles north of Berlin, there is a group of lakes to which the gentry of that once great capital used to go for their weekends. One of these lakes, probably because of its rather swampy, marshy lands, did not seem to attract too many visitors and it was there on the shore of Lake Fürstenberg where, shortly after the outbreak of war, a concentration camp for women was sited and for the first time in 1939 figures on the official papers of the SS show a recognised concentration camp named Ravensbrück.'

At one end of the court sat the judges. The president was an English major-general in full uniform with a King's Counsel in wig and gown at his side, and five other uniformed military judges on the bench, including one Frenchman and one Pole. Directly in front of the judges were the sixteen defendants, each wearing a black number on a square of white cardboard on their chest.

All pleaded not guilty to charges of committing war crimes involving the ill treatment and killing of Allied nationals. Seated in front of the defendants were their lawyers, eleven robed German doctors of law.

The witnesses, waiting to be called, largely former women prisoners, were from France, Belgium, Holland, Denmark, Norway, Austria, Poland, Czechoslovakia, Switzerland, Germany and Britain. In the centre of the courtroom was a table for the interpreters and shorthand writer. The press bench was on one side and the prosecution bench on the other. Vera sat just behind Stewart and da Cunha. Her presence attracted the interest of the journalists opposite, but they were not told her name. Vera at the trial was later described by Tickell as 'a smooth, utterly impersonal figure in WAAF uniform'. There was little or no heating in court. Vera wore her thickest uniform and two of the defendants, Carmen Mory and Vera Salvequart, wore fur coats.

Stephen Stewart proceeded to give the court an overview of the evidence. Ravensbrück camp, he said, was built in 1939 for six thousand prisoners but the population had reached forty thousand by January 1945. In those years 120,000 women had passed through the camp, of whom 92,000 had died. The first women to be brought to the camp were Germans and Austrians, then followed Czechs, Dutch, Poles, Danes, and soon Russians began to arrive en masse. Many prominent women passed through the camp: including Geneviève de Gaulle, General de Gaulle's niece, who had worked with the French resistance. There were writers, doctors, scientists, artists, mothers, peasants, gypsies and prostitutes. There were many women who had never been identified at all. And all the prisoners were divided into categories; among them were political prisoners, Jews and 'asocials', who included lesbians, prostitutes and gypsies. The staff were drawn from numerous other concentration camps but Ravensbrück was primarily known as a training camp for SS women guards. Himmler visited the camp often.

Stewart went on to outline the way the inmates lived, sleeping 250 to a hut, three to a bed, lining up for hours a day in the freezing cold for parades, feeding on watery soup and boiled potatoes and shuffling through stinking excreta in the most primitive of sanitary huts. Those fit enough were forced to carry out back-breaking labour in quarries, factories or fields while others took jobs in the camp itself as prisoner-guards. Stewart outlined how they died, often at night in bed, simply of starvation or ill health or of one of many epidemics. The living lay alongside the corpse, even if it was in the same bed, until morning, when a barrow would come round the blocks collecting bodies to burn in the crematorium.

If the women died at work, their bodies would also be wheeled off in barrows to the crematorium. Many died in the punishment block, which consisted of 78 cells, each 2 metres wide by 2.5 metres long, where prisoners were locked for days and taken out from time to time for 'punishment' – whipping or beating on naked buttocks. Most passed out after ten strokes and many died, but a doctor was on hand to take the pulse of the victim and if they revived they were given the full twenty-five-stroke punishment.

Prisoners died also during or after medical experiments in Block 17 or during abortions or sterilisation. Many prisoners lost their minds and were held in a special block for 'lunatics' – Block 10 – where the defendant Carmen Mory strapped and shackled them until, as she had testified in one statement, 'foam came from the ears and nose'.

In the early days those selected for extermination – by reason of age or ill health – were shot or hanged and their bodies thrown into the crematorium, although sometimes they were transported to Auschwitz. In the autumn of 1944 a gas chamber was built in which seventeen hundred women were murdered in the single month of November. Between January and April 1945 the killings were accelerated and 6993 women, girls and children – the majority Jews – were gassed.

Witnesses were then invited by the court to tell their own stories.

First to speak was Sylvia Salvesen, wife of the physician to the Norwegian king, and a prominent figure in the Norwegian resistance, who told the court what had happened to her from the moment she entered the gates.

'When you enter something you only enter it through a door and we entered it through a big porch and we saw that this was in a wall and there was a big fence. Later we learned it was an electric fence. We had to wait a few hours before we were let into what we later learned was called a bath. There was a room about as big as this courtroom and there were no baths in it but there were a few openings in the roof and from these came water; but we had to wait naked at least two hours before any water came. When you think of it we had been eighteen days on the road and we were longing for water but we had to be four under every one of these showers and the water only ran for moments. We got a little bit of soap in our hands and what they would call perhaps a towel but it was no bigger than a handkerchief. When that was finished I am sorry to say most of us had lost the small piece of soap because the water came so quickly and we lost it between the ribs and the floor. Then we had to wait. I do not know how long because time runs so slowly when you are naked for the first time in your life with a lot of unknown people, and then something happened which gave us the biggest shock, the first big shock in Ravensbrück. There entered two men dressed in uniforms. Later we were to hear that one was a doctor and the other a dentist. We were then put in rows and then, still naked, we had to pass them and they looked, as far as I can remember, only at our teeth and our hands. I am afraid we had the feeling of shame because we had not yet learned that shame was not ours but theirs. We had a feeling that they were selecting us for something. We were very naive. We thought we should get our dresses again and we were shown a lump of clothes and we had to grab something – some sort of dress, sort of underwear, stolen from other prisoners. We got some wooden shoes.'

She went on: 'After we left the "bath" we were to stand in rows of five outside the "baths" and again had to wait. This was perhaps my first real glimpse of the camp because standing the first few hours there we saw the other prisoners pass. This for me was looking at a picture of Hell. Why should I use that word? Because I had seen pictures by our best artists of how they supposed it would be in Hell. And that was not because I saw anything terrible happen but because I saw for the first time in my life human beings that I could not judge whether they were men or women. Their hair was shaved and they were thin, unhappy and filthy. But that was not what struck me most. It was the expression of their eyes – they had what I would call "dead eyes".'

As witness followed witness the court learned every detail of the layout of the camp, and every routine of the prisoners' day and every characteristic of the tormentors in the dock. Dorothea Binz always had her hair well done, the court was told – undercurled and bobbed – and she always carried a whip and had a little English terrier with her. She often observed the beatings in the punishment block, standing hand in hand with her SS lover, Edmund Braenung, another guard.

They heard too about the *Jugendlager*. The word meant 'youth camp', but this sub-camp, just outside the main perimeter, was in fact the extermination annexe, opened in January 1945, when the gassings increased. Here up to ten thousand women were packed together in conditions worse even than those in the main camp, so that many died before their day came for extermination. Each prisoner in the *Jugendlager* had been issued with a pink card, which meant they had been selected to die, because they were too ill to work or simply because they had grey hair. A pink card could be handed to a prisoner at any time of day or night. And in the *Jugendlager* parades were held randomly, so that all the inmates lived in constant fear that they could be selected. Those selected were often stripped in front of the block to see what clothing they had on, and then given back only their dresses before being taken away on a truck in the evening and not seen again.

Girls between eight and eighteen were picked out for special 'experiments' on their reproductive organs which involved injections into the uterus and Fallopian tubes. The girls were usually gypsies and many died of infections.

As the evidence poured out, occasionally there would be a release of tension – something small might happen which would suddenly make everyone laugh in a manner out of all proportion to the event. But mostly the horror was relentless. At any moment a witness might summon up a new and yet more ghastly image: rats eating the eyes and noses of the dead left lying near the 'hospital', the sight of bleeding dog bites running up a woman's legs.

From time to time Vera would write a note and pass it forward to Stewart or da Cunha. But mostly she kept quite still. After the day's proceedings she might relax by going to the state opera, revived among the rubble, with the interpreter, Peter Forrest, another Austrian and friend of Vera's. Or she might go for a drive with the Deputy Judge Advocate General, Carl Stirling KC, who had taken a shine to her. In the evening Vera often found the company of Sara Jensen most relaxing. Sara took it upon herself to 'shepherd' Vera, while Vera shepherded the witnesses.

Then the proceedings would begin again. Towards the end of the prosecution case came perhaps the cruellest evidence of all. In the winter of 1944 the birth of babies was allowed in Ravensbrück. Until then pregnant women underwent forced abortions, normally in the seventh or eighth month, or the babies were strangled at birth and one of the prisoner-nurses then burned them in the boiler room. But in September 1944 the policy changed and children were born, by then mostly to Polish political prisoners, who were arriving in various stages of pregnancy.

The first baby to be born was treated 'like a prince in the camp', said the Norwegian Sylvia Salvesen, who had tried to help care for the new-borns. All the women wanted to see this child and news of the birth went round the blocks in a flash. And, for reasons nobody ever understood, others were allowed to be born, and at first mothers were allowed to stay with their babies.

But soon the mothers were kicked back to slave work or to their dirty blocks and the babies were left with no milk and bits of rag and they started to die.

As Sylvia Salvesen described the first of the babies' deaths the chief German defence lawyer, Dr Von Metler, protested that the translator had wrongly stated that a particular group of babies had died because they had turned over and could not breathe, whereas in fact the witness had said that it was because no nurse was present. But, as the evidence continued, it became quite clear that babies born in Ravensbrück died simply because they could not live. They were left alone without mothers, milk or warmth. Of 120 babies born in January and February 1945, 80 died. And then the court heard that in March 130 babies and pregnant women were suddenly taken away to be gassed in a railway wagon.

As the testimony continued a witness would from time to time mention one or more of Vera's dead girls – Cicely Lefort, Violette Szabo, Denise Bloch or Lilian Rolfe. Little of the evidence was new to Vera and she rarely reacted to what she heard.

Even so, under questioning from a judge or a lawyer, or in conversation outside the court, a witness would remember something in a way that even Vera had not heard before.

Sylvia Salvesen had seen Cicely Lefort just before she was gassed and described how, while she was in the main camp, Cicely had become very ill and could not tolerate standing for roll-calls so she had volunteered to go to the newly opened *Jugendlager*, believing there was no roll-call there and that conditions were better. But prisoners in the sub-camp had to stand for seven hours for roll-call, starting at 3am. Everyone had dysentery. Fifty died each day from exhaustion. At least one hundred women were taken away each day from the *Jugendlager* and never seen again. So sick was she by then that Cicely was picked out for extermination almost as soon as she reached the *Jugendlager*.

Another witness told the court: 'The women were put on one side and a few hours later taken away in motor lorries. I was told a few days later they had been taken to the railway siding in the village, put in a van and gassed.'

Several witnesses remembered the strength and cheerfulness of Violette. One woman recalled her talking incessantly about 'my baby, my baby'. A woman who saw Violette, Lilian and Denise in the punishment block before they were taken away to be shot described all three as emaciated, dirty and weak; so weak was Lilian, said the witness, that she had to be carried to the place where she was shot.

Sitting in court, it was impossible for Vera to overlook even the smallest detail as every word of every witness was meticulously translated over and over again into various languages, in at least three of which Vera was fluent. And the way the story was presented here – from beginning to end – gave Vera a perspective she had not had before. Sitting on the prosecution bench, she was for the first time able to view the fate of her girls in the context of the camp as a whole, which until now she had had little time to consider. For the past year she had been so busy hunting down evidence and trying to understand the technical aspects of the case that when the court proceedings in Hamburg began she suddenly found she had time to reflect.

———

I hoped that in her letters home Vera might at last feel freer to say what she thought now that the case was under way, but they were as bland as always. 'Dearest Ma, We were a bit cold at times and also furiously busy with one thing and another. It is really a most interesting case,' she wrote from Hamburg in January 1947, signing off by thanking her mother for a hairbrush she had posted to her.

'In court I think Vera saw it partly as her job to keep emotions – others' as well as her own – under control,' said John da Cunha. 'And at the time, you know, we all adjusted to it. You do, I'm afraid. You get hardened to it. You almost become coarsened by it.'

Had Vera become hardened?

'She must have been, of course. But it was so much more difficult for her. She knew many of the victims. It was much more personal for Vera.'

'Do you think she was feeling emotion?'

'I am sure she was. I have no doubt at all,' da Cunha said. 'One could tell. She was always exhausted by it. I think it all totally drained her. I used to go up to her room at the end of each day to talk over the evidence and prepare for what was coming next. When I went in she would be sitting at a table with her hair down, holding her hairbrush. It was the only time I saw her with her hair down. And as we talked she would start brushing her hair and she brushed it over and over again. I always thought it was probably her way of releasing tension.'

Da Cunha said that when it was all over the press had clamoured at her door and he was posted outside her room to keep them away. 'She just wanted to be alone at that time. Some on the prosecution side wanted to celebrate; it had been a long, hard trial. But Vera never wanted to celebrate in any way. She certainly showed no sign of feeling any anger towards these people. Like the rest of us, I think she just felt a mixture of disgust and pity.

'And Schwarzhuber was very important to Vera. He was her most important witness. I remember he said how impressed he had been with the bearing of Vera's girls when they were executed. Perhaps that was some consolation to her.'

————

On day thirteen Johann Schwarzhuber, the camp overseer, took the stand. Vera had taken his statement about the deaths of Violette, Lilian and Denise nine months previously. Had it not been for his capture she might never have learned of their fate. As on that occasion, Schwarzhuber once again seemed ready to talk and give the court all the information that he could. Unlike other witnesses, he at no stage sought to deny his role in events. He even seemed to try, from time to time, to catch the eye of prosecution lawyers.

A father of three children, born in Bavaria, Schwarzhuber told the court he was a printer by profession. He said he had worked as an SS guard in Dachau, Sachsenhausen and Auschwitz before being transferred to Ravensbrück in January 1945. He had a remarkable memory for detail, telling the court that from January to February thirty to thirty-five women died every day, but from February to the middle of March sixty to seventy died each day, purely as a result of illnesses. At the end of February, he said, he had been called to see the Kommandant, Fritz Suhren, and told to organise the mass gassing of prisoners because the killing was not going fast enough. He was reluctant to do this: 'I had done it at Auschwitz and did not want to do it a second time.'

The gassing nevertheless went ahead. 'I attended one gassing in which 150 women were forced into the gas chamber. They were ordered to be undressed as if to be deloused and taken into the gas chamber. Then the door was locked. A male prisoner with a gas mask then climbed on to the roof and threw a gas container into the room through a window, which he closed. I heard groaning and whimpering in the room. After two or three minutes it grew quiet. Whether the women were dead or just senseless I cannot say.'

Mass killing had become a routine, daily event, but for reasons he was never asked to explain, Schwarzhuber still recalled in detail the particular deaths of Violette Szabo, Lilian Rolfe and Denise Bloch. After they reached the punishment block in early January nobody had known what happened to them because they could not be seen or contacted by other prisoners. But Schwarzhuber was able to tell the court – as he had first told Vera, but in more detail now – what happened next. 'One evening towards 1900 hours they were called out [of the punishment block] and taken to the courtyard by the crematorium. Camp Kommandant Suhren made these arrangements. He read out the order for their shooting in the presence of the chief camp doctor, Dr Trommer, SS Sergeant Zappe, SS Lance Corporal Schult, SS Corporal Schenk and the dentist Dr Hellinger. I myself was present.'

Schwarzhuber continued: 'I accompanied the three women to the crematorium yard. A female camp overseer was also present and sent back when we reached the crematorium. Zappe stood guard over them while they were waiting to be shot.

'All three were very brave and I was deeply moved. Suhren was also impressed by the bearing of these women. He was annoyed that the Gestapo did not themselves carry out these shootings.'

The shooting was done by SS Lance Corporal Schult with a small-calibre gun fired through the back of the neck. 'They were brought forward singly by Corporal Schenk. Death was certified by Dr Trommer. The corpses were removed singly by the internees who were employed in the crematorium and burned. The clothes were burned with the bodies.'

22

'A VERY FINE MANNER'

When Johan Schwarzhuber had completed his evidence at the Ravensbrück trial, in mid-January 1947, Vera disappeared from court for several days. She told colleagues she had to clear up 'loose ends' in Bad Oeynhausen. In fact, as colleagues began closing speeches in the Ravensbrück case, Vera was on her way to reopen her investigation into what had happened to Nora Inayat Khan.

Vera also had a second, related mission, which she hoped to accomplish in her break from the Ravensbrück trial. News had reached her from Bill Barkworth that Hans Kieffer had finally been run to ground and was being held in prison in Wuppertal. The development was timely, and Barkworth agreed that Vera could interrogate him there in a few days' time.

It was now nine months since Vera had closed the investigation into Nora's case. In April 1946 she had concluded that Nora was one of four girls taken from the prison in Karlsruhe to Natzweiler concentration camp, where she, Andrée Borrel, Diana Rowden and Vera Leigh were killed on 6 July 1944 by lethal injection and their bodies cremated. Nora's family had been given this version of events. Nora's murder had been part of the case made against the Natzweiler camp staff at their trial. And this story had formed part of the citation which had recently secured for Nora a mention in dispatches. But Vera had never found it easy to fit the pieces of Nora's story together and it had taken a single letter from a woman she had never met and knew nothing about to show her that the story she had so painstakingly constructed about Nora's death was wrong.

————

I knew by now the trouble Vera would take to ensure nobody ever knew she was wrong. On one occasion in her later years she gave a lengthy talk to a group of FANY officers about her war crimes investigation, which was taped. Afterwards she realised that in her talk she had mistaken the name of an SS officer. She then insisted that a FANY officer should go to her home with the tape and tape recorder, and together, over many hours, they replayed the tape and located each mention of the misnamed officer, so that the error could be erased. Then, speaking into the microphone at precisely the right moment, Vera stated the correct name.

Vera appeared to have gone to even more extraordinary lengths to ensure that nobody thought she was wrong about Nora. According to the published official record of the Natzweiler trial, held in May 1946, Vera was not wrong about the identities of the dead women when she gave evidence to the court on oath. In this 'official verbatim record' of the trial, edited by a leading barrister for publication as a book in 1949, Vera told the court: 'During the course of investigations in Karlsruhe I was able to establish that the four who left [Karlsruhe] were Andrée Borrel, Vera Leigh, Diana Rowden and a fourth woman whose identity I was and am unable to ascertain.' I knew this 'official verbatim record' could not be right because other evidence showed quite clearly that Vera had told the court that the fourth woman was Nora, and at the time she firmly believed this to be correct.

Then a specialist researcher, burrowing in the National Archives at Kew, found a second 'official verbatim record' of the same trial. This second document was made public only in 1976 and was the original contemporaneous transcript of the trial, unedited and with no commentary. It told a different story. Here Vera said on oath: 'During the course of investigations in Karlsruhe I was able to establish that the four who left [Karlsruhe] were Denise [sic] Borrel, Nora Inayat Khan, Vera Leigh and Diana Rowden.'

The 1949 version had obviously been changed to remove all mention of Nora's name. As the publisher had ceased to exist and the editor was dead, it was impossible to know exactly how the rewriting of the 'verbatim record' had been arranged. But there could be little doubt that in order to hide her mistake Vera herself had found a way to ensure history was rewritten, scotching from the records what she had said on oath.

———

The atmosphere in Bad Oeynhausen in January 1947 was very different from when Vera had first arrived a year before. The victorious powers were by now more interested in rebuilding Germany than punishing war crimes. The US target was to complete all war crimes trials by the end of that year. It was evident to Vera that, in this climate, new evidence about what happened to Nora would be harder to find and might soon be buried for good. Criminals would from now on find it easier than ever to slip through the net and would be less willing to talk about the past.

Yet snippets of Nora's story were now suddenly emerging on several fronts. Others as well as Vera had been uncovering new evidence. In January 1947, Nora's brother, Vilayat Inayat Khan, had also received a letter from Yolande Lagrave, the prisoner who had known 'Nora Baker' at Pforzheim. Nora had evidently managed to pass to Madame Lagrave not only the Taviton Street address, but also the address of a friend in Paris through which Madame Lagrave had passed a letter to Vilayat. And Vilayat had also heard about Nora from a second, entirely new witness, who had taken pity on an English parachutist at Pforzheim. Vilayat wrote to Norman Mott in London:

I have received corroborative accounts from two different sources relating to the presence of my late sister, Miss N. Inayat Khan – sometimes known as Miss Nora Baker – in the local jail at Pforzheim in the winter of 1944.

This information does not tally with the official announcement that you gave of her death at Natzweiler on 6 July 1944 and I wonder if the evidence could not be examined officially on its merits.

One of my informers is a French girl who served a sentence at Pforzheim and has since returned: they exchanged addresses on their mugs without giving names and she traced the family. Therefore I cannot see a priori why I should mistrust this information.

The girl states that my sister left Pforzheim in September 1944 for an unknown destination. In November 1944 the

internees were massacred and my informant managed to get
away.

Vilayat went on to say that his second informant was a German
woman who worked at the jail and had managed to get information out
quite recently through a United Nations representative in Pforzheim.

The information forthcoming from this source states that one
morning at the time when Strasbourg was taken by the Allies (I
cannot place the date very accurately but this could be
determined) all the internees were taken by the Germans to be
executed and subsequently my sister was buried in the local
cemetery. The jail keeper who is said to have beaten up my
sister has been maintained in his post as jail keeper to this day.
  I am giving you, sir, this information on its face-value
hoping that it will help piece up what is, I imagine, a difficult
reconstruction of an obscure past where information, often
unreliable, is knit together piecemeal for want of more data,
and hope it might help to sort out other inter-related problems
in retracing missing personnel.

Finally he said: 'May I ask you to be so kind, Sir, as to communicate
with me, and not my mother, who becomes hysterical at the mention
of my sister's name. She has been so deeply grieved.'

As well as the information which had fallen into the hands of
Vilayat, Vera knew that other evidence had also emerged about Nora,
quite independently of her own enquiries.

A war crimes lawyer named Alexander Nicolson had been assigned
to take over investigating the Karlsruhe Gestapo case, with a view to
preparing it for trial, after Vera had left Bad Oeynhausen the previous
summer. In early November 1946, when Vera was back in England,
Nicolson had come across the case of Nora Baker. He had never heard
the name before and had opened a file on the case. 'In the course of
interrogations at Karlsruhe about another British subject, Nora Baker
has been ascertained as a victim. She was detained at Pforzheim from
27 November 1943. It appears that Squadron Officer Atkins did not
investigate this case,' he noted at the time. Nicolson, the son of a
German historian who had emigrated to England before the war and
changed his name from Karl Nowack, had been assiduous in his inves-

tigation. Dissatisfied with all the depositions Vera had taken, he had reinterrogated several suspects himself. It was when he reinterrogated a Karlsruhe Gestapo officer named Alfred Lehmann that he first heard about '*eine Englischerin*' – an Englishwoman – sent to Germany from Paris in late 1943, but apparently still unidentified in November 1946. Lehmann had been interrogated by Vera the previous summer and had told her he remembered the case of the French girl Lisa Graf. But, according to the statement Vera took from Lehmann, he remembered nothing about any Englishwoman. In talking to Nicolson, however, Lehmann found his memory dramatically improved. He remembered particularly the arrival from Paris of a single Englishwoman in November 1943 because he had been told she was 'extremely dangerous' and was to be treated as 'a most important case'.

He recalled: 'The Englishwoman had made two attempts to escape in Paris and during the second attempt she was caught but only at the last moment.' On security grounds, therefore, shackling had been ordered. Further questioning by Nicolson had elicited the fact that this woman was sent to Pforzheim prison.

Nicolson then went to Pforzheim and found the prison governor, a man of seventy-four named William Krauss, who had worked there for thirty years. Krauss had retired since the war but remembered the English girl well because she had to be kept in solitary confinement and was shackled in chains and kept on the lowest of rations. He had been ordered to detain her under the *Nacht und Nebel* order; he too was told she was very dangerous. Krauss told Nicolson he had taken pity on the girl. She was called Nora Baker.

Vera had now come to Bad Oeynhausen to read the Nora Baker file before pursuing her own lines of enquiry. In particular she wanted to read the latest detailed testimony taken from Yolande Lagrave. Following up his own enquiries, Alexander Nicolson had recently sent a colleague to Bordeaux to see Madame Lagrave and to take a full statement from her about Pforzheim. The officer who carried out the interrogation, a young French-speaker, Lieutenant Basil Hargreaves of the Rifle Brigade, had just returned to Bad Oeynhausen.

I the undersigned, Yvonne Yolande Lagrave, born on 27.12.02 at Mérignac (Gironde) of French nationality and by profession a shorthand secretary, declare the following facts on oath.

A political deportee, I was arrested owing to denunciation along with a friend who died at Dachau on 16.6.43 by the Gestapo arriving eventually at Pforzheim on 25.1.44. I occupied cell Number 12 with two friends: this cell was on the ground floor and was at the corner of a little passage leading towards the door which gave access to the courtyard of the prison; our window gave a view over the courtyard which allowed us to watch the men during their walk.

Nora Baker had cell No. 1; the cell which was opposite us was Number 2 cell. Number 1, then, being well apart from the other cells and on the other side of the little passage, which was bordered by two gratings which could be locked. So, as regards ours, Nora Baker's cell was after the second grating and almost opposite the office.

This cell was always shut; when we went for our walk all the cells were open except for No. 1 and we often wondered what could be there.

One day one of the people in my cell, Rosy Storck, began to say: 'If we were to write on our mess tins to find out if there are other Frenchmen . . .' It is thus that she wrote on the bottom of the mess tin with a knitting needle: 'Here are three Frenchwomen.' Our mess tins were taken away to be cleaned and replaced at 5pm. As soon as we received our own mess tins our first thought was to see if a reply had been made to our message. In fact we saw this message. 'You are not alone. You have a friend in cell 1.' This was the beginning of our correspondence.

Madame Lagrave recalled that, near American Independence Day, the girl in cell 1 wrote, 'Here's to the Fourth of July' and on 14 July she wrote, 'Long live free France, for that keeps us together', and added two flags, one English and one French.

Her statement continued: 'In the course of our "correspondence" she let us know that she was unhappy, very unhappy, that she never went out, that her hands and feet were manacled, that except when they brought us soup or changed our water they never opened her cell door, or the small opening through which they made us pass our mess tins.'

Yolande Lagrave said that when they asked for the prisoner in cell

1 to give her name she said at first she could not give it but eventually she wrote out 'Nora Baker' and gave two addresses – one in London and one in Paris, which Yolande had kept in the hem of her skirt.

Vera had seen other evidence of the manacling of Nora. The governor of the prison had told Nicolson that he decided to remove the chains soon after Nora arrived, as she was so miserable. But he added that soon afterwards he was reprimanded for doing so by the Karlsruhe Gestapo and was forced to put them on again. Alfred Lehmann, the Gestapo officer, had told Nicolson that when Nora first arrived from Paris he had also questioned whether it was necessary to have the girl chained while in prison but was told that Berlin had expressly required it. He also recalled that the prison governor at Pforzheim had telephoned the Karlsruhe Gestapo, shortly after she arrived, to ask for the shackles to be made looser.

'The governor said he had spoken to the prisoner and was of the opinion that it would suffice if the prisoner was fettered on one hand and this was connected only loosely to the bed. I agreed so as to spare the prisoner pain, the chains should be loosened or even completely removed, as long as the governor could assure me that escape could be ruled out.'

It was during the brief period when Nora was unfettered that Yolande Lagrave caught sight of her out in the courtyard. 'On one occasion in the afternoon, we heard some footsteps in the courtyard. Immediately we thought it must be Nora Baker who was really going out. Rosy Storck, then Susan Chireiz and I in turn, climbed on to the bed to see her. We saw her and she raised her eyes towards our cell and smiled at us. At that time she had not yet got her prison clothes.'

The women saw Nora Baker three times only and then never again. But she was still able to scratch messages on the back of her tin. 'She wrote to us: "Think of me; I am very unhappy; give me some news if you hear of any" and we told her all we could get to know. She asked us if we belonged to the Alliance [a French intelligence circuit] or to the French Section (I forget the exact title). Then she added never to tell her mother that she had been in prison.'

After Nora was chained up again the prisoners tried their best to keep up her spirits, Yolande Lagrave said. One day two friends in cell 3 tried to communicate with her and 'sang' news to her. 'Immediately we heard a warden named Trupp open the door of the cell and suddenly hit Nora and he took her to the dungeon which was below ground. We heard cries, so clearly that all three of us were struck still. We said: "Poor Nora."'

Yolande added: 'Another time, the chief warder, Guiller, saw that the judas [peep-hole in the door] was open. He went into Nora's cell, shouting, and then Nora replied with great dignity that it was not her who had raised the judas. According to my friend Rosy Storck, she spoke very good German and was holding her own with Guiller. We heard blows that Guiller gave her. Nora continued to reply. She had a very fine manner.'

When the Allied forces began to advance towards Germany, Nora had been taken away.

Eventually one day – the date escapes me but it was September or October 1944 – the mess tin arrived with this message 'I am going' written in a quick and nervous hand.

Poor Nora. She was no longer with us. Where had she gone? Our grief was great. We thought that in view of the advance of the French, for people said they were at Saarbrücken, she had been sent to a camp. But we all knew the end was near now and with Nora's address we hoped one day to celebrate victory with her. Then, on 30 November 1944, we were all woken at 5am to go to an unknown destination.

Yolande Lagrave's fellow prisoners were then taken away, but at the last minute, for reasons she never learned, she was told that she alone was staying at the prison. She was repatriated on 1 May 1945 and a fortnight later she heard that a burial place had been discovered 2 kilometres from the Pforzheim prison and all her group had been massacred. She discovered the women in the group were all raped before being shot and thrown into a mass grave. 'I have thought, had Nora on her departure been transferred elsewhere or been massacred like my unfortunate companions? I will never know. I could give you the names and addresses of all my companions, men and women who were detained with me, but alas they are dead.'

The final piece of evidence in Nicolson's file on Nora Baker came from a man named Marcel Schubert, a prisoner who had become an interpreter at Pforzheim. He claimed to have witnessed several cases of maltreatment of prisoners, including the 'sad case of a British woman parachutist whose hands and feet were bound at nearly all times even during meals for months on end'. He said: 'The prisoners thought she was a Russian Countess but she told me herself that she was British. She spoke French rather well.'

Schubert had noticed that the British woman's name was never written in the prison register. 'It seems to me that this was done on purpose for it to be easier to get rid of her. I don't know what happened to her but my opinion is that she died there, the same way as so many others did.'

By now Vera needed no more convincing that Nora had been at Pforzheim, and she already had her own ideas about what might have happened to her next. She also had her own ideas about who would know.

Vera had never expected to return to Tomato, the little British prison near Minden where the previous year she had spent so much of her time interrogating suspects, but, once again, she was sitting in a Mercedes as it wound its way down the icy track leading to the jail. Tomato was fuller than ever, according to Tony Somerhough, although few of the prisoners there were now expected to face trial. German lawyers representing war criminals were gaining confidence, sending in letters protesting that their clients were being unfairly held without charge. The wife of one Karlsruhe Gestapo prisoner had written saying she could 'scarcely imagine' why her husband was being held. German church leaders were also beginning to speak out for the first time since the end of the war, calling for a new period of healing.

Elsewhere internment camps were increasingly impossible to police, complained Somerhough. 'Bodies' were regularly mislaid in the system and escapes were commonplace. One of two men Vera had been keen to reinterrogate for the new Nora Baker investigation had simply been 'lost' by the Americans. She had asked for Christian Ott to be transferred to Tomato from the US zone, but an entirely different Christian Ott had been handed over by mistake. The other 'body' Vera was interested in reinterrogating – Max Wassmer – had, however, been found and it was he that Vera had now come to see for a second time. She hoped that Wassmer would be able to confirm what she already believed had finally happened to Nora.

Yolande Lagrave and others had talked of massacres of Pforzheim women prisoners near the prison and Vera now knew that hundreds of bodies had been exhumed from a mass grave – most of them identified as French deportees, although some were too badly decomposed to identify. However, she did not consider it likely that Nora was among those randomly killed near Pforzheim. Nora, she believed, was taken to a concentration camp, like all the other SOE girls. And, like the others, she was almost certainly executed on the specific orders of Berlin.

Vera also thought she knew which concentration camp Nora had been taken to, and it was not Natzweiler, as she had first believed. As yet she had no new evidence to support her theory and she certainly had no new witnesses. On the contrary, what she had was old evidence, but she was reading this old evidence in a new way.

When Vera was first investigating the Dachau case the previous summer, she had acquired statements from several members of the Karlsruhe Gestapo, but none was as important as those of Christian Ott and Max Wassmer. These men provided the crucial evidence which enabled Vera at last to clear up the case of Madeleine Damerment, Yolande Beekman and Eliane Plewman, the second group of girls imprisoned at Karlsruhe, whose fate had remained a mystery for so long. The evidence of Ott and Wassmer showed that the three women had been taken from the prison in Karlsruhe to Dachau concentration camp, where they were killed by shooting.

Ott's evidence had been particularly detailed and helpful. The descriptions he had given of the women and their ranks were clearly – as far as they went – accurate.

However, in certain respects Vera had found Ott unreliable. For one thing, throughout his statement he talked of four, not three, women being taken to Dachau. He said, for example, that 'four women' were collected from Karlsruhe prison. He also said that 'four women' had been handcuffed 'two by two in the usual fashion'. There were 'two French and two English'. Ott also said in his original statement that the fourth woman 'was brought from Pforzheim' and joined the other three at Karlsruhe before they all left for Dachau.

When Vera then interrogated Wassmer he denied ever having said to Ott that he was present at the shootings. However, he clearly corroborated the main elements of Ott's story. He said he too had accompanied the women to Dachau as Ott had described and he also spoke about the journey; the girls had brought bread and sausages from the prison to eat in the train and they had chatted in lively fashion, showing no fear when the train had to stop for an air raid. On arrival at Dachau,

Wassmer said he had delivered the women to the SS guards and had not seen them again. He said he had been told the next morning that they had been shot and was given a 'receipt' for the bodies. And he, unlike Ott, was willing to accept Vera's suggestion at the time that there were probably only three women involved and not four.

As a result of statements taken from these men Vera had concluded back in August that the three women she was then looking for had indeed been executed at Dachau, discounting the evidence that a fourth was present. In her report to London Vera had attached both Ott's and Wassmer's statements, but the section of Ott's statement referring to a fourth prisoner, who was brought from Pforzheim, was omitted from her report.

Now, however, Vera realised that Ott's evidence of a fourth woman at Dachau could no longer be ignored. Her main purpose therefore in seeing Wassmer again was to secure a new statement from him saying there were four women killed and not three. Vera also hoped he might be able to give a description of the fourth prisoner, brought from Pforzheim.

Max Wassmer, a policeman before he joined the Gestapo, was in his late fifties with a full white beard. Considered a safe pair of hands, he was responsible for the transport of Gestapo prisoners, usually to concentration camps. He was also said by colleagues to be 'good at settling women'.

Vera explained to Wassmer why she had come to see him a second time. She then took a sheet of plain paper and wrote across the top: 'Notes on reinterrogation of Max Wassmer' and began to take him through his story once again.

Six months after their first meeting, Wassmer had even less to say than before. His memory, which had always been weak, was even weaker now. At the end of the interrogation Vera's jottings barely filled one side of paper. Wassmer's story, though, had not changed. According to Vera's notes, he described the journey just as he had done in his first interrogation. 'Wassmer came from Bruchsal'; 'Changed trains Munich for Dachau'; 'Arrived Munich at 8pm'; 'Arrived Dachau 11–12pm'; 'Did not tell them on outward journey purpose of journey other than destination Dachau'.

What Wassmer had to say to Vera about events at Dachau was also unchanged: he knew almost nothing. In particular, he continued to deny Ott's claim that he ever said he was present when the execution took place. All Vera could grasp from Wassmer this time about what happened to the girls was contained in these three little notes: 'Some officers arrived and took women away'; 'Wassmer slept till 7.30'; 'At 10am got the execution slip from official'. And then Wassmer was on his way back to Karlsruhe. 'Caught train from Munich with Ott.'

On the question of who had given the orders for the women to go to Dachau, Wassmer also had nothing to add to what he said before. Vera noted: 'Rösner gave order to Wassmer, who did not want to go' and 'Gmeiner ordered Rösner to order Wassmer.'

On the most vital question for Vera, though – whether there was a fourth girl in the group – Wassmer gave the answer she now wanted. Yes, he said, there were four women, not three. Wassmer even managed to give Vera the briefest of descriptions of the four. It was just one or two adjectives in each case, but she nevertheless noted down what he said with very great care:

'1 small round face (Dussautoy)

'1 tall blonde a little German (Beekman)

'1 ordinary (?Plewman)

'1 very thin (?Madeleine).'

And then Vera rose from her interrogation and Wassmer was led back to his cell.

Feeble though it was, the evidence Vera had secured from Wassmer, combined with other evidence already gathered, supported her new conclusion that Nora had been killed with the other three women at Dachau. Having drawn this conclusion, Vera was now able officially to revise Nora's story. But the end remained very difficult to write. Despite these latest discoveries, Vera still knew very little about how Nora – or any of the Dachau girls – had actually died.

In the Natzweiler case the evidence of how the women had died had been presented virtually minute by minute, from numerous different angles, in the most harrowing detail. The deaths of the four women who died at Ravensbrück had been harder to piece together, but Vera had secured reliable and adequate testimony about their time in the camp, their last few days in the punishment block and even their final moments before they were shot.

In the case of Dachau, however, nothing at all was known about what happened to these four women after they were handed over to the SS guards at the Dachau gates. Nothing was known about where they spent the night, or what happened the next morning. The evidence given by Wassmer was that they were shot. But Vera knew nothing about their treatment before they were shot, or their bearing at the time or the manner in which they were shot. No witnesses had been interrogated who had seen anything at all of these women inside Dachau concentration camp.

Vera had for the most part discounted the only account of the deaths she had heard. This was the account Christian Ott had given in his first deposition, which he, in turn, had claimed was given to him by Wassmer, who Ott said had been present. According to this version of events, the women were told 'to kneel down with their faces towards a small mound of earth' and were then shot through the back of the neck as they held hands.

While this account was apparently credible, Wassmer from the start denied relating it. Vera then rejected it altogether because Ott, when later reinterrogated, said he himself never believed it. Alexander Nicolson, the war crimes investigator who had taken the Karlsruhe Gestapo case over from Vera, had himself reinterrogated Ott (who had eventually been found interned in the former concentration camp at Dachau) and had challenged him directly about what Wassmer had really told him about the Dachau deaths. Ott then repeated the same details, but this time he also talked of the conversation he had with Wassmer after Wassmer had finished his description. Ott told Nicolson: 'So I said to him, "but tell me, what really happened?" And Wassmer turned to me and said: "So you want to know how it really happened?"'

Nicolson asked what Ott had taken Wassmer to mean by this comment. 'I knew that what he meant was that what he had told me was just a story – "*eine Geschichte*" – that he had made up, and I wouldn't want to know how it had really happened.'

——

The Dachau war crimes trial was held by the Americans. But when I examined transcripts of the trial in the US National Archives, I found no evidence that any Dachau camp staff were ever charged with the killings of these four women, and no evidence to throw light on the way they died.

Baron Arthur Hulot, a leader of the Belgian resistance and a prisoner in Dachau, told me: 'I never heard mention of these women. If the murders took place outside the crematorium it was far from the camp and nobody would have known. Anything could have happened.'

There was nothing in Vera's war crimes files to suggest that she ever sought to find out more herself at the time. On Ravensbrück and Natzweiler Vera's papers were detailed and extensive; her Dachau file contained only a few newspaper cuttings. Perhaps after probing the depths of horror at the two other concentration camps, Vera was now well and truly exhausted and simply did not wish to know more.

Nor did she, apparently, wish to return to the other mystery, thrown up by the new development concerning Nora. If Nora was not Stonehouse's 'No. 2', who was? It must now have been obvious to Vera that Sonia Olschanesky was a real name, or at least a real alias. Yet Vera left it to others, many years later, to find out exactly who Sonia was.

Into the vacuum surrounding the final hours of the Dachau girls, the story told by Wassmer was freely inserted and over the years gained common currency. The story was perhaps a comforting and heroic one, telling of how the four women, holding hands, went to their deaths bravely, from a single shot to the head. I found the tale – embellished and sanitised – reproduced as fact in several official accounts of the women's last hours.

Families and friends of the dead, though, seemed to know instinctively that Wassmer's story was not true. Diana Farmiloe, Yolande Beekman's sister, said she had been told many years ago, by Nora's brother Vilayat, that the girls had all been tortured before they died. 'He said they were all beaten in some way. I remember him saying it was not how we had been told.'

Lisa Graf, who had befriended Madeleine Damerment in prison in Karlsruhe, told me she had visited Dachau years after the war and seen the plaque in memory of the four women, which said they were 'cruelly murdered'. 'What did it mean – "cruelly murdered"? I know for sure they were not killed nicely. I am sure that was never true.'

23

KIEFFER

Vera had almost given up hope of meeting Hans Kieffer. At first she thought he would turn up in an internment camp, or be picked up at a border. But he had been too clever for that. Each time she had circulated his name to the Americans' rogues' gallery the reply came back 'rogue not met'.

A great deal of information about Kieffer had by now been passed to Vera from her own people who had been imprisoned by him at Avenue Foch. She had heard how he kept his prize agents on the fifth floor; how he had befriended Bob Starr, who even drew his portrait; and how his 'favourites' would sometimes be called down to his office for a meal or a chat. In the eyes of some of Vera's agents Kieffer appeared almost to have won a certain respect. And he clearly commanded respect among his own men, as she had discovered more recently when his staff had finally been run to ground and interrogated.

One of the reasons Kieffer had been so difficult to find was the intense loyalty he appeared to have inspired among most of his closest colleagues, who had refused to say, even under interrogation, precisely where he was. And his men rarely tried to shift blame for what had happened on to their boss. Rather, they tried to protect him, saying they were sure Kieffer had no idea that agents were sent to concentration camps. They were sure he expected all agents to be given a trial. And they doubted very much that any torture ever took place with his authority.

Vera, however, had never been deceived by Kieffer, and she was certainly under no illusion about what he really knew. He had sent scores of her people to concentration camps, albeit on orders from above. And, of course, he knew what a concentration camp was – no SS officer of his rank could not have known. She was also under no illusion about what 'treatments' he authorised for his own prisoners. Agents living under Kieffer's roof were fed and nurtured and generally encouraged to feel 'at home'. One agent, Maurice Southgate, had even been allowed to order accountancy books so that he could study the subject while he was locked up at Avenue Foch.

Torture, though, while not condoned at Avenue Foch, was quite clearly authorised at the 'house prison', as Kieffer called it, at Place des Etats Unis. Josef Stork, Kieffer's driver, had been placed in charge of the prison and had confessed under interrogation to several 'cures' and 'treatments', as he called the torture there. A favourite at the prison was to submerge victims in ice-cold water until they decided to talk. In one case, Stork had confessed, a prisoner drowned while undergoing the water 'cure'. And Kieffer employed a fellow known only as 'Peter Pierre', a kind of special protégé, who liked to use a riding whip on prisoners.

Kieffer was always astonishingly well informed about what happened within his department, largely because Stork, as well as his enforcer, was also his 'eyes and ears'. But he never 'knew' about the torture, and was never present when the torture took place. For Kieffer, therefore, the torture was always deniable.

In the end, though, Kieffer had committed a crime he had been unable to deny. Despite the fact that his prime enemy throughout the war had been SOE, the one atrocity that he was accused of when finally captured was not committed against any SOE agents. He had ordered the murder of five SAS paratroopers. And the person who had finally secured the capture of Kieffer was Bill Barkworth, because it was Barkworth's people who had been killed.

Kieffer's crime was committed in the very last days of the German occupation of Paris. A few weeks after D-Day, at the beginning of July 1944, a group of twelve uniformed SAS soldiers were dropped by parachute to carry out sabotage operations but fell straight into the arms of Kieffer's men, who knew about their arrival through a radio playback.

In the ensuing firefight five of the SAS men were taken prisoner, three were wounded and four were killed. When he sought instructions from Berlin about what to do with the prisoners, Kieffer was told to keep them in his 'house prison', but this was very overcrowded, so he asked Berlin for further instructions. After some delay he eventually received orders from Berlin to shoot the SAS men. It was all to be done in strictest secrecy. Even Berlin recognised that shooting uniformed prisoners was illegal under the Führer's own Commando Order, so Kieffer was ordered to remove their uniforms and dress them in civilian clothes before the shooting.

After some hesitation Kieffer had obeyed Berlin and instructed his men to dress the SAS soldiers in civilian clothes and shoot them. The five uninjured prisoners were driven to woods near Noailles, given sandwiches on the way, then lined up to be shot. Two men escaped, one by opening his handcuffs with a watch spring at the very last minute and running off into the trees. The remaining five were murdered. Kieffer told Barkworth he had tried his best not to implement the order. He had refused to shoot the wounded SAS men, whom he had been told to kill too. But in the end he had no choice but to kill the others. He would have been shot himself had he refused, he claimed, insisting that after the attempt on Hitler's life on 20 July 1944, any German officer who refused to obey an order was executed.

And now here was Kieffer at last, standing before Vera in his cell at Wuppertal. He had finally been picked up by Bill Barkworth's men at Garmisch Partenkirchen, following a tip given to Vera from one of his captured colleagues, Karl Haug. Kieffer had been living quite openly in Garmisch, working as a caretaker in a hotel. He had even registered with the town hall, and had not changed his name except to remove one 'f' to make 'Kiefer'. Even during the war Kieffer did not use aliases.

At the age of forty-seven Hans Josef Kieffer was a good-looking man who seemed taller than he was, owing to a thick mop of wavy, black hair. He was stocky and muscular with an almost boyish face, a small, slightly upturned nose, deep-set eyes and thick, black eyebrows. He appeared relatively relaxed in the circumstances and not much like a man who had been on the run or had a great deal to fear. His conditions were good here, he said. And Vera observed that he had a small desk, with pen and ink. Pinned to the wall was a single photograph of a young girl – chubby-cheeked with fair, thick, wavy hair and wearing a floral dress. She was quite obviously a daughter.

Kieffer said he had been allowed to invite his daughter here over Christmas. Major Barkworth had allowed her to stay in his cell.

————

The picture pinned to the wall in Kieffer's cell was of Hildegard, his youngest daughter, then aged nineteen. When he wrote to her from prison he began, '*Meine liebe Moggele*' ('My dear squirrel'), using her pet name. Hildegard showed me the letters her father wrote and she picked out little phrases. 'Look, here he says, "In the end it [the arrest] all happened quite suddenly." But I don't think he was surprised to have been arrested.'

Hildegard said that her father had been picked up, as he feared he would be, just a few weeks after his old friend Karl Haug had left Garmisch Partenkirchen. Vera herself had interrogated Haug, who fell into British hands – again, just as Kieffer predicted. I showed Hildegard Haug's deposition. 'I last saw Kieffer in Garmisch. He may have stayed there,' were Haug's words to Vera, which Hildegard was now reading from the statement.

'This is very interesting,' said Hildegard and she signalled to her brother, Hans, and sister, Gretel, to come and read the document. 'You see, we always thought it must have been Haug who talked. But until now we never had proof.'

When the Kieffer family first agreed to help me they said it was because they wanted to give an 'objective' view of their father to his grandchildren. Hans Kieffer, the son of a barrel-maker, had followed an elder brother into the police. His skill at getting information out of people without threats or violence was spotted and he was quickly moved into intelligence work. 'As a father he was like that too,' said his son Hans. 'He was not intimidating or frightening – but I just remember this feeling that I could never lie to him.'

When war broke out Kieffer was transferred to the Gestapo, to the investigation department at Karlsruhe. 'Was he in the Nazi Party?' I asked.

'Yes, of course,' said Hans.

'But if you ask if he was interested in politics I would say no. He was interested in his profession. In being a policeman.'

And were they, Hans, Gretel and Hildegard, in the Nazi Party at the start of the war? They looked around at one another. 'Yes, of course,' said Hans. 'Look, from 1933 we were all young Nazis. It looked different then. Our parents were in the party and we children were in the *Jungvolk*. We enjoyed it. We went singing and talked about our heroes of the First World War. Everybody did it.'

I asked if their father visited them all in Karlsruhe when he was working in Paris. They said he used to come from time to time with his driver, Stork, because he had business still in Karlsruhe. But he never talked about his work. Did he talk about the British agents he captured? 'No', they answered, although they all remembered 'Bob', who gave evidence in Kieffer's defence at the trial. 'And Peter Churchill,' said Hans, suddenly remembering another name. 'I have a knife of Peter Churchill,' and he looked at me with a grin. Hans explained that his father had given him the knife as a trophy sometime in 1943. It was a hunting knife with 'PC' engraved upon it.

I asked Hildegard how her father seemed when she visited him in prison. 'He didn't want me to visit him in the beginning because he was uncertain about how things would turn out,' she said. He had many other worries too: his wife, Margarete, had died of stomach cancer the previous year and her father had also lost two brothers in the war. But by the time she did visit, at Christmas, his mood had improved. And with the English officers they had had quite a Christmas party.

Did Hildegard remember anything about a woman WAAF officer visiting her father in January? Her father never spoke of her, she said. But she remembered a Major Blackwood or Backwood. I suggested that perhaps it was Major Barkworth, and she thought it probably was. He had been kind and reassuring.

By mid-January her father was feeling quite confident, said Hildegard. 'He did not think he had done anything wrong. Look, here,' she said, pulling out another letter written to her in January. 'He is just concerned that he won't have his suit in time for the trial. I don't think he ever thought at that time that he would be hanged.'

Vera had not come to interrogate Kieffer in a formal manner. She certainly wanted to hear what he had to say on a number of important matters. On the question of Déricourt, for example, Kieffer was to be Vera's prime witness, for only he would know the true extent of this man's treachery. And Kieffer was also the only person who would know the answer to the Prosper conundrum. He would be able to tell Vera once and for all if there had been a pact with Prosper.

But Vera approached this meeting more as a chance to have a long and private chat. Though at the end she would ask Kieffer to sign a deposition, she wanted first to talk things over, to settle in her own mind – more than for the public record – questions which she knew only he could answer. More than anything, she wanted to know which of her people had helped Kieffer and which had not.

Vera introduced herself as the intelligence officer from the French Section in London and Kieffer immediately responded with respect for her and for her section. Her name was known to him, as were most names of F Section's London staff. He told her that he had always had the greatest concern for her agents, and admiration for many of them too.

'Berlin attached extraordinary importance to the French Section,' said Kieffer, and he explained that his chief in Berlin, Horst Kopkow, and his department worked on all the French Section cases. All instructions concerning captured British officers came from Kopkow or even from Gruppenführer Heinrich Müller himself, the head of Department IV of the RSHA. The Führer also took a personal interest in the French Section, as did the head of the SS, Heinrich Himmler. Berlin had 'again and again' shown an interest only in French Section matters. As a result he had been obliged to neglect other resistance circuits. 'Berlin considered the French Section particularly dangerous.'

Kieffer said he had got to know many of the agents well and he had tried to ensure they were treated fairly. He talked almost affectionately about the 'English gentlemen', as he called some of the agents. He had found the English more 'honourable' than the French, he said. It was obvious from the way he talked that Kieffer had his favourites among the prisoners and one of these, as Vera knew, had been John 'Bob' Starr. Vera asked Kieffer to tell her about Bob and his work at Avenue Foch.

'I very soon recognised Bob's real talent for drawing,' Kieffer told Vera, 'and I gave him more and more work to do of this kind, which, however, mainly consisted of illustrations and designs from which he, as a member of a hostile power, was unable to learn anything and then possibly divulge and betray it.' He had allowed Bob to go back to his Paris flat to collect his painting materials, on condition he gave his 'word of honour' not to escape.

'Bob was in a cell directly next to the guardroom where a four-man guard was permanently present. Any escape seemed to me at that time to be out of the question. After I was convinced that Bob would not escape I gave him drawing tasks which had to be kept secret. Because he knew so much I impressed upon the guards again and again that however affable and obliging Bob might be, his lodging was to be carefully guarded.'

In the next weeks and months Bob was even used for 'wireless plays', said Kieffer, explaining that Bob checked messages to make sure they were in typical English. 'It was by means of this activity that Bob gained a great insight into our counter-espionage work and got to know numerous arrested agents,' said Kieffer. 'It was precisely at this time that the capture of the woman W/T operator Madeleine took place.' Vera showed Kieffer a picture of Nora, and he recognised her as Madeleine but said he had never known her real name.

'She told us nothing. We could not rely on anything she said. I cannot remember her real name but I am sure in this she also lied to us,' said Kieffer, as if her refusal to cooperate still infuriated him even now. Kieffer had never won Madeleine's trust or respect. It was obvious to Vera that Nora had never fallen for Kieffer's tricks. Unlike many other F Section agents, she seemed to have treated him with contempt from start to finish.

In the end, Kieffer said, he asked his senior interpreter, Ernest Vogt, who was good at setting people at their ease, to try to befriend her. Vogt had spent hours talking to Madeleine and learned more than most. She was treated extremely well, and was even served English tea and biscuits, which she refused, although she accepted the English cigarettes. But Nora's stubborn refusal to cooperate never weakened. It was also evident to Vera that, although Nora had maddened Kieffer, he had also greatly admired her courage.

'One night,' continued Kieffer, 'at about three in the morning, I was awakened in my room by the guard to say Bob and Madeleine had escaped. They, with the French resistance leader, Colonel Faye, had broken through the iron bars in the cells leading to the window of the ceiling and they climbed up on to the flat roof. By means of strips of blankets and sheets, knotted together, they let themselves down on to the balcony on the third storey of a neighbouring house and there smashed a window and entered the apartment. Had they not been recaptured it is assumed that all the radio plays which were in full swing would have been finished.'

Starr had described this incident on his return to London, saying

Kieffer was in such a rage after the escape attempt that he made all three of them stand against a wall on the fourth floor of Avenue Foch to be shot. But Kieffer had hesitated and in the end ordered them back to their cells.

Kieffer now told Vera that after the escape attempt he was indeed angry and had insisted that the three give their word of honour not to escape again, but only Starr agreed. 'It was difficult for Bob to make amends for the mistrust which had surfaced against him with us.' So he had talked to Starr about what had happened and had been persuaded by him that he had not really broken his word of honour because, as Kieffer then realised, his word of honour first time round had been given only in relation to a specific case: 'namely that he would not escape while travelling to his flat to get his painting materials'.

However, Kieffer added: 'First of all I completely dispensed with Bob's assistance for some time because he had disappointed me too much by his escape. I talked with him about the reasons for this escape whereupon he told me that Madeleine had approached him with the escape plan and that if as a woman she had the courage to escape and had succeeded in doing so she would have made life impossible for him in England had he not displayed the same courage as a man.'

Soon Kieffer and Bob made a pact and became friends again. 'I let him do this work again only after he had given me with a hand-shake his explicit word of honour in the presence of witnesses that he would not undertake an attempt to escape again and that he would also not work against us.'

———

According to his second wife, Starr was bitter about his treatment by Vera and Buckmaster after the war. When eventually he returned to London from Mauthausen concentration camp after getting out on a Red Cross convoy, he found nobody to meet him and discovered he was being blackballed. He wrote a long report for HQ about every-thing he learned inside Avenue Foch; giving details of the radios the Germans played back and describing how they did it. He said he had gathered all the information with a view to passing it to London if he managed to escape.

But Starr's report completely disappeared. 'All his life he would say: "What happened to my report?" but he never found out. I don't think they wanted people to know what it said,' said his wife.

'And he had learned so much. He was always trying to get information, not to give it. He was somebody who knew how to play the game. Yes, he checked the spellings and made Kieffer's drawings pretty. Kieffer was delighted. And Bob respected Kieffer. Kieffer and Bob even stripped off one day and swam alone in the pond at Avenue Foch. You have to be open and honest with somebody if you see him in his nudity like that – two men just swimming together. You understand?'

Her husband, she told me, had always said that if there had been real suspicion of him there should have been a trial in England. He should have been accused. 'He just wanted it to be clear.' But there was no trial. 'They found it easier just to tell people he was a traitor. But Kieffer saluted my husband when the death penalty verdict was given at his trial. Kieffer would not have saluted a man who was a traitor to his country.'

———

There was to be no pact, however, with Madeleine, continued Kieffer to Vera. He explained that Madeleine and Colonel Faye were then immediately sent from Avenue Foch to Germany. 'They refused to give their word of honour not to attempt further escapes.'

Vera asked Kieffer where he had sent Madeleine. 'She went to Karlsruhe, and later I heard she had been sent to Pforzheim because the prison in Karlsruhe was over-full,' he explained. She then asked him why he sent Nora to Karlsruhe in the first place and why he had sent the other women there later. He said he wanted Nora to be somewhere he could reinterrogate her further if necessary, as they continued playing back her radio after she was sent away. The jail in Karlsruhe was well run and he presumed the women had remained safe there until the end of the war, he told Vera.

'It was nice for you to select Karlsruhe for the women for your convenience, since you happened to live there,' Vera replied. 'It was nice for you to have an excuse to return from Paris whenever you felt like it.'

Vera then told Kieffer that Madeleine had been held in chains throughout her time in Pforzheim. That was harsh, he admitted, but it was important to understand that she was considered a 'dangerous' prisoner because of her escapes. He himself had requested that she be put in restraints to prevent further escapes. If she had escaped again she would certainly have been shot. Most Gestapo officers would have shot her after her first attempt.

Then Vera told Kieffer that Madeleine and other women he sent to Karlsruhe had been taken to concentration camps, where they were killed. Kieffer looked up, quite obviously surprised. He began to cry. Vera told him: 'Kieffer, if one of us is going to cry it is going to be me. You will please stop this comedy.'

Next Vera asked Kieffer to tell her more about the other agents and he mentioned others that had refused to cooperate with him: Antoine – the Mauritian France Antelme – and Bertrand – the Canadian Frank Pickersgill – who had tried to escape and been shot.

On the whole Vera found Kieffer to be frank, but when she asked specifically for names of prisoners whom he had 'turned' and persuaded to work for him, he looked uncomfortable. Most more or less helped, though not necessarily voluntarily, he said. 'Most were made to feel they had nothing to lose because we knew so much already.' Archambaud [Gilbert Norman] had helped a lot, he said eventually. In the end there were many who helped because they felt they had no choice.

'The French Section had no traitors then?' asked Vera, now prompting Kieffer to volunteer the information she was sure he had. 'There was nobody who willingly betrayed us?'

At this Kieffer suddenly looked up, surprised. 'You are asking me if there was a traitor in your ranks? But why are you asking me? You know yourself there was one. You recalled him to London – Gilbert.' Suddenly Kieffer was not at all uncomfortable. Clearly he had no qualms talking about Gilbert, because he was not one of his informers. 'He was Boemelburg's agent,' he told Vera, referring to his boss, Karl Boemelburg, head of the Sicherheitsdienst in France. 'For Boemelburg in fact he was more than an agent. He was a friend going back a very long time. And Boemelburg alone dealt with him. He had the symbol BOE 48. "BOE" for "Boemelburg". He was Boemelburg's forty-eighth agent.'

'And who exactly was BOE 48?' Vera asked.

'Well, I think you know,' he said observing her curiously. 'Of course you know. It was Henri Déricourt.'

Here at last was the credible confirmation Vera had for so long sought of the treachery of Henri Déricourt, alias Gilbert. All other evidence against Déricourt had been viewed by MI5 and by

Buckmaster as tainted or open to alternative explanations. Even Dr
Goetz might have been protecting his own position in some way. But
now Vera had Kieffer's testimony that Déricourt was working for
the Germans. His evidence was more valuable than that of any other
witness, not only because he knew more, but because, on the traps
of the gallows, he had nothing to lose by telling the truth. For order-
ing the deaths of the SAS soldiers, Kieffer knew he would almost
certainly be hanged.

What exactly was Boemelburg's arrangement with Déricourt? Vera
then asked.

Kieffer didn't know how Boemelburg had come to know Déricourt.
'Boemelburg was very secretive about Gilbert,' he said. He had come
to understand, however, that under his deal with Boemelburg, Gilbert
offered to show him the agents' mail and to inform him of any landings that were taking place coming from England. In return
Boemelburg agreed that the landings should take place undisturbed.
Gilbert also insisted that the agents should not be followed from the
landing fields and that if arrests were to be made they should be at an
agreed distance. Generally, Kieffer told Vera, agents were only shad-
owed and not arrested, in order not to implicate Gilbert. He had his
own wireless officer, and generally he told the Germans where he was
transmitting from so that they did not arrest him.

'Was he paid?'

'Boemelburg gave him a lot of money. Boemelburg wanted to
buy Gilbert a property; his grand dream was that Déricourt would
tell him the date of the invasion. Boemelburg thought Déricourt
was his "super ace",' said Kieffer, an expression Vera had also heard
from Dr Goetz. 'He arrived with masses of papers which had to be
photographed so we could use them in interrogations. Everything
had to be photostatted very quickly in the night. Then I kept the
papers in my safe.'

'When was Gilbert's mail first used?'

At first he had not attached a great deal of importance to Gilbert's
material, Kieffer said. Then he added: 'It was, however, put to very
good use in the interrogation of Prosper.'

Tell me about Prosper, said Vera, who had waited patiently for the
right moment to ask Kieffer about Francis Suttill. Suttill was the
most important French Section agent to fall into Kieffer's hands,
but so far he had not been mentioned at all. More than anything,

Vera had wanted to ask Kieffer for the truth about the Prosper collapse.

'I remember that in the summer of 1943 I started the drive against Prosper,' he told her. 'Prosper was arrested in his house after the house had been watched.'

'How did you know the address?'

'Possibly through Boemelburg. Possibly we did get Prosper's address through Déricourt. We watched his flat for fourteen days. One day he walked in. We would never have caught him otherwise.' After Prosper was caught Boemelburg had passed to Kieffer copies of Prosper's mail, which Kieffer, in turn, passed to an officer named August Scherer, who first interrogated him.

'I remember that Scherer was very happy to have all this material to use in the interrogation against Prosper. And Prosper was astonished that we knew this and that.' Soon after Prosper, Archambaud and Denise (Andrée Borrel) were also arrested.

'Prosper, however, did not wish to make a statement,' said Kieffer. 'But this was not the case with Archambaud, who had not the integrity of Prosper and made a very full statement.'

They talked about Prosper for some time further. How had the Gestapo learned of the locations of all the arms dumps, after the arrests of Prosper and Archambaud? How did they seem to know exactly which resistance men had worked with the Prosper circuit? Did Kieffer offer Prosper a pact under which lives would be saved in return for information? Did Horst Kopkow in Berlin agree to the pact? Or was the story that Prosper had done a deal with Kieffer just that – a story told to break the confidence of other agents?

All these questions Vera asked, and she considered Kieffer's answer carefully in each case. But few of the answers were noted down. The words exchanged about Prosper were part of the 'private' conversation and nobody else needed to know. So when Vera drafted a terse two-page deposition for Kieffer to sign, it contained little information at all on Prosper.

Kieffer signed the statement in bold, slanting script, and below his name Vera signed her own pinprick signature.

———

For more than fifty years the formal deposition that resulted from Vera's interrogation of Hans Kieffer was kept secret. When it was finally made public with the opening of the SOE files, it contained the bare minimum of information. Given Kieffer's importance to SOE's history, this thin little offering was hard to believe.

I had found other ways of piecing together something of what was said during this encounter. Vera had jotted notes and in her private papers were two additional statements taken from Kieffer, one on Nora and one on Bob Starr. I had also picked up many comments made by Vera over the years about the meeting.

The puzzle about the formal statement was not only its brevity, however, but also its ambiguity. Vera abhorred muddled writing. Annie Samuelli, her Romanian friend, told me how, as a young secretary in Bucharest, Vera was much sought after because of the clarity of her writing; people often asked her to improve their own letters or prose. Jerrard Tickell once described the words in Vera's minutes or notes as 'a neat little row of scalpels'.

Yet the deposition Vera took from Kieffer was a masterpiece of ambiguity. Furthermore, it was clear from the early drafts that she had deliberately constructed the ambiguities herself.

Nowhere was the statement more ambiguous than on the question of whether Prosper made a pact with Kieffer. Kieffer was evidently a man who liked making pacts. Vera had taken a detailed three-page statement on the 'pact' he made with the agent Bob Starr, which was of far less importance to F Section history. Yet the word 'pact' does not appear in connection with Prosper. All Vera recorded was that, although Prosper 'did not want to make a statement', the information Kieffer had received from Déricourt 'was put to very good use in the interrogation of Prosper'. What use was this information put to exactly? Vera must have asked Kieffer. But she did not give us his answer.

Clearly Kieffer admired Prosper more than he did Gilbert Norman, saying Norman 'had not the integrity of Prosper', which left open the possibility that Prosper, unlike Norman, did not talk at all. On the other hand, Vera chose Kieffer's words for him carefully, saying Prosper 'did not want to make a statement'. She did not say that he did not make a statement once he was persuaded, perhaps, that it might save lives.

The deposition Vera took from Kieffer fitted a familiar pattern; throughout her post-war investigation she had shown a reluctance to pass on details of what she found. Sometimes her reasons for silence were understandable. The families of the victims were told the bare minimum, perhaps in the belief that they would be spared pain. Vera often chose not to pass on all she found out of loyalty to Buckmaster. But her readiness to manipulate information for less admirable reasons – for example, to cover her own mistakes or the mistakes of SOE – had also been evident.

By the time Vera saw Kieffer, in January 1947, bitter controversy was raging in France over whether or not Prosper had sold out his loyal French followers in a futile bargain with the enemy, causing hundreds of needless deaths. By guarding what Kieffer said for herself, Vera was depriving Prosper survivors of the truth, and the bitterness would always remain. Furthermore, she was letting down Francis Suttill's own wife and sons. After the war a slur stuck to Suttill's name. No open accusation was ever made against him by Vera or Buckmaster, but their silence on his case was somehow worse. Margaret Suttill sensed that her husband had been blotted out of SOE's history and she blamed Vera. 'My mother hated Vera Atkins,' said Anthony Suttill. 'She felt others had been helped after the war but she had not.' To make matters worse, Margaret Suttill never received confirmation of her husband's death and always expected he might come back.

Over the years Margaret Suttill's anger deepened. If any word was said against her husband she went into a rage. So embittered did she become as she watched other SOE heroes and heroines fêted in post-war years, she refused even to talk of her husband to his two boys, who grew up knowing nothing of their father. 'My only memory of him is a bare bottom,' said Anthony Suttill, who was a baby when his father left for the field. 'I suppose I must have been in a bathroom with him as a toddler and that is what stuck in my mind.' Francis junior, born in 1940, had no memory of his father at all. It was only after their mother died in 1996 that the sons were able to start to get to know their father. They began to find little remnants of his life hidden around the house. In an airing cupboard Anthony found a box of negatives containing scores of tiny pictures and they turned out to be little portraits of his father, each with a slightly different expression. Suttill's two sons also started trying to find out what had really happened.

Talking to them in a London pub, I heard how they had just found out about the trial of Sachsenhausen camp staff held behind the Iron

Curtain in 1947. They had discovered that at the trial evidence was given about their father's execution, but it was still not clear if he had been hanged or shot. 'I know that at other camps, when they hanged the agents, often they just hooked them by the collar to a meat hook so they were slowly throttled,' said Francis, looking at Anthony, who winced. 'I know my brother doesn't like me to talk about it like that, but that is how it happened. Even when they killed them, they wanted to humiliate them as much as possible. The story about one agent being taken to his death with a German guard of honour because he had been so brave is obviously total rubbish.'

Vera's failure to record any detailed testimony from Kieffer on the question of Henri Déricourt was even harder to fathom than her silence on Prosper, especially because – as she was well aware when she met Kieffer – Déricourt had just been arrested by the French.

At about the same time as Kieffer was captured the French charged Déricourt with treachery and held him in prison in Fresnes while they prepared a case against him to be heard before a military tribunal.

Any evidence from the senior Sicherheitsdienst officer Déricourt worked for would, as Vera knew, be of vital importance to the French prosecutor's case. And Vera had learned enough detail from Kieffer virtually to guarantee Déricourt's conviction. Kieffer had confirmed in the most credible terms that Déricourt was BOE 48, Boemelburg's forty-eighth agent. He had also confirmed that Déricourt passed agents' mail directly into German hands. And he had confirmed that he and his officers knew about every landing from England organised by Déricourt. Yet Déricourt's name appeared only twice in the formal deposition that Vera took from Kieffer and was mentioned almost in passing.

Then I discovered that Vera had been building up her own file on Déricourt. She showed it to Francis Cammaerts, the former F Section agent, in early 1947.

Cammaerts had told Vera he was intending to speak in his defence at Déricourt's trial, and Vera tried to discourage him. 'As far as I was aware, Déricourt was a very good thing,' Cammaerts told me. 'Nobody had ever told me otherwise. Then Vera took me aside. She didn't say anything. She just took me into a room quietly and showed me a file on him and then left me to read it. It didn't take me long to see that he was a double.' So what happened to the main body of Kieffer's evidence against Déricourt?

When the trial of Henri Déricourt did eventually take place, in Paris in June 1948, it was a travesty of justice. By then Kieffer lay buried in an unmarked grave. He had been convicted of the SAS murders at a British military trial in Hameln in June 1947 and was hanged by Albert Pierrepoint, the last British hangman. Bob Starr had testified in court to *Sturmbannführer* Kieffer's humane treatment of F Section prisoners at Avenue Foch, but his words carried no weight.

Had anyone suggested it, British prosecutors could easily have offered to defer Kieffer's execution to allow him to give evidence against Déricourt. Contemporary papers showed that war criminals were often 'loaned' to others for trials and then returned for sentence or execution. However, at no point, apparently, did the British suggest making Kieffer available for the Déricourt case and at no point, it seemed, did the French request him.

Furthermore, when the military tribunal convened to try Déricourt there was no statement from Kieffer – not even Vera's paltry deposition – before the court. And, most extraordinary of all, there was nobody from SOE to give evidence against the accused. The only SOE staff officer who appeared at Déricourt's trial gave evidence in his defence.

Much to everyone's astonishment, Nicholas Bodington made an eleventh-hour appearance, telling the military tribunal that he personally had been in charge of Déricourt's work in the field and vouching for his total loyalty. He said that Déricourt's contacts with the Germans were known about in London and fully authorised for counter-espionage purposes. As a result of Bodington's evidence, Henri Eugène Déricourt performed his greatest con trick yet and walked away from his military tribunal a free man.

Once again Déricourt and Bodington appeared to be acting in tandem, and nobody seemed to know why. Diplomats in London were so perplexed by Bodington's appearance that they asked an MI6 officer based in the embassy in Paris to make enquiries among former F Section people and come up with an explanation. In reply a fellow diplomat and former SOE man, Brooks Richards, said Déricourt's evidence 'bears no relation whatever to the truth as it was known to F Section in London' and that it was 'fresh evidence of his unreliability' and 'a piece of perjury'.

Vera made her disapproval of Bodington's appearance in the court quite clear in later years, when she often told a story of how she 'cut' Bodington as a result of it, saying: 'I don't know you, Nick', and then never spoke to him again. Nor, it seems, did anyone else ever speak to Bodington about his French trial appearance. Damned by former colleagues as a 'perjurer', he ended his career as a sub-editor on the *Western Morning News* and died in 1974.

Yet in many ways the mystery of Bodington's apparently unauthorised appearance at Déricourt's trial is perhaps a red herring. The more important question is why nobody from SOE or from the government appeared in an official capacity to present evidence against the man they now knew had hastened scores of British agents to their deaths. Perhaps the Foreign Office refused to countenance any official presence at the trial for fear of ruffling French sensitivities at a time when Britain was trying to heal post-war rifts with the French. De Gaulle had always been deeply suspicious of SOE and its real intentions in France. French men and women who worked with British-run SOE circuits were accused by De Gaulle of being mercenaries, and after the liberation of 1944 he had, on occasion, even ordered SOE agents off French soil. For a representative of SOE now to appear officially in a French court – especially when it meant washing dirty British linen – might have been considered both unwise and embarrassing. And yet there were no British papers to show that this was the Foreign Office view. French records on the affair remain closed.

And, on the other hand, there were many people in London who wanted to see Déricourt convicted; none more, it appeared, than the woman who had spent so much time investigating his treachery. Déricourt's conviction would have been a fitting finale to Vera's 'private enterprise'. Whatever her impulse to guard F Section secrets, she must have wished to see justice done, if only for the sake of her dead men and women. Remarkably enough, however, Vera was not even in court to listen to the case. There was no coverage of the trial in the British press. Until the late 1950s the name Henri Déricourt remained entirely unknown in Britain.

However, Déricourt was by no means the only person to walk free at the end of Vera's war crimes investigation. The case of Horst Kopkow was in some ways an even greater scandal.

Horst Kopkow was the senior counter-intelligence officer with the Reich Security Head Office, in Berlin, and was responsible for all enemy 'parachutists', which included all SOE agents captured in France. As Vera had established time and again, it was Kopkow who passed down orders to men like Kieffer relating to the agents' capture, interrogation, imprisonment and death.

By the end of 1946 Kopkow was also in British custody and being 'very helpful', but he coolly denied responsibility for the murder of F Section people, saying that it was Heinrich Himmler, the Reichsführer and head of the SS, who had personally decided on their fate. He even revealed, for the first time, what happened to the agents held at the Ravitsch fortress: Himmler had directed that they be taken to the concentration camp at Gross Rosen, in Poland, and shot.

Kopkow, however, was less cool when he was questioned about the case of the MI6 man Frank Chamier, dropped into Germany in April 1944. Vera, on MI6's behalf, had established that Chamier had once been in Ravensbrück men's camp, where he used his alias, Frank of Upway 282. By the end of 1946 evidence suggested he had been brutally tortured on Horst Kopkow's orders in order to get him to talk. Evidence suggested he was later executed. Asked about Chamier by British interrogators, Kopkow at first 'nearly fainted' and 'asked for a glass of water', so frightened was he of the charges he would face over the Chamier case. Kopkow, however, had nothing to fear.

In 1948, when the war crimes investigator Alexander Nicolson checked on progress in the Kopkow prosecution, he was told that Kopkow, by then detained in London, had died in British custody of natural causes. A letter dated 15 June 1948 and marked 'secret', in a newly opened war crimes investigation file in the National Archives, certified Kopkow's death. The letter, addressed to the War Crimes Group and from a Lieutenant Colonel Paterson, said: 'The above [Horst Kopkow] as you know was sent to England about ten days ago for special interrogation and when he arrived here he was found to be running a temperature and after two days was sent to hospital, where we regret to say he died of Bronchopneumonia before any information was obtained from him.

'We enclose a certificate of death issued by the Hospital Authorities and would request that you duly advise his relatives of his decease. He has been buried in that portion of the local Military Cemetery allocated to prisoners of war who have died here.'

Kopkow, however, had not died. A pact was made with him, sparing him prosecution for the SOE deaths and the torture and death of Frank Chamier so that he could be released 'for special employment'. He was released from custody to work for British and American intelligence.

The evidence of this pact was contained in Vera's file on the Chamier case. MI6 has never spoken about Chamier – the secret service never speaks about its agents. Chamier's family have never even been told about his mission to Germany or his death.

Kopkow's 'special employment' was helping the West catch communists. As well as rounding up SOE agents, Kopkow had spent the war gathering intelligence for Germany on the 'Red Orchestra', a Russian communist spy network first based in Antwerp. After faking Kopkow's death, therefore, MI6 issued him with a new identity and used him to help them fight the Cold War.

Karl Boemelburg, head of the Sicherheitsdienst in France, also escaped the net; he eluded capture by taking a false name under which he continued living in Germany until, in 1947, he slipped on a piece of ice, cracked his skull and died. Neither Dr Goetz nor Hugo Bleicher was ever charged with any crime. Dr Goetz returned to Germany as a schools inspector.

Several minor officials were in the end released. Wassmer and Ott, for example, the two men who transported Vera's women to Natzweiler and Dachau, were freed after it was concluded that they were only carrying out orders. And Hermann Rösner, of the Karlsruhe Gestapo, who instructed Wassmer and Ott to take these women to the concentration camps, was also freed as he too was only doing as he was told. In the 1960s Rösner was hired by the British to provide intelligence for NATO. Of the concentration camp staff, many eluded capture, the most notable perhaps being Dr Heinrich Plaza, who, with Dr Rohde, had injected the four SOE women before they were cremated at Natzweiler.

At the conclusion of the Ravensbrück trial eleven of the camp staff, including Johann Schwarzhuber, Dorothea Binz, Vera Salvequart and Carmen Mory, received death sentences for crimes against humanity, although Mory killed herself with a razor blade hidden in the heel of her shoe before she reached Albert Pierrepoint's noose. Fritz Suhren, the camp Kommandant, was eventually recaptured and executed by the French.

As for Kieffer, Vera clearly had her doubts about whether he should have been hanged at all. If it had not been for the SAS killings, 'he would have been a free man today', she said after the war. 'We [SOE] had nothing against him.' Just before he was taken from his cell at Wuppertal, Kieffer removed the photograph of his daughter Hildegard from the wall and asked for it to be posted to her with a note on the back: '*Moggele*, I bless you in my last hour. Your father.'

Although Vera would always keep to herself much of what Kieffer had told her, she was determined to make public some of the evidence she had drawn from him. While burying the mistakes of SOE, Vera was just as eager to promote its successes. Kieffer's evidence had, above all else, proven the extraordinary bravery of Nora Inayat Khan. When Vera got home from Germany in early February 1947 she therefore had one more task to perform before finally leaving 'this game of war crimes'. She was determined to put Nora up for a George Cross.

Three years after the end of the war it was not easy to persuade the powers that be that Nora's recommendation for a gallantry award should be rewritten for a fourth time. First she was proposed for a George Medal, then for an MBE, then a Mention in Dispatches and, now that the truth about her courage appeared to have emerged, she was to be put forward for the highest award for bravery anyone could receive. The correspondence between Vera and Eileen Lancey of the Honours and Awards Office showed Vera endlessly battling to prove that this time she had got the facts for the citation for Nora right. First Miss Lancey seemed to doubt the evidence that Nora had really been held in chains in Pforzheim. Then there was doubt about how she could have communicated via the prison mugs. 'How they exchanged mugs I cannot say but that they did is proved by the fact that Mlle Lagrave was in possession of Madeleine's names and address and many other details concerning her,' wrote Vera in an exasperated reply to the official. In the end it was Kieffer's evidence of Nora's escape, and of her absolute refusal to give any information, which counted more than anything towards

her award. Although Kieffer's evidence was not available to convict
Déricourt, it was crucial in securing Nora her George Cross. Vera
quoted Kieffer as the source for the fact that the escape with Starr
and Faye was 'Madeleine's idea'.

Nora's George Cross was finally made public in 1949. 'G/C for
Braver Than They Thought Girl', said one newspaper headline.
And it was under this headline that Vera revealed how Kieffer cried
when he heard of Nora's death at Dachau.

> In London yesterday a woman executive of the Top Secret
> Department described Nora's heroism and said: 'Since the
> war I have seen Sturmbannführer Hans Kieffer, Gestapo
> chief at Avenue Foch, Paris. It was he who sent her on her
> way, describing her as intractable and highly dangerous. Bully
> and hard man though he was, the reminder of her courage
> and patriotism caused him to break down and weep bitterly.'

————

After concluding her interrogation of Kieffer in January 1947, Vera
had nearly completed all she had returned to Germany to do: she
had assisted the prosecution at the Ravensbrück trial, established
where Nora died and interviewed the man who captured her agents.
Before she returned to England, however, she went briefly to
Hamburg, where sentences were about to be passed on the sixteen
defendants.

By the time the former Ravensbrück guards were brought into the
dock for the verdicts, Vera had resumed her seat on the prosecution
bench. As the sixteen lined up she took a small scrap of paper and
down the left-hand side, in tiny black writing, she wrote the number
of each defendant, one to sixteen, with a full stop after each. As the
sentences were read out she noted them down. Against the number
of the five defendants who received a prison sentence she wrote
the number of years each was to serve in jail. Against the number of
each of the eleven defendants sentenced to death she marked a tiny
black cross.

PART IV

ENGLAND

CONSPIRACIES

'Any history of SOE would seem to be in the nature of self-vindication which as a secret service is in my opinion undesirable and unnecessary. That other people will seek to claim the honour and glory should, I think, leave us unmoved,' wrote Leslie Humphreys in September 1945, when SOE was considering how its work should be recorded, once the organisation had been closed down.

The Whitehall establishment was content to bury all memory of SOE after the end of the war. MI6 could not snuff out its awkward wartime rival fast enough and the Foreign Office was delighted to see an end to the organisation which had interfered so much with quiet diplomacy, particularly in France, where Buckmaster's celebratory tours – his so-called 'Judex' mission – had led to vitriolic attacks on him in the French press. As one diplomat put it: 'To a certain extent Buckmaster is himself to blame. He has courted post-war popularity in France and has enjoyed the floral tributes of a resistance hero. Now that spirit has changed he is getting the rotten eggs.'

Officially, Humphreys's view that SOE should rest in silence prevailed. (Humphreys himself had soon retired from intelligence to become a schoolmaster at Stonyhurst.) The Special Forces Club was formed in 1946 to keep SOE memories alive and to provide a network for job hunters, but all members were instructed never to speak again of their wartime work. The best of the SOE rump were offered work in MI6 or other departments, but Vera was offered no such position. After she failed 'by one place' to achieve her MBE in the 1946 Birthday Honours, a further attempt to secure her an honour, in recognition of her war crimes work, was unsuccessful. Although she received a Croix de Guerre from the French in 1948, Vera was, as she put it, 'undecorated' by Britain. When she arrived back from Germany in early 1947 she was also unemployed.

Sometime in early 1947, probably soon after returning from Germany, Vera wrote again to Dick Ketton-Cremer's brother, Wyndham, asking if he had any more news. She received this reply:

> Dear Miss Atkins, I was so glad to hear from you again and to know your address though I am afraid I have no good news to tell you about Dick. There can now be no doubt that he was killed in Crete on or about 23 May 1941, during the German attack on Maleme airfield, where he was stationed. We heard from a man in the squadron to which he was unfortunately attached in Crete, who found him badly wounded and practically unconscious during the fighting. He thought he had very little time to live and could do nothing to help him. We know no more, and have heard nothing at all about his grave.
>
> It is unbearable to think of this even now, and I am afraid it will grieve you very much.
>
> While he was in the Western Desert in 1940, he made a codicil to his will with various bequests to his friends. Among those bequests was one to you, and I shall send you a cheque for the amount as soon as we have settled his affairs.

The news that Dick died at Maleme must already have reached Vera, through her contacts with the RAF and the Red Cross. But the finality – 'There can now be no doubt' – of Wyndham's brief account must have compounded Vera's grief. And what she would not have known until now was that she had been mentioned in Dick's last will.

In his fourth and final letter to Vera, Wyndham Ketton-Cremer sent a cheque 'which represents Dick's legacy to you, plus interest but less tax'. He added: 'I did so much appreciate your letter about Dick. As you say, the whole story is just heartbreaking.'

I obtained a copy of Dick's will, hoping it might contain further clues about his intentions towards Vera.

The codicil began as follows:

'I Richard Thomas Wyndham Ketton-Cremer of Felbrigg Hall Roughton Norfolk England on this date 5 July 1940 at Maaton Baguish Western Desert Egypt make the following bequests and legacies extra and above those previously made.

'I HEREBY BEQUEATH the sum of £1000 (One thousand pounds) to' – and here the page turned – 'Mrs Billie Pelmyra Gordon née Rhoads, American citizen, present address c/o American Consulate Funchal Madeira or might be traced at St Cloud Florida USA with much love and in memory of an association no less delightful because it could not be final I hereby bequeath to Miss Vera Atkins of "Magazine" Winchelsea Sussex (Rumanian citizen) the sum of 500 pounds with love & in memory of a delightful friendship I hereby bequeath to Mrs Theodora Greaves now of 4 Walsingham Terrace, Hove, Sussex the sum of £300 with love and in gratitude for much friendship and worldly advice . . .' and so on.

The will contained sparse punctuation and it was hard to say, at first, if the phrase 'with much love and in memory of an association no less delightful because it could not be final' applied to Billie or to Vera. At first I liked to think it applied to Vera but on reflection I decided, reluctantly, that it belonged with the £1000 Dick left to Billie. Vera got the lesser sum of £500 and 'love and memory of a delightful friendship'.

I read on through the rest of the codicil, which included a series of bequests: Dick left his horse Jester to the local rector; his auto-cycle to the Felbrigg chauffeur; a sum to the Norfolk and Norwich Aeronautical Club; and his Ford car, Fluff, to a friend.

The document was witnessed by Pilot Officer John Ward of 113 Squadron RAF and was signed on 10 July 1940.

The will was a further indication that Vera was important to Dick. But precisely how important she was remained ambiguous.

Shortly after Vera returned from Germany for the last time, she disappeared on her own to Wales for many weeks. She went to stay in a remote cottage on the Pembrokeshire coast and saw nobody there apart from a local farmer who helped her carry her suitcase up a track to the house. 'I always thought she had gone there to be alone after all that happened, and to mourn,' said Mary Williams, Guy's girlfriend, who remembered his sister's disappearance at that time. There were suddenly so many for Vera to mourn.

Then, in May, Vera's mother died. It had not been expected. Hilda Atkins was cremated and then interned at a small family ceremony in the Jewish cemetery at Golders Green, north London. Ralph, in a letter to his 'dear baby sister' on 8 June 1947, said: 'It is frightful to think that our dear mother is no more, she was our rallying point and stand-by in our troubles. I always had the feeling that she sensed if one of us had something on his mind without even telling her about it . . . It doesn't seem so very long since we were all at Crasna. What a lot of things have happened since then.'

Whatever yearnings Vera or her brothers still had for their childhood home, Crasna – along with all of Romania and eastern Europe – were now disappearing behind the Iron Curtain. A friend who had lived with the Rosenbergs at Crasna wrote to Vera from Australia after the war saying the news from Crasna was 'very sad' and that he was sending food parcels to 'the Flondors', the Rosenbergs' former neighbours there.

Ralph was himself nearly stranded behind the Iron Curtain. The letter he wrote to Vera about their mother's death was sent from Bucharest, where he had returned in 1946 in the hope of working normally again in the oil business. Now the communist clampdown was beginning to tighten and he was desperate to get out. Exit permits were already hard to come by and he had not even been able to leave to attend his mother's funeral.

After her stay in Pembrokeshire Vera returned to London, where she eventually found work in one of the many new post-war bodies set up to foster international understanding, established by UNESCO, the United Nations' education and culture body. Her new employer, the Central Bureau for Educational Visits and Exchanges, arranged student exchanges throughout the world. The post of office manager, which Vera took up in October 1948, was secured for her by Francis Cammaerts, the former Jockey circuit organiser, who became the Bureau's first director. The post was perhaps not the top-flight one Vera might have hoped for after the war, but she was soon promoted and became head of the organisation in 1952 when Cammaerts left. And Vera still had a time-consuming job to do for SOE.

Whatever Leslie Humphreys might have ruled, Vera, along with Maurice Buckmaster, had already begun to claim 'the honour and glory' for F Section and they had no intention of ceasing now. Their promotion drive had started well before the end of the war, when Buckmaster began composing citations for as many F Section agents as possible. Then, no sooner were surviving agents back from the field in 1945 than they were persuaded by Vera and 'Buck', as so many now called him, to go immediately on lecture tours, even to the US.

The fact that by 1946 SOE had been shut down and its files closed was no impediment to Vera and Buckmaster's publicity efforts. Vera carried all the information needed (and more than was in the files) in her head. Authors, screenplay writers and, later, TV producers contacted Buckmaster first about their projects and Buckmaster then passed enquiries on to Vera. 'Miss Atkins's memory is so much better than mine,' he always said.

Stories about glamorous SOE agents were therefore rarely out of the newspapers in the immediate post-war years, and Vera and Buckmaster worked as a duo, just as they had during the war. Their success was measured in the cuttings which I found spilling out of Vera's files.

Odette Sansom, the tortured heroine, who had escaped from Ravensbrück and become the first woman to receive a George Cross, was the darling of the press, along with Peter Churchill, her organiser, who was arrested with her. When, in 1947, Odette left her first husband and married Churchill, a media fairy tale came true. The biography of Odette, by Jerrard Tickell, was published in 1949 and was publicised by a series of sensational articles about SOE in the *Sunday Express* entitled 'Set Europe Ablaze'.

'"I am not sure," said a German spy chief, "whom we shall hang first when we get to London. Winston Churchill or Colonel Buckmaster,"' read a caption on a picture of Buckmaster.

Vera's personal copy of Tickell's book contained the author's handwritten inscription, acknowledging just how much he owed to his prime source of information. 'For Vera Atkins':

'Onlie begetter,' midwife, vamp.
Doubling Will Hews with Mrs Gamp,
Invisible as Mrs Harris,
In Baker Street, Berlin and Paris,
For each part, in each latitude,
Accept an author's gratitude.

There were many SOE stories to be told. The *Daily Herald* ran a series called 'The Commando Girls' which told of Pearl Witherington's 'adventures with the *maquis*'. The poignant tragedy of Violette Szabo's daughter, little Tania, continued to capture imaginations. In another article in the *Sunday Express*, Violette's last escorting officer was quoted as saying that, as Violette departed from the field: 'She zipped up her flying suit, adjusted her parachute, shook her hair loose and climbed laughing into the aircraft.' The quote obviously came from Vera.

Vera had cut out numerous pictures of Violette's daughter, whose little dresses were weighed down by more and more of her mother's medals as the years went on.

From Vera's letters it was clear that some of those projected into the limelight did not always welcome it. Yvonne Baseden received a call from Vera one day in the mid-1950s asking if she would agree to appear on *This Is Your Life* with Eamonn Andrews. Yvonne, who had not yet fully recovered from the trauma of her imprisonment at Ravensbrück, detested the very idea, but was persuaded by Vera.

Pearl Witherington at first declined to go on a lecture tour which Vera had organised. 'Only if you absolutely insist, Vera, will I go,' she wrote. Pearl had already been embroiled in controversy over her civilian MBE. The FANYs who survived the war found they were caught in yet another legal loophole. Having agreed to join a civilian organisation, to get around the bar on women in the military bearing arms, these same women were now told that as mere FANYs they could receive only civilian awards. 'There was nothing civil about what I did,' protested Pearl, who in the weeks before D-Day took command of a group of at least a thousand resistance fighters. She sent her civilian award straight back.

These were busy times for Vera. Soon promoted within the Bureau, she also moved from Nell Gwynne House, where she had lived since 1940, to a small but airy new apartment on the top floor of a stucco-fronted terrace in Rutland Gate, just off Knightsbridge, which was convenient for the Special Forces Club, as well as Harrods.

After the book about Odette came the film, with Anna Neagle as Odette, Trevor Howard as Peter Churchill, Marius Goring as their captor Hugo Bleicher and Maurice Buckmaster as himself. Vera now found herself rushing up and down to Ealing film studios with

Buckmaster for rehearsals, checking screenplays and briefing reporters. In her files was a letter to Vera from J. Arthur Rank saying photographs were enclosed, and here they were: Vera standing in a svelte suit with the film's stars. Vera had also preserved a note to 'My dear Vera' from Neagle herself.

The film, *Odette*, opened amid great acclaim in 1950, with the King and Queen, as well as Vera and Buck, in the audience. 'The Queen and the Heroine,' said one headline describing how Odette arrived at the opening 'wearing evening crinoline of black lace and champagne lace underskirt'. 'I'm quite ordinary,' said Odette as she faced the press.

Buckmaster by now had also published his own book on SOE, *Specially Employed*, and later came *They Fought Alone*. If more proof were needed that the head of SOE's most important country section was a man who struggled to distinguish fact from fantasy, these books provided it. As Buckmaster himself candidly admitted inside Vera's personal copy: 'Dedicated to Vera who knows more accurately than I do how, when and why these events occurred (I might also add "whether").'

Then the publicity started to backfire. On 3 August 1949 Vera had received to her flat a petite young woman with short, cropped auburn hair and a plain but pleasant face. Jean Overton Fuller wanted to research the life of Nora Inayat Khan. From the moment Jean began writing, Vera lost control over the SOE story.

During the war Jean lived in Bloomsbury a few doors away from where Nora's family then lived, and the two young women became closely acquainted. One day in May 1943 Nora told Jean she was 'going on foreign service' and then vanished. Nora's brother Vilayat never seemed to have been told for sure what had happened. Jean read the citation for Nora's George Cross in the newspapers in 1949 and decided to find out more. She had never heard of SOE but she was referred through the War Office to a Colonel Buckmaster, who said he was not sure he could remember Nora, and referred Jean straight to 'Miss Atkins'.

Jean Overton Fuller was cultivated and determined. She had also had a deep distrust of official secrecy ever since learning that her father's death in 1914, during the attack on Tanga, German East Africa, was an 'official secret'. She gave an account of her first meeting with 'Miss Atkins' in a preface to one of her books: 'She said she did not know if the names of the schools in which my friend had trained had yet been taken off the security list. Nor could she tell me anything about the people Nora had been sent out to work with, who were, in any case dead.' Vera did, however, offer Jean suggestions about people she could talk to and among them was John 'Bob' Starr. He was, of course, a perfect contact because he could describe Nora's bravery at Avenue Foch, but, as Vera well knew, he was embittered and very likely to reveal the damaging secrets of the 'radio game'. So Vera warned Jean that should Starr 'begin to spin some sort of story in which he is perfectly justified and the Section seems to have done everything wrong', she should not believe him.

For some months Vera continued to help Jean as she pursued her research and the couple dined together to talk about Nora. When *Madeleine* was published in 1952 Vera was generally pleased with the book, which revealed few damaging secrets, saying nothing about Nora's radio being played back. Vera had some small objections to the way she herself was portrayed, and she invited Jean to 'talk over' these points with her but by and large she considered the book 'a very striking portrait of Nora' which 'exposes her character as a live and lovely compound of intelligence and warmth, timidity and courage, simplicity and love of truth'.

Jean replied gratefully but evidently did not take up Vera's invitation to 'talk over' the book, so Vera wrote a letter inviting Jean to dinner. In another note, preserved by Vera, Jean replied that she could not go on the day suggested by Vera and proposed a meeting at her own flat a week later. 'I would like to prepare a little dinner – nothing terribly elegant but I will try to make something tasty to eat.'

In a further little note that Vera had kept, Jean wished Vera well after she had been ill over Christmas. Jean wrote: 'I do hope you are feeling better now, as it must be miserable to spend Christmas in hospital.' The two women seemed to have become quite close.

Well before Jean's next book, *The Starr Affair*, however, Vera and Jean's friendship had irretrievably broken down. Early in her research for *Madeleine* Jean had spoken to Starr at length not only about Nora but about the way the Germans had captured the British radios and fooled London by playing them back. She found Starr 'credible' and wrote: 'I realised I had stumbled upon an inconvenient secret.' Vera had either been astonishingly naive in believing

Jean would not pursue what Starr told her, or she was deceiving herself even then about the seriousness of what Starr knew. In any event, Jean now immediately widened her investigation. Tracking down all surviving witnesses to Nora's captivity, she found they were not all dead, as Vera had told her, and she even found Ernest Vogt, the interpreter at Avenue Foch, who had played a large part in interrogating Nora. When Jean told Vera she had found Vogt she expected her to be pleased, but Vera advised her in the strongest terms to stay away from him. The idea that Jean should talk to one of Nora's German captors clearly horrified Vera, though Jean could not understand why.

Jean chose not to confuse her biography of Nora with an exposé of German penetration. In her next book, however, her sole purpose was to unveil the 'radio game', revealing at the same time how Starr had been victimised after the war because he knew too much. While she was writing *The Starr Affair*, a book entitled *London Calling North Pole*, by the former head of German counter-espionage in Holland and Belgium, Lieutenant Colonel H.J. Giskes, was published in 1953, revealing that the Germans had operated the 'radio game' with devastating success in those two countries. Giskes's revelations prompted questions in the Commons, which the Foreign Secretary, Anthony Eden, answered by saying they were largely true.

Jean Overton Fuller's revelations that British and French women and men had similarly been parachuted into Gestapo hands in France prompted no official comment at all. However, other writers, as well as former SOE members, noted what she wrote. Vera opened a 'controversial books' file, which from now filled up rapidly. 'There was no Starr Affair until you started it,' wrote Vera to Jean when the book was published in 1954. 'I did not mean to offend you personally,' Jean replied.

By the mid-1950s Vera was advising another young writer, Elizabeth Nicholas. Elizabeth had known Diana Rowden and once again there were dinner invitations from Vera, but it soon became clear that Elizabeth, like Jean Overton Fuller, would ask the wrong questions. To deter her, Vera was not only uncooperative: on one matter she quite clearly lied.

One question Elizabeth Nicholas sought to answer was the identity of the fourth woman to die at Natzweiler, who, as far as she could see from the published record of the trial, was 'unidentified'. Not realising that the record itself had already been altered to cover up Vera's initial error of identifying Nora as the fourth woman, Elizabeth then asked Vera if the identity had ever been established. Vera had known since 1947 that the fourth woman was Sonia Olschanesky, but she did not give Elizabeth her name. 'All Vera Atkins could tell me was that she had not been sent to France by SOE'; in other words, the fourth woman was locally recruited in France to work with an SOE circuit. It was not until eight months later that Elizabeth found Sonia's name for herself. She discovered that she was a former ballet dancer, a Jew, and the daughter of Russian parents. Sonia had also been astonishingly brave, staying on to work as a courier for an F Section circuit near Paris after the collapse of Prosper. Elizabeth also discovered that Sonia's fiancé and family had never been informed of her fate, although they had made desperate attempts to trace her.

I found it hard to reconcile the callous streak in Vera, which had now begun to show itself, with her dedication in searching for the missing. The failure to tell Sonia's family what she had discovered was not the only example of callousness. For reasons never explained, Nora's family were never officially told the full facts of her death at Dachau. Although Vilayat had gathered his own evidence that Nora did not die at Natzweiler, it was only when the family read Nora's citation for her George Cross in 1948 that they learned the final official version of what happened. The sudden news of an entirely different horror at Dachau produced a second devastating shock for Nora's mother, who died ten days later.

However, some people who knew Vera well were not surprised by this toughness in her character. 'She was treated like a man, she had to behave like one,' said Vera's war crimes colleague and close friend Sacha Smith. Vera had once been close to the SOE agent Francis Cammaerts, who secured her the job at the Central Bureau for Educational Visits and Exchanges. But when I met Cammaerts it was clear that he and Vera had become estranged. 'She was always a cold-blooded professional,' he said. She was the person the agents 'trusted to lie'; in other words, she could be trusted not to tell their families the truth about their fate.

After the war, Cammaerts claimed, Vera only helped her 'favourites'. She avoided those 'who might rumble her'. A teacher by vocation, Cammaerts said: 'For a teacher, having favourites was always the worst thing.'

When I asked why he had fallen out so bitterly with Vera, he told me he had discovered she was 'a racist'. In the 1960s Vera had visited Cammaerts in Africa, where, after leaving the Central Bureau for Educational Visits and Exchanges, he taught at the University of Nairobi. He was shocked at the way Vera treated his black colleagues and staff.

When Elizabeth Nicholas's book *Death Be Not Proud* was published in 1958 new questions were asked about how agents could have been flown to penetrated circuits, with London apparently unaware that SOE radios had been captured. In the case of Nora's captured radio, Nicholas posed 'a truly dreadful theory': that London deliberately dropped France Antelme, Madeleine Damerment and Lionel Lee as part of a 'double bluff'. She explained: 'London had known very well that the "Poste Madeleine" had been taken over by the Germans and was busily feeding to it false information to deceive the enemy. More than this, in order to convince the Germans that London believed the "Poste Madeleine" was still in British hands, London had prepared to send agents deliberately to a reception committee organised by the Germans so as to maintain the deception.' She admitted she had been 'unable to confirm that this was the case' but added that 'a number of people, including officers of SOE, believe it was'. On the other hand, she continued: 'the point has also been made that such action would demand a logical and cruel ruthlessness such as the British never employ, even in war'.

Buckmaster dismissed 'Nicholas's nonsense' in a piece in the *Empire News*. But conspiracy theories about SOE's darker purpose were now being circulated as fast as the sanitised sentiment, epitomised in the 1958 film about Violette Szabo, *Carve Her Name with Pride*, on which Vera advised. Violette's portrait painter, Douglas Pigg, complaining about the film in a letter to Vera, wrote: 'It was to my mind a great pity that the internment scenes were as brief. Surely it was here that the true fortitude and strength of the girls were most evident. How the girls would have wished it was as quick to the end as depicted.'

Buckmaster's complaint to Vera was not about the portrayal of Violette but 'the nauseating presentation of ourselves'. He wrote:

'My agent tells me that in law we cannot stop the portrayal of ourselves either with our true names or with fictitious names, if the latter merely cover up well-known personalities (as believe it or not, we are).'

And, on top of everything else, the Churchills' story was unravelling. Peter and Odette faced accusations, particularly in France, that instead of arming the resistance they spent their time in bed together, which was precisely where Hugo Bleicher, the Abwehr officer, found them when they were arrested in 1943 at a hotel in St Jorioz. A rumour also now spread that Odette had been spared at Ravensbrück because she became the mistress of the Kommandant, Fritz Suhren. There was no evidence for this claim. Sylvia Salvesen, the Norwegian prisoner, vouched for Odette's heroism, saying she had spent eleven months at Ravensbrück in an underground cell. But so fixed did the tale become in F Section's burgeoning mythology that Selwyn Jepson – who, as 'Mr Potter', had been Odette's SOE interviewer – repeated the claim as a fact in a taped interview he gave to the Imperial War Museum in 1986. Jepson, who in civilian life had been a crime writer, was cut short by the embarrassed museum official, who changed the subject.

It was also being said that Odette had lied about having her toenails pulled out, though Stephen Stewart, the prosecuting barrister at Ravensbrück, asserted categorically that on this point her story was true. By the mid-1950s the fairy-tale marriage of Odette and Peter Churchill was over, and Peter wrote to Vera to say he was living alone in a caravan in the South of France 'with a loaded gun behind the door to frighten away newspaper correspondents'.

Vera, though, by now had more to worry about than the portrayal of agents in books and films. She was deeply anxious about how the Conservative MP Dame Irene Ward might portray her in the House of Commons. An indomitable character, Ward had once hoped to be an opera singer, but used her powerful voice instead to remonstrate with ministers on behalf of her Tynemouth constituents and in fighting for unpopular causes. In the early 1950s she was writing a book on the history of the FANY and, like Jean Overton Fuller and Elizabeth Nicholas, had come across the cases of the SOE girls. Irene was particularly intrigued by the case of Henri Déricourt, which had by now been explored by Jean Overton Fuller in her third book, *Double Webs*. Here Jean traced Déricourt himself, who told her he had indeed handed agents' mail over to the Gestapo but had been acting on instructions from a high authority in London. This claim then fuelled a theory that Déricourt himself was planted inside SOE by MI6. Perhaps MI6 was using Déricourt to keep tabs on the SOE camp and to further its own plans to deceive the Germans.

Writing to the Foreign Secretary, John Selwyn Lloyd, in 1958, Irene Ward warned she was 'going to be an awful nuisance' unless she got some answers to certain questions. One of these questions was: 'whether Gilbert was working for one of our secret service organisations, and put into SOE to keep an eye on what was going on there, or was he working for the Germans?' The MP was also campaigning for Odette's George Cross to be rescinded. 'She is a phoney. Buckmaster must have known,' wrote Ward in a note in 1959.

Ward was directed in the first instance to Vera for her answers. 'Miss Atkins', she noted, 'was extremely pleasant but I gained absolutely nothing. To tell you the truth it ended with my being questioned.' Soon after this meeting Ward turned her sights on 'Miss Atkins' herself.

'HOME OFFICE Minister's case R20340/3 Rosenberg Vera May alias Atkins,' was the heading on the papers relating to Ward's questions about Vera. She had heard a rumour that Vera Atkins was Romanian and demanded to know whether F Section's intelligence officer had been naturalised and, if so, when. Reluctantly the Home Office revealed Vera's Romanian origins to the MP, giving the date of her naturalisation in February 1944. Realising that Vera had therefore been an enemy alien at the time of her employment with SOE, Ward demanded to know more. How many naturalisations were granted by the Home Office in 1944 and in what circumstances?

She was told that in 1944 549 certificates of naturalisation were issued, of which 472 were in respect of persons who were being readmitted to British nationality, having previously held it. In all other cases naturalisation was not granted during the war except in cases of 'national interest'. Vera's naturalisation must therefore have been granted 'in the national interest'. Now Ward wanted the names of Vera's sponsors.

Vera would certainly have appreciated the full damage the MP's attack could cause. During the war it had been virtually a matter of life and death that her origins remain secret, a central tenet of clandestine operations being that agents in the field should trust implicitly their handlers in headquarters. The stakes may not have appeared so high now in peacetime, but Irene Ward's campaign nevertheless struck at Vera's very reputation.

If any suggestion emerged in public that there had been an enemy alien in SOE headquarters, conspiracy theorists already hunting for more controversy would have had a field day. Such was the climate of suspicion that Vera would herself have been caught up in those very conspiracies she had tried to dispel. The subtext of Ward's question was evident: she was exploring the possibility that Vera herself might have been playing some sort of double game. Certain conspiracy theorists were already developing suspicions of Vera – among them one of her own former agents.

In Vera's files were numerous letters from a man named Pierre Raynaud, who, as a young soldier, had escaped from France in 1942. He was snapped up by F Section and parachuted back into France as an agent. Immediately after landing he escaped capture by the Gestapo only by a fluke. Raynaud had been due to link up on landing with the Canadians Frank Pickersgill and John Macalister, who had been dropped the night before, and was to have travelled with them, but, horrified by Macalister's French accent, he decided to travel alone.

After the war Raynaud discovered numerous blunders committed by London which could have landed him – like Pickersgill and Macalister – in German hands. He decided that no intelligence body could have been so stupid as to commit these errors. Like Elizabeth Nicholas, Raynaud wondered if it was all part of a bigger strategy. He decided it was and that the strategy was to fill agents with false information in the knowledge that they would be captured and pass it to the Germans.

In the 1970s and 1980s new writers took up the theme, embellishing it with details from newly released papers on 'Cockade', the Allied plan to trick the Germans about the date and location of the D-Day invasion. It was now claimed that Henri Déricourt must have been deployed by MI6, or perhaps directly by Claude Dansey, the assistant chief of MI6, as part of the plan, ensuring that agents' mail containing phoney hints about D-Day reached the Germans. In his last years Buckmaster himself suddenly miraculously recalled that MI6 had indeed sent messages directly to some of the captured SOE radios. By this time most who had followed Buckmaster's delusions over the years ignored him. However, his thoughts were taken seriously by some and helped feed new conspiracy theories so enticing that they were put into a novel, Larry Collins's *Fall from Grace*, published in 1985.

Like Vera, I had a pile of letters from SOE's arch conspiracy theorist, Pierre Raynaud, who invited me to the Canary Islands to see his archive. I didn't go, but I did try to challenge him, saying that what happened could be only too easily explained by F Section bungling, which was allowed to run unchecked. But Raynaud told me that 'Buckmaster's stupidity' had always been 'the excuse'. He said Vera was SOE's 'official liar', appointed to cover up the truth. And he expected me to write her 'official hagiography'.

Back in 1955 Vera could have had no idea how far the conspiracy theories about SOE might develop, but she certainly didn't want to be drawn into them. On 7 November 1955 the Home Office came to her aid by stopping any more questions about her origins. Exasperated by Irene Ward, who still had 'the bit between her teeth', an official wrote: 'Miss Ward seems to be gathering ammunition for some sort of attack on Miss Atkins. I see no objection to telling her when Miss Atkins first came here but if more intimate questions follow we must call a halt.'

It was puzzling that the Home Office refused to divulge the name of Vera's sponsors, as such a list of eminently English names – Kendrick, Rogers, Pearson and Coverley-Price – all proclaiming Vera as 'English to the core', would surely have been reassuring. Ward did win one battle, however. It was largely due to her campaigning that a historian called M.R.D. (Michael) Foot, a young lecturer at Oxford, was appointed to write an officially sponsored history of the French Section of SOE. 'However,' said the Prime Minister, Harold Macmillan, in a note to Ward, 'I doubt in fact it will ever be possible to establish exactly where praise or blame may have lain in all these intricate clandestine operations.'

Just as the Home Office was closing down Irene Ward, however, others were beginning to ask questions about Vera's loyalties which were potentially of an even more threatening kind. The Cold War was by now being fought, not only across the Iron Curtain, but in the corridors of Whitehall and anywhere where the spy-catchers of MI5 might sniff out a traitor. In 1950 a German-born scientist, Klaus Fuchs, who came to Britain in 1933 after fleeing the Nazis and was interned at the start of the war, had been caught passing US nuclear secrets to the Russians. Then, in 1951, came the dramatic flight to Moscow of two of the 'Cambridge spies', Guy Burgess and Donald MacLean. The intelligence agencies now clamped down, imposing positive vetting on all secret services and opening files on suspect individuals in any walk of life, on the most meagre of pretexts. The domestic security service, MI5, opened a file on Vera May Atkins.

Exactly when the file on Vera was opened was a matter of guesswork, because it had been destroyed, but I knew it was in existence by the 1950s and I knew that at this time her card was also marked within the Foreign Office. When her name was proposed as an intermediary between the British government and a leading French trade unionist, diplomats immediately vetoed Vera because of her 'left-wing views'.

Also guesswork was the reason why the file on Vera was opened. Most people who knew her in her later years had gained the impression that she was, and always had been, right-wing; some thought her contacts were not with the Soviet Union, but with the CIA. Sacha Smith, her former war crimes colleague, even recalled that Vera once told him she was 'advising the CIA, on restructuring' and being paid for it. Though he did not press her on what she meant, he guessed that her CIA contacts went back to the war, when she had contact with members of the Office of Strategic Services (OSS), the American counterpart of SOE and precursor of the CIA.

Then I found people who had gained an entirely different impression of Vera's politics. One of her former agents, Tony Brooks, remembered how she loathed De Gaulle and always emphasised the importance the communist groups had played in the resistance. When I revealed to Brooks that Vera was an eastern European Jew, he took no more convincing that she was herself a communist. But then Brooks himself had spent much of his career as a spy-catcher for MI5.

Some of Vera's very closest friends often wondered about her. Most were light-hearted in their musings: 'The only drawback to you of course,' wrote the former Chancellor circuit organiser, George Millar, in a letter to Vera in the early 1960s, 'and it is minuscule really by contrast with your bounties, is that you are by nature so very discreet. So discreet indeed as to seem mysterious, if you are not mysterious.'

Other friends, though, including Jerrard Tickell, became over the years more serious in their suspicions of Vera.

Jerrard's son Sir Crispin Tickell, former British ambassador to the United Nations, recalled how, as a teenage public schoolboy, he often met Vera when his father was writing his biography of Odette. 'I have an image of her with a slightly blonde moustache uttering quite left-wing sentiments at Sunday lunchtime. She was a slightly sinister lady and my mother hated her. One always wondered who she was working for,' he said. 'She made a number of comments which struck me at the time as not so much politically left as inclined to the Soviet Union and Soviet Empire, along the lines of H.G. Wells or George Bernard Shaw – fed up with our society and there was a new Jerusalem over the hill. I know my father became very suspicious of her. She made me uneasy.'

Sir Crispin asked me what Vera had done after the war. I said she had worked for an educational body, sponsored by UNESCO. Certain bodies created by UNESCO at that time were used as little more than front organisations, he suggested. In the 1950s the Bureau for Educational Visits and Exchanges, which Vera worked for, might well have been 'an umbrella for the Soviets', he claimed.

But what precisely had brought Vera under suspicion of being a communist or a communist sympathiser? Perhaps it was her early friendship with Francis Cammaerts. MI5 certainly had a file on Cammaerts, who at the outbreak of war was a conscientious objector, which immediately marked him out as a left-wing radical. 'They had files on anyone,' Cammaerts scoffed when I asked him for his views on Vera's politics. 'MI5 and MI6 were the stupidest people I have ever known. Of course Vera was not a communist. She had the politics of a right-wing Kensington lady, which was what she wanted to be.'

Vera's links with another left-winger, Landon Temple, prominent in Communist Party politics in London in the 1950s and 1960s, may have aroused even more suspicion. During his most active years as a communist, Temple was Vera's deputy at the Central Bureau. Vera was always 'tolerant' of his political views, he recalled, as well as a good friend and respected colleague.

When Temple was sacked from the Bureau in 1961, for voicing pro-Soviet, anti-American sentiments while on a Bureau visit to Poland, Vera had defended him. This may have brought suspicion of 'the establishment' upon her, he said. It may even have contributed to her own resignation from the Bureau, ostensibly over lack of funding, later the same year. But such 'witch-hunts' were all part of the 'Anglo-American, anti-communist conspiracy of the times', said Temple, who never considered that Vera was particularly left-wing herself, and he thought it 'very unlikely' that she was ever a communist.

'Her life was very compartmentalised, but I always had the impression that she was socially rather stuffy and she had a lot of right-wing people around her. On the other hand, Vera was not a conventional person. She was highly intelligent and intelligent enough to be interested in many points of view. She was certainly understanding of mine and on some things I'm sure we agreed.'

Mistrust of Vera may also have sprung from suspicions of her younger brother Guy, on whom MI5 also had a file. Guy was an obvious target for the spy-catchers. Jewish, born in Romania, educated at Oxford and at Prague in the 1930s, he took a job in 1948 lecturing in Bantu languages – learned with the East Africa Rifles during the war – at SOAS, London University's School of Oriental and African Studies, which was considered a left-wing campus.

And yet I found no evidence that Guy had ever shown an active interest in politics of any kind. Former colleagues at SOAS remembered mostly his 'brilliance and wit' and considered that his 'contempt for humbug' was such that he probably steered away from politics.

Jean Overton's Fuller's typing was wobbly at eighty-eight, but her meaning was crystal-clear. She could not tell me what she knew about 'Miss Atkins' until after the publication of her next book on SOE, which was not due out for several months. In it she intended to reveal certain things about Vera which would cause 'great shock'. She apologised for being so tantalising, but I would have to wait.

Eventually we met at her cottage in a quiet Northamptonshire village. 'What did you make of it?' she asked me as soon as I was in the door. Jean's latest book had been published and now she felt free to talk. Before waiting for me to answer she said: 'The oddest thing was not so much what she said but that she said it to me like that. Why? Why did she say it to me? Then?'

'Why do you think?'

'I felt it was dangerous. It worried me deeply,' said Jean as she disappeared into a tiny kitchen to make coffee. I tried to find a seat, but it was hard, because the room was strewn with papers, manuscripts and other debris of a restless mind. All over the walls were marvellous pictures, painted by Jean, of cats. She emerged with coffee and we began to discuss the revelation in her book: that Vera Atkins might have been a Soviet spy.

Jean published this claim in 2002 in *Espionage as a Fine Art*. The main body of the book was a collection of fictional short stories, written by Henri Déricourt, about his life as Gilbert. Déricourt died in Laos in 1962 when the small plane he was flying, carrying gold bars to pay for opium, crashed on landing. Well before his death he had told Jean about his short stories and all these years later she had the opportunity to publish them with a detailed commentary. It was in the somewhat surreal context of her commentary on Déricourt's labyrinthine short stories that Jean made the claim about Vera.

In one story Déricourt wrote about a woman in the Baker Street headquarters of SOE named 'Lucy' who was a German agent. Lucy, said Jean in her commentary, was supposed to be Vera. This in itself was extraordinary: the SOE tangle of conspiracy theories had at last come full circle and had indeed caught up Vera. Here was the traitor Déricourt, whom Vera, above all people, had always mistrusted, turning the tables and now accusing her – in the guise of 'Lucy' – of being a traitor, all in a work of fiction published after his death.

This little paradox, however, was not Jean Overton Fuller's point. In her commentary she went on to explain that 'Lucy' was obviously meant by Déricourt to be Vera, because Déricourt had also referred to 'Lucy' as a lesbian. 'He had told me he believed she was a lesbian,' she wrote. 'Was she? Her exceptionally low-pitched, exceedingly husky voice and something in her face and figure had reminded me of Marlene Dietrich; on the other hand, I had never heard of her having a woman-friend or, for that matter, a man-friend either. She lived behind iron bars, which she had had set across the window of her small flat in Nell Gwynne Mansions, Chelsea. In case of burglars, she said, which made me think she must house secret files.'

However, Jean's commentary continued: 'If Déricourt ever toyed with the idea that Vera Atkins could be a German agent he was on the wrong tack. Her loathing of the Nazis was, I am sure, genuine.

She was after all Jewish, which made that natural.'

Jean went on to write that Vera, far from being a German sympa-thiser, was 'very far to the left'.

When Jean had first encountered Miss Atkins, she told me, she had found her 'not unsympathetic'. She was 'obviously very reserved but I thought that natural for somebody in that job. Just out of curiosity I asked her then what she had done before SOE. She said: "Just this and that."'

Jean then explained how her suspicions of Vera were first pro-voked at a dinner for just the two of them, in Vera's flat, soon after they met. At the dinner Jean told Vera she had traced one of the Germans at Avenue Foch, Ernest Vogt, and hoped to interview him. Jean was cock-a-hoop and thought Vera would be pleased too, but she was not. 'She said I would be spending my money on an expen-sive train journey to Germany and would learn nothing. I thought at the time, Why doesn't she want me to see this man? I thought there must be something she knew he would tell me. I didn't know what it was exactly. I just knew she had something which she feared Vogt might tell me. The atmosphere was thick. I felt something was wrong.'

Adding to Jean's anxiety that evening was Vera's apparel. Jean recalled that when she arrived Vera greeted her in a black lacy evening dress. 'I remember thinking this was very elegant, but it was very transparent and the shoulder straps were showing – there was a lot of lace. What has happened to the lining? I thought. It was quite transparent. I thought it was very strange.'

When did the 'dangerous' conversation take place? I asked.

It was not until after *Madeleine* appeared, in 1952, and it took place in Jean's tiny flat, on the occasion Jean had offered to make something 'tasty to eat'. That evening she had expected Vera to want to talk about the book on Nora. But Vera hardly mentioned it. Instead she raised the case of Klaus Fuchs, who had recently been arrested and charged with spying for the Soviet Union.

Vera told Jean: 'I don't think of him as a traitor. During the war we shared all our secrets with the Russians, and after it he just went on. I don't call that being a traitor.'

Jean was surprised and said nothing. 'This was while we were still eating,' she told me. 'Miss Atkins was facing me across a very narrow table.'

I asked what Vera was wearing that evening. Was she dressed provocatively this time too?

'Oh, no,' said Jean. 'Then she was dressed quite differently. Rather dowdy, in a grey suit, if I remember.'

After the meal Vera and Jean moved to more comfortable chairs and Vera said she had never been to America and would never go because of all the questions that would be asked. '"Are you a communist? Have you known a communist?" You just have to decide whether you want to go to America and if so tell the necessary lies.' She said she didn't think it was worth it.

I pointed out to Jean that it was not so surprising that Vera should have talked like this. After all, it was true that Russia had been an ally for much of the war and Vera herself would have liaised with Russians who worked with SOE and been quite used to sharing secrets with them.

Jean was not persuaded. Vera had spoken of the Soviet Union with great 'earnestness'. Vera told Jean: 'I do believe in democracy – with perhaps a little more freedom than is possible in Russia at present – and I don't see why that should be impossible to achieve.'

It was the way Vera said the word 'achieve' which struck Jean. 'In England we generally thought of ourselves as living in a democracy and the natural word would have been "preserve" rather than "achieve".'

I suggested that Jean's own suspicion had perhaps been influenced by the Cold War paranoia of the times. She said: 'My main thought was: why is a person who is always so discreet about her views and private life, who never offers any information suddenly – and so deliberately – making these indiscreet disclosures?'

'And what did you conclude?'

'I thought she was sounding me out for possible sympathy. If I showed the least interest in what she was saying she was going to recruit me. I was very frightened by it.'

'Did you tell anyone?'

'Who on earth should I tell?'

Then I looked at Jean's face. Even at eighty-eight, the horror she had felt remained written in those alert and darting eyes. 'Can you imagine how this felt?' she said. 'I was all alone. I could tell nobody. I wanted her out of my flat. She smelled of danger.'

*

For a while after meeting Jean I pursued the theory that Vera was a Soviet spy. If true, it could explain her defensiveness, her extraordinarily secretive nature and her sometimes utterly inexplicable loyalty to Buckmaster. She was certainly clever enough to have got away with it. As the SOE man George Millar had said to me: 'She could have been anything she was so bloody clever.'

I met a Soviet defector in the Home Counties and asked him over borscht and smoked salmon to discuss the possibility. Was she the right profile? He said it was not impossible but unlikely. 'On a scale of one to ten,' I asked, did he think she was a Soviet spy? 'Two she was, eight she wasn't,' he said.

I then discovered that there had been countless Soviet agents operating in Britain during and after the Second World War but that, to this day, we don't know who most of them were. Their wireless signals to Moscow – known as the Venona traffic – were partly decoded after the war and were all now on file in the National Archives. I thought of examining the decoded Venona signals myself. I would have enjoyed trying to identify Vera's 'fist'. But I soon had more productive avenues to pursue.

25

BELGIAN LADIES

Early in my research into Vera's life I had a call from a woman named Judith Hiller, a close friend of Vera's and widow of the SOE agent George Hiller, who wanted to know if I knew about 'a Belgian lady'. No, I said. What Belgian lady?

There was a Belgian lady at Vera's funeral, said Judith. I should talk to her. She had helped Vera escape from Belgium early in the war. There had been some sort of incident with the Gestapo on a train. Vera was not in Belgium at the beginning of the war, I said. She was in England. She had arrived here from Romania in 1937 with her mother. She stayed here and joined SOE in 1941. She had never worked for SOE in the field.

Judith Hiller said perhaps I should find the Belgian lady. She had lost the name and address but recalled that she lived in Kensington.

'What did she look like?' I asked.

'She was a little dumpy,' said Judith.

The funeral service for Vera May Atkins took place at the Church of St Thomas the Martyr, Winchelsea, on Monday 3 July 2000. Vera had supported Winchelsea church over the years, although her views on religion were always closely guarded. She once told a friend she had read the whole Bible through from start to finish but when asked if she was religious she simply responded: 'I think I have a reasonable line to God.'

The death notice, which appeared in *The Times*, the *Daily Telegraph* and the *Rye Observer* on 23 June, said the funeral was for close friends and family only. At the service the different groups from different compartments and periods of Vera's life did not mingle. Judith Hiller, however, noticed that the lady in the pew in front of her knew nobody at all. She appeared a little nervous and was carrying a Marks & Spencer plastic bag containing sandwiches.

Outside the church, when the coffin had departed, somebody asked if anyone had left a plastic bag. Judith swiftly reunited the bag with its owner, who was already leaving to catch a train home. Judith offered to give the lady a lift to Winchelsea station and it was in the car that she heard the story. Peter Lee, the former SOE staff officer, was in the car too.

The lady told Judith that she was Belgian (Peter Lee thought she said Dutch) and had met Vera somewhere in Belgium (Peter Lee thought Holland) in the early years of the war, after the German invasion of the Low Countries in May 1940. There was an incident on a train with the Gestapo. Vera needed help and had to go into hiding as it was already dangerous for Jews. The Belgian (or Dutch) lady helped Vera to find a safe house. At that point in the story they arrived at the station.

I found nobody else who remembered a Belgian or Dutch lady at Vera's funeral. Most of Vera's SOE friends said the tale was obviously untrue. If she had really ever operated in the field, the fact would have been hard to conceal after the war, even for Vera. The poor Belgian (or Dutch) woman must have been deluded. SOE attracted fantasists. And what on earth would Vera, a Jew who had already fled Europe, have been doing on the Continent at that time? After the German invasion all ports were closed.

Yet there was something intriguing about the story. Winchelsea was not an easy place to reach for an elderly lady, Belgian or otherwise, and funerals are not events to attend without good reason. The mystery lady had not trumpeted her story of rescuing Vera; on the contrary it was pressed from her by Judith Hiller, who seemed to believe it.

Furthermore, the trail Vera had left of her pre-SOE years in England had always made me uneasy. There were long gaps I had not properly filled in. Was she really playing bridge with divorcees in South Kensington all day, as one acquaintance had recalled?

*

British intelligence was, like the rest of the world, totally unpre-
pared for the German invasion of the Low Countries on 10 May
1940, but sabotage operations – 'Scarlet Pimpernel missions', as
one writer put it – were launched. One venture was a spectacular
mission to Amsterdam to snatch industrial diamonds from under
the Germans' noses. The man involved in the diamond swoop
was Montague 'Monty' Chidson, the MI6 officer who had once
proposed to Vera in Bucharest and by 1940 was attached to Section
D, MI6's special operations department. Any number of Vera's
intelligence contacts from her Bucharest days could have drawn
her into clandestine work on the eve of war, including Leslie
Humphreys himself, the man who eventually recruited her for
SOE. Thomas Kendrick, who later sponsored Vera's naturalisation, was back in England in 1939, having been expelled from
Vienna by the Germans. And another of Vera's four sponsors,
Reginald Pearson, was by 1939 based in Basle, working for yet
another 'secret show', known as the Z network, a deniable spying
organisation within MI6 run by Claude Dansey, then assistant
chief of the secret intelligence service. The Z network had its
headquarters in Switzerland in 1939, with agents operating all
over Europe.

Vera, as noted on her naturalisation files, had made two trips to
Switzerland in early 1939, travelling presumably on her Romanian
passport, as her only British identity paper was an Aliens
Registration Certificate. I had proof that both trips were ostensibly
skiing holidays: a photograph of Vera as Bluebeard during the first
trip and pictures of her in the mountains with Dick Ketton-Cremer
for the second. Nevertheless, it had always seemed surprising that
Vera should have travelled to Switzerland twice on the eve of war.
On her Home Office form she was vague about the purpose of the
second trip and even vaguer about the dates she was away, saying
only that the trip lasted thirty-nine days, which was a long and costly
skiing holiday for a woman short of money.

There was, however, no record on the files of Vera's involvement
in any secret work immediately before she joined SOE, I was told.
But then equally, I was told, even if she had been involved, there
would not be any record. When I wrote to one intelligence source,
asking what Vera might have been up to in Belgium or Holland, I
received a tantalising reply: 'I do not feel the need to unburden

myself about Vera's pre-SOE connections. There are secrets, which don't and shouldn't die, and perhaps this is one of them.'

A few months later I was sitting in a house in Woodditton, in Cambridgeshire, with a Belgian lady named Gilberte Brunsdon-Lenaerts. Born Gilberte Lenaerts in Antwerp, she had married a British military officer named Roger Brunsdon and lived in England from 1945. Gilberte had been to Vera's funeral. I had finally found her through the military attaché at the Belgian embassy. She had been until recently president of the Amicale des Anciens Combattants Anglo-Belges.

Gilberte was only nineteen when she first encountered Vera Rosenberg in Antwerp in the winter of 1940–1, she told me. Her father, Jean Lenaerts, worked in the diamond trade and helped Jewish diamond traders escape at the outbreak of war. Gilberte helped her father by delivering messages. Later she became famous as the 'heroine on a bicycle' who helped rescue British pilots behind enemy lines.

Vera had come into contact with Gilberte's father through a well-known Antwerp Jewish family. 'I went to meet her in the *Schule* near Pelikaan Straat in the diamond district. Others were there too,' said Gilberte, and then she paused. I could see she was uneasy and trying to think back.

'Now I will stop for a second and tell you a few things,' she said. 'What do SOE say about all of this? What does her family say?'

They know nothing of it, I told Gilberte.

'Surely there must be papers. Somebody else must know something,' she said, suddenly worried that she was the only person who knew of this. Then she added: 'Personally I think that this Rosenberg person led a double life,' saying 'double life' with an anxious sort of lilt.

'What was she doing in Belgium?' I asked.

'That I don't know, dear. I had learned never to ask questions. You say: "What is your name and where do you want to go?" and that's it. And, of course, you are always looking out for German infiltrators. That was the time for it, wasn't it – the time to get German infiltrators across?'

'But do you know how Vera had got to you? Where had she come from?'

'She said she had come down from Holland, from Rotterdam, I think, or perhaps Amsterdam. You see, many of them thought parts of Belgium might remain free. And then they got stuck there too. I think her story was just that. That she was caught on 10 May and the Germans, as you know, only took five days to take Holland and in Belgium it took eighteen days. Well, you know, eventually we got our backs to the sea but just the same we did fight for eighteen days. And it is all very well of them to say now we should have fought longer. *Chapeau* to the Belgian Army, I say. *Chapeau*.'

I pointed out that if Vera had 'got stuck' in Holland after 10 May it had taken several months before she arrived in Antwerp to seek help. 'There are certainly gaps in this lady's story, but it was definitely winter when I saw her. It is always better to get people out when it is winter because of the early curfew, so you can move them across the border.'

'Where did she go next, after she left you?'

'I do not know, dear. You see, they went from one place to another. Organised escape lines had not yet come into existence. Later there was the Comet line and the Ligne Libertas.

'And you have to remember that in that mêlée-mêlée you have Jewish people wanting to leave and remember the banks were closed, so you start bartering with diamonds. You have to have people who are willing to take you over the border. It costs a lot of money.'

'Did you take Vera Rosenberg somewhere?'

'You know, my dear, I don't recall. She was one of hundreds that passed through my hands. I don't remember all of them.'

'But you do remember Vera Rosenberg?'

'Yes,' she said, but she could not explain quite why.

'You know, my dear, there is something wrong here. *Il y a quelque chose qui cloche*.'

'When you remember her, in Pelikaan Straat, what do you see in your mind's eye?' I asked.

'I had gone on my bicycle to the *Schule* to investigate who was there. They were all there. They were panicking, but she was not. She came in. She was tall. She seemed in charge. She was most insistent – arrogant – no, there is a better English word for it. She was haughty. You know. And at that point the impression it made on me was: My God! You know. In charge! She did the talking. She gave the impression she was important and that she knew important people in England. Although she was tall she had flat feet. Now why do I remember that? She had that Jewish walk. I remember that. She was wearing a hat and coat. She said: "I must get back. Can you help?"'

'Was she with the rest of the group?'

'She was with a man. The man was not English. They spoke German together. They clung together in a way. I am sure there was a man,' said Gilberte, suddenly sounding unsure.

'What nationality did you think she was?'

'I think she spoke to me in French but I thought she was Dutch because she had come from Holland.'

Gilberte paused again to think and twist her rings.

'It has always worried me – no, bothered me, that is the word. Why did I never trust that woman? We had to be extremely careful who we helped.' And then she said: 'You know, my dear, my feeling is we are dealing with a double agent here.'

'You mean a German double agent?'

Over recent weeks I had been told first that Vera worked for the CIA, then that she was a Soviet spy and now somebody was seriously suggesting she was a German agent. My mind returned to Déricourt's bizarre depiction of Vera as 'Lucy', the German agent in Baker Street.

'You see, it was the time, as I say, wasn't it – to get them to England? And when you have been asked to help somebody like that you think it might be a German agent, especially if they are not from Belgium but *de passage*.'

I said the suggestion seemed, on the face of it, preposterous, given all I knew about Vera. For a start, why would she have gone to look for all the missing agents if she was a German spy?

'To make sure they were dead, perhaps. To make sure that those who might have learned something about her were dead. Or to look in the German papers and see what they knew.'

I looked hard at Gilberte, with her thick, jet-black hair, darting eyes and pale complexion. She had seemed quite lucid and had been credible in most respects. And yet, sitting in her tiny black velvet slippers, her black dress drawn high up to her neck, she worried me. The house was neat and dotted with delicate porcelain ornaments. Her suggestion that Vera was a German agent made me doubt some of her story. Was it really my Vera that she met, or somebody else?

I wanted to be absolutely sure too that she had been at Vera's funeral and not somebody else's. Had she kept the order of service? I asked. She had not. Did she recall somebody giving her a lift to the station? 'No, my dear. I went by car. I almost always had a driver who drove me to these things.'

If she had gone to Winchelsea by car, obviously she would not have needed a lift to the station and could not have been Judith Hiller's 'Belgian lady'. And yet she insisted she was there. How had she heard about the funeral?

'As secretary of the Amicale I was often called upon to go to these things,' she said. 'And after all, you see, I had met Vera Rosenberg again after the war. So I wanted to go and pay my respects.'

'How did you meet her after the war?' I asked, intrigued again.

'She called me on the telephone. I was living in London by then. She must have got my number through the embassy or the diamond club. I think she said she had gone to some trouble to find me. She said we could meet for a chat. 'She suggested Fullers in Regent Street. It was a little tea-house on the corner opposite a bank. It was quite small and discreet. And many years later she called again. That time we met in Fortnum & Mason.' Gilberte had just named two of Vera's favourite meeting places.

'Why had she wanted to meet you?'

'I never knew. Both times I went away wondering what it had all been about. But now I think she was meeting me to sound me out – to see if I ever talked, or said something indiscreet. Of course I hadn't. And she was relieved.'

I asked Gilberte to tell me more about the meetings, to see if she could describe Vera.

The first meeting must have been in the late months of 1946, said Gilberte, who remembered telling Vera she would be noticeably pregnant. Her son was born in January 1947.

'How would you recognise her?'

'She said she would wear a flower. And she came wearing a flower. She was quite different from how I remembered her – very English, in a twin set and pearls. She was more English than the English, really. She was very careful how she spoke. She was artificial in her speech, with her posh accent, you know. You know what I mean, dear, she had that particular way of enunciating.'

'What did you talk about?'

'I didn't ask questions. I said only, "Did you get back safely?" She said yes. She had lost touch with the man. She told me she was doing research, she had been in Germany. I didn't ask what research. She mentioned her mother, I think. Her mother was elderly and had "not settled" well. That was the expression she used: "not settled". They were living in a small flat in Chelsea, she said.

'I asked her if she had settled down now in England – you know, married or anything – but she did not reply. She said something about a brother in America – but that might have been the second time.'

I told Gilberte that Vera's brother, Guy, was in America in the 1960s, then asked: 'Did you talk about Antwerp at all?'

'She asked me if I was still in touch with my old friends, that sort of thing. But just in general.' Gilberte stopped to consider. 'You know, dear, she was always cagey.'

I had heard the word 'cagey' to describe Vera probably more than any other.

'That is the word I would use about her – cagey. *La vie cachée*. We are talking about a woman with a double life.'

I wondered why Vera had called her, just at that time in 1946. Gilberte said she too had always wondered about that. 'I think she might have seen this,' she said, then felt around in an envelope and pulled out a cutting from the *Evening Standard* which showed a picture of Gilberte as a young girl and told the story of how she had helped British pilots. Gilberte had just been awarded the Belgian Croix de Guerre. The story appeared in September 1946. 'I think she saw that and saw I was in England and thought she must get to me to see what I was saying, what I was like, if I knew anything.'

I asked how the second meeting came about.

'It was many, many years later – in the sixties or seventies. Perhaps something was happening which made her worried. And she would have seen my name with the Amicale perhaps, laying wreaths and so on.'

This time they arranged to meet by the Jermyn Street entrance to Fortnum & Mason, so they could not miss each other.

'What did you talk about this time?'

'Oh, again, this and that. I think she was living near Harrods by then. She asked me again if I was still in touch. I said my father had died. Perhaps that was what she had wanted to know. Perhaps she wanted to know something from my father, or if he was still alive. I didn't hear from her again.'

'Did you ever call her?'

'No, dear. I didn't ask for her number.'

Then I got out my photographs to see whether Gilberte recognised Vera.

She looked at one or two of Vera in later life, and nodded. And then she looked at others. I had brought a variety of photographs: Vera in France, Vera in uniform in Germany, at memorials in England, on her eightieth birthday.

'You see how she is a chameleon,' said Gilberte, holding up the picture of Vera at the opening of *Carve Her Name with Pride*. 'In this she is "*Voilà*", you know, "Here I am."' And then she held up a picture of Vera with a stiff perm in a tweed suit. 'This was more how she was when I saw her the second time in London.'

Gilberte put the pictures down, looking more anxious than ever. The more she was sure that my Vera was also her Vera, the more she became agitated. 'You know, my dear,' she said plaintively, 'this woman had a hidden life, of that I am now sure. I have been saying it a lot, I know, but I have a feeling in the back of my neck. It is a silly thing. But it is the silly things, you see. How can I call it? – "fishy". I do not believe my mind has gone. I don't think I would have made a mistake. At my age you are careful what you say. *Mais, il y a quelque chose qui cloche dans la vie de cette dame.* It is an instinct, you know. I feel it. And she was very shrewd. You will never find out because she has destroyed everything. Do you have to write this book? Is it really necessary?'

Soon after seeing Gilberte, I called Judith Hiller to say I had found her Belgian lady – at least, I thought I might have found her.

Delighted, Judith asked what I had learned. I said she was charming and had told a fascinating story. 'What was the name of her road in Kensington?' asked Judith. I said she lived in Cambridgeshire but had recently moved from London. She used to live in St John's Wood. I said I thought Judith might have confused the two. 'I never confuse anything with Kensington,' came the reply. 'Did she recall my taking her to the station?'

'No,' I said, 'she seemed to think she came by car.' I realised that

I had found a Belgian lady but the wrong one. Either Gilberte had made her story up, or there was a second mystery Belgian lady at Vera's funeral who had also helped her 'escape' and who I would also now have to try to find.

I started my enquiries again. This time I began by asking Vera's family and friends to rack their brains for any mention of Antwerp, or Belgium or Holland in any conversation with Vera. Then I went back to Winchelsea, thinking the clue to finding the second Belgian (or Dutch) lady might still lie at the funeral scene. Canon Basil O'Farrell, who conducted the service, had checked his records and there was no list of mourners and no plate for donations either. If mourners wished to make a donation they could give money to Vera's favourite charity, the Sue Ryder Foundation, and they were requested to do so through the funeral directors.

Two years later, it seemed unlikely that the funeral directors would still have the list of donors, but I called Ellis Bros., in Rye, just in case. A helpful woman said she would get out the file and within a moment she had found the list of donors. She read them out for me. There was a woman on the list who lived in Kensington, West London. Hers was a name I had never heard before.

When I knocked on the door of the woman's Kensington home, a man came to the door in a grey tweed jacket with a poppy pinned to a lapel. Yes, he was the husband of the person I was looking for and, yes, she had been to Vera Atkins's funeral. His wife was Dutch. But she wasn't in.

'And I should just warn you of something,' he said. 'My wife's memory is sometimes confused especially when it concerns the war. You might learn something from her, but some of what she will tell you will be a jumble.'

But her memory had become confused only in recent years, he added. She had known Vera Atkins well before that.

So they were definitely old acquaintances – that was not a confusion?

'No, that was not a confusion,' he said. He himself remembered going to dinner with his wife at Vera's flat sometime in the 1950s. 'Rutland Gate, wasn't it?' he asked. She had made quite an impression, and he remembered in particular how adept she was at cooking in a tiny kitchen while entertaining her guests at the same time.

'Was she a lesbian?' he asked. 'She didn't marry, did she?'

I told him I wanted to ask his wife about the story she had told to Judith Hiller: about helping Vera escape from Holland during the war. He said he himself had been a naval officer and had never been involved in anything clandestine. But his wife had certainly been in Holland during the war.

'So might it be true?' I said.

'Well, this is my dilemma,' he sighed. 'Some of the things she says turn out to be true. I could give you lots of examples of where she has been right. There are lots of grey areas. You will have to judge for yourself. At least she keeps a good house, so I can't complain.'

A few days later I returned to Kensington for my meeting with the second mystery 'Belgian lady' who had been at Vera's funeral, and whom I now knew to be Dutch. An elderly woman came to the door with very light-grey hair folded in a turnip-shaped bun on top of her head. She was called Beatrice, and she was carefully dressed in a tweed pleated skirt, brown suede pumps and a maroon cardigan. She offered coffee. She appeared very alert and the room was immaculate, though rather dark. I explained why I had come. She seemed willing to help and began talking.

She told me she was born in The Hague and grew up in Holland. She met Vera Atkins in Amsterdam early in the war, when she was working in Amsterdam as a social worker, looking after the children of prostitutes. The story so far was clear. How did she come into contact with Vera?

Beatrice said she had had contacts with a man in the Amsterdam National Bank. The man was Vera's brother, and he said his sister was about to be deported and needed help. Beatrice now became hard to follow. Neither of Vera's brothers ever worked at the Amsterdam National Bank. Yet Beatrice talked a lot about 'the man at the bank' in sentences that did not seem to join up in sequence. There was a lot of garbled matter. She seemed to be saying that she had been told to go and find Vera Atkins. It would be hard to identify her. So she was told to go to the red-light district, where she would have to recognise her. She would be under cover and posing as a prostitute.

What exactly did Beatrice mean? Her answer was hard to follow but I think she was telling me that she had been told Vera Atkins would be sitting in the window, posing as a prostitute, in one of the brothels in the red-light district. That was where Beatrice had been told to go and find her. There would be a sign, she said.

I tried not to give up. Beatrice had moved on now and was talking about being on a train. All the time I tried to pick out names, places, facts that might be relevant and discard the jumble around them. It was as if Beatrice's thoughts had been through a tumble-dryer and everything had got tangled up.

Among the web of sentences was talk of Princess Alexandra and President Trudeau; Maurice Buckmaster seemed to be tangled in there too. Then suddenly I caught a flash of Judith Hiller's account and tried to hold on to it. There was a crowd of people who were being deported to some sort of camp for Jews at a village near Apeldoorn. Beatrice went to the station in Amsterdam and got on a train with these people and managed to persuade the Germans on the train that she lived near the village and that Vera lived there too, so they both managed to get away from the others and Beatrice took Vera to a family of Jehovah's Witnesses who also lived in the village near Apeldoorn. The family sheltered Jews. She said Vera then hid in a barn and later Vera showed her a photograph of herself working in the hay barn at the farm in the village.

'Trudeau would know everything,' she said and then the thoughts got tangled again. Audrey Hepburn was in the barn too.

'Whose barn was it?' I asked.

It was a barn owned by Beatrice's family. Her family lived in the village, she said, and showed me a photograph of the barn with its name on it. 'It was a place where a lot people hid,' she said. Vera had never talked about this, I told her.

Beatrice then said: 'Ah, but there were two Veras. I know now that there were two Veras. The other one was a proper English lady.' And now she was wondering if 'our Vera' was perhaps really 'a tart'.

'Why?' I asked.

'Because of the way she used to walk up and down Knightsbridge.'

'How do you know she did that?'

'I used to see her.' Then Beatrice said that Vera was a 'very shrewd woman'.

I asked if she saw Vera again after the war, and she said she did. She first bumped into her at Sloane Square tube station and then saw her a lot in the 1950s, but less in recent years.

'You must have felt close to her to go to the funeral,' I said.

'We had shared experiences. But there were two Veras. I know that now. I realised that ten minutes ago. Sometimes there were three.' The she said: 'It's a bit jumpy for you, isn't it? It's hard for you to follow,' as if she were reading my mind.

Beatrice got a map out and started finding places on it, as if to provide reassurance that she was not mad. She pointed out the village near Apeldoorn. Then she looked in the Dutch telephone directory and found the name of the family of Jehovah's Witnesses and gave me the telephone number, suggesting I call them. I said I would.

Now, as I got up to leave, Beatrice was talking about how people get too concerned with the marmalade and the details of life. Her husband talked so much about the marmalade.

However confused Beatrice's story had been, it was not inconsistent with Gilberte's story. Gilberte had told me that when she met Vera in Antwerp she had 'come down from Holland' – from Amsterdam or Rotterdam, she thought. Both women talked of Vera being with a man, perhaps a brother. The man was older than Vera.

It was frustrating that neither story had given any answer to the most important question: why was Vera in Holland or Belgium at that time? But in this Gilberte and Beatrice were also quite consistent: neither had asked and neither had ever been told.

The fact that Vera approached Gilberte through the diamond industry suggested that diamonds might have been a possibility. Annie Samuelli, Vera's friend from Romania, considered it quite likely that the Rosenbergs would have put their money into diamonds before the war. Many Jewish families chose to do this, and Vera's South African family had once owned a diamond mine. Perhaps Vera suddenly needed a lot of cash, but for what reason, I did not yet know.

26

HEROINE

Although hard information about Vera was difficult to come by, anecdotes about her were plentiful, and many were about money. Generous bequests from her South African grandfather, Henry Atkins, who died in 1937, had ensured she always had private means, but she watched her money grow in the bank or invested it on the Stock Exchange, rather than spent it. 'She would take yesterday's cold dinner with her on the train up to London rather than pay for a sandwich,' said Christine, her cleaner.

In the 1960s, with her elder brother Ralph, Vera went into business, importing 'Tuppit' teapots. The Tuppit had an inbuilt strainer to stop tea leaves floating around, but the idea did not take off.

Vera also enjoyed a flutter – on the National Lottery, for example. A neighbour related how she had once been woken at midnight by an anxious-sounding Vera demanding a lift. Expecting an emergency, she found instead that Vera wanted a ride to a late-night store. She had forgotten to buy a Lottery ticket.

Because Vera didn't like to spend her money, it was sometimes said that she was mean. 'But I never had to ask for a rise,' Christine told me. And I heard many stories of her generosity. Her niece Zenna remembered the most interesting anecdote about Vera and money. Vera had once had to take a large sum of money on a long and dangerous journey, Zenna told me.

When was that? I asked.

She wasn't sure at first. It was a story she heard her father, Guy, and Vera tell many times when she was a child. It came up when the two grown-ups were discussing the meanness of their mother, Hilda. They would reminisce a while and then Vera would always say: 'Well, Mother wasn't mean on that occasion. Oh, no!' A story was then told about how early in the war a relative was in danger of being deported to a concentration camp. So, with Vera's help, Hilda got together money to help the relative. Vera then had to travel somewhere, either to collect or deliver the money. Zenna could recall no more. But she said it must have happened just after her father was posted to Africa.

'Why then?' I asked, and she recalled another anecdote.

There was a lot of one-upmanship between Guy and Vera, said Zenna, and in this same conversation the siblings would talk about how Vera had undertaken the dangerous journey and not Guy. (Ralph was *en poste* in Istanbul at the time.) Then Guy would defend himself by saying how he couldn't have helped because by then he was serving with the East Africa Rifles. When did he go out to Africa? Zenna could not be precise, but her father's papers suggested it was some time in 1940. I wondered if this mystery journey was linked to Vera's appearance in the Low Countries. But who was the relative who needed help?

While most of Vera's German relatives had fled to Chile, Palestine or the US, several Rosenberg cousins, sons and daughters of Max's siblings, were still on the Continent at the outbreak of war. The Cologne cousins, Klaus and Gert, had stayed in Germany, but little was known of them. The rumour in the family was that Gert joined the Luftwaffe and became one of Goering's pet pilots. He was killed in an air raid in 1943. His brother, Klaus, somehow survived the war in Germany, but was impossible to trace.

Vera's cousin Aenne, daughter of her Aunt Bertha, had stayed on in Berlin. She was an artist and married another, Manfred Pahl, and they had a daughter named Beate, who was already eighteen when war broke out. At first Aenne believed she would not be persecuted by the Nazis, because her husband was not a Jew. But by 1940 the family were in great peril and were forced into hiding in Berlin. Beate was safely hidden. Aenne, however, was eventually arrested, although, astonishingly, she was not sent to a concentration camp. Instead she was imprisoned in a jail for favoured Jews in Wedding, in north Berlin. She was released after the war, traumatised but, miraculously, alive. Beate (now Beate Orasche) never learned how it was that her mother had been spared, although there was talk that a friend with influence may have intervened to save her life. This talk did not involve Vera, as far as Beate knew.

Vera's strongest family ties had always been with the Romanian branch of the Rosenbergs. At the outbreak of war her uncles Arthur and Siegfried, and Arthur's sons Fritz, George and Hans, were still living in Vallea Uzului. Even though the family company in Germany had by now been Aryanised – in other words, forcibly taken over by non-Jews – life in Vallea Uzului was still largely insulated from the threat of fascism. As Uncle Siegfried wrote in his memoir: 'Until 1940 all went quite well.' During that year, however, the Rosenbergs' confidence began to shatter.

By mid-1940 Romania was being dismembered and the Rosenbergs of Vallea Uzului faced the prospect of losing their homes and, later, of deportation to Auschwitz, along with hundreds of thousands of other Romanian and Hungarian Jews. The full extent of the threat was brought home when Fritz Rosenberg, Vera's cousin, who had by then taken over the family business in Vallea Uzului, was imprisoned in Hungary.

Fritz Rosenberg, I knew, had emigrated after the war to Canada and died there in 1998, and I had been told that he left many papers. The papers were in the shed, in Rawdon, Quebec, where Uncle Siegfried's memoir had come from. By the time I was able to travel to Canada to find out more it was nearly winter again.

Karina Rosenberg, an engaging fair-haired woman in her mid-fifties, picked me up from Montreal and as we drove to Rawdon, about 100 kilometres to the north, she talked eagerly about her Rosenberg roots. Karina was the daughter of Fritz and Karen Rosenberg. Fritz had married Karen when she worked as the housekeeper at Vallea Uzului. Born Gehlsen, Karen was an educated German girl from a Lutheran family and much more down-to-earth than any Rosenberg, said Karina. Unlike a Rosenberg, Karen liked to talk, so everything Karina learned about the family came from her mother. 'My mother thought the Rosenbergs were very snooty,' she said. 'She thought they had all been raised in a very rarefied atmosphere.'

Karina said that Fritz's father, Arthur – one of Vera's three uncles – had not approved of Fritz marrying her mother. 'The maids were good enough for the Rosenberg men whenever they wanted, but it was not good enough to marry the housekeeper,' she told me. 'And they were always conflicted about who they really were.' They were always changing their name, their religion or their nationality. But the one Rosenberg that Karina's parents, Karen and Fritz, had always admired was Vera. Nothing was ever said against Vera. She was somehow different. 'In the family, she was the one we always looked up to. She had an almost mythical status for my parents.' I asked Karina why, but she didn't know.

We arrived at Rawdon, a small, white-boarded town, and headed on through forests towards a great white lake, and there, right on the water's edge, was Karina's house. A quiet and wooded place, it could almost have been in the Carpathian foothills. We pulled up at the house and I was shown to a room that overlooked the lake and was piled high with boxes. Fritz's papers had by now been rescued from the shed.

Unlike his cousin Vera, Fritz had tried to open up his past in later life and re-examine it. Most of the papers in the boxes were used in Fritz's fruitless lawsuits seeking compensation from the German, Hungarian, Romanian and Swiss governments. To support his cases he had gathered everything he could find: photographs, certificates, letters in German, Hungarian, Romanian and English. In a long statement to the embassy of the Republic of Hungary 'regarding Hungarian Restitution Laws for Losses 1939–1949', Fritz set out the family story, as Siegfried had, but in more detail, asserting again and again the family's birthright as Germans. He described how he and his twin brothers had been brought up in Germany and educated in Munich, but forced to abandon their studies in 1933 'for obvious reasons'. There were numerous photographs of the three boys – Fritz small and dark and the twins tall and much fairer, good-looking, in lederhosen, in bathing suits, in suits and ties. It was hard to tell them apart.

From Fritz's papers it seemed that until 1938 all was still going well in Vallea Uzului, but early that year there were signs that he was concerned about the future. Karen had become pregnant. A civil marriage certificate dated 27 April 1938 and a birth certificate for Peter Rosenberg dated two days later were both issued in Eastbourne, suggesting that Fritz wished to cement ties with England by marrying there and ensuring his son was British-born. Had he thought to stay in England as a refugee, this would have been the time to do so. 'Fritz arrived in London,' wrote Hilda in her diary. But Fritz had soon taken his new family back to Romania, hoping no doubt that war could still be avoided.

From now on the files showed that Fritz was busy obtaining numerous statements testifying to his length of residence in Vallea Uzului, his good character and his Catholic credentials. But, a year later, on 23 May 1939, Fritz's German passport was stamped with a large red 'J'. On 10 May 1940 the Germans invaded the Low Countries and then surged into France. From now on, even if Fritz had wanted to reach England, he was well and truly cut off.

Closer to home, the carve-up of Romania was beginning: Germany and Italy were about to force it to hand over north Transylvania to Hungary. The deal which cemented the transfer, known as the Ribbentrop–Ciano agreement or the Vienna Diktat, was signed on 30 August 1940. From that date the province of Cuic, in which Vallea Uzului was situated, would be under Hungarian – and therefore German – control. For Jews living in these territories the future could only bring terror. Fritz put it simply: 'The situation changed with the signing of the Ribbentrop–Ciano agreement.'

Immediately the pact was signed Hungarian police were sent to Vallea Uzului to requisition the company. The Rosenbergs tried to convince themselves that the Hungarian takeover was only a temporary setback. But soon the Hungarian police were telling them they could not tolerate foreigners, let alone Jews. The Rosenbergs protested that they were German nationals, but the Hungarians said that made it worse. Fritz's father and uncle said they had won the Iron Cross in the First World War. 'For a while they listened but not for long,' wrote Fritz.

Siegfried and Arthur went to Budapest to seek some sort of protection for the family and the company, while Fritz stayed in Vallea Uzului with Karen and the new baby, Peter. Fritz still had faith that the German embassy in Budapest would set things right for them. 'Our family was of German nationality, and enjoyed the best reputation in European forestry and lumber circles.' And he added that 'friends in Berlin' now tried to intervene to 'sort things out'.

But just as the Rosenbergs' company in Cologne had been Aryanised, so the company in Romania was now 'Hungarianised'. The Compania de Lemne became Uzvoglye Faipar RT. As a 'foreigner' Fritz was now refused permission to work in his own timber business and was told to pack up and leave. Fritz and Karen prepared inventories so that there could be no mistakes when the family returned to reclaim their possessions. Fritz must have believed that he might one day return to the Valley of the Uz because he had even gone to the trouble of getting receipts for his hunting rifles. 'Confiscated, in other words stolen,' he had written on the receipt.

The inventories from Vallea Uzului were here in these boxes. Every piece of machinery from the timber plant had been described and counted. Every book in the house had been named and entered. And every piece of linen had been folded, packed and carefully checked and double-checked. Carrying little more than a few clothes and their precious inventories, Fritz, Karen and baby Peter left for Hungary on 23 September 1941. When the train they were travelling in stopped at the Transylvanian town of Marosvasarhely, Fritz was immediately arrested and locked up in prison.

In Budapest, meanwhile, Fritz's father, Arthur Rosenberg, and his Uncle Siegfried were still frantically seeing German and Hungarian 'contacts' to find somebody reliable to 'take charge of the business for a few years'. More urgently now, they were pleading with anyone they could for Fritz to be freed from jail.

Here in this file I now found evidence that the family had been in direct contact during these terrifying months with their old friend – the highest German contact they could have – Count Friedrich Werner von der Schulenburg, whom they had known as Germany's ambassador in Bucharest in the early 1930s and who had to move on to be ambassador in Moscow. How they reached Schulenburg, now back in Berlin after the German assault on the Soviet Union, was not clear. But he was swift to intervene. He had not forgotten his former friends and hosts from Vallea Uzului and wrote in person to the German embassy in Budapest with the all-important instruction: '*Die Rosenbergs sind als Deutsche zu betrachten*' ('The Rosenbergs are to be regarded as Germans'). However, I had not yet found what I was really hunting for: evidence that Vera had somehow also played a role.

I asked Karina and her brother Peter if they had ever heard about Vera's intervention to help their father. They had heard nothing definite, but Karina, for one, had always wondered if Vera had helped. Perhaps, if she had, it would explain why she was always spoken of in such hallowed terms.

Had she ever been here to visit? I asked. They said she hadn't, which seemed strange given that Vera did visit friends and other relatives in Canada from time to time. But the family here had been shown all the photographs of Vera and they had read every book which mentioned her name.

'So you never met Vera?' I asked Karina.

Yes, she had, she replied. She had visited London once as a teenager during a tour of Europe and Vera had invited her to her flat at Rutland Gate. Karina found Vera distant but impressive. 'She told me very little. But she had such a presence. And, you know, she really surprised me one day with something she said. We were having dinner – just the two of us – and afterwards she sat down next to me and said: "Karina, did your mother ever tell you what a brave woman she was during the war?"' Karina had been taken aback and said, no, she hadn't. Vera then said something very general about how brave Karen had been, before making clear that she wanted to say nothing further.

When Karina got home to Canada, however, she asked her mother about the story and learned a little more. She learned that her father had been in terrible danger when the Hungarians took over, because he was a Jew. Karen had therefore gone to the husband of a German friend of hers, a lawyer in Berlin named Hans Fillie, and asked him to help secure a new passport for Fritz. Fillie had got the passport and the couple had managed to escape to Istanbul. In Istanbul they were tracked down by German secret agents and Karen was blackmailed into agreeing to provide information to the Germans. Karina explained: 'She said these German "bloodhounds" had come to her and talked about the accidents that could happen to her family back in Germany and to her baby boy. She went to the British and told them everything about it and the British got my parents and Peter out of Istanbul to Palestine. On the way my mother was debriefed by the British in Cairo.'

The story was intriguing. But what interested me most was why Vera had so very deliberately raised this episode with eighteen-year-old Karina all these years later. It seemed most unlike her to have risked opening up a chapter from the past which could so easily have been left closed. Karina had also clearly been left a little uneasy by Vera's question. And, to me, she suddenly expressed the view more confidently than before that Vera had indeed had some role in helping Fritz. Perhaps it was something her father had said to her. Or perhaps there was some mention of it in the files. I returned to check.

As I continued to read through Fritz's papers I looked out carefully for any trace of this story. At first it seemed that Schulenburg's intervention in 1941 might have eased Fritz's plight as records showed he was released from prison in October 1941. But within weeks Uncle Siegfried had been arrested at the Romanian–Hungarian border and after talking his way out of trouble went into hiding in Romania. Arthur, Fritz's father, whose health was failing badly, was by now back in Bucharest, hiding in a Catholic seminary.

Fritz and Karen remained in hiding in Budapest 'to avoid deportation to an extermination camp'. Fritz wrote: 'My wife and I had to be extremely careful not to be arrested in the streets and we had to find new sleeping quarters on every second day. I need not mention the cost.'

Then he added, almost as an aside: 'During this time I was supported by my uncle Siegfried and my English cousin Vera Atkins.' I hunted through the papers to find any more mention of 'my English cousin Vera Atkins'. How had she helped him? She was thousands of miles away in London, on the other side of Nazi-occupied Europe.

In the early hours of the morning I was still opening files. Fritz had rehearsed the story of his flight from Romania many times in statements for various legal actions. Each statement contained slightly different details and I hoped still to find something more about Vera's 'support'. I did not. Instead I stumbled on the answer to a quite different question.

Opening yet another brown folder – this one contained statements in support of Fritz's Swiss claims – I found a newspaper cutting clipped to a single piece of paper.

It was from the *New York Times* of 1999 and was about new evidence that the United States government had ignored warnings of euthanasia killings in mental asylums in Germany and Austria at the start of the war. 'In the fall of 1940 death notices started appearing in suspicious numbers and the families who placed them used strikingly similar phrases about the fates of their loved ones who were in mental asylums,' said the piece. 'The notices would all say something like: "we received the unbelievable news of the sudden death of . . . or we heard the incredible story of the unexpected death of . . ."' The accumulation of thousands of these notices was noticed by US officials in Germany but ignored.

The paper attached to the cutting was an affidavit, which had been translated:

'I the undersigned Fritz Rosenberg declare that my brother George and myself are the only surviving children and heirs of my deceased parents Arthur and Nina Rosenberg. My second brother Hans (the second of three children) having been liquidated in 1941 whilst a patient in the Sanatorium am Steinhof near Vienna, Austria.'

I looked further in the file for any more information about Hans's death. When did the family learn of it? As Fritz himself faced the possibility of deportation to a concentration camp, did he have any idea about what had become of Hans? Could Vera conceivably have heard of it? But Fritz made no further mention of his brother's death. Only because Swiss lawyers wanted proof of who the rightful claimants in the family might be, should any compensation be agreed, was Fritz forced to refer in writing to the gassing of Hans, or, as he put it, to his brother's 'having been liquidated'.

By now I had been reading so long that a watery pink dawn was beginning to break across the frozen lake. I copied the document word for word for fear that this pathetic little piece of paper might somehow get lost; it was the only evidence of what had happened to the good-looking boy (if it was not his identical twin) sitting on a horse, two down from Vera in the photo of the Whitsun picnic in Vallea Uzului in 1932. Hans, the slightly taller one, was the one who, Annie Samuelli first told me, had had a nervous breakdown. He was also the boy with the broad smile, the boy Uncle Siegfried put his arm around. Hans Rosenberg was gassed by Hitler and his family had never spoken about him again.

The next morning I took up Fritz's story. On 25 November 1941 Fritz and Karen's position became even more perilous when a law was passed under which German Jews outside their country would lose their German nationality forthwith without regard to their religion. From now on Fritz's German passport was useless except as proof that he was stateless and a Jew.

He wrote: 'Due to the intervention of a friend in Berlin, new German passports were issued in Budapest with the condition that we leave at once for Istanbul.' This 'intervention' appeared to be a reference to the episode described to me by Karina the previous day. She said that one of her mother's oldest friends, Liselotte, had been married to a German lawyer, Hans Fillie, who had offered to help Fritz get a new passport. On 3 September 1942 Fritz miraculously received his new passport.

And here, in another box, were Fritz's old and new passports. On the front of each were the words '*Deutsche Reich Reisepass*'. The first passport, Reisepass no. 418, was issued on 23 April 1939 and, on 23 May 1939, had a large red 'J' stamped on it. The bearer was stated to be a Fritz Rosenberg, a businessman, born in Galatz on 16 November 1911. A stamp inside said Fritz went to Budapest in May 1941 with permission to stay until 22 May 1942.

The second passport was issued in Budapest and dated 2 September 1942. In this one, the bearer, Fritz Rosenberg, was born in Munich. The stamps showed that in September 1942 he left Budapest and travelled through Bulgaria, Yugoslavia and over the Turkish border and on to his destination, Istanbul.

That hair-raising journey from Budapest to Istanbul, through German-occupied Bulgaria and Yugoslavia, had left an impression on Peter Rosenberg though at the time he was only four years of age. Peter told me that even today he remembered his parents' fear each time they stopped at a station. And later in life his parents talked of how Fritz had been hauled up by a German train patrol and accused of being a Jew and nearly ejected from the train there and then. 'Only when they made him drop his pants did they let him go,' said Karina. 'Because my father was baptised a Catholic he was never circumcised. Otherwise none of us would be here today.'

Fritz claimed that when he reached Istanbul in November 1942 he 'worked for the intelligence section of the British embassy', though he did not say in what capacity.

He also wrote that his persecution by the Germans did not stop when he left Budapest. On arriving in Istanbul he was tracked down by German agents and harassed. He was also told that Karen's friend Hans Fillie had been sent to the Eastern Front as a punishment for helping the family escape. Fritz and Karen were then advised by the British embassy to leave for the safety of Palestine, which they did on 6 June 1943, finally emigrating to Canada in 1948.

Before packing the files back in the boxes I spent some time reading letters sent to Fritz by relatives and friends in the immediate post-war years. These were always in a guarded code as the writers did not always know who knew what, about what had happened or what others in the family might have gone through in the war. In the case of senders still in Romania, the letters showed the full force of the post-war communist rule was taking effect. A relative, Daisy Mendl, writing to Fritz from London in 1951, had received a letter from another relative, Nora, in Bucharest, which had come via Italy and in which Nora asked people to write to her on postcards and not mention names or addresses. 'It is all terribly sinister and distressing,' said Daisy.

Fritz had evidently spent time in England, utterly destitute, before emigrating to Canada. There were packets of kind letters here from friends and family in England offering him blankets, cutlery, children's clothes and advice. Writing to Fritz at this time, Vera's brother Ralph asked: 'Have you thought of changing your name, old boy? I only mention it as it does complete the assimilation and will help your children no end.' But there were no kind letters from Vera, or if there had been they had disappeared. In fact there was no further mention of Vera in any of Fritz's papers until the early 1990s, when, sparked by an approach from Fritz, a correspondence started between the elderly cousins, but even now Vera's letters to Fritz were only scraps – dry missives with no personal touch at all.

One of the newsiest letters was among the last, written in 1997: 'I have had a strenuous year selling Northden [Vera's first Winchelsea house] landing in hospital twice, making two short visits to France, receiving a CBE investiture at Buckingham Palace and now Christmas!'

I packed some of the documents I had not had time to read properly into a suitcase to bring back to England. Among the items I had not read were pocket diaries kept by Karen between 1932 and 1951. The writing was in old German Sütterlin script, which could hardly be read, even by her daughter. When I opened the years 1940–3 to see if I could make anything out, several four-leafed clovers pressed inside fell out.

I also brought back with me an old wallet belonging to Karen stuffed with tickets and cards dating back to the war, as well as lists with words I could just make out, like '*Schokolade*' and '*Kartoffeln*'. Curiously, it appeared that Karen had kept dozens of very old shopping lists.

On my return I asked the SOE adviser whether there was any trace of Karen or Fritz Rosenberg's contacts with British intelligence, as mentioned in Fritz's files. There was none, I was told, but the name Karen Rosenberg had come up in a different context. A German intelligence officer, who was interrogated by the British in 1944, had named Karen Rosenberg as one of his contacts. The German was named Willi Goetz (no relation to Dr Goetz of Avenue Foch) and said Karen had worked for him in Budapest and Istanbul.

From the summary given to me on the phone it seemed that Willi Goetz was telling the same story that I had read about in Fritz's files, but from a very different angle and with one or two significant differences.

A few days later a document came through my letterbox which stated: 'SIME (Security Intelligence Middle East) Report (no. 1, 21 November 1944). Interrogation of Dr Willy [*sic*] Goetz, an agent/employee of Abwehr Department I/T or IH/T (Espionage against foreign countries – Military Technical Intelligence).'

The three pages of typescript provided a snapshot of the lives of German spies operating in and around Nazi-occupied Europe during the war. Willi Goetz was a German radio operator, based in the Balkans, Turkey and Middle East. At some point in 1944 he came over to the British side for a 'chat' and was subsequently arrested, interned and interrogated.

He told a story to his interrogators of how he and his Abwehr colleagues moved between capitals – Istanbul, Budapest, Sofia and Berlin – under false names and using false cover companies, meeting informants in hotel lobbies and sending scraps of secret information about enemy movements on postcards in letter codes.

Asked who he had worked for, Goetz named several senior Abwehr officers, including a certain Dr Hans Fillie. Fillie, he said, was a barrister from Berlin who worked for the Abwehr Department I/T: espionage against foreign countries – military technical intelligence.

Dr Hans Fillie travelled widely, recruiting agents and passing on information. He was able to move about in the guise of a businessman and he had a cover company, Afropan, based in Antwerp and Rotterdam. His partner in this company was a Dutchman named Hans Schmidt, who had a German passport. Schmidt also travelled widely in Holland, Switzerland, Hungary, Bulgaria and Romania.

Dr Fillie visited Budapest almost every six weeks and it was on one such occasion that Goetz was recruited by Fillie to provide military intelligence in Turkey. He was to transmit his intelligence through another Abwehr agent, code-named Klatt, who was based in Vienna.

Klatt, actually a Jewish businessman named Richard Kauders, I later learned, was one of Germany's most notorious spymasters, who ran a huge espionage network for the Abwehr stretching across Europe to the Soviet Union and the Middle East. Oddly, his network was code-named 'Vera' and was based in Vienna, Sofia and Budapest. After the war British counter-intelligence was baffled by Klatt because nobody seemed sure if he had been a German double agent or whether he was really working for the Russians. In any event, his transmissions had troubled the best brains in Britain throughout the war. Intercepted and cracked by the British, his messages were often passed on to Moscow by Kim Philby and Anthony Blunt.

Goetz was also questioned about his informants. Among a list of twenty-one such people in his network he named Karen Rosenberg. 'Karen Rosenberg is a German Aryan woman who was married to a German Jew,' he told his interrogator.

He had learned about Frau Rosenberg early in 1942 and was told she was anxious to leave Hungary as her husband was Jewish. Goetz learned that Karen Rosenberg had already spoken with Fillie, whose wife Liselotte, he was told, happened to be a close friend of hers. Fillie had said he could provide new passports for her and her husband as long as they left for Turkey and gathered information for the Abwehr from Istanbul.

Goetz was instructed to obtain the passports, which he did. Before the couple left Budapest, Goetz met Karen Rosenberg. He informed her that in Istanbul she would be contacted by somebody who would collect any information she had obtained and send it back to Hungary.

Goetz then explained that he arranged with 'a man called Klatt' that Klatt would transmit Frau Rosenberg's material on to Fillie in Berlin.

So Karen Rosenberg had not simply been exposed to a few small-time German blackmailers as she sought to secure her husband's escape, but had been drawn into close contact with one of the most infamous intelligence networks run by the Abwehr in Europe.

The interrogation report then said that once Goetz had handed over the new passports to the Rosenbergs, they made their way to Turkey. Here Goetz himself made contact with Karen Rosenberg in the Hotel Novotny in Istanbul, where they were staying, to receive her information.

The Abwehr was swiftly disappointed by Karen Rosenberg's failure to provide anything useful. It knew of her contacts with the British consulate in Istanbul. Specifically, the Abwehr knew of her contacts with two people at the consulate, one of whom was a Mr Atkins. Willi Goetz told his interrogator: 'In Turkey, Frau Rosenberg was in touch with Mr Atkins and Mr —.' The second name had been removed either deliberately or accidentally from the paper, but 'Mr Atkins' was clearly a reference to Vera's brother Ralph.

Details of Ralph's war service had proven impossible to obtain, and seemed to have been deliberately kept secret. Ralph Atkins never breathed a word of his war years to his son, Ronald. I had established, however, that Ralph remained in Istanbul at the outbreak of war with his oil company and that, like almost every other British expatriate in Istanbul during the war, he had become informally involved with intelligence work for the British consulate. Nothing more was said by Goetz about those contacts with 'Mr Atkins', whose role in the Karen Rosenberg affair was left extremely unclear. But Ralph Atkins had evidently been a good contact for the newly arrived Rosenbergs in Istanbul. Furthermore, Ralph almost certainly had means of communication with London throughout this period, and hence with Vera.

Soon Karen's failure to produce useful information led to threats from her Abwehr minders. Goetz was sent to the Hotel Novotny to tell Frau Rosenberg that Fillie had been sent to the Eastern Front as she had 'not provided a single item of information'. Goetz stated that Fillie had been charged with accepting a sum of fifty thousand Hungarian pengos from Karen in return for the new passports. The Abwehr severely punished any of its officers who took bribes, particularly if the bribe helped a Jew escape. Frau Rosenberg was now asked to come up with better information, in order to get her friend's husband back from the Eastern Front, and restore his credibility. 'She promised and subsequently gave Goetz a few titbits which were incorrect (e.g. Britain's intention to invade Turkey).'

The British then arranged for Karen to be sent on to Palestine to remove her from Goetz's threats. But before the Rosenbergs left Istanbul, Goetz gave her another mission for Palestine, where Fritz had been promised a job on a British military base. She was to send information on shipping in Haifa and on troops in that district. 'This she was to write down in the form of a simple code (e.g. Dear aunt = ships; chocolate = destroyers etc.) and send the letter through the post to a man called Amenak Seutyan whom Mr Rosenberg had once met on business.'

Goetz emphasised that it was clear to him that Frau Rosenberg undertook to supply information only because of her need to help her Jewish husband escape persecution in Germany. 'She was definitely not a pro-Nazi. Furthermore, her husband knew nothing of his wife's mission.'

I now compared Goetz's matter-of-fact report with the story of terror and flight told by Fritz. In some respects the two versions meshed perfectly – the provision of the false passport, the escape from Budapest and the harassment by German intelligence agents in Istanbul. When Karen had talked years later to her family of German 'bloodhounds' sent to threaten her she was evidently referring to Willi Goetz.

But the differences between the two stories were also glaring. Although Fritz made reference to the fact that his wife had been blackmailed into promising information to the Germans in Istanbul, at no stage did he say that Karen had promised to give information in return for his new passport. He made no mention at all of a large sum of money being paid to the Abwehr in return for his passport. And, most important of all, he made no mention of the fact that his wife's friend Hans Fillie was himself an Abwehr agent, and the very same Abwehr agent who had taken money from his wife for his passport. In 1941 50,000 Hungarian pengos was worth £3000 (£100,000 in today's terms).

It seemed that Karen kept the truth about her dealings with the enemy hidden from her husband. Goetz himself said: 'Her husband knew nothing of his wife's mission.' Karen had also kept key elements of the story hidden from her own children. When I spoke to them, Karina and Peter Rosenberg certainly knew about Hans Fillie, as the man who came to their father's aid by securing a new passport. But they had no idea that he was an Abwehr officer and were never told that their mother paid him a large sum for the passport. So where had Karen obtained the money? Vera's comment to her niece Karina now rang very loud in my ears: 'Did your mother ever tell you what a brave woman she was during the war?' It was as if Vera had been sounding out Karina to see what her mother might have told her.

Karen had certainly been brave. She had dealt with the enemy at dangerously close quarters in order to save her husband's life. And she had done so without ever telling him the whole truth, holding on to hope as she collected four-leafed clovers.

And yet Vera's question to Karina begged a series of other, far more disturbing questions. How much of Karen's bravery had Vera herself known about? Did Vera know, as she worked in Baker Street at the heart of British secret intelligence, that her close relative had done a deal with the Abwehr to help her cousin, Fritz?

There was no reason why Karen should have known that, through her dealings with Fillie, she had been put in touch with one of Germany's biggest spy networks. Perhaps the infamous Herr Klatt transmitted some of Karen's 'titbits'. Perhaps they were intercepted at Bletchley, read by Philby and passed on to Moscow.

But did Vera know how exposed Karen had been? If she did, she also knew how devastating it would be for her if the facts of the episode ever came out. All the time Vera was working for SOE she had a relative who was on the books of enemy intelligence, making Vera herself a prime target for German blackmail.

But was Vera perhaps implicated in Fritz's affair far more deeply than this?

Already there was evidence from Zenna that Hilda had provided a large sum of money to help a relative when he or she was facing deportation to a concentration camp. In his papers Fritz stated that he received 'support' in his difficulties from 'my English cousin Vera Atkins'. Quite possibly the large sum of money Zenna had heard about was raised to pay Fillie for Fritz's new passport. According to Zenna, the money was delivered by Vera. But how did Vera secure such a large amount of cash? And how did she pass it over to the Abwehr?

Fritz's peril was evident from early 1940 as the future of Vallea

Uzului hung in the balance, and negotiations to secure a new passport for him could have begun from then. Vera's movements throughout 1940 had always been hard to pin down.

I had found no evidence about how Vera might have reached the Continent at this time. Her Romanian passport was missing from her papers and she had no other. Possibly her old intelligence contacts – particularly those now in Section D who had known her family – offered help. But in any event it was most likely that she left England before the Germans seized the Low Countries and France, in May 1940, and then found she could not easily get back.

What I had found were the compelling stories, told independently by two women, of Vera's appearance in Holland and Belgium early in the war.

Beatrice's memory was certainly confused, but much of what she had told me had proved quite accurate. I spoke to Beatrice's sister and her very elderly father, who both lived in Holland, and established that her parents did live precisely where she had indicated, as did the family of Jehovah's Witnesses. And Beatrice's family did have a barn and they did hide Jews during the war, although they did not know their names.

Gilberte Brunsdon-Lenaerts's credentials as a heroine of the resistance in Antwerp could not be faulted. But why would Vera have taken the money for Fritz to Holland or Belgium?

Willi Goetz had now provided a possible answer. Hans Fillie and his partner Hans Schmidt used their Rotterdam- and Antwerp-based cover company Afropan to allow them to travel incognito all over central Europe, making visits to Budapest every six weeks.

Goetz does not tell us how Karen Rosenberg set about raising the fifty thousand pengos to give to Fillie, and he probably did not know. Karen's own family were certainly not wealthy enough to have produced that much money, but messages urgently asking for cash could well have been passed to Vera in England. Whoever raised the alarm must have carried great authority, given the seriousness with which Vera and her mother took the warning.

In any event, the quickest way of getting the money to Karen and Fritz would have been through Fillie's company Afropan, and probably through his associate Hans Schmidt, who travelled so regularly from Antwerp to Budapest. And if, as Annie Samuelli had speculated, Hilda's cash was tied up in diamonds stored safely in an

Antwerp bank, it would have made all the more sense for the bribe to be handed over in Antwerp.

When I first heard of a mysterious Belgian lady who appeared at Vera's funeral telling a tale of Vera's 'escape' from Antwerp during the war, it was hard to piece the episode together with the known facts of Vera's life. Gradually, however, the weight of evidence had accumulated, so that I now felt sure it must have happened. Though certain details of the story remained hazy, the outline was clear. Sometime early in the war, probably before she joined SOE, Vera travelled in dangerous circumstances through Holland to Belgium in order to pass over money to a contact, to buy Fritz Rosenberg a new passport which would save his life.

Then, quite unexpectedly, I found more corroboration. During my research I had asked Zenna to think again whether Vera ever mentioned Antwerp in any context. When she was growing up, did Antwerp feature in any conversation at all?

'Oh, yes,' Zenna suddenly said as a memory was triggered. 'When you put it like that, it did.' Vera had certainly been to Antwerp, she told me. She remembered this because Antwerp had come up in the course of another story Vera had told her as a child.

Food was another subject which provoked anecdotes about Vera. Vera, it was often said, would eat almost anything – even raw eggs. One day when Vera had taken Zenna out for a special meal she told a story about all the different foods she had once eaten on a long and dangerous journey. 'It began with how Vera had had nothing to eat but raw eggs for a long time. She was in a barn, hiding somewhere, and it was all a big adventure, is how I remember it. They lived on nothing but these raw eggs which they found in the barn. Then they had to get somewhere and it was exciting and took a long time.

'And after this long, exciting journey the whole story ended with a delicious meal in Antwerp. They had friends in Antwerp and they met up and finally sat down together for this meal.'

Zenna didn't recall Vera mentioning anything dangerous about her journey to Antwerp – 'but it was a story told for a child'. What she did remember, however, was the excitement with which her aunt spoke about having to 'hide out' and 'get away'. Every place on the journey had a connection with a certain food and the denouement was definitely in Antwerp. 'If I could remember the other food we talked about I might be able to remember where else she had been,' said Zenna.

So Vera had not been able to bury the story of her mission entirely; she had passed it on, safely disguised as an adventure, in a tale she told to her young niece, who had no reason to make anything of it. And then I realised that Vera had also told the story to somebody else.

The story of Vera's mission and Fritz's final escape to Canada must have been the same story which spilled out in bits and pieces, over dying embers of a fire, into the failing ears of Vera's elderly neighbour Alice Hyde.

As Alice had already told me, she used to keep Vera company in their old age in the evenings in Winchelsea, and often Vera would tell her a long, 'heartbreaking' story which came to a conclusion in Canada. Alice could remember almost no details of the story and believed that Vera only talked to her about her past because she was 'too muddled and deaf' to hear or remember anything.

But Alice did remember that the story always ended in Canada and she remembered the ringing words with which Vera always concluded: 'The family told me not to be afraid. They said I would always be remembered by them as a heroine.' And she remembered those words because Vera uttered them over and over again, after the story was over. The words must have been spoken to Vera by Fritz and Karen, who would always remember Vera as a heroine because she had helped save Fritz's life.

The revelation of Vera's secret mission rang true for another reason. It explained, for the first time, the cause of her excessive secrecy. It was quite natural that Vera should have been defensive about her past; after the war many Jewish refugees chose to pull down a curtain, and never spoke of their losses or the horrors they had experienced. Yet Vera protected her early life as if she were protecting a wound. Nobody, but nobody – even in her old age – was allowed to get even close to it.

The fact that Vera had a relative who worked during the war as an Abwehr agent – albeit in circumstances of life and death – was incriminating enough to explain some of this protectiveness. But for history to reveal, years after the event, that Vera herself had passed a large sum of money to the Abwehr to secure a passport would have been a bombshell indeed for SOE. History would almost certainly have judged Vera kindly. Friends and admirers, of course, would have viewed her mission to save a relative from the death camps as an act of extreme bravery and self-sacrifice. But, as Vera knew, those whom she had worked so closely with during the war would not have seen it in that way.

When Vera joined SOE she clearly took a decision not to avow her mission to the Low Countries and, having kept it secret, she had to keep it so all her life. All the time, though, she must have worried that it might leak out.

After the war Vera could never drop her guard. She constantly built up cover in case anyone should look too closely at her past, thus fending off any possibility that the few who knew anything of the story might talk.

The convention accepted by Vera's generation – that one didn't ask questions about other people's lives – clearly helped her. Occasionally individuals like Irene Ward MP posed a threat to Vera by challenging that convention, but Dame Irene was seen off. M.R.D. Foot, the official historian of SOE, was given unique access in the 1960s to SOE's personal files and could well have chosen to reveal that an influential F Section desk officer was an enemy alien. In fact, before the book was published, Foot was taken quietly aside by Vera and persuaded not to mention her Romanian roots.

But how long would it be before the record of an interrogation like that of Willi Goetz, sitting in a Whitehall file, would surface?

Vera adopted many techniques to divert people's interest from her past; and as a result some who came into contact with her were confused and drew surprising conclusions. Gilberte Brunsdon-Lenaerts, who had helped her in Antwerp, sensed that Vera was leading a double life and, given the backcloth of her own war experience, concluded that she was a Nazi double agent. Jean Overton Fuller also sensed Vera's double life. At the outbreak of the Cold War, Jean's conclusion was that Vera was a Soviet spy.

Both Gilberte and Jean were right that Vera had something to hide but wrong about what she was hiding.

Those words of admiration, spoken by Karen and Fritz, 'to us you will always be a heroine', were treasured by Vera, all the more because they were the only recognition of her heroism that she would ever receive. Once Vera's mother and then Ralph and Guy were dead, nobody else could ever be allowed to know the secret. Even the most important beneficiaries of Vera's heroism – the next generation of the Rosenberg family – were not allowed to find out.

Knowing that questions from the children, and the grandchildren, were certain to come sooner or later, Vera erected the only defence she could: she simply shut herself off from her Rosenberg family roots. For decades after the war she had no contact at all with Fritz or Karen, fearing that this would bring the story to life. When contact was made in the 1990s it was limited to those dry little cards I had found and cold Christmas greetings.

I found no evidence either that Vera had ever sought to make contact with Fritz's surviving brother, George, who lived simply as a labourer in Romania until his death in 1988. Vera certainly never mentioned the second twin, Hans. From a Holocaust research group in Vienna I received confirmation that Hans was a victim of the Nazi euthanasia killings, as Fritz had revealed in his papers. According to the registration books of the mental hospital, Am Steinhof, near Vienna, where he had been a patient, 'Hans Israel Rosenberg' [the name 'Israel' was given by the Nazis] was deported from Steinhof to Hartheim Castle, in Alkoven, Austria, on 17 August 1940 where he was murdered.' Hartheim Castle was a 'specialised euthanasia killing institution, where more than 18,200 handicapped and mentally ill patients were killed by gas'.

Similarly, Vera cut herself off entirely from the German branch of the Rosenberg family – even from her Uncle Siegfried. Uncle Siegfried knew better than anyone the story of Fritz's rescue. 'During this time I was supported by my Uncle Siegfried and my English cousin Vera Atkins,' Fritz had written of his period in hiding. After the war Siegfried was the only one of Vera's father's brothers still alive. He returned to Cologne and struggled to get back on his feet. Vera, however, had almost no contact with Siegfried and when he died in Cologne in 1964 she was too busy to attend the funeral.

Vera's relatives in Stuttgart were also cut off entirely by her after the war. Her cousin Aenne Pahl, to whom both Vera and her mother had once been particularly close, had suffered appalling trauma at the hands of the Nazis during her imprisonment in Wedding jail. Yet, as far as the family knows today, Vera made no attempt to contact Aenne or her daughter at any time after the war.

In the 1960s Aenne's sixteen-year-old granddaughter, Iris, turned up at Rutland Gate on her first trip to England, eager to meet her Aunt Vera, who – although she never visited – had always been spoken of with awe in Iris's family. Young, pretty and highly intelligent, Iris had been told nothing of her own background – 'only tales'. Away from home for the first time, she looked forward to meeting her English aunt, hoping she would tell her more about her Rosenberg roots. Vera, though, was deeply fearful of the questions this young girl might ask and presented her very coldest face, which deterred Iris from asking any questions at all. Iris, now a child psychologist, recalled the meeting in chilling terms. 'Vera certainly had an aura and I was quite impressed. But she was also very distant and I found her very cold. I remember thinking all the time I was there I mustn't let my teacup fall off this saucer. I never saw her again. In later years when I came to London I always called but she was always busy or not available. For me Vera was a completely blank screen.'

SECRETS THAT DON'T DIE

One day in the early 1960s another pretty young woman arrived for tea at 34 Rutland Gate. This woman was not a member of Vera's family, but Vera was nevertheless fearful once again about the questions her visitor might ask.

Now in her early twenties, Tania Szabo had been living with her grandparents in Australia since the age of eight, when the family emigrated, in part to avoid the publicity surrounding Violette. Vera had never been in contact with Tania during this time.

When she arrived back in London everyone wanted to see Tania, remembered as the little girl who had received her mother's George Cross. But the person Tania most wanted to meet was Vera Atkins. 'I don't remember why I wanted to see her or how I found her,' said Tania, now sixty-three, in a flowing skirt and trailing scarf. 'But I do remember I wanted so much to please her. Then when we met it was all rather formal and she seemed distant and cold. I think Vera disapproved of me.'

In the 1960s there had been a further attempt to lay the SOE story to rest with the publication of the official history, *SOE in France*, by M.R.D. Foot. For most the book became the long-awaited authoritative account of SOE, although not for Vera, who was angered that anyone should claim to know more about the subject than her. When I met her in 1998 she expressed her opinion that: 'Some consider it the Bible. It's about as accurate as the Bible.' For some critics the history simply raised more questions than it answered. Though Foot meticulously analysed the disasters and the treachery, he found no conspiracies and blamed few, concluding that the errors were largely due to the fog of war. 'To the question why people with so little training were sent to do such important work, the only reply is the work had to be done, and there was nobody else to send,' he wrote. Foot also blamed 'sensation mongers' for making 'ghastly imputations' about what happened to women agents, who, he said, would have wanted no special treatment.

No history, though, official or otherwise, could provide answers for the young Tania Szabo, the first of the offspring of SOE agents to make her way to Vera's door in the hope of finding out more about what really happened to their parents, uncles or aunts. Immediately after the war the questions Vera faced were largely from writers, MPs or former SOE agents themselves, but from the 1960s on she faced questions from the children of the dead and these were much harder to answer. I suggested to Tania that perhaps the reason Vera appeared so cold and distant at their first meeting was not because she 'disapproved' of Tania but because she feared the questions she might be asked. Perhaps Vera feared Tania would blame her in some way.

'She certainly didn't want to get too close to me,' said Tania. 'That's why I thought she disapproved.'

'What was it you felt she disapproved of?' I asked.

'Oh, well, you know, it was the sixties and I was young and doing not very much. I think she expected more of me. And I think I had a feeling that she didn't want me to be bothering her. Here I was in London, alone – perhaps she thought I would always be at her door. It must have been very difficult for her. She thought she might have me on her hands.'

Had there been any contact while she was in Australia?

'None at all,' said Tania. Tania and her grandparents had not even been invited to attend the launch in 1958 of the film about her mother, *Carve Her Name with Pride*.

I asked Tania if she did blame Vera in any way for what happened. 'Oh, no,' she said. 'Of course I didn't blame her. It was war.' Then she added: 'Though she might have thought I would blame her. It was understandable she should think that, I suppose. She certainly didn't open the gates, as it were. But I had the impression she was somebody who didn't want to open the gates. Ever.'

That day at Rutland Gate, Tania must have been about the same age as her mother was when Vera first met Violette. We wondered if Vera might have seen a likeness. I showed Tania a tribute to Violette, written by Vera after the war. It read:

I first met Violette in the early autumn of 1943 when she volunteered for work in occupied France with the French resistance. She was twenty-two, recently bereaved, her daughter little more than a year old. She was beautiful with great natural gaiety and vitality but she had been deeply hurt. Often her eyes would have a hooded look and there would be little silences, small leaks in her brave armour. She sought an outlet in action, preferably exciting and demanding.

Tania read the little piece carefully, then said: 'I think there was always something particular between Violette and Vera. There was an understanding. I had a sense of that. It was an instinct. It had to do with the way she talked about Violette. I think it was why she went out to Germany: to find out what had happened to Violette. And if she hadn't done it we would never have known.'

After Tania came many others. As the offspring of the dead agents grew up, many suddenly discovered they knew nothing about their parents, whose mission, capture and death were doubly hard to learn about because they were officially secret. Who could they ask? Letters usually found their way first to the Historical Sub-Committee of the Special Forces Club, and then to Vera.

'All these letters would come in and she just squirrelled them,' said the former agent Tony Brooks, doing a squirrelling action – a kind of pawing – with his hand. 'She squirrelled every single one of them,' he said, doing the action again. 'Never told the rest of us what was even in them. Wanted them all for herself.'

I found these letters, still hidden away, in lots of brown envelopes in Vera's files. In their first approaches to Vera, most of the sons or daughters, nephews or nieces, sought names of people and places, any clues, however slight, about how to begin their search back in time. Some found in Vera a conduit to the past or a source of guidance and advice. Others, like Alain Antelme, nephew of France Antelme, who was dropped into the hands of the Gestapo, were treated warily by Vera. 'She kept her discretion,' Alain told me.

Many of Vera's correspondents then started to make their own enquiries and wrote to Vera to check a detail, and that detail was also squirrelled away here. The more I opened envelopes the more I realised that among this mass of little notes and cards were vital snippets of new information, and the more I realised that the story could not yet be laid to rest because it was still being told. Not only did relatives write, but so did others who had known the agents yet never spoken up before. A prisoner who shared a cell at Fresnes with Violette Szabo, before her deportation to Germany, suddenly wrote years later with vivid memories. 'When she arrived in Fresnes jail she was wearing the same dress as when she left London: a new one, in crêpe de Chine, with blue and white flowers. She was also wearing a shirt in black crêpe georgette with yellow lace.' The writer also recalled that Violette had talked in prison of a traitor in London who had betrayed her. Letters also came from people who read the many books about SOE now published and who had still more new information. One of these correspondents was a man named Wickey.

There was nothing on the envelope to indicate who Wickey was, and at first sight the contents were puzzling. On top of the papers was an official-looking letter. It was from the Canadian High Commission in London and was addressed to Vera. The letter was dated 9 May 1975 and said: 'Dear Miss Atkins, Thank you for your query about Colonel H. J. Wickey, which has been passed to National Defence Headquarters Ottawa. You will be advised once we are in receipt of their reply.' There was no sign of a reply. Underneath was another letter – this time a faded copy – dated April 1958. The address of the sender was given as 'Stony Mountain, Man.' and the letter was addressed to 'The Editor' of Pan Books in London.

Dear Sir, Some time ago when browsing through the book section in one of the large departmental stores in Winnipeg I chanced to see one of your books entitled *Born for Sacrifice*. I picked up the book and glanced through it. Immediately I recognised some of the names in it and so purchased the book.

From perusal of the book I can see there is still some doubt about how the wireless operator, Miss Inayat Khan (code-name Madeleine, cover name Jeanne-Marie Renier) was disposed of after being taken from Karlsruhe prison. Thinking that the enclosed document may be of some value I would greatly appreciate if you would be good enough to pass it on to Miss Jean Overton Fuller, the author of the said book as I do not know how I could contact her except through your office.

Yours truly H. J. Wickey. Lt Col OC Intelligence Coy., Winnipeg Manitoba.

Cc: War Office, London, England.

Attached to the letter were three pages of single-spaced typescript – obviously a copy of the original: it was Wickey's document on the 'disposal' of Nora. And along the sides of one of the pages was some barely legible handwriting.

Lieutenant Colonel Wickey explained first that during the war he worked for Canadian intelligence. As a fluent speaker of French and German he was used behind the lines as a courier and had 'contacts on both sides of the fence'. After the war he became Military Governor of Wuppertal-Eberfeld, in the British zone. He also worked on war crimes investigations.

Now if my memory serves me well, I believe that on the trial agenda were Herren Kiefer [sic] and Knochen, who both had been on the staff of the Geheime Sicherheitsdienst at Avenue Foch. It came to our notice that the question of Miss Inayat Khan was to come up . . .

But, as stated above, I was the Military Governor of Wuppertal and with some four regiments then stationed in the vicinity (British, French, Dutch and some Russian small formations) social life was somewhat heavy and also on account of my own duties, my movements were restricted. However, I managed to go under cover and sneak out. I frequently mingled with all sorts of people, house parties, slums rendez vous, even black market operators. Thanks to my training and dual nature, I once more felt quite at home, and, of course, I was after information. All this was to the dismay and consternation of my own staff who obviously could not always know where I was. In due course of time my 'suspicious movements' were reported to British HQ then at Düsseldorf.

Now on my staff, my police section was headed by two officers, both of whom were, I think, on the London

Metropolitan Police staff, but of this I am now not too certain. In any case, one of these officers, from the very first day I arrived in Wuppertal, greatly detested me, perhaps not personally, but perhaps because I was a Canadian, a 'colonial' and, further, because a foreigner (as I am not Canadian born, just naturalised) was in command.

These officers, said Wickey, often sent 'distorted reports' of his 'suspicious behaviour' to HQ, but nevertheless he continued with his underground investigations into the Nora Baker case.

That was how many of us Canadian officers were treated after the war to make room for unemployed British officers . . . and at that time I regret to say that I did not trust British HQ. So much information that I had previously passed on had leaked out and especially information on Russian agents who were trying to establish contacts with London, with the view of obtaining industrial diamonds for the operation of certain type of machinery.

Eventually, said Wickey, he came across a 'certain German officer' who had worked as an interpreter and once spent some time at Dachau.

While there some camp officials had told him that a few days previously they had received a group of special prisoners, four women who had arrived from Karlsruhe. These women were to be kept absolutely separate from other inmates of the camp.

The four women were French but one of them, somewhat more swarthy in complexion, looked much like a Creole. She was considered to be a 'very dangerous' person and to be given the 'full treatment'.

Now, if we remember that agent Nora was of Indian descent, she would as such look much like a Creole. In Europe any person who shows an appearance of not being pure white is often referred to as a Creole.

The German officer gave Wickey the name of one of the Dachau camp staff who had somehow managed to get away before the Allies arrived and was by then living in Hamburg or in a village close to it.

'This official had been present to the last hours of these four women and, of course, would know well about all that had happened. Upon this hot tip, which I considered most reliable, that same evening I commandeered my car and driver and left for Hamburg.'

With assistance of the military government of Hamburg and the Hamburg police, Wickey eventually found his man.

At first and quite naturally he denied all knowledge but when I assured him that there was no action contemplated, at least just now, he began to talk. At first I made a bargain with him that for the information wanted I would not mention his name to anybody. He said they did receive a group of four women, three typical French and one looking more of a Creole type. The three French women were taken, after some two or three hours of their arrival, near the crematorium where they were partially undressed, they were in rags anyhow, and shot with pistols. They were handled very roughly, one of them had her face several times slapped, they were all kicked several times before being shot.

The Creole was kept outside, chained and almost naked. She was subjected to ridicule, was slapped and kicked several times, apparently by this same man who was very fond of this type of sport. She was left all night long lying on the floor in a cell and the next day, rather than drag her along to the crematorium, they gave her some more rough handling. Finally in a cell they shot her with a small pistol and dead or half dead she was carried by some other inmates and thrown into the furnace. That the person was the unfortunate Inayat Khan is well nigh 99 per cent certain.

Wickey concluded by saying that he had never presented his report to the war crimes command because when he returned to Wuppertal he was summoned to Düsseldorf and charged with taking a joyride to Hamburg without first requesting permission.

'I was so angry with this attitude towards Canadians that although my pockets were bulging with hot information I destroyed the whole thing and requested to be returned home.'

I then turned the paper around to try to read the handwriting scrawled along one edge. It wasn't Vera's writing. I could just make out one sentence: 'This bears more resemblance to the horrible report from Gibraltar than to Wassmer's account given to Miss Atkins.'

I looked again for a reply that Vera might have received from the National Defence HQ in Ottawa, but it wasn't here. Presumably she had requested information about Wickey to check his reliability, and perhaps also to see if he was alive or dead.

So I contacted the Canadian Defence Department and was put in touch with Colonel Wickey's son, John Wickey, who said his father died in 1994. He sent me newspaper cuttings and obituaries, as well as a record of his father's war service.

The documents painted Hippolyte John Wickey (known as John) as something of an adventurer. Born in France and educated in Switzerland, he served with the French Foreign Legion in the First World War, before moving to Canada. In 1944 he was seconded from the Canadian Army to train in England with SOE and was parachuted into France in 1944. This was presumably when he operated as a 'dual agent', as he put it. It was not possible to verify every aspect of Wickey's life story. However, his service with the Canadian armed forces and his tenure as Military Governor of Wuppertal-Eberfeld in 1945–6 were very clearly substantiated.

Reading Wickey's report, I immediately thought of Max Wassmer's comment to Christian Ott: 'So you want to know how it really happened?' and of the sanitised story he had first told about how the women had died, all holding hands. The Wickey report also reminded me of a conversation I had with Zenna Atkins about how Vera thought Nora might have died. The conversation arose in a roundabout way. I had asked several people if they thought Francis Cammaerts was right to say that Vera was racist. Several thought he was. 'But only in the way women of her generation were,' said Phoebe Atkins, her sister-in-law. Zenna, however, did not believe Vera was racist in her views and she recalled how Vera once told her that Nora had been singled out for particularly horrific treatment by the Nazis because of the colour of her skin. 'I think this distressed Vera more than anything,' Zenna told me. Vera believed that not only had Nora been appallingly beaten but she had also been raped.

When I first interviewed Vilayat Inayat Khan I didn't know about Wickey or his story and so couldn't ask him about it. But I went to see Vilayat a second time. Again, I didn't raise Wickey's evidence, but

Vilayat did so very early on. And I discovered that he knew every
detail of the Canadian's story and had done for a very long time.

We were talking again in his house in Suresnes, this time sitting in
the living room surrounded by Indian artefacts. There was a strong
smell of teak and incense. I wanted to ask Vilayat again about Nora's
cyanide pill. I told him I had heard that Vera advised Nora not to
take the pill with her on her mission, fearing she might swallow it
when it was not absolutely necessary, in order to be sure she would
not give anything away.

Vilayat repeated, however, that he had seen the pill and was sure
Nora had it with her.

'But, of course, the Nazis took it away from her,' he continued. 'They
knew these agents had the pill and made sure they took it from them.'

'Would she have used it?'

'To get out of being tortured, yes, I think she would. And, of course,
she was tortured in Dachau. In fact, she was beaten to death. I don't
know if you have a copy of a report by a man who contacted me – a man
who said he was present when she was beaten to death and said she was
covered in blood and said like this she was thrown into the oven.'

As Vilayat spoke he got out some papers from a pink folder and
flicked through documents he had accumulated over the years. I
could see that the paper he handed me was Wickey's report.

I asked Vilayat whether he had managed to come to terms at all
with what had happened to Nora.

'Well, it is still not resolved,' he said. 'I am just reliving it every
day. I am living representing in detail in my thoughts everything she
went through day and night. Not just in general – but I am visualising, first of all, that moment.' He paused as if visualising right there.

'And, you see, we still don't know if she was killed with the others
or on her own, so I always try to visualise how it happened. She was
probably brutally taken from Pforzheim and brutally thrown in a
lorry and when she landed in Dachau she was brutally thrown on a
floor. I don't know if it was in a room, or if it was raining or cold or if
it was outdoors, but according to what we know the Gauleiter kept
on kicking her with his big boots and she must have had sores all
over her body and spent the night in agony. Whether it was in the
open or not, I don't know, but if she was out there in the open, then
others would have seen her when she was beaten to death.

'And there she was after a terrible night and there was the waiting

and she knew she would be killed and then the Gauleiter kept kicking and beating her until she was – what did he say? – a "bloody
mess". And again I have been trying to represent to myself' – here
Vilayat coughed – 'what it would have been like with her nose
bleeding and her eyes bleeding – I don't know.'

I didn't recognise the phrase 'bloody mess' from Wickey's report.
I asked Vilayat if he had ever received a letter from somebody in
Gibraltar. Again he reached for his pink folder, and handed me
another piece of paper. It was a copy of a handwritten extract, obviously from a different letter. The light was fading outside and we
had only an oil lamp in the room, but I managed to make out the
words: 'Afterwards I spoke to Yoop, who told me that it was terrible
what had happened. When Ruppert got tired and the girl was a
bloody mess, he told her that he would shoot her. First she had to
kneel and the only word she said before Ruppert shot her from
behind the head was "*liberté*".'

Vilayat coughed again and shifted a little in his chair. 'And then, you
see, for my eightieth birthday I conducted the B Minor Mass in
Dachau.' Vilayat Inayat Khan, like all his family, was a talented musician
and studied as a boy under Stravinsky. He shifted again and smiled.

'I don't know how to say this. Let's see. Well, there is a picture of
Noor there at the museum. It was a grey day, like today. And I am
conducting and thinking, How can I communicate with Noor about
what is happening?

'Maybe she is alive, I thought. And I thought maybe I saw a smile
on that picture. No. Then I thought, I need evidence that she is
here.' He paused and sniffed. 'I said: "No, I want you to give me a
more tangible sign." So, then, all of a sudden, the sun came out
from behind the clouds, and then went in again, just at that moment.
How meaningful it is, I don't know.'

I asked Vilayat how he received the Wickey papers. He could
not remember exactly. They had come to him with the extract
from the other letter. He thought the papers had all been sent on
to him from his younger brother, Hidayat, who lived near The
Hague. This fitted with the story of the provenance of these
papers, which all went back to Jean Overton Fuller, Nora's biographer. After publication of the first edition of her book on Nora,
Madeleine, Jean Overton Fuller received, via her publisher, the so-
called 'Gibraltar letter', which referred to a 'Yoop' and a 'Ruppert'.

All Jean could recall today of the provenance of the letter was that it was posted in Gibraltar and the writer signed himself 'Peters'.

'It was so sadistic that I thought it must have been written by somebody who was actually there. All that remains in my memory are the words "the girl was a bloody mess". The writer was revelling in it and it was disgusting.' Jean's instinct was to destroy the letter, but she was loath to incur the responsibility of destroying a historical document, so she kept a brief note of the contents and sent the original to 'Miss Atkins'. This must have been in the mid-1950s. The fact that I had not found the 'Gibraltar letter' in Vera's papers suggested that she had almost certainly destroyed it.

In 1958, after publication of a second edition of *Madeleine*, retitled *Born for Sacrifice*, the Wickey letter also reached Jean, via her publisher, and it resembled the 'Gibraltar letter' but was less detailed and less 'sadistic'. Jean told me she kept the original of the Wickey letter herself for her records. Wickey stated that he had sent a copy of his letter to the War Office, so Jean saw no reason on this occasion to send the letter on to Vera.

Years later, in the 1970s, when Jean was revising her biography of Nora again, she had a new publisher in Holland who wanted her to include the sanitised 'official' story of Nora's death at Dachau. Jean had never believed that version of events, and, having read 'Wickey' and 'Gibraltar', she refused to repeat it. To show her publisher why she felt so strongly, she sent a copy of the Wickey letter and a description of the contents of the 'Gibraltar letter'. She also scrawled a note on the side of Wickey's report, pointing out that it bore more resemblance to the 'Gibraltar letter' than to the evidence Wassmer gave to Miss Atkins. Jean also requested that her publisher keep the material strictly to himself, but he passed the material on to Hidayat Inayat Khan, Vilayat's brother, whom he knew. Obviously Hidayat then passed the papers to Vilayat.

In the light of this complicated sequence of events, the question that puzzled me was: how and when did Vera receive the Wickey papers? Given that she wrote to the Canadian Defence Department in 1975 to enquire about Wickey, it would appear that she could only have just received the papers at about that time. Presumably, therefore, the copy Wickey sent to the War Office in 1958 never reached Vera. In any event, as I now realised, Vera's copy was obviously not from the War Office as it had Jean Overton Fuller's scrawled note to her publisher on the side.

The only explanation for this was that Vilayat, having received the papers from his brother, then passed them to Vera. Not for the first time, it appeared, new and ever more shocking details about Nora's death had inexorably found their way out. And not for the first time, it may well have been Nora's brother Vilayat who passed on the new information to Vera about his sister's fate, and not the other way round.

The 'Gibraltar letter', which arrived in the mid-1950s, had been impossible for Vera to pursue. But such was the detail in the Wickey evidence that Vera felt obliged to follow it up, writing to Canada's Defence Department.

So had Vilayat passed the papers to Vera?

He might have done, he said, although he had not seen Vera for many years after the war. 'It is the sort of thing I might have done, though. I would have thought, Well, she should know everything about what happened to my sister because only by knowing all the whole truth can anyone understood her real spirit, her real strength.'

Then he recalled that Vera had come to a ceremony the family held in Suresnes many years after the war to erect a plaque on the wall of the house in Nora's memory. 'Perhaps I gave her the papers then – I don't know. Both Vera Atkins and Buckmaster came on that occasion.'

What Vilayat remembered very clearly was how Buckmaster had broken down in tears at the ceremony. 'I think Buckmaster had fought with his conscience all that long time and maybe he managed to forget about it all for many years. But finally he was devastated by his conscience and when he came here he could fight with it no more. He told my sister Claire that he bitterly regretted sending Nora. You know, seeing Claire might have reminded him of Nora. He told her he was overcome with remorse and said he could never forgive himself.'

'Did Vera say anything of that sort?'

'I did not talk to her so much. I think she was disappointed in me by then.'

'What makes you say that?'

'I think she looked at me and saw the long beard and the clothes. I think she thought, He used to be such a dashing naval officer, and now look at him – a phoney guru.'

'Did she show any emotion?'

'No. I think in her case she was able to bypass her conscience more easily. She was much more cold-blooded than Buckmaster.'

'What makes you say she was cold-blooded?'

'With Buckmaster, I think that when he sent these people out to their deaths he was acting in defiance of his conscience because he knew that it was what he had to do for the war. But deep down he was emotionally devastated. As far as Vera Atkins was concerned, I don't think she was emotionally devastated, which is what makes me say she was cold-blooded. Or possibly she hid it – in which case she hid it even from herself because it was all justified in a good cause.'

'But Vera did go and look for them all. Buckmaster did not. What was her motive then?'

'I think Buckmaster was so . . . devastated he knew there was nothing now he could do about it. Of course, it was of interest to find out what happened to people, but it would not bring them back. So he was more readable. More visible – readable. "Readable" – is that the word? Yes, and Vera Atkins was harder to read.'

'Why did she do it? Why did she go to look for them then?'

'My impression was that Vera Atkins was the intelligence officer who really wanted to find out what happened. She wanted to sort things out – to be clear about things. She didn't want to allow any details to escape her.'

'You mean she just wanted to find out and that was it?'

'Yes, she wanted to know. That was it.'

'And perhaps she was hiding the emotion – even from her own self.'

'And when she was sending these people out she was simply following a course. She would be quite capable of following a course – even if it meant lying. And, of course, she was good at lying and, what is more important, of remembering her lying – because a lot of people get caught when they forget their lies.'

'Do you think she lied to you?'

'Well, that was the thing, of course – they sent a girl who could not lie to be used in the big lie.'

What did he mean? I asked.

'Well, you see, we know now that all that time they were holding out hope that Nora was free, it was just because they didn't want the Nazis to know that they knew that she was captured. They just wanted to make the Nazis believe that they believed she was free, so that the Nazis could receive agents over her radio who would give them information that was wrong. And so that the Nazis could receive messages over her radio saying where the British were going to land, which was wrong. This is the irony. Nora could never lie but she was used for the big lie.'

So Vilayat too believed the conspiracy theories.

I asked how he had come to believe all this. Where was his information from? He suggested some books for me to read, all of which I had read, and all of which expounded different versions of this conspiracy theory. I said I was surprised that he had accepted at face value what was in these books. There was a large amount of evidence that the capture of the agents was due simply to terrible incompetence and tragic mistakes. But Vilayat seemed not to hear.

He told me he didn't mind if books written about Nora were fact or fiction as long as they honestly preserved her memory. As he talked some more he seemed not to distinguish between information he had received which was supposed to be true and that which was not. The truth of how she died and the conspiracy about why she died were now all tangled up in his mind.

Vilayat's wife, Mary, came in to give us some more light. Had she met Vera Atkins?

'Once,' she said, when she came for the ceremony. 'She did not strike me as interesting at all. She was somebody who made no impression – a kind of non-person almost. She seemed to have no personality. A quiet figure – mouse-like.'

'She was a little bit aloof,' continued Vilayat. 'It might just have been her English character.'

'You know she wasn't English?' I said.

Vilayat paused. Then he laughed. 'Well, that is really surprising because her accent was very English. Like Leslie Howard – I would never have thought he was Hungarian.' And he laughed again.

Then I asked Vilayat: 'Can people really hide these things from themselves – these emotions that Vera must have felt?'

'Yes, of course. People are continually hiding their guilt from themselves because their self-validation is so precious that if one admits one's guilt it gets worse and so one finds it very difficult to admit that one hates oneself, so one is lying not really to other people but to oneself. So it has to be hidden, or bypassed. I think in Vera Atkins's case she bypassed the responsibility.'

'How could she bypass such great responsibility?'

'There is only one way to bypass it. Like a doctor or a surgeon you have to be cold-blooded. You have to have strong self-control. That is what she had. That is what I sensed that she had.'

I said I thought that Vera had been very fond of Nora and I quoted something she once said to Jean Overton Fuller about her. 'Her motives were so pure – of such a high spiritual order – it was as if she was from another world.'

I asked if Vilayat thought that Vera, like so many others, was in love with Nora. 'I think Nora was somebody who Vera Atkins respected,' he said. 'But she was still able to use her to tell the lie.'

'But you were grateful to Vera Atkins at the time that she returned from her search in Germany,' I said, and I showed him the card he had written to Vera which had tumbled from an envelope in the shed in Zennor. 'To Vera Atkins. With gratitude – a feeling I know Nora would have shared for your enterprise in following in her tracks in the German wilderness of the aftermath.'

He looked at his words, facing a photograph of Nora, and said: 'Ah, yes. I was always grateful to everyone. I would not write that now.'

When I returned to London I looked once more for any sign of the 'Gibraltar letter' in Vera's files, but there was none. That piece of evidence – the cruellest of all – had, it seemed, been well and truly destroyed. But with her new knowledge of Nora's suffering and of her bravery, what more could Vera realistically have done? Thirty years after the crime was committed, the criminals had long since died or disappeared and it was inconceivable that the case could be reopened. Nora's citation for gallantry had already been rewritten four times between 1944 and 1948. Her published story could not now be changed yet again.

Nora – and all the other dead agents – could, however, now be properly remembered. It was not until the early 1970s – about the time that this last information appeared about Nora's death – that the first F Section memorials started to go up at concentration camps, more than twenty-five years after the victims died. In the end it was only because Vera and others campaigned for memorials that they were ever erected. Britain offered an insulting £200 as a contribution towards the memorial stone for the four women agents who died at Natzweiler, a sum which hardly paid the airfare of a single WAAF or FANY delegate, so the French ended up paying for Britain's stone.

Prime Minister Jacques Chirac attended the unveiling. The British just sent a defence attaché from the embassy in Paris.

Vera not only devoted time to raising money, but also to finalising the tiniest details for the memorials, including composing the inscriptions. One of her greatest supporters was Airey Neave, who became a friend of Vera's and had himself escaped from Colditz.

Her correspondence showed that Vera took enormous care about the design of the memorials, sketching her own ideas, and frequently admonishing others who made errors with the spelling of a name or wrongly remembered an award or date. In a note to Neave in 1974 about the choice of stone for the Natzweiler memorial, which was to go up in the crematorium where Andrée Borrel, Vera Leigh, Sonia Olschanesky and Diana Rowden died, it was clear that Vera's attention to technical detail and linguistic precision was as acute as ever. 'On the choice of material it would probably look best in marble with the flags in colour and the rest of the lettering in black,' she wrote. And she suggested that the memorial should give only one Christian name in full and leave out initials. 'As not all the girls achieved the Croix de Guerre would it not be nice, Airey, to forget about decorations which all so obviously merited?'

And, finally, she added:

'I enclose a very sketchy effort at layout and have tried to find a brief form of words to give minimum information. What do you think of the quotation, which is taken from a poem by Walt Whitman (American 19th century)? It appeals to me because it raises our sights from the sordidness of the surroundings and places their sacrifice in the realm of timelessness. It does this for me but how does it strike you?: "Only the dark, dark night shows to our eyes the stars."'

EPILOGUE

The plane took off from Stansted Airport at 6am and we were soon over the Channel and following the loops of the Loire, before landing at Tours. Travelling with me was Yvette Pitt, daughter of Yvonne Cormeau, one of F Section's women agents, who was parachuted into southern France. Vera saw Yvonne off on her mission from Tempsford airbase, north-west of Stansted village, in August 1943.

Yvette was only two years old at the time and was placed in a convent of Ursuline nuns where she stayed until she was five. 'I don't remember much about the convent but I do remember telling everyone there: "I have got a mummy. I know I have got a mummy." And people would ask me where she was. And I would say: "I don't know."'

Yvette complained about the recently released film of the novel *Charlotte Gray*, which tells the story of a fictional SOE woman agent. The heroine of the film volunteers to parachute in behind enemy lines, mainly because she sees her mission as a chance to find her lover, a pilot, whom she believes has been shot down over France.

'It is quite wrong to say that these women did what they did for romance,' said Yvette. She told me her own mother volunteered because she wanted to 'do something'. She wanted 'to save France from the Nazis'.

I was coming to France for the annual ceremony in memory of all of the F Section dead, an event which began in 1991 with the inauguration of a spectacular memorial in the small town of Valençay, in the Loire Valley. Since 1991 Vera, with a small coterie of SOE loyalists, had made an annual pilgrimage here every May.

'What happened was this,' said Vera's friend Judith Hiller. 'I would motor down to Winchelsea in the Rover the night before, picking up Peter Lee on the way. There were usually at least two others squeezed in the back. Then we'd stay in a B&B overnight, ready to leave early next morning. Vera would prepare the picnic – usually four sorts of sandwiches and hard-boiled eggs with cheese sticks to nibble. It was such fun. Vera always sat in the front and chattered while everyone in the back strained to hear her.'

I asked Judith why she liked Vera so much.

'I liked to be part of her tapestry. And I enjoyed her mystery,' she said.

I had with me a little booklet about the F Section memorial which provided a map of all the circuits. Our route along the River Cher now took us between the Ventriloquist and Wrestler circuits, and along the southern reaches of Prosper. Water meadows, blanketed with buttercups, ran down to the river's edge. Henri Déricourt chose several of his landing fields near the banks of the Cher and the Loire.

Valençay was chosen for the memorial in part because it was close to many early SOE operations. It also happened to be close to where Pearl Witherington (now Madame Cornioley) lived and near where, as 'Pauline', she had taken command of Wrestler. Pearl was to lay the wreath at this year's ceremony.

The Lion d'Or, in Valençay, was where Vera's 'retinue', as one observer put it, always stayed on the occasion of the memorial service. I found the hotel bar quite empty apart from a small group of elderly women – probably Vera's retinue – talking quietly around a crochet-clothed table. From another room came a high-pitched wailing which nobody appeared to notice.

The landlady told me she had no recollection of a Vera Atkins, though she knew Pauline very well. Pauline was, she said, '*une des grandes ici*'. And then she asked if Vera Atkins was perhaps '*la dame qui a toujours pris la chambre 2*' and she affected a haughty pose. Yes, she remembered Vera now. '*C'était une très belle chambre. La meilleure.*'

The wailing became louder as an elderly woman in black moved towards me with hands outstretched, as if to speak. But just as she was about to grab my arm she moved away, still wailing. I was evidently not who she thought I was.

I went to join Vera's retinue. They too were talking about the 'travesty' of the latest controversial film about SOE, *Charlotte Gray*. Vera also would have considered the film a travesty, had she been here, we all agreed. The Valençay booklet, which Vera had partly written, stated: 'All, men and women alike, were motivated by a loathing of Nazi ideology, a love of freedom and a desire to make an individual contribution to the liberation of France.'

Until the very end of her life Vera had found herself defending the decision to send women behind the lines. In 1996 she picked up her pen yet again to rebut criticism of the decision to send Nora Inayat Khan to France. On the back of a PEPS statement, in a now faltering hand, Vera drafted a letter to the *Daily Telegraph* describing how Nora had evaded capture, made two escape attempts, given nothing away and was kept in chains as an exceptionally dangerous prisoner. 'This is the record of Nora Inayat Khan and her answer to those who doubted her,' Vera concluded. The letter was also her answer to those who doubted her; because every claim that the women should not have been sent was, by implication, an attack on Vera herself. After two years researching her life, there remained many unanswered questions about Vera, but of one thing I was now quite sure: an important key to her character was her overwhelming sense that she was always right.

As I talked to Vera's friends the hotel bar began to fill with SOE veterans and families. There was a little flurry across the room as another carload arrived from England, among them the SOE adviser in his French beret and red V-neck jersey, and his assistant Valerie, *SOE in France* under her arm.

And then the woman in black appeared again, still wailing, but apparently recognising one or two of the new arrivals. I noticed now that her face was deathly pale and her eyes bloodshot. She clutched an SOE veteran and started speaking to him very fast in French, occasionally breaking off to cry. The man patted his supplicant kindly while clearly trying to extricate himself if he possibly could.

He later explained that the woman came every year. She was still mourning her fiancé, who was killed while serving with SOE in France, but she had never been told quite how he was killed or where he died. I wondered whether the woman in black had grabbed Vera's arm and how Vera had responded.

I had not always been able to make sense of Vera's mixed responses to the survivors and the families of the dead. 'Before joining, the agents had been warned that their chances of survival were estimated at about evens. But in fact something like three agents in four survived,' stated the Valençay booklet. As everyone here knew, had it not been for Vera, very little would ever have been known of the fate of those who did not survive.

I had found letters from the bereaved spilling from Vera's files. To many she offered emotional and financial support until the end of her life. Latterly, for example, the case of Francine Agazarian, wife of Jack Agazarian, who was hanged at Flossenburg, had taken up a great deal of Vera's time. 'I am most grateful for the cheque, and deeply touched by your kindness; once again let me thank you with all my heart,' wrote Francine in 1988. On another occasion: 'For many years I felt it was not right that I should be alive. I should have gone when they did and in the same manner.'

And yet, precisely because I had seen such examples of Vera's sympathy and understanding, the examples of her coldness in other cases were so hard to comprehend. Vera's heartless disregard, in the immediate post-war years, for the family of Sonia Olschanesky, who were never informed that she died at Natzweiler, was the starkest example. Often the most needy were shown the coldest face. Occasionally Vera's reserve even had the paradoxical effect of transferring a sense of blame or guilt to the other person. When, in her early twenties, Tania Szabo came to see Vera to talk about her murdered mother, she found a distant and disapproving Vera. Yet, far from feeling let down by Vera, Tania left the meeting blaming herself for having 'disappointed' her, and hoped to make amends.

On other occasions, when Vera feared accusation she automatically played down her personality, as if to hide herself. Vilayat Inayat Khan's wife, Mary, told me when she met Vera at Nora's memorial service in Suresnes she was 'mouse-like' and 'made no impression'. This must have been deliberate on Vera's part. The former F Section agent George Millar, an admirer of Vera's, once told me always to remember one thing about her: 'Everything Vera did was deliberate.'

Many I spoke to detested this coldness in Vera. Some saw it as sinister. But others saw it as another facet of her inability to concede that mistakes might have been made.

Close friends felt only sympathy for Vera. Behind that controlled façade they sensed that she was all the time suppressing her own emotion and her own guilt. From time to time Vera would – just momentarily – lose that control. Nigel Smith, an amateur historian, who worked with Vera on securing the SOE memorials, came to know her well in later years. On one occasion, in the 1980s, when Vera was talking to him about Violette Szabo, she started to describe what Violette was wearing the day she saw her off to France. She recalled every tiny detail of Violette's clothes – her shoes, the shirt and the dress – and she described them several times. 'I think the dress was of blue and white flowers,' said Nigel. 'It was as if she had never shaken the image from her head. That was the only time I saw her show emotion. She was obviously moved.'

'She was imperturbable – *contrôlée*,' said the former F Section agent Jean-Bernard Badaire. After surviving Neuengamme concentration camp, Badaire managed to escape from a train which was transporting him to Belsen, two days before the liberation, and miraculously he made his way to the British lines. His friendship with Vera after the war was as close as anyone's. Yet she had never once shown concern for what had happened to him in German captivity. '*Jamais une question*,' he said with a flourish of his hands. 'But just occasionally something would suddenly come out,' he added. 'One day a subject came up, and she suddenly began to talk about a German she had interrogated who had murdered little children. She told me she said to this man: "How could you do such a thing?" And he said to her: "Like pictures, I hung them all along the wall."' Badaire had evidently been very struck, not so much by the German's comment, but by the way Vera had repeated it all those years later. '*Elle a dit ça*,' he said, looking at me. '"Like pictures I hung them along the wall." I think she was haunted by that phrase. It had come out in a moment she wasn't thinking. When she wasn't in control.'

Badaire believed that Vera could not talk to him about the concentration camps precisely because she knew he had seen everything. 'I think if you talk to somebody who has been in a camp and has seen all the horrors you are wary of him, if you feel he might think it was you who sent him there. That is what Vera feared, that we might think it was her who sent us there.' He paused. 'It is . . .' he said, and he struggled for a word. '*En français on dit "rancune"*. You understand?' He explained. The word meant a grudge. 'Particularly for the families of the girls. Vera always feared that *elles ont gardé une rancune contre elle*. This, perhaps, was the key to her comportment.'

Some of Vera's other closest friends had made similar observations. And Vera's niece Zenna Atkins was quite sure that her aunt's 'mental wiring' meant she was able to control her emotions. 'But I think when she discovered all that awful horror it was like a series of body blows. Then she spent the rest of her life recovering from those blows.'

As we milled around waiting to take our seats for dinner, Pearl appeared, followed by a TV crew complete with cameraman and sound recordist. Channel Four had interviewed Pearl recently for a documentary on *The Real Charlotte Grays*. Now the BBC were filming her for a new programme about Violette Szabo.

The producers had interviewed a woman who had shared a cell with Violette and who broke down on camera as she described how Violette had been raped by a German guard. The TV investigators had also apparently discovered that Violette's famous battle, holding off her German captors with her Sten gun, was probably a fabrication. The story had formed part of Violette's citation for her George Cross.

Those early attempts to sanitise the stories of agents, as in the case of Violette, and then embellish their heroics, was another manifestation of Vera's determination to be always right. It also sprang from an understandable determination on the part of Vera and Buckmaster, supported by many former F Section colleagues, that SOE should be valued and remembered. The sense of deep betrayal at the end of the war, when SOE was closed down, to be forgotten, cannot be overstated. 'They all just wanted us scrubbed off the face of the earth,' one F Section staff member told me, referring to MI6, the Foreign Office and other Whitehall antagonists.

Yet the publicity drive only diverted attention from the true heroism of several of the agents. At Ravensbrück, Violette's cheerful spirit and defiance in the face of unremitting Nazi degradation was an inspiration to weaker prisoners. Whichever of the women it was who scratched the face of Peter Straub, the Natzweiler executioner, as she was pushed, drugged, into the furnace, surely deserved to be remembered for such extraordinary resistance. Letters in Vera's files suggested the woman might have been Vera Leigh, because she was once put forward for a George Cross; although, inexplicably, the proposal was not pursued. None of the citations for Nora Inayat Khan mentioned that her last word to those who had already beaten her to certain death was '*liberté*'.

The publicity drive had another unintended result: it fuelled conspiracy theories, which then obscured the very success stories which Vera and Buckmaster had hoped to promote.

Around the table at Valençay most people tried to find something kind to say about Buckmaster, whose last job was public relations manager for the French champagne industry. Former colleagues still remembered him as the grand old man of F Section but ever since his death in 1992 there had been much talk of his 'gullibility' and 'naivety'. Some said he had arrived at SOE with a chip on his shoulder – perhaps because he had not taken up his exhibition to Oxford. Then, when he unexpectedly secured the post as head of F Section, he felt a need to prove himself and secure, in the words of Colin Gubbins, 'the highest possible dividend' for F Section – but zeal and patriotism, and a link to the old-boy network, were not enough. Perhaps Buckmaster sensed, as Gubbins said after the war, that he got the job 'because there was nobody else'.

When things went wrong, Buckmaster, rather than face up to reality, retreated into fantasy, from which he rarely seems to have emerged. In his later years, when confronted with the facts of his gaffes, he, like others, took refuge in conspiracy theories, saying, for example, that he had known all along that Déricourt was a double agent but he had been following orders from on high. Sometimes when confronted with the facts, Buckmaster simply cried.

The question of Buckmaster, of course, always led back to the question of Vera's wartime role. How much had he really depended on her? Here, at the Lion d'Or, Vera was considered by most to have been his 'number two' and everyone considered her to have been 'Buckmaster's brains'. 'We saw her as "*la vraie patronne*",' said Bob Maloubier, the tips of his white moustache curling up in affectionate memory. 'Vera was the real boss.'

Yet the greater the influence ascribed to Vera within the organisation, the more questions arose about her role in the flawed decision-making. If she was the brains behind Buckmaster, why did she not warn him – or others if he would not listen – of the errors? And why did she continue to protect him so vehemently after the war?

One answer is, of course, that Vera was not, as she insisted, always right. While cleverer than most of those around her, she was an amateur like all the rest, and in the confusion and chaos of war Vera was quite capable of being wrong. When I met her at Winchelsea in 1998 I asked when she first believed that Nora was captured. Her answer gave a small hint of the acute anxiety which had surrounded that 'wrong' assessment in December 1943 that Nora was free. 'The Germans captured several radio operators. There were many mutilated messages. When she was arrested in October we were suspicious. By January we felt she must be all right.'

Furthermore, indispensable though Vera became to F Section, the simple fact was that she joined the organisation as a mere secretary and by the winter of 1944 still held only a junior officer's rank and was both a Jew and a woman. It was perhaps partly because of her 'inferior' status that she felt such an overwhelming need to cover up mistakes.

On top of these considerations, Vera had her own exceptional reason for feeling personally insecure. For most of the war her status as an enemy alien meant she was highly vulnerable and could not afford to rock the boat. And then, tucked away somewhere inside British intelligence files, the case of Karen and Fritz Rosenberg was lurking. The consequences for Vera, had details of her mission to the Low Countries ever emerged during the war, would have been grave indeed. Had it become known that she had passed a large sum of money to pay a bribe to the Abwehr, there is little doubt that she would have been ejected from SOE and packed off to some place where she could do no harm. Whatever she may have suspected about captured wireless operators, whatever she may have thought about Buckmaster's judgements, Vera could not risk losing Buckmaster's support or provoking any investigation into her own past. Her own survival was at stake.

Although after the war Vera remained loyal to Buckmaster, the character of their relationship changed. Her loyalty to him in later years, though still respectful, became almost maternal. Perhaps her indebtedness to him for his protection during her difficult times was such that she instinctively protected him in return when he came under attack for F Section's failings.

There were occasionally small chinks in that loyalty – signs, almost, of rivalry. Asked once about the long hours Buckmaster worked at F Section, Vera scoffed, saying he was 'the worst clock-watcher of all'. And she also allowed a difference of opinion to open up with her former boss over Déricourt. She had told me she never trusted Déricourt and I soon discovered that in older age she had made a point of telling many people the same thing, even giving interviews for TV documentaries on the subject. Yet nobody pressed Vera to explain why, if that was the case, she had not ensured his conviction back in 1948.

While Vera's failure to speak out about errors during the war could be explained, her failure to ensure that evidence against Déricourt was put before the French tribunal in 1948 remained one of the greatest puzzles of all. Déricourt could not be held responsible for anything like all of F Section's failings but his treachery had clearly hastened many agents to their deaths. The Foreign Office may well have advised former SOE officers in 1948 that this was a French affair and a British presence could stir up sensitivities. But such advice would not have deterred Vera from trying to convict Déricourt. Revenge was never a motivating factor in her 'private enterprise', but she certainly wanted to see justice done. Yet when Déricourt went on trial, Vera stayed away.

'Imagine,' said the French SOE agent Bob Maloubier, giving one credible explanation: '"Antelme, captured on landing." "Damerment, captured on landing." "Lee, captured on landing." "Michel", captured on landing."' And his list of agents 'captured on landing' went on and on. Twenty-seven SOE agents were named in the Valençay booklet as captured on landing or very soon afterwards. 'They would not have wanted to be in court to hear that.'

The next day Valençay was covered by low, grey cloud as we all headed off for the service at the SOE memorial, which stands at one end of an avenue of plane trees. At the other end of the avenue are the gates of the Château de Valençay, famous as the home of Talleyrand, Napoleon's foreign minister. The sun was trying to break through, although most people were hovering under trees waiting to see whether it would rain.

Soon everyone was surging around the memorial. There was quite a crowd. Judith Hiller was standing upright, proudly wearing her husband's medals on her royal-blue suit. The SOE adviser was talking to a man who had come down from the embassy, who was bemoaning the fact that 'On a perdu le soleil.' Examining the list of names on the memorial, I noticed someone was missing. Sonia Olschanesky, captured while working as a courier for F Section, and murdered as an F Section 'spy' at Natzweiler, was not on the memorial to F Section's dead. Vera had forcefully argued for Sonia's name to be included, I was told, but she was overruled by a committee which decided that, as a local recruit, not commissioned in the British armed forces, Sonia Olschanesky could not be remembered here.

Somewhere in the mêlée I bumped into Prosper's son Anthony Suttill. He and his brother Francis had recently found more evidence to undermine the theory that their father had made a pact with the Germans. Yet, as Anthony knew, the truth about the pact was now unlikely ever to be known, because Vera had taken it with her to her grave.

Just before Vera died, Anthony Suttill travelled down to Winchelsea in the hope of coaxing Vera to tell him, once and for all, everything she knew about his father's case. He took Vera out for lunch at the New Inn, so they could chat about his father in a relaxed atmosphere. They talked about many things, but the subject of Prosper was never raised. 'I waited for Vera to say something but she said nothing about it at all. And for some reason I felt it wasn't up to me to raise it,' Anthony told me.

'Why not?'

'I don't know. I wish to God I had.'

Now a group of French resistance veterans, several in jeans, appeared with fifteen different flags and trumpets. An estimated 200,000 French men and women died in Nazi concentration camps during the war, and more than a million French were deported.

We were all waiting for Pearl. I flicked again through the Valençay booklet, which set out the achievements of the SOE circuits in organising the French resistance. The SOE agents were 'messengers of hope' to the resistance. The booklet quoted the words of General Eisenhower, the Supreme Allied Commander, who wrote in May 1945 that resistance action on D-Day 'played a considerable part in our complete and final victory' – words often quoted by those defending the creation of SOE.

Eventually Pearl appeared, still trailing her film crew, who shone a glaring arc light upon her. Tributes were spoken to the dead. Pearl struggled to the podium in front of the memorial, which stands 15 metres high, a long, graceful, stretched piece of arching metal, set amid a bed of flowers.

The traffic stopped and Valençay was quiet as Pearl laid the wreath. The sun came out. We stood a while. Pearl spoke most movingly of those who had died. And then we moved away.

Back in the shed in Zennor I had come to take a last look through the remnants of Vera's files. It was another wet and windy day. Phoebe was bed-ridden with arthritis. Zenna was here visiting with her two small children. But Vera was no longer with us. The urn carrying her ashes had been removed from the window sill of the conservatory; she must finally have been laid to rest.

There was unlikely to be more to learn here in the shed. I now knew just how systematically Vera had 'weeded' her own papers before her death. Mark Seaman, the SOE historian at the Imperial War Museum, had told me he was periodically summoned by Vera in her last years to 'go through her files'. This meant watching her pluck papers from brown envelopes, examine them and say: 'That's not interesting', and the paper would go in the bin. 'She was a bit of a tease really,' Mark admitted. 'She let us all know what she wanted us to know.' I picked up a notebook belonging to Guy Atkins. It was full of aphorisms: '"It is better to light a candle than curse the darkness."'

Here were those photographs again, showing Vera at endless dinners. Vera arranged things in her later years so that she was rarely alone. When she wasn't visiting friends she entertained and probably partied more in her seventies and eighties than she had since her Romania days. There were many intimate dinners for her favourites at Rutland Gate and countless functions at 'the Club'. When Vera finally won her CBE in 1997 she took over the Special Forces Club with a party at 'happy hour'. The delay in granting Vera an honour had raised many eyebrows, as the letters in her CBE file showed. Well-wishers commented on how the award had been 'a long time coming' and 'was well overdue'. In fact, Vera's chance of securing an honour had been stuck for over fifty years, ever since MI5 had opened a file on her, suspecting her of communist sympathies. Only in 1995, when the French made Vera a Commandeur de la Légion d'Honneur, the order's highest rank, did the British finally wake up to the fact that a British gong for Vera was overdue. Even then, Vera's case had been quite hard to 'get unstuck', as one senior official put it.

*

In her very old age Vera was still busy with SOE affairs, as her cleaner Christine had told me. 'She'd sometimes have me stand in front of her desk on a Monday morning and she'd say: "Now, dear, I shall be in Paris next Thursday and in London Monday and Tuesday, and so you must redirect the mail and would you type some letters on Tuesday, polish the silver on Wednesday and change the linen on Thursday", and I almost expected her to say: ". . . and parachute into France on Friday".' Christine laughed, then said: 'She did once look at me and say: "Yes, I might have given you a job."'

In the evenings Vera preferred the telephone to the television for company. 'When I went to stay,' said Mavis Coulson, widow of John Coulson, whom Vera had known in Romania, 'I had to be exactly to her schedule. I do remember the drink hour punctually began at seven. And the phone started to ring thereafter and all her friends would call and she sparkled on the phone, often breaking into French. You would think that every man was her lover and it was rather strange and rather sweet really. That was the hour of the day for her.'

Vera continued to travel widely in later life, often with Alan Nightingale, an old friend from her war crimes days, and here were the pictures, including snaps of her in Egypt which I had not looked at before. I wondered if she went to Egypt to see Dick's name, inscribed on the Alamein Memorial, erected in memory of Commonwealth servicemen and -women with no known grave. She would have found Dick's name on column 241.

Lying loose in a drawer, I found a newspaper clipping from the *Daily Telegraph* about Felbrigg Hall, reporting that, after the death of Wyndham Ketton-Cremer in 1969, the house was left to the National Trust. There were no heirs.

The most important romantic love of Vera's life was surely Dick Ketton-Cremer, but it had been hard to tell how important Vera was to Dick.

Shortly before she died Vera visited Ann Eagle (née Rogers), her old friend from Bucharest days, who lived in Norfolk in later life. Out of the blue, Vera asked Ann to drive her down to Felbrigg Hall. 'I had no idea why she should want to go there. The house was closed when we arrived, so we drove around a little and then she said: "You know, Ann, all this might have been mine." It was a funny thing to say, but, you know, Vera could be funny like that. So I didn't comment and we drove back home.'

After obtaining Dick's will, in which he left £500 to Vera, I had found John Ward, one of the named witnesses, hoping he might have heard Dick talk about Vera, but he had not and he thought Vera was probably 'just one of many'. 'He certainly liked the girls,' said John, a bomber pilot who had shared a tent with Dick in the desert. Was there anyone special? He said not, but then he paused a moment, as if considering whether to tell me something. 'There was one he used to talk about. I had the impression he had travelled a lot before the war. I don't know where it was exactly, but somewhere maybe in the Far East. He had a native girl. He used to talk about her.'

'What did he say?'

'Oh, just how she used to come and live with him for weeks on end and then go back again to her family. I don't think she was important, though. It was just the sort of thing one did if one was travelling. She was the only one he talked about. I think she was just useful to him at the time.'

I had found many other indications, however, that for Dick Vera was not just 'one of many'. He had asked the RAF Standing Committee on Adjustment to inform Vera, albeit privately, should he go missing. He had named her in his final will, although second to another woman. He had kept a photograph of Winchelsea church, probably taken on his visit to meet Vera's mother, in July 1939. Most important of all was the unsigned love letter which I first found in the shed here, with its address torn off. A handwriting expert had confirmed that the letter was almost certainly in Dick's hand. 'My Sweet, My lovely, My Darling – Cross out the possessives if you like, but you are – My Darling My Sweet.

'Please – My love – I love you. Dear Sweet.'

It seemed probable that Dick's love for Vera was sincere but, given her background, it was a love that he, as a Norfolk squire, knew he would never be able to avow. As he wrote to her: 'Cross out the possessives if you like'.

Poking around the back of the shed, I spotted a musty old box which somehow I had overlooked entirely on my first visit. I pulled out a thick brown envelope addressed to Guy Atkins and sent from

Stuttgart in 1973. When I opened it I found, much to my surprise, a copy of Siegfried's memoir. This was the same memoir that had been sent to me from another shed, in Canada, after the snow melted. Yet, all along, a copy had been lying here, and neither Zenna, Vera's niece, nor Phoebe, Guy's widow, had known about it.

I noticed that the package was sent to Guy by Aenne Pahl, the Rosenberg cousin in Stuttgart, yet Aenne's own granddaughter, Iris Hilke, had known nothing of the memoir when I had spoken to her in Stuttgart some months before. She had said she had met Uncle Siegfried as a child and he had told her wonderful tales about Romania – fairy tales, she thought – about 'forests full of bears and great balls with ladies in long gowns'. So I had sent her my own copy of the memoir posted from Canada, and only then did she realise that 'the fairy tales were true'.

'There were so many taboos,' Iris said. 'As children we were not told about the past and we did not ask. It was a great mistake. It just confused the next generation.'

I asked her how she thought Vera had coped with a life so full of secrets. 'She had probably retreated in some way a long time ago,' she said. 'Think of the age when everything went wrong for her. She was an attractive, clever young woman. Until then she had been protected. She too probably did not know she was a Jew for a long time. She probably grew up with taboos as well. So much would have been hidden from her. And then suddenly she was confronted with the terrible fears and realities of being a Jew at that time. There had perhaps been so many deceptions she had had to practise over the years.'

Before leaving the shed for the last time, I looked through the papers on Vera's death and funeral. In 1980 she had paid fifty guineas to reserve a niche next to her mother in the crematorium at Golders Green Cemetery. In her will Vera left a total of £800,000; evidently her investments had done very well. The money was divided up among her closest family and generous donations went to godchildren, of whom she had several.

Back indoors, I asked Phoebe and Zenna whether Vera's ashes had gone to Golders Green? No, they said. Vera had changed her mind before she died and told them she wanted to 'go in' next to Guy, who was buried in the little churchyard of St Senara in Zennor.

'How did Vera die?'

'Killed by the NHS,' said Zenna.

Shortly after her ninetieth birthday Vera had gone into hospital in Rye suffering from a nasty skin complaint which had produced itchy blisters. Just as she was recovering she was moved to a nursing home, where she fell and broke a hip. She was then taken to a hospital in Hastings while her hip mended and she caught the MRSA 'super-bug'. 'She didn't give up. She just wanted to get out of there. She was battling to get home. But then she weakened and had to battle with hallucinations as well,' said Zenna.

'The thing that bothered her most about the hospital was that all the young nurses called her Vera,' recalled Phoebe. 'She kept saying: "Will you please call me Miss Atkins."'

Phoebe seemed still to be grieving over Vera's death. 'Before she died I said there will be a time when I am here and you are not here and I cannot bear that. I cried during the first winter after she died. It seemed to go on and on for ever.'

I walked down to the village to look at Vera's grave. St Senara is a twelfth-century granite church, famous for its legend of a mermaid who once sang here and led a young village boy down to the sea, never to be seen again. Hikers pass by on their way to the Tinners pub or on to the coastal path, which traverses one of the wildest and most spectacular stretches of Cornwall's coast. Vera had come to rest a long way from Galatz.

In the graveyard, I couldn't see her headstone immediately, but then there it was, nestling against a drystone wall. Phoebe had arranged for Vera to share a stone with Guy. I read the inscription 'Vera May Atkins CBE' and then the words 'Coix guerre'. The stonemason had missed out both the 'r' of 'Croix' and the 'de' and I almost expected to see a couple of marks in black ink correcting the errors. When I returned to the house I told Phoebe about the stone-mason's mistakes. She would have to get it put right, she said, or Vera would turn in her grave.

SOURCES

OVERVIEW

Archives and documentary material

The most important material for the story of Vera Atkins's life and the reconstruction of her war crimes investigation came from her personal archive. Part of this archive was held by Phoebe Atkins at her home in Zennor, Cornwall, and part of it at the Imperial War Museum in London.

For the story of SOE I relied largely on primary sources, mainly in files opened recently at the National Archives (NA), and in papers deposited with the Imperial War Museum.

I also referred to other private archives in the UK, as well as material held in archives in Germany, France, the US and Canada.

Numerous individuals have allowed me to read their contemporaneous diaries, correspondence and other relevant papers.

Interviews

I interviewed dozens of former SOE agents and Baker Street staff in the UK and France, as well as their families. I also interviewed Vera's former war crimes colleagues and relatives of murdered SOE agents. For details of Vera's earlier life I spoke to relatives in Britain, Canada, the US, France, Germany and Romania, as well as friends and acquaintances.

Several historians and individuals with specialist knowledge gave valuable assistance. Where possible, I also visited places where important events in Vera's life took place and talked to those I found there who had relevant memories or documents.

MORE DETAILED SOURCES

PART ONE

Archives

From Vera's personal archive I drew details of her appointment with SOE and background on individual F Section agents. The files 'Correspondence on Casualties', 'Correspondence on Tracing', 'Paris Files' and 'Avenue Foch' provided information on the early stages of her search for missing SOE agents, including the debate on the posting of casualties, contacts with next of kin and early interrogations with returning agents. I also drew extensively on interviews Vera gave for the IWM's sound archives. Vera's naturalisation file was shown to me by the Home Office (R20340/2/Nat.Div), for which I am grateful to John M. Lloyd.

For details on F Section I referred in particular to SOE files in the NA series HS4, HS6, HS7, HS8 and HS9. I relied heavily on Vera's own SOE personal file, HS9/59/2.

MI5 interrogations concerning Henri Déricourt, Nicholas Bodington, Hugo Bleicher and related files were largely in the KV2 series. Related papers on SOE operations were also in Air2, Air20 and Air 40.

For the tracing of agents immediately after D-Day I relied in particular on HS6/438, 439 and 1440. For war crimes-related material I referred also to NA papers in the series WO32, WO309, WO311 and WO323 and related files. Among interrogations of returnees I relied in particular on statements from Maurice Southgate, John Starr, Harry Peulevé, Jean Argence, Eileen Nearne, Yvonne Baseden, Odette Sansom, Brian Stonehouse and Armel Eugène Guerne.

Others sources and archives

For the story of Nora (Noor) Inayat Khan I drew on Nora's personal file (HS9/836/5) and on the biography by Jean Overton Fuller, *Madeleine*. The author also generously provided original documents. Vilayat Inayat Khan spoke about Nora's background and provided documents. I relied on my own interview with Vera.

For the wider F Section story I also drew on the IWM sound archives and was grateful to the First Aid Nursing Yeomanry (FANY) for access to their archives. Francis Suttill provided documents. Tim Buckmaster kindly showed me his father's contemporary diaries. Peter Lee and E.H. Van Maurick showed me their memoirs. John Pitt at the Special

Forces Club assisted with research. *SOE in France* by M.R.D. Foot was a regular point of reference.

Interviews

For the portrayal of Vera at Baker Street and at the airfields, I relied on my own interview with Vera and on interviews with numerous SOE agents and staff officers, in particular Nancy Roberts (formerly Fraser-Campbell), Yvonne Baseden, Penelope Torr, Hugh Verity, Francis Cammaerts, Elizabeth FitzGerald (née Norman), Lise de Baissac, Margaret Jackson, Kay Gimpel, Peggy Heard, Robert Sheppard, Peter Lee, Roddy Clube, Peter Lake, Jacques Poirier, Bob Maloubier, Tony Brooks, George Millar, Ralph Beauclerk, Jean-Bernard Badaire, Sir Brooks Richards and Sir Douglas Dodds-Parker. Joan Astley, co-author of *Gubbins of SOE*, gave advice. Lynette Beardwood advised on the FANY.

On the collapse of the Prosper circuit I interviewed agents involved, including Gaston Collins, Bob Maloubier, André Watt, Lise de Baissac and Roger Landes.

Robert Sheppard gave first-hand memories of Avenue Foch and of Hans Kieffer.

PART TWO

Archives

Vera's letters, address books, photographs and pocket diaries were an essential source. Her naturalisation certificate and a post-war passport were in her archive. Her curriculum vitae for the Central Bureau for Educational Visits and Exchanges provided several pointers.

Ronald Atkins, Vera's nephew, provided further family papers, including information about his father, Ralph Atkins. Zenna Atkins, Vera's niece, provided additional documents relating to Vera and her father, Guy Atkins.

In the NA I referred again to Vera's SOE personal file and records of name changes by deed poll relating to Hilda, Ralph and Guy Atkins. Hilda Atkins's birth and marriage certificates were in the Family Records Centre.

Foreign Office files in the NA confirmed details about Vera's associates in pre-war intelligence. I am also grateful to BBC archivists for assistance on Vera's pre-war intelligence links. Duncan Stuart, the SOE adviser; Gillian Bennett, the Foreign Office historian; Nigel West, the military historian, also assisted in this field. Stonyhurst College provided

background on Leslie Humphreys and Valerie Chidson provided information about Montague Chidson, and photographs.

For the wider Rosenberg story I drew extensively on Siegfried
Rosenberg's memoir, and on Fritz and Karen Rosenberg's papers. I am
grateful to Karina Rosenberg, her husband Michael McCardle and her
brother Peter Rosenberg for granting access to Fritz Rosenberg's papers
and for help and advice. I am grateful also to Filip Heilpern, for further
background on the Rosenbergs, and Michael Styrcea and Johann
Romalo for details on Crasna.

The Stadtarchiv in Kassel, Germany, provided documents on the
Rosenberg family history.

On the wider Atkins family story I was assisted by Vera's cousins
Joan Atkins, Janet Atkins, Rabbi Hillel Avidan and Barbara Horak. De
Beers Consolidated Mines Ltd provided details on the family's dia-
mond interests.

For background I drew on material from the Wiener Library and the
German Historical Institute, both in London, as well as Yad Vashem, the
Holocaust Memorial Authority in Jerusalem, and the Simon Wiesenthal
Centre for Holocaust Studies.

In Romania I was assisted by Prince Mihai Sturdza, Mihai Alin Pavel
and Ion Rizescu. For assistance in Galatz I am grateful to the Galatz City
Archives and the Galatz Jewish Community Centre. I also drew on advice
from Leah Benjamin at the Jewish Community Centre in Bucharest.
Boris Voldavsky, investigative journalist, uncovered material in Vienna.

For historical background I am grateful to Professor Dennis Deletant,
Dr Maurice Pearton, Dr Jonathan Eyal, Ivor Porter, Sir Dennis Wright,
Professor Andrei Pippidi and John Wimbles. Lady Gowrie (Adelheid
Schulenburg) provided background on Friedrich Werner von der
Schulenburg. Lord Weidenfeld gave historical advice.

Interviews

Vera's own memories of Romania were relayed to me by her friends
Barbara Worcester and Alice Hyde. I am indebted to Annie Samuelli
for many hours of discussion and to Ann Eagle (née Rogers) and
Teresina Mendl for their memories of Vera in Romania. Other members
of the Mendl family offered family trees and memories.

I am particularly indebted to Zinovia Iliut in Crasna and to Princess
Ileana Sturdza in Bucharest. Despina Wittgenstein kindly provided
information about her husband, Peter Wittgenstein.

For Vera's life in Bucharest I also relied on contemporary writing, including the memoirs of the *Times* correspondent Archie Gibson, and I drew on Hilda Atkins's pocket diaries. I am particularly grateful to Mavis Coulson for lending her husband's letters.

An invaluable source of information on Vera's life after arriving in England in 1937 was Mary Williams. I also drew on information in Vera's naturalisation file and on information provided by Pat Holbeton and Mimi Rocke. Vera's oral testimony given to the IWM and files on her membership of ARP were helpful.

The story of Vera's relationship with Dick Ketton-Cremer came first from Barbara Worcester, Mary Williams and Christine Franklin. I am grateful to the National Trust and in particular to Jim Watt, Mari Chalk and Joan Chapman at Felbrigg Hall for showing me Dick's papers and photographs, and to Lady Wilhelmine Harrod for her advice.

PART THREE

Archives

Vera Atkins's Papers

For the reconstruction of Vera's investigations in Germany I relied primarily on her own papers, some of which are duplicated in files in the NA.

Among Vera's war crimes papers I relied particularly on 'Correspondence on Casualties' for details of agents still missing in January 1946, and on 'Movements and Orders' for the terms of her appointment as an investigator and for plotting her travels around Germany.

Her files on 'Karlsruhe Prison' contained interrogations of prison staff and former inmates, including Fräulein Becker, Hedwig Müller and Lisa Graf and related correspondence. 'Karlsruhe Gestapo' and 'Natzweiler' contained interrogations, reports and correspondence used for the reconstruction of events at Natzweiler and Dachau, including Brian Stonehouse's drawings. The interrogation of Franz Berg, as well as Vera's handwritten notes of this interrogation, were in 'Natzweiler'.

For other phases of her investigations in Germany I relied on further files, including 'Ravensbrück', 'Sachsenhausen', 'Ravitsch', 'Mauthausen', 'Flossenburg', 'Dachau' and 'Gross Rosen'.

Correspondence with next of kin, and with Norman Mott, including Vera's monthly reports to London, and letters about honours and awards, were mainly in 'Personal Correspondence'.

Later stages of Vera's investigation, including her enquiries into penetration of F Section and the treachery of Henri Déricourt, were pieced together from her interrogations of Avenue Foch staff, particularly Dr

Josef Goetz and Hans Kieffer, and her notes on these meetings, which were largely contained in 'Avenue Foch' (personal archive) and 'Paris Files' (IWM).

Numerous papers in Vera's own files provided colour and background, including letters and notes from colleagues, as well as her own writings about her search, letters home from Germany, maps, drawings and newspaper cuttings.

A file kept by Vera in her personal archive on the case of Frank Chamier, the MI6 agent, and Horst Kopkow, the German intelligence chief, contained details never revealed before about this case.

National Archives

For background on Germany under Allied occupation I referred to contemporary Foreign Office and War Office documents in the NA and to those in Control Commission files. I also referred to Foreign Office Historical Branch papers, particularly volume no. 3 (1989) and other publications in the NA library.

I consulted war crimes files in the NA to supplement Vera's files on her investigation. Those relating most closely to her work were contained in the series WO 309 and WO 235, relating to the Judge Advocate General's (JAG) department; files in the HS9 series, containing SOE personal files; files on enemy intelligence, particularly WO 204/1257; and the KV2 series, containing MI5 personal files.

Of particular importance to the first half of Vera's investigation in Germany were WO 309/282 on the Karlsruhe Gestapo investigation; WO 309/1022, covering the investigation into Nora Inayat Khan's imprisonment at Pforzheim and death at Dachau; and WO 235/336, containing a contemporaneous transcript of the Natzweiler trial. I also relied on the personal files (HS9 series) of Nora Inayat Khan, Violette Szabo and Francis Suttill and on the files on Hans Kieffer's trial, WO 235/560 and 235/711.

New evidence surrounding German penetration of F Section and Déricourt's treachery was contained in several security service files, particularly KV4/20, and in the diaries of Guy Liddell, KV4 (185–96), and in Nicholas Bodington's report on the Prosper collapse.

SOE personal files (HS9 series) revealed the scale of the penetration, in particular the file on Noor Inayat Khan (HS9/836/5), which contained the original telegram warning of her capture. Security service interrogations of Nicholas Bodington (KV2/830) and Hugo Bleicher (KV2/164 and KV2/166) further illustrated the penetration.

Private papers

Vital details of Vera's early investigations came from Anghais Fyffe's personal diaries, now in the IWM, and Yurka Galitzine's report on Natzweiler-Struthof (December 1944) a copy of which was provided by Anthony Kemp.

I drew from the diary of signaller Freddie Oakes (provided by his son William Oakes) and descriptions of war crimes work by the Home Office pathologist Keith Mant (given by his son Tim Mant).

John da Cunha, the war crimes lawyer, provided vital papers and photographs relating in particular to the Ravensbrück trial, as well as poignant memories of Vera. Jane Hamlyn kindly lent photographs of Bad Oeynhausen.

Anthony Kemp gave permission for use of his interviews with Vera and with Gerald Draper in his book The Secret Hunters.

Depositions before the French military tribunal which tried Henri Déricourt were provided by Robert Marshall. I was assisted by Martin Sugarman of AJEX (Association of Jewish Ex-Servicemen and Women)

German archives and sources

Dr Manfred Koch at the Stadtarchiv in Bad Oeynhausen provided information on the period of the British occupation.

Staff at the Generallandesarchiv, Karlsruhe produced documents of the period, including files on Hans Kieffer and files relating to the Office of the Military Government of the United States (OMGUS) detailing life in Karlsruhe under Allied occupation.

Dr Michael Stolle of Karlsruhe University provided extensive briefings on the Karlsruhe Gestapo and documents. Dr Angela Borgstedt of Karlsruhe University gave information on denazification. Josef Werner provided contemporary documents and background on Karlsruhe under occupation.

Stadtarchiv archivists in Pforzheim, Gaggenau, Hameln, Garmisch Partenkirchen and Rastatt also provided relevant documentation.

Christiane Fischer, owner of the Villa Degler in Gaggenau, showed me her house.

I also drew on information provided by: the Bundesarchiv in Berlin; museums at Dachau and Natzweiler concentration camps; Monsieur Jean Simon, Natzweiler concentration camp historian; Baron Arthur Hulot, a witness at the Dachau trials; the US National Archives, Washington, DC; the Centre Historique des Archives Nationales, Paris; and the Association Nationale des Anciennes Déportées et Internées de la Résistance, Paris.

Interviews

Throughout Part Three interviews with witnesses provided essential background and information. For descriptions of life in Germany, and particularly at Bad Oeynhausen, Baden Baden, Gaggenau, Hamburg and Berlin, I interviewed several war crimes lawyers, former SOE members, and 'Haystack' investigators, including John da Cunha, John Hodge, Sacha Smith, Arribert Volmar, Freddie Warner, John Buckingham and Phillip Worral. Julia Draper, Mary Kaiser and Jane Stewart kindly gave information on their husbands' war crimes work. Amy Crossland provided information about her father, Eric 'Bill' Barkworth.

In Karlsruhe several people passed on information or memories of the events, including Franz Becker, nephew of Fräulein Becker; Heinrich Graf, chief warder at the prison in Riefstahlstrasse; and Erich Johe, son of Elise Johe, an inmate of Karlsruhe prison.

Hans, Hildegard and Gretel Kieffer, as well as Karl Schuhmann, spoke about Sturmbannführer Hans Kieffer, and provided letters, documents and photographs.

Yurka Galitzine gave several interviews and showed documents.

Lisa Graf gave testimony of imprisonment in Karlsruhe prison.

Relatives of the victims who kindly passed on memories of Vera and relevant papers include: Francis and Anthony Suttill; Diana Farmiloe (sister of Yolande Beekman); Helen Oliver (sister of Lilian Rolfe); and Vilayat, Hidayat and Claire Inayat Khan.

Vera's former SOE colleagues Sir Brooks Richards, Bob Maloubier, Nancy Roberts and Robert Sheppard, as well as the writer Anthony Kemp, provided information or recalled interviews and conversations with Vera which helped me piece together her 'private chat' with Hans Kieffer. Robert Marshall was among several authors who recalled conversations with Vera about Déricourt.

My own interview with Vera also provided vital information on her war crimes search.

PART FOUR

Chapter 24

Archives

On the post-war period, Vera kept newspaper cuttings, screenplays, videos, correspondence with writers and legal documents.

I drew from her papers on the Central Bureau for Educational Visits and Exchanges. Vera's miscellaneous files included pictures and correspondence about the Tuppit Teapot venture, her financial investments and her will.

NA series HS6, HS7 and HS8 contained records of SOE after the war, including on publicity and French attitudes towards Buckmaster.

PREM 11/5084/1047/143 contained reports of Irene Ward's intervention and debate on publication of the official history of SOE.

I referred to Irene Ward's personal papers deposited with the Bodleian Library, Oxford. Minister's case R 20340/3, relating to Irene Ward's request for information about Vera, was held in Vera's naturalisation file.

My sources for information about an MI5 file once held on Vera and on Guy Atkins and other references to her left-wing sympathies in official files requested anonymity.

Jean Overton Fuller's commentary on Vera's political views is contained in her book *Espionage as a Fine Art*.

Francis Suttill provided three original research papers.

Oral testimony

Agents including Yvonne Baseden, Tony Brooks, Francis Cammaerts, Nancy Roberts and Pierre Raynaud spoke or corresponded about aspects of post-war writing on SOE, as did Francis and Anthony Suttill and authors Larry Collins, Robert Marshall and Jean Overton Fuller. Professor David Dilks advised on the demise of SOE.

Background on Vera's alleged communist sympathies was provided by the former communist and SOE agent Ormond Uren, Landon Temple and SOE agents Tony Brooks and Francis Cammaerts. On Vera's political loyalties I drew on discussions with Barbara Worcester, Jean Overton Fuller, Annie Samuelli, Oleg Gordievsky, Nigel West, M.R.D. Foot, Sir Crispin Tickell, Ronald Atkins, Zenna Atkins and intelligence officers.

Details on Dick Ketton-Cremer in Part Four were drawn from his will, provided by the Probate Registry, and from papers provided by the International Committee of the Red Cross (ICRC) and the Air Historical Branch (RAF). The Lord Chancellor's Advisory Council on National Records and Archives assisted with access to Dick's casualty file. Sebastian Cox of the Air Historical Branch gave advice. John Ward allowed me to read his diaries and hear his memories of Dick.

Chapters 25 and 26

Oral history

For Vera's mission to the Low Countries I drew first on information from Judith Hiller, the Belgian Embassy in London, Canon Basil O'Farrell in Winchelsea, Ellis Bros Funeral Services in Rye, Zenna Atkins and Alice Hyde. Subsequent interviews were conducted with Gilberte Brunsdon-Lenaerts, a 'Dutch lady' (real name withheld) and her family. Karina and Peter Rosenberg, Iris Hilke and Beate Orasche provided family background and Ludwig Linden of the German Embassy in London helped with research.

I am grateful to the Belgian historian Etienne Verhoeyen and the Dutch historian Frans Kluiters for extensive research in Holland and Belgium, and to Eric Laureys of Ceges/Soma, Centre for Historical Research and Documentation, in Brussels.

Documents and archives

The account of the Hungarian takeover at Vallea Uzului drew on Siegfried Rosenberg's memoir and on Fritz and Karen Rosenberg's files. In addition I drew on SIME (Security Intelligence Middle East) Reports (No. 1 of 21 November 1944 and No. 4 of 10 January 1945), provided by the SOE adviser, and related SIME material in the WO series of the NA. Iris van Vlaardingen of the Gemeenteachief in Rotterdam provided documents.

Background was drawn from the Joods Museum van Deportatie en Verzet, in Mechelen, Belgium.

For information on the murder of Hans Rosenberg I relied on Fritz Rosenberg's files and on material from the Documentation Centre of Austrian Resistance (DÖW), Vienna.

Chapter 27

Vera's personal archive contained letters from next of kin, researchers and other correspondents seeking information about agents after the war. For details of new evidence about the death of Nora Inayat Khan I drew on a letter and report from John Wickey, in Vera's archive. Gabrielle Nishiguchi of the Canadian Defence Ministry in Ottawa and John Wickey's son John kindly provided documentation.

Jean Overton Fuller clarified the provenance of the Wickey papers and of the so-called 'Gibraltar letter', and Vilayat Inayat Khan granted a further interview and shared material.

For the history of SOE memorials and awards I drew on Vera's papers and was assisted by John Sainsbury and Nigel Smith. Tim Buckmaster gave information and extracts of his father's diaries for the post-war years, and his sister, Sybil Beaton, also spoke of her father and Vera. BBC producer Robin Punt advised on Violette Szabo.

During each part of the book researchers helped me accumulate documentary evidence. I would particularly like to thank Andrew Smith, Richard Smith, Uwe Günther, Alice Ceresole, George Mireuta, John Powell and David Harrison.

EPILOGUE

For an understanding of Vera's later years I am particularly grateful to Barbara Worcester, Nancy Roberts, Susan Roberts, Sacha Smith and Judith Hiller as well as several of Vera's neighbours and friends in Winchelsea, who shared memories of her. Information on Vera's will was in her archive. Her grave is in the churchyard of St Senara, in Zennor.

BIBLIOGRAPHY

Andrew, Christopher, *Secret Service: The Making of the British Intelligence Community* (Heinemann, 1985)

Andrew, Christopher and Mitrokhin, Vasili, *The Mitrokhin Archive: The KGB in Europe and the West* (Allen Lane, 1999)

Annan, Noel, *Changing Enemies: The Defeat and Regeneration of Germany* (HarperCollins, 1995)

Atkins, Ronald, *Fair Shares and Romanian Oil* (The Book Guild, 2005)

Bakels, Floris, *Nacht und Nebel* (Lutterworth Press, 1993)

Beevor, Antony, *Berlin: The Downfall 1945* (Viking 2002)

Beevor, Antony and Cooper, Artemis, *Paris after the Liberation* (Hamish Hamilton, 1994)

Beevor, J. G., *SOE Recollections and Reflections 1940–1945* (The Bodley Head, 1981)

Binney, Marcus, *The Women who Lived for Danger* (Hodder & Stoughton, 2002)

Bower, Tom, *Blind Eye to Murder* (Little, Brown, 1981)

Boyle, Andrew, *The Climate of Treason* (Hutchinson, 1979)

Breitman, Richard, *Official Secrets: What the Nazis Planned: What the British and Americans Knew* (The Penguin Press, 1999)

Buckmaster, Maurice, *Specially Employed* (Batchworth Press, 1952)

—— *They Fought Alone* (Odhams Press, 1958)

Camp 020: MI5 and the Nazi Spies (Public Record Office, 2000)

Cave Brown, Anthony, *Bodyguard of Lies* (Harper & Row, 1975)

Clare, George, *Berlin Days 1946–1947* (Macmillan, 1989)

Collins, Larry, *Fall from Grace* (Simon & Schuster, 1985)

Colvin, Ian, *Colonel Henri's Story* (William Kimber, 1954)

Cookridge, E. H., *Inside SOE* (Arthur Barker, 1966)

Cornioley, Pearl, *'Pauline'* (Editions Par Exemple, 1996)

Cremieux-Brilhac, Jean-Louis, *La France libre* (Gallimard, 1996)

Déricourt, Henri, with commentary by Jean Overton Fuller, *Espionage as a Fine Art* (Michael Russell, 2002)

Elsberry, Terence, *Marie of Romania: The Intimate Life of a Twentieth Century Queen* (Cassell, 1973)

Escott, Beryl, *Mission Improbable* (Patrick Stephens, 1991)

Farago, Ladislas, *The Game of the Foxes* (Hodder & Stoughton, 1972)

Favez, Jean-Claude, *The Red Cross and the Holocaust* (Cambridge University Press, 1999)

Foot, M. R. D., *SOE in France* (HMSO, 1968)

—— *SOE in the Low Countries* (St Ermin's Press, 2001)

Foot, M. R. D. and Langley, J. M., *MI9 Escape and Evasion 1939–1945* (The Bodley Head, 1979)

Ford, George H. (ed.), *Frank Pickersgill: The Making of a Secret Agent* (Ryerson Press, 1948)

Galbraith, John Kenneth, *A Life in Our Times* (André Deutsch, 1981)

Gellately, Robert, *Backing Hitler: Consent and Coercion in Nazi Germany* (Oxford University Press, 2001)

Gilbert, Martin, *Second World War* (Weidenfeld and Nicolson, 1989)

—— *Never Again, A History of the Holocaust* (HarperCollins, 2000)

Giskes, H. J., *London Calling North Pole* (Kimber, 1953)

Gleeson, James, *They Feared No Evil* (Corgi, 1978)

Herwarth, Johnnie von, *Against Two Evils: Memoirs of a Diplomat-Soldier during the Third Reich* (Collins, 1981)

Jenkins, Roy, *Churchill: A Biography* (Macmillan, 2001)

Joffrin, Laurent *La Princess Oublie* (Robert Laffont, 2002)

Jones, Liane, *A Quiet Courage* (Bantam Press, 1990)

Kemp, Anthony *The Secret Hunters* (Michael O'Mara 1986)

Ketton-Cremer, R. W., *Felbrigg: The Story of a House* (Century, 1962)

King, Stella, *'Jacqueline': Pioneer Heroine of the Resistance* (Arms and Armour, 1989)

Kramer, Rita, *Flames in the Field* (Michael Joseph, 1995)

Larteguy, Jean and Maloubier, Bob, *Triple Jeu: L'Espion Déricourt* (Robert Laffont, 1992)

Macdonald, Bill, *The True Intrepid* (Timberholme Books, 1998)

Mackenzie, W. J. M., *The Secret History of SOE*, ed. M. R. D. Foot (St Ermin's Press, 2000)

Manning, Olivia, *Great Fortune, The Spoilt City, Friends and Heroes* (The Balkan Trilogy) (Heinemann, 1960–2)

Marks, Leo, *Between Silk and Cyanide* (HarperCollins, 1998)

Marshall Robert, *All the King's Men* (Collins, 1988)

Masterman, Sir J. C., *The Double Cross System in the War of 1939–1945* (Yale University Press, 1972)

Millar, George, *Maquis* (Heinemann, 1945)

Minney, R. J., *Carve Her Name with Pride* (Wyman, 1956)

Nichol, John and Rennell, Tony, *The Last Escape* (Viking, 2002)

Nicholas, Elizabeth, *Death Be Not Proud* (Cresset, 1958)

Overton Fuller, Jean, *Madeleine* (Victor Gollancz, 1952)

—— *The Starr Affair* (Victor Gollancz, 1954)

—— *Double Webs* (Putnam, 1958)

—— *Déricourt: The Chequered Spy* (Michael Russell, 1989)

Philby, Kim, *My Silent War* (MacGibbon & Kee, 1968)

Poirier, Jacques, *The Giraffe Has a Long Neck* (Leo Cooper, 1995)

Porter, Ivor, *Operation Autonomous: With SOE in Wartime Romania* (Chatto & Windus, 1989)

Read, Anthony and Fisher, David, *Colonel Z* (Hodder & Stoughton, 1984)

Rezzori, Gregor von, *Memoirs of an Anti-Semite* (Pan Books, 1983)

Rolf, David, *Prisoners of the Reich* (Leo Cooper, 1988)

Russell, Lord E., *The Scourge of the Swastika* (Cassell, 1954)

Sadler, Cynthia, *Lilian War Journey* (Artemis, 2003)

Salvesen, Sylvia, *Forgive but Do not Forget* (Hutchinson, 1958)

Samuelli, Annie, *Woman Behind Bars* (Frank Cass, *1967*)

Sebastian, Mihail, *Romania Journal 1935–1944* (Pimlico, 2003)

Sheppard, Bob, *Missions secretes et deportations*, 1939–1945 (Heimdal, 1998)

Simon, Jean (ed.), *Le Camp de Concentration de Struthof, Konzentrationslager Natzweiler, Temoinages* (Essor, 1998)

SOE Syllabus, Lessons in Ungentlemanly Warfare, World War II, Introduction by Denis Rigden (Public Record Office, 2001)

Spender, Stephen, *Journals, 1939–1983* (Faber & Faber, 1985)

Stafford David, *Churchill and Secret Service* (John Murray, 1997)

Stent, Ronald, *A Bespattered Page? The Internment of His Majesty's Most Loyal Enemy Aliens* (André Deutsch, 1980)

Stolle, Michael, *Die Geheime Staatspolezei in Baden* (Konstanz, 2001)

Sweet-Escott, Bickham, *Baker Street Irregular* (Methuen, 1965)

Tickell, Jerrard, *Odette* (Chapman & Hall, 1949)

Trial of Major German War Criminals (HMSO, 1946–51)

Tsarev, Oleg and West, Nigel, *The Crown Jewels* (Yale University Press, 1999)

Vader, John, *The Prosper Double-cross* (Sunrise Press, 1977)

Vassiltchikov, Marie 'Missie', *The Berlin Diaries (1940–1945)* (Chatto & Windus, 1985)

Verity, Hugh, *We Landed by Moonlight* (Crécy, 2000)

Walker, David, *Adventure in Diamonds* (Evans Bros., 1955)

Ward, Irene, *F.A.N.Y Invicta* (Hutchinson, 1955)

Wasserstein, Bernard, *Britain and the Jews of Europe 1939–1945* (Clarendon Press, 1979)

Webb, A. M. (ed.), *The Natzweiler Trial* (William Hodge & Co., 1949)

West, Nigel, *MI6* (Panther Books, 1985)

Wighton, Charles, *Pin-stripe Saboteur* (Odhams, 1959)

Wilkinson, Sir P. A. and Astley, Joan Bright, *Gubbins and SOE* (Leo Cooper, 1993)

INDEX